EVEREST: THE FIRST ASCENT

RB7

EVEREST: THE FIRST ASCENT

How a Champion of Science Helped to Conquer the Mountain

HARRIET TUCKEY

LYONS PRESS
Guilford, Connecticut
An imprint of Globe Pequot Press

To buy books in quantity for corporate use
or incentives, call **(800) 962-0973**
or e-mail **premiums@GlobePequot.com.**

Lyons Press is an imprint of Globe Pequot Press.

Project editor: Meredith Dias
Layout: Melissa Evarts

Library of Congress Cataloging-in-Publication Data is available on file.

ISBN 978-0-7627-9192-7

Printed in the United States of America

10 9 8 7 6 5 4 3 2 1

For Netia, Lizzie, and Rosie

CONTENTS

Contents

LIST OF ILLUSTRATIONS

Map of the Three Expedition Routes
Griffith Pugh

BLACK-AND-WHITE PLATES

Some of the pictures are the author's own, with details of exceptions listed below.

1. The Queen and the Everest team at the fortieth anniversary gala party in 1993 (© *John Cleare*).
2. Members of the 1953 Everest team at Bhadgaon near Kathmandu. Left to right, top row: Tom Stobart, Griffith Pugh, Wilfred Noyce, Charles Evans; middle row: George Band, Michael Ward, Ed Hillary, Tom Bourdillon, Mike Westmacott; bottom row: Alf Gregory, George Lowe, John Hunt, Tenzing Norgay, Charles Wylie (© *Royal Geographical Society*).
3. Part of the Everest Icefall, with climbers like ants in the vast landscape (© *Royal Geographical Society*).
4. Pugh in Switzerland in 1938.
5. The Hôtel des Cedres, Cedars, near Beirut (*courtesy of the Koorey family*).
6. The ski company moves off (*courtesy of the Koorey family*).
7. James Riddell, Chief Instructor at Cedars (*courtesy of the Koorey family*).
8. Eric Shipton (© *Royal Geographical Society*).
9. Michael Ward (© *Royal Geographical Society*).
10. Tom Bourdillon (© *Royal Geographical Society*).
11. George Band, the 1953 expedition joker (© *Royal Geographical Society*).
12. Tom Stobart (© *Royal Geographical Society*).
13. John Hunt, Ed Hillary, and Tenzing Norgay cope with the media at London Airport after the 1953 expedition (*Pathé News Ltd.*).
14. Pugh at the start of the 1953 expedition, telling the locals about his exceedingly large box of scientific equipment. (© *Royal Geographical Society*).
15. Illustration of closed- and open-circuit oxygen sets (© *Royal Geographical Society*).

GRIFFITH PUGH

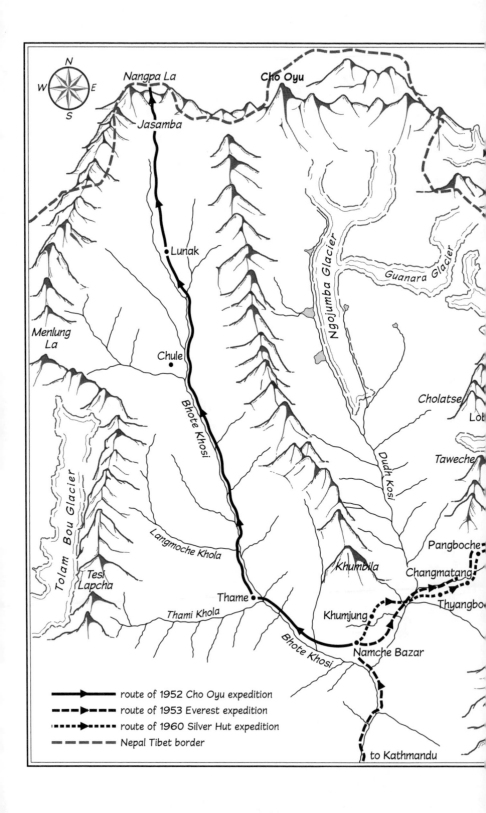

N
W E
S

Nangpa La

Cho Oyu

Jasamba

Lunak

Menlung
La

Chule

Ngojumba Glacier

Guanara Glacier

Bhote Khosi

Cholatse

Lot

Taweche

Dudh Kosi

Tolam Bou Glacier

Langmoche Khola

Tesi
Lapcha

Khumbila

Pangboche

Changmatang

Thame

Khumjung

Thyangbo

Thami Khola

Bhote Khosi

Namche Bazar

route of 1952 Cho Oyu expedition
route of 1953 Everest expedition
route of 1960 Silver Hut expedition
Nepal Tibet border

to Kathmandu

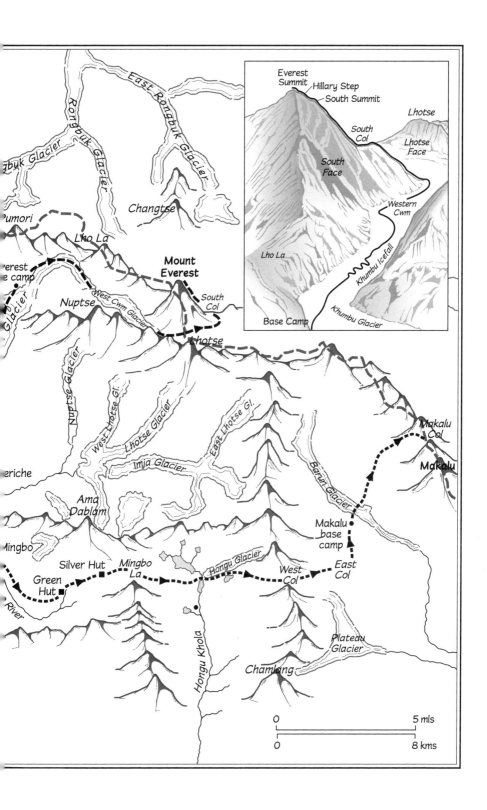

East Rongbuk Glacier

Rongbuk Glacier

Rongbuk Glacier

Pumori

Changtse

Lho La

Everest base camp

Glacier

Nuptse

West Cwm Glacier

Nuptse Glacier

West Lhotse Gl.

Mount Everest

South Col

Lhotse

Lhotse Glacier

East Lhotse Gl.

Imja Glacier

eriche

Ama Dablam

Makalu Col

Makalu

Barun Glacier

Makalu base camp

Mingbo

Silver Hut

Mingbo La

Hongu Glacier

West Col

East Col

Green Hut

River

Hongu Khola

Chamlang

Plateau Glacier

Everest Summit
Hillary Step
South Summit

Lhotse

South Col

Lhotse Face

South Face

Western Cwm

Lho La

Khumbu Icefall

Base Camp

Khumbu Glacier

0   5 mls

0   8 kms

Introduction

The Anniversary Lecture

Seldom since Francis Drake brought the Golden Hind *to anchor at Plymouth Sound has a British explorer offered to his Sovereign such a tribute of glory as Colonel John Hunt and his men were able to lay at the feet of Queen Elizabeth for her Coronation Day.*
— THE TIMES, JUNE 2, 1953, COMMENTING ON THE RECENT "CONQUEST" OF MOUNT EVEREST

One evening in May 1993, I found myself struggling to push my father, in a borrowed wheelchair, into the crowded lecture hall of the Royal Geographical Society, my mother following close behind. Forcing our way through throngs of people, we moved him toward a row of seats near the front that had been reserved for the members of the 1953 expedition to Mount Everest. My father, Dr. Griffith Pugh, had been the oldest member of the expedition. The lecture we were about to hear was a celebration of the fortieth anniversary of the "conquest" of Everest.[1]

I was only six in 1953, but I can still remember the euphoric public reaction to the news of the British triumph. Everest was climbed on May 29. The story was rushed home in the greatest secrecy, but then held back and released on June 2 in a blaze of nationalistic publicity on the morning of the coronation of the youthful Queen Elizabeth. It seemed as if the Everest prize was being laid at the feet of our new Queen to remind her of the underlying greatness of her loyal subjects, crushed by postwar austerity and the loss of empire. Young boys felt surging pride and patriotism. It was a cheering, uplifting moment, and now it was being celebrated, forty years on, with an illustrated lecture given by members of the expedition, to be followed by a glittering reception, at which Queen Elizabeth would be the guest of honor.

The members of the 1953 expedition had been allocated seats in the second row, directly behind the Queen and other members of the Royal Family. There was an air of tension among the officials, who were trying to make sure that the large audience would be in their seats in time to rise, respectfully, at the royal entrance. Suddenly it occurred to them that my father's wheelchair might be an obstruction if it was allowed to remain near the front, and, after much dithering and chopping and changing, they resolved to leave my mother at the front and shunt my father to the very back of the lecture hall where he would be out of the way. There I left him, sitting alone in his wheelchair in the back aisle, a diminutive, hunched figure who had once been so tall, strong, and athletic. His unruly red hair, which had faded to the color of ripe corn but betrayed no trace of gray to testify to his eighty-three years, was plastered down with Trumper's Oil, and his thick spectacles drooped, slightly askew, on his nose.

I had reluctantly agreed to go to the RGS, and that was only because my mother had persuaded me to help with transport for this prestigious occasion. My father had become partially disabled from a series of accidents, and my mother, who was not strong, felt unable to handle the wheelchair herself. He had been a remote and irascible parent. I didn't get along with him, and I had never asked him about his work and knew little about it, though I had always been vaguely aware that my mother felt he hadn't received fair credit for his achievements. It crossed my mind that his current position at the back of the lecture theater seemed to underline this point rather acutely, since the organizers had known for a long time about Griffith's infirmity. Still, I found a spare aisle seat a few rows in front of him and prepared to watch the lecture, expecting to be bored.

As the lecture progressed, however, I became captivated. Magnificent slides showed a chaotic mass of huge ice boulders barring the way up Everest's infamous "Icefall." The climbers were tiny specks in a vast and threatening landscape. Members of the expedition spoke about the brilliant leadership of Sir John Hunt, about the peerless logistical support given by George Band, the consummate organizational abilities of Charles Wylie, and the skill and determination of Sir Edmund Hillary and his climbing partner, Tenzing Norgay. Then a tall man with thick, graying hair, whom I had never seen before, stood up to speak. He was introduced as the expedition doctor, Dr. Michael Ward. His opening words took the audience by surprise:

> *We have been hearing a great deal this evening about the extraordinarily brilliant leadership provided by Sir John Hunt on the 1953 Everest expedition, but there had been eleven previous expeditions to Mount Everest, many of which had excellent leaders, and they failed.*
>
> *We have been hearing about the great skill of our climbers, but there had been many highly skilled climbers on previous Everest expeditions yet they failed to get to the summit.*
>
> *We have been hearing about the brilliant logistics, but there had been other well organized, well planned expeditions which all failed.*
>
> *What I want to talk about tonight is the most important reason why the 1953 expedition to Mount Everest succeeded where all its predecessors failed, and that is the work of the unsung hero of Everest . . .*[2]

At this point he paused for effect, and a perceptible hush descended as the audience gave him their full attention. Then he spoke the name emphatically: "Dr. Griffith Pugh."

I felt a jolt of surprise. As the speaker began to describe the series of scientific innovations that had played a pivotal part in the success of the expedition, a few unexpected tears came into my eyes. Turning back to look at my father, I saw his chin rising with pleasure and pride.

The audience remained in thrall until Dr. Ward had finished speaking, and, at the prestigious party that followed, Griffith Pugh became the center of attention, the celebrity of the evening. The Queen spent several minutes bent over his wheelchair, talking to him; Rebecca Stephens, the first British woman to reach the summit of Everest (and a renowned beauty), stooped down to take his hand and gaze into his eyes. He was surrounded by attentive people. On the way home afterward, he said, with great satisfaction, that the Queen had been "very gentle," and made no further comment.

Within a few months he was bedridden and demented after a series of small strokes; a year later he was dead.

Not long after, I read the official book about the Everest expedition of 1953, *The Ascent of Everest,* written by the leader John Hunt, and I was mystified to find that Hunt had chosen not to reveal the true extent of my father's role in the expedition. Michael Ward had explained how Pugh had designed the all-important oxygen and fluid-intake regimes, the acclimatization program, the diet, the high-altitude boots, the tents, the down clothing, the mountain stoves, the airbeds. He claimed that Pugh's work had been crucial to the expedition's success. Why, then, had Hunt only mentioned my father's part in designing the Everest diet? Had Ward been exaggerating? The book was full of elaborate praise for all the many people who had helped the expedition, right down to the "indefatigable" efforts of "the committee on packing," and the "wonderful work" of the ladies who had sewn the climbers' name tapes into their expedition clothing. But details of my father's practical and scientific work had been shunted to the back of the book in the appendices—indeed, behind six earlier appendices. No wonder the general public had no idea about his real contribution.

My father never promoted himself. Even his own children were unaware of his true role. However, if Sir John Hunt feared he would be criticized for having failed to sing the praises of one of the heroes of his incomparably famous expedition, perhaps he was relieved when, a few days later, he received a letter from the Queen's private secretary, full of thanks and effusive praise for a most excellent lecture which the Queen had found "riveting."[3]

The evening at the Royal Geographical Society made a profound impression on me, and kindled the first small thought that I might one day try to tell my father's story. But the relationship between us was so bad, and, rightly or wrongly, I felt so let down by him as a parent that it was another ten years before I found the emotional strength to focus my mind on him and begin.

The trigger was watching the BBC gala film *Race for Everest,* produced in 2003 to celebrate the fiftieth anniversary of the climbing of Everest. It did not mention either Griffith's name or his role in the expedition, forcing me to acknowledge that the fascinating part he had played in the Everest conquest had almost vanished from the historical record. Unless someone took action, it might be lost forever, and Griffith's descendants might never find out about it.

When I began my research, I knew practically nothing about Griffith. I was in the habit of thinking of him purely as my difficult, bad-tempered father, not as a person in his own right. The trouble started with the onset of adolescence. Suddenly every conversation between us seemed to descend into argument. At the age of sixteen, I left home and went to live with my aunt in London, though I still often returned home on the weekends, managing an uncomfortable, uncommunicative coexistence with my father. A small but typical event some twenty years before the lecture at the Royal Geographical Society illustrates the lack of rapport between us. I was twenty-six and Griffith was in his sixties.

Griffith, a tall, thin man with untidy hair and pale skin stained by numerous sunspots, stands in the open back door of our large house at Hatching Green, a suburban hamlet, a mile to the south of Harpenden in Hertfordshire. He is naked except for a brief green loincloth, brown suede shoes, and a pair of thick spectacles perched crookedly on his nose. Supporting himself on metal crutches he leans forward on the door frame and, obviously furious, shouts at me: "Go away and never cross my threshold again!"

The loincloth was acquired at Stanmore Orthopaedic Hospital, where Griffith had recently undergone a successful operation to replace a painful arthritic hip joint which had been damaged in a car accident eleven years earlier. The weather was very hot, and he was dressed in a way he regarded as "physiologically appropriate" for the exacting postoperative program of rehabilitation he had carefully devised for himself. This included a long series of ballet exercises executed to music and frequent walks around the circumference of the large lawn at the back of our house. He wore his loincloth from morning to night that hot summer, quite oblivious to the fact that visitors to our house found his appearance a little odd—even a little unsavory. Hatching Green was a deeply conservative neighborhood, but what other people thought was generally a matter of total indifference to Griffith.

Like his red hair, Griffith's temper was fiery. He was easily provoked, and, when angry, he often said immoderate things. On that particular occasion I had parked my car in the "wrong" place in our driveway, and had shown insufficient remorse for the transgression. I knew, of course, that his anger would soon subside; I would be able to return to the house a little later, and nothing more would be said. But his words still made an impact and were not forgotten.

The day of real rapprochement after our years of strife did not come in my father's lifetime. When, at last, I began to study his life, I was shocked by how little I knew about him either as a man or as a scientist.

I became a diligent researcher, scouring archives and libraries and searching out Griffith's former colleagues. I was taken aback by how kind, helpful, and interested they proved to be. Many agreed that his achievements had never been fully acknowledged, and said they thought he "deserved" a biography. In addition, the hunt through the archives brought with it an exciting realization: I was unearthing facts about the British Everest quest that no one had noticed— or remarked upon—before. The Everest story was often characterized as the last "innocent adventure" of the ghost of the British Empire. Few authors had taken a deeper look at the swirling conflicts behind the scenes, conflicts that embodied the political, cultural, and social changes that were dragging the outdated fabric of British society into the modern age after World War II.

When I turned to my father's personal life, there was one glaring gap in my knowledge that seemed insurmountable. I could find out practically nothing about his character as a young man. My knowledge was limited to sketchy family traditions, a few stories he had told my brothers, and snippets from my mother. My mother and most of Griffith's close friends were long since dead. I visited the surviving few but found that men and women of his generation rarely articulate their emotions or talk about other people's psyches. They helped as much as they could, but I was almost in despair about how to get beneath the opaque surface of my father's young character to understand his complex motivations and make sense of his irascible and dismissive behavior.

In 2006 I struck gold. For two years I had been pestering Sarah Strong, an archivist at the Royal Geographical Society and expert on the Everest papers, with frequent queries. Then, one day, out of the blue, Sarah telephoned me and said, "I think you should come and see us. I've got something here that I am sure you will find interesting."

I went at once. When Sarah walked into the reading room, she was carrying a battered leather suitcase, held together by a strap. Slowly, she unbuckled the strap and opened the case. Inside were bundle upon bundle of old letters—my father's personal letters to and from his parents when he was a child, letters from youthful lovers, and letters from my mother before they were married and during World War II. For years the suitcase had remained hidden in the loft at our old house, which had changed hands twice since my mother had died in 2000, and was being renovated for the second time when the suitcase was found. Thoughtfully, the owners had contacted the RGS because they knew the house had once belonged to a member of the Everest expedition of 1953. The suitcase was brought to London and collected from Euston station by Sarah Strong.

The contents proved to be entirely personal and of no interest to the RGS. If the suitcase had been found at some other time, or if Sarah Strong had not been so plagued by my questions, she might have returned it, and it might have ended up in a landfill. Realizing, however, that I would want the letters, she kindly gave me the case and its contents.

It allowed me to enter the previously hidden world of my father's youth.

The first half of this tale of Griffith's life lifts the veil on the power struggle and skullduggery behind the scenes of the British quest for Everest, and describes the contribution Griffith made to the expedition. However, Everest was not the end but rather the beginning of the most fruitful period in his career, when he did his most significant scientific work—work which is still saving lives and influencing the behavior of ordinary people today, sixty years later.

The subject of this book is the expeditions, adventures, and discoveries of a uniquely talented, turbulent man whom former colleagues described as "in his way, truly great." But it is also a voyage of discovery of a daughter provoked to find out about the father she hardly knew, and, in so doing, attempt to banish forever a troubling ghost of past conflict and resentment.

1

The Man in the Bath

In the spring of 1951, Michael Ward, a tall, handsome young doctor with a graceful, easy stride, walked into a large and forbidding building in Hampstead to keep an appointment with physiologist Griffith Pugh. There was no receptionist at the entrance of the building, which housed the Medical Research Council's Division of Human Physiology. Ward searched along wide, dark corridors, eventually finding Pugh's laboratory on the second floor.[1]

Entering the laboratory past crowded shelves of scientific equipment, Ward was confronted with a large, white Victorian enamel bath in the middle of the room, full to the brim with water and floating ice cubes. In the bath lay a semi-naked man whose body, chalk-white with cold, was covered in wires attached to various instruments. His blazing red hair contrasted sharply with the ghostly white pallor of his face. The phantom figure was Dr. Griffith Pugh, undertaking an experiment into hypothermia. Ward had arrived at the crisis point when, rigid and paralyzed by cold, the physiologist had to be rescued from the bath by his technician. Ward stepped forward to help pull him out of the freezing water. So began a long, fruitful collaboration and friendship.

A recently qualified doctor in his mid-twenties, Ward was a passionate climber, drawn to visit Pugh by his frustration with the complacency and lack of drive of the British climbing establishment. The objects of his discontent were the Alpine Club and the Royal Geographical Society (both gentlemen's clubs founded in the nineteenth century) that had organized and financed every British expedition to Mount Everest since the early 1920s.

Between 1921 and World War II, a voluntary committee drawn from the two had sent seven expeditions to the world's highest mountain, all of which had failed. Six British climbers had reached 28,000 feet—a thousand feet below the summit—but none had been able to climb higher. The altitude record of just above 28,000 feet set on Everest in 1924 had never been broken.[2] It was as if there was a glass ceiling 1,000 feet below the summit barring further advance, and yet no one was trying to find out why.

In the thirty years of its existence, the Everest Committee had always been a conservative body, the province of former diplomats, senior civil servants, ex-army colonial types, and old-guard climbers and explorers. The chairman (also president of the Alpine Club) was Claude Elliott, the provost of Eton. Young climbers complained bitterly—but to no effect—that there were too few active climbers on the committee.

Coming fresh to the Everest question after the war, Ward suspected that the real reasons for the repeated failures were the terrible physical problems caused by Everest's high altitude. At the beginning of 1950, not a single one of the fourteen mountains in the world above 26,250 feet had been successfully climbed. The best efforts of the world's finest climbers had been to no avail. Lives had been lost. It seemed increasingly obvious to Ward that altitude, rather than the technical severity of the climbing challenge, was the biggest problem, yet the difficulties of climbing at high altitude had never been seriously addressed by the committee. Everest expeditions were organized by amateurs, for amateurs, and it wasn't part of the amateur tradition to adopt a professional or scientific approach.

With his medical training Ward scoured reports written by the early Everest climbers for evidence of the impact of altitude on their health and climbing performances. He collected his findings into a table of what he described as "symptoms of altitude." However, he needed specialist advice, and an acquaintance had suggested that Griffith Pugh was one of the few men in Britain with the skills and experience to help.

Also a qualified doctor, Griffith Pugh had become an expert on survival in the mountains while serving in the Royal Army Medical Corps in Lebanon during the war. He had recently joined the Medical Research Council's human physiology division, set up after the war to study the problems faced by soldiers and sailors operating in extreme climatic conditions. When Ward met him, he was testing his ability to tolerate immersion in cold water as part of an investigation into hypothermia. He had been in the bath for 25 minutes when Ward found him in a state of collapse. Earlier a hardy Channel swimmer had lain in the same ice-cooled bath quite comfortably for more than three hours, eating chocolate and reading the newspaper.

Ward helped Pugh across the large room to a tiny makeshift office in a windowed turret in a far corner, where they found Pugh's diary buried beneath a jumble of papers. Their appointment was not in the diary. Even if it had been, there was no guarantee that Pugh would have seen it; his absent-mindedness was legendary among his colleagues. The latest story doing the rounds was that a few weeks earlier he had forgotten where he had parked his car in a London street, so he took a train home and informed the police that it had been stolen—the only way he could think of to get it found.

Pugh and Ward had a disjointed conversation, and Ward realized he would have to come back another day. Thinking Pugh "rather shambolic," he made sure their new appointment *was* written into the diary.

Returning a few days later, Ward found the bedraggled, shivering figure of his previous visit transformed into a tall, well-built man with striking blue eyes, a Celtic complexion, and a strong, interesting face. About forty, Pugh was scruffily dressed in shirtsleeves with the cuffs undone, a pair of baggy old beige trousers, and scuffed, brown suede shoes. His most recognizable feature from their previous encounter was the leonine mass of wavy red hair.

Ward had come armed with photographs of a proposed route up Mount Everest he was hoping to investigate in the autumn. Pugh, who in his youth had been an Olympic skier, examined the prints and immediately endeared himself to the young climber by declaring that he thought he could ski down most of the route, so mountaineers should be able to climb up it. Better still, when Ward produced his matrix of "symptoms of altitude," Pugh grasped exactly what he was talking about, having cut his physiological teeth working on similar problems. He had read the Everest histories too. As Ward put it, "He knew it all already."

The young doctor and the older physiologist took a long walk on Hampstead Heath and discussed the problems of Everest. Edward Norton, the first climber to reach 28,000 feet on Everest in 1924, had described the extreme exhaustion he experienced at high altitude, the penetrating cold, the seeing double, the nausea and sleeplessness, his feet as cold as stones, finding it impossible to eat enough and always feeling thirsty. Raymond Greene, the popular doctor on the 1933 expedition, wrote vividly of the "appalling panting" at high altitude: "The air starvation, the rapid pulse, the lassitude which made of every step a struggle, the sleeplessness, irritability, mental deterioration, grinding headaches, mountain sickness and loss of appetite."[3]

Pugh and Ward discussed the litany of illnesses—sore throats, persistent coughs, diarrhea—that had weakened expedition after expedition. But the subject they talked of most was the shortage of oxygen.

At 20,000 feet, there is 50 percent less oxygen than at sea level. At 29,029 feet—the summit of Everest—there is nearly 70 percent less. The human body responds to a lack of oxygen by breathing faster and panting harder when exercising, so more air passes through the lungs, giving them a chance to absorb more oxygen. As the air becomes thinner and thinner higher up, the ascending climber needs to pant harder and harder to keep going. Panting uses up a lot of energy in its own right, on top of the energy needed for climbing. Eventually the climber reaches a point where he cannot climb and pant at the same time, and thus has to keep stopping to catch his breath. "Our pace was wretched," Norton recalled. "My ambition was to do twenty consecutive paces uphill without a pause to rest and pant elbow on bent knee; yet I never remember achieving it—thirteen was nearer the mark."[4]

Pugh likened progress above 28,000 feet to "a series of 100-yard sprints, except that instead of 100 yards, only 10 yards is covered at each burst." Apart from the problem of exhaustion, this interrupted pattern of climbing was so slow that the early Everesters never had time to reach the summit from their highest camp and get back down in daylight. "The trouble was," Norton wrote, "that one went so miserably slowly. I only mounted something under 100 feet . . . in my last hour."[5] Wearing the typical clothing of the 1920s and '30s, they did not believe they could survive the intense cold of an overnight bivouac near the summit, so they always turned back well below the top.

What puzzled Ward was that, since 1921, oxygen had been taken on every Everest expedition. The supplementary oxygen should have helped the climbers to ascend faster, and with less effort. If they moved faster, they would feel the cold less and get to the top quicker, so their chances of reaching the summit and returning to a camp before nightfall should have been substantially improved. But nearly all the climbers who tried oxygen concluded that the apparatus was so heavy and unwieldy that its weight canceled out any benefits. "It didn't seem to give them a boost," as Ward put it.

During their conversation, Pugh made no allowances for the fact that Ward was new to the subject of high-altitude physiology. Walking along extremely fast and speaking in physiological jargon, he expected Ward to keep up with him. Far from being irritated, Ward was flattered by this refusal to talk down to him, and rushed off afterward to read up on altitude in the famous physiological textbook, *Samson Wright*. The only thing that mattered to this determined young man was that he had found the person he was looking for.

2

Gallant Failures

The question of whether Everest could be climbed without the help of oxygen equipment had been debated incessantly for thirty years by the time Pugh and Ward turned their minds to the subject. The climbers on the seven Everest expeditions between 1921 and 1938 could not agree about it—nor could the most eminent scientists.[1]

Oxygen had been taken on every expedition since 1921, mainly because, as Hugh Ruttledge, the leader in 1933, explained, "We could not afford to dispense with anything which might contribute to success."[2] But attitudes toward it were at best lukewarm, and most of the climbers did not want to use it. Bill Tilman, the charismatic leader of the 1938 expedition, summed up the common view: "My own opinion is that the mountain could and should be climbed without, and I think there is a cogent reason for not climbing [Everest] at all, rather than climb it with the help of oxygen."[3]

Yet like all previous Everest leaders, he, too, reluctantly concluded that he could not afford to refuse to take oxygen with him: "Whether to take oxygen or no was an open question which was finally decided in the affirmative for the rather cowardly reason that if we encountered perfect conditions on the last two thousand feet and were brought to a standstill purely through oxygen lack, not only might a great chance have been lost but we should look uncommonly foolish."[4] But like most of the other leaders, Tilman did not arrange for the oxygen to be used for his team's attempts on the summit.

Many prominent Himalayan veterans were convinced that oxygen was unnecessary. Edward Norton was quite sure that if man could climb to 28,000 feet without oxygen, he could manage a further 1,000 feet without.

The Scottish mountaineer and writer W. H. Murray thought the same. But Charles Warren, medical officer on the 1935, 1936, and 1938 Everest expeditions, drew precisely the opposite conclusions from the same evidence, writing: "Although climbers have already struggled to 28,000 feet there is no reason to suppose they are bound to be able to climb the last thousand feet without using oxygen."[5]

The scientists who had been debating the issues since the early 1920s were just as divided. Oxford professor Georges Dreyer, who had designed the oxygen equipment used by British fighter pilots in World War I, believed that oxygen was necessary for a safe summit assault.[6] The head of another Oxford department, Professor John Scott Haldane—perhaps the most eminent physiologist of his day—disagreed, declaring that there was "every reason to hope that, apart from the physical difficulties, men could with the help of acclimatisation get to the top [of Everest] without oxygen."[7] But the younger generation of academics tended to disagree.[8]

The oxygen taken to Everest in 1921 was not used.[9] It was first tried in 1922 on the second expedition, at the instigation of George Finch, who was considered by the then president of the Alpine Club to be one of the best mountaineers he had ever seen.[10] The team, led by Brigadier General Bruce, included such legendary climbers as the formidably handsome George Mallory, Edward Norton, Howard Somervell, and Tom Longstaff, all stalwarts of the English Alpine Club. Finch, an outstanding chemist at Imperial College, and later, a fellow of the Royal Society, applied his rigorous scientific mind to the preparations for the expedition. Almost by accident he discovered the benefits of oxygen. In an effort to improve the climbers' Primus stoves, which did not burn well at high altitude, he visited Oxford University, where Professor Dreyer had one of only two pressure chambers in the country for simulating high altitude.

While working in the pressure chamber, Finch breathed oxygen through a tube to compensate for the thin air, and was amazed by how much better and more alert he felt with it, than without. On the back of this revelation, Dreyer convinced him that oxygen was the key to success on Everest, and a slightly reluctant Everest Committee was persuaded to provide it.[11] The breathing equipment was based on the standard RAF apparatus, modified by Finch with the help of Dreyer and RAF experts at Farnborough.[12]

By the time they reached base camp, many of the climbers already suspected that Finch's heavy, clumsy oxygen sets would spoil the pleasure of climbing and unbalance them on difficult terrain. They also argued that it would be unsportsmanlike to use oxygen. Finch pointed out that they would probably view oxygen as acceptable if it came in the form of a pill, and tried in vain to persuade them that it was no more of an artificial aid to climbing than boots or Thermos flasks.[13] When several climbers reported that the weight of the sets neutralized any perceptible benefits from the oxygen, the news was welcomed by the skeptical as evidence that oxygen was of no use anyway.

Unfortunately Finch fell ill and was unable to take part in the main push for the summit in 1922, which was undertaken without oxygen by Mallory, together with Norton, Somervell, and Major H. T. Morshead. They reached 26,800 feet.

By the time Finch recovered, all the experienced climbers were exhausted, and he was forced to make the first-ever oxygen-assisted bid for the summit of Everest with a novice climbing partner, Geoffrey Bruce, the transport officer. They failed, but set an altitude record of 27,320 feet, ascending higher in bad weather than the stronger main assault team had climbed in better weather without oxygen.[14] The record only lasted until 1924, when it was beaten by Norton climbing without oxygen, but the achievement made a deep impression on George Mallory.

Finch was an outspoken character, unpopular with the rest of the Everest team. He had consistently been refused membership to the Alpine Club, and while his record climb in 1922 finally gained him acceptance as a member, he was excluded from the next Everest expedition in 1924 because of a dispute with the Everest Committee.[15] In his place, the committee selected Andrew "Sandy" Irvine, a handsome, membership-worthy Oxford undergraduate. Julie Summers, Irvine's great-niece and biographer, admitted she was baffled about "why Sandy was ever considered as a possible candidate for the 1924 expedition. He was so much younger than any of the other expedition members . . . he was sorely lacking in real mountaineering experience, and his height record to date was 5,800 feet, some 23,200 feet lower than the summit of Mount Everest."[16]

Irvine, a third-year chemistry student, was put in charge of oxygen because he was "rather good with his hands." With no real experience he made fundamental changes to the apparatus Finch had prepared for the expedition, while simultaneously writing home to a friend: "I really hate the thought of oxygen. I'd give anything to make a non-oxygen attempt. I think I'd sooner get to the foot of the final pyramid without oxygen than to the top with it . . . Still, as I am the oxygen mechanic, I've got to go with the beastly stuff."[17]

As "climbing leader" on the expedition, Mallory planned the summit assaults and chose which climbers would take part.[18] He never admitted to being influenced by Finch, yet he decided to use oxygen for his final attempt on the summit, selecting the novice Irvine as his climbing partner. "Irvine has done the principal engineering on the [oxygen] apparatus," Mallory explained to his wife, "so Irvine will come with me."[19] On June 8, 1924, Mallory and Irvine set out on their final climb with Irvine's modified equipment, never to return.

There are many who hold to the romantic view that Mallory and Irvine—or Mallory alone—may have reached the summit before dying on the way down. But there are cogent reasons why this was unlikely. Mallory and his team had spent the best part of the preceding month at high altitude, undertaking grueling maneuvers (without oxygen). As a result, Mallory told his wife, "the physique of the whole party has gone down sadly."[20] On top of this general loss of condition, Mallory had been suffering from persistent stomach problems and a severe sore throat, "with bursts of coughing fit to tear one's guts . . . headache and misery together."[21] He doubted his fitness to take part in the second (oxygenless) summit attempt of June 1–2, but joined in regardless. When that failed, he went on to make his third attempt less than a week later, without recuperating at lower altitude in between.

The route to the summit from the northern side is difficult even for modern professional climbers.[22] Mallory was tackling it accompanied by an inexperienced partner who was suffering from "the prevalent throat trouble" and "appalling sunburn," and had spent the whole of the previous week at the punishing altitude of 23,000 feet.[23] They had, at best, a meager and uncertain supply of oxygen; in fact, the expedition leader, Edward Norton, suspected the equipment might have had "some mechanical defect."[24] Without an appreciation of the need to keep the body hydrated and without modern lightweight equipment, the probability that they succeeded must be virtually nil.[25] There is a complete lack of evidence that either of them did—only wishful, romantic speculation.

Following the deaths of Mallory and Irvine, oxygen was not used for a summit attempt on Everest again for twenty-eight years. Finch never returned to the Himalayas, but was always present on the sidelines, furiously castigating later Everest teams for failing to make proper use of oxygen, and for indulging in their "futile" debate about the ethics of using artificial aids to climbing.[26]

However, oxygen was not the only problem. Everest mountaineers could not agree when it came to acclimatization—the gradual process of adjustment to the lack of oxygen at altitude.[27] Many of the unpleasant symptoms of oxygen shortage, such as headaches, nausea, sleeplessness, disturbed breathing, fatigue, and loss of appetite are alleviated, if not entirely eliminated, by acclimatization.

Some early Everesters believed it was essential to ascend the mountain slowly, allowing time for acclimatization. The 1933 team, led by Hugh Ruttledge, paused for a few days at each camp on the way up. Ruttledge reported that this resulted in better fitness and improved climbing performances. But Tom Longstaff, medical officer on the 1922 Everest expedition, declared himself "an unbeliever in the fetish of acclimatisation," arguing, "It is far better to try to rush the peak with men who are under-acclimatized than to lose perhaps the only chance of good weather."[28]

There were further disagreements, too. In the 1920s, Finch claimed with remarkable prescience that climbers continued to acclimatize up to a height of roughly 21,000 feet. However, above that—and certainly above 23,000 feet—the advantages of adaptation were outweighed by the physical deterioration caused by the altitude: Sleep would always be fitful, and it was impossible to recover from fatigue or to regain a lost appetite, resulting in a rapid decline in health and strength. Therefore, time spent at or above 23,000 feet, Finch argued, should be kept to an absolute minimum.[29]

In 1933, Ruttledge's team ignored Finch's advice and spent an extended period at 23,000 feet. They descended in extremely poor shape, claiming they had not known "how long it was safe to go on acclimatising." "We have learned our lesson," the expedition doctor, Raymond Greene, admitted.[30]

But the lesson was not learned. The leading climber Frank Smythe, who took part in the Everest expeditions of 1933, 1936, and 1938, rejected the idea that time spent at camps above 23,000 feet should be minimal: "Contrary to the belief of some, recuperation of physical energy is possible at a height exceeding 27,000 feet, and I would go even farther and say that for a period of two or three days at least, acclimatisation more than counterbalances deterioration at this altitude."[31] And the Everest veteran Noel Odell—the last person to see Mallory and Irvine alive—refused to accept that the debilitating effects of extreme altitude could outweigh the benefits of acclimatization, insisting that: "Acclimatisation to an altitude of 27,000 feet has been demonstrated, and there seems no valid reason why it should not be possible to 28,000 feet, or to the top of Everest."[32]

Acclimatization issues aside, rations were a further problem. The leading climbing manual of its time, *Mountain Craft,* written by Geoffrey Winthrop Young, an influential member of the Alpine Club, recognized that, because high altitude suppressed the appetite, climbers should be provided with "pleasant luxuries that go down easily."[33] "Food that is not palatable or eaten with pleasure is of little benefit," he emphasized.[34] This was affirmed by Raymond Greene, the Everest doctor in 1933: "Not only must all the food [on Everest expeditions] be of the highest quality, but the individual tastes of every member must be studied with the greatest care and without any regard for economy."[35]

Accordingly, the early expeditions took large quantities of food with them, including delicacies such as foie gras and truffled quails, together with supplies of wine, champagne, and whiskey. However, Greene complained that expedition organizers often failed to apply their own principles. In 1933, for instance: "There were plenty of complaints about food. The choice had been left to the secretary in London who had asked us all for our suggestions and then took no notice of them . . ."[36]

In the 1930s an influential group of climbers rejected the lavish approach. Pioneering a new lightweight style of expedition, consisting of just a few skilled climbers supported by a handful of local Sherpas, the renowned climbers Eric Shipton, Bill Tilman, and Frank Smythe adopted the principle of eating local food at lower and intermediate altitudes, and taking supplies from England only for the high-altitude stages. But as local foodstuffs were often in short supply, the climbers frequently went hungry.

Uncharacteristically, Tilman and Shipton took professional advice on high-altitude rations from an expert in nutrition, but the advice did not take into account the fussy appetites of mountaineers at high altitudes, nor did Tilman and Shipton follow it completely.[37] When leading the 1938 expedition, Tilman pared down the food to an absolute minimum to keep the weight of the baggage as low as possible, causing his team to complain bitterly of hunger and to blame the plague of ill health that bedeviled the expedition mainly on the inadequacy of the food.[38]

As early as 1923, Finch pronounced it vital to eat the right food at the highest camps, and recommended that "high-altitude food parcels" be planned and prepacked in England.[39] Again, his advice was ignored. Fifteen years later, after four more unsuccessful expeditions, Frank Smythe, apparently unaware that he was only repeating what Finch had said long before, suggested that high-altitude rations should be carefully prepared in advance and taken up the mountain in "small, labelled boxes." In reality, however, they were far from carefully planned: "The usual procedure is to plan out some food for high-altitude camps, and when one gets to Camp Three, one lumps as much as one can remember of it into a rucksack and takes it up."[40]

Everyone recognized that diet was important, but this did not lead to concerted action. Time after time climbers descended from periods at altitude with wasted muscles and haggard faces, drained of energy and having invariably lost large amounts of weight.

Even more important than poor diet was the inadequate consumption of fluids. Tom Longstaff, argued that "[t]he loss of body fluids by evaporation is, in my belief, a grave element in mountain sickness. Thirst is a terrible trial at great altitudes . . ."[41] Dr. Hingston, medical officer in 1924, recognized that in addition to evaporated sweat, high-altitude climbers lost large amounts of water by exhaling warm, wet air from their lungs and breathing in dry, cold mountain air in its place.[42] He suggested that dehydration might be one of the key causes of the high-altitude deterioration that undermined the performance of climbers.[43]

However, it was out of tune with tradition to worry about fluids. Geoffrey Young's *Mountain Craft* advised that "a certain amount of liquid is essential in action," but insisted that climbers must keep their thirst under strict control. Thirst was "merely feverish," and "impossible" to satisfy. It was a "delicious temptation," but to indulge it too freely "swamps and upsets the human machinery. . . . Some resolute men . . . train themselves not to drink at all during the day," and "a good manager should never fail to remark a man who is constantly stopping to drink in passing streams. Spartan example in abstinence will do much to check him."[44]

Young suggested various ways of resisting thirst, such as sucking a prune stone or a pebble, letting water "run through the mouth, swallowing as a special indulgence only a mouthful or so." For those on the point of collapse, he advised that "[a] man showing signs of exhaustion should not be allowed to drink more than a mouthful or two at longish intervals."[45] What the climbers did not recognize was that dehydration had a severely debilitating effect on their bodies.

Driven to the limits of human endurance by lack of oxygen, dehydration, and inadequate food, Everest climbers also struggled with poor equipment. They suffered dreadfully from the cold, and regarded frostbite as an unavoidable hazard. "The cold, out of the sun, is almost the coldness of space, and this combined with oxygen-lack must inevitably freeze people," wrote Frank Smythe in 1938.[46]

In 1922 George Finch commissioned his own outfit of feather down encased in hot-air balloon cloth. His diary shows that he felt very superior, watching his colleagues shivering in their tweed and gabardine clothes: "Everyone felt the cold except myself—my eiderdown coat, trousers, flying boots and flying helmet keeping me as warm as toast all through."[47] He imagined his fellow climbers were envious, but he was wrong. They simply poked fun at his eccentric costume behind his back. With a tribal love of the old uniform which confirmed one as a member of the upper classes, the Everesters continued to wear their Norfolk jackets, conventional knickerbockers, gabardine suits, Shetland sweaters, and trilby hats, and thus continued to be beset by cold and frostbite. As late as 1951, Noel Odell advised the New Zealanders Edmund Hillary and George Lowe that they needed no special equipment for the Himalayas, but "should take just exactly what we used [for climbing] in New Zealand, an ordinary Alpine tent and the clothing we wore in the Southern Alps."[48]

Down clothing did not become the norm for British climbers until after World War II.

On top of the problems caused by the cold, Everest expeditions were plagued by ill health. Sore throats, flu, laryngitis, respiratory infections, and stomach upsets invariably sapped the strength of the climbers. A few doctors questioned whether this was inevitable. Greene, for instance, was keen to improve the hygiene of the local cooks:

> *It is impossible to deny the danger to health of the filthy habits of native cooks in a country where dysentery is endemic. The Sherpa or Butia sees no sense in the cleaning of pots or washing of dishcloths. Himself apparently immune to any but the most virulent dysentery, he looks upon the boiling of water or milk as an insane whim of the doctor. Only unceasing vigilance will ensure his cooperation . . .[49]*

One of the doctors on the 1922 expedition wrote to the *Alpine Journal* suggesting that high infection rates among local Tibetans and Sherpas might be a contributory factor in the "high-altitude throat" that played havoc among expedition members. He also recommended the strictest medical supervision of the cookhouse to ensure the best possible sanitary conditions, worrying, rightly, that such issues "might be overlooked" on future expeditions.[50]

But later leaders, such as Shipton in 1935 and Tilman in 1938, took the view that ill health could not be avoided on Himalayan expeditions. Strict supervision of the cookhouse was simply not Tilman's style. Shipton and Tilman's unfussy, almost casual approach to mountaineering and their desire to blend in with the local ways were part of their appeal for many young climbers.

Over the years, the indefatigable expedition doctors who studied these subjects came to the conclusion that the climbing of Mount Everest was "as much a physiological problem as a mountaineering feat."[51] However, none of them was a specialist in the field.[52] Hingston was an RAF doctor. Charles Warren was a pediatrician. Above all, their work revealed the need for systematic study of the problems by specialists. But the idea of taking non-climbing scientists on expeditions—be they physiologists, geologists, naturalists, or geographers—had never been popular, and became even less so with the small-expedition ideal. Bill Tilman did not even want to take a doctor with him in 1938, and had to be forced to do so by the Everest Committee.

In 1937, Dr. Charles Warren suggested that high-altitude deterioration "required a great deal more investigation."[53] But nothing happened. After the expedition of 1938, Raymond Greene taunted the Everest Committee: "Supposing we go on sending out expeditions which return one after another but get no nearer the summit than the last; people will get rather tired of Everest expeditions and ask, what is the interest of these continued failures? Everybody will know, of course, that they are gallant failures . . . but the fact remains that one party after another fails to reach the top."[54] Greene pointed out that vast sums of money had already been spent on failed expeditions that kept coming home with nothing to show for their efforts, and things were getting worse. It was regrettable, he believed, "that [scientific work] on the more recent expeditions to Everest has been in no way encouraged, but rather discouraged by those responsible both for their organisation and their leadership."[55]

Insisting that the situation could no longer be justified, he called for future expeditions to be "planned primarily on a scientific basis" so that even if they failed, they would, at least, bring home some useful information. Provocatively he went on to suggest the unthinkable: The next expedition to Everest "should go out primarily as a scientific expedition accompanied by a small climbing party which, if the opportunity arises, will undoubtedly reach the top."[56]

Suitably horrified, Dr. Tom Longstaff stood up and intoned: "The idea of sending a scientific expedition to Everest is really deplorable; there could be no worse mixing of objectives."[57] At which point the British efforts to climb Mount Everest were interrupted by World War II.

3

Mountain of Destiny

Had it not been for Michael Ward, there would have been no British Everest Reconnaissance in 1951. The British had halted all attempts to climb Everest during World War II, and had disbanded the Everest Committee. It was not until 1947, the year of Indian Independence, that the Royal Geographical Society and the Alpine Club formed a new Himalayan Committee and began to think, unhurriedly, about reviving the Everest campaign.[1] Ward and other young climbers like him were frustrated by this lack of urgency from the old guard.

The climbing establishment's leisurely attitude toward Everest was partly due to their perception that changes in the political landscape had blocked off any viable access to the mountain. Previous expeditions had approached Everest from the north through Tibet. But Tibet had closed its borders to outsiders in 1947, and in 1950 it was invaded by the Chinese, who enforced their own ban on Western visitors. The only other route to Everest was from the south, through Nepal, a country that had been closed to almost all foreigners for the previous hundred years. Now, however, Nepal was gradually relaxing its restrictions, and the first Western expeditions were beginning to explore and map its territories, which included eight of the fourteen highest summits in the world.

In 1949, a small Swiss expedition, led by René Dittert, reconnoitered mountains on the border between Nepal and Tibet and claimed a virgin summit; in 1950, the French stunned the climbing world by making a successful ascent of Annapurna, the tenth-highest mountain in the world, and the first peak above 26,250 feet to be climbed.[2] Later that year, two members of a small American-led exploratory expedition, Charles Houston and the English Everest veteran Bill Tilman, briefly reconnoitered the southern approach to Everest. Misreading the mountain, they pronounced an ascent from that side unlikely to be feasible.[3]

Believing that the chances of climbing Everest from the south were at best "forty to one against," the Himalayan Committee remained apathetic.[4] Besides, the British had enjoyed priority over Everest for so long that they remained confident no other country would presume to muscle in on their territory. Michael Ward and his climbing friends, however, were shocked by the exploratory trips in Nepal, especially when they heard that yet another party who was "not English" was planning to visit Everest. In early 1951, fearing the British were about to be "caught napping by foreigners," Ward took positive action.[5]

First, he had to determine whether Everest could be climbed from the south. Poring over forgotten photographs in the library at the RGS, he discovered what he thought was a feasible route to the summit and began to agitate for an immediate British reconnaissance of the south side of the mountain. He had great difficulty, however, in drumming up any enthusiasm from the committee, who regarded him as a young whippersnapper.

Refusing to admit defeat, Ward organized his own trip with the help of the top Scottish climber and mountaineering author, W. H. (Bill) Murray, with whom he had climbed in the Alps in the 1940s. Murray rejoiced at the prospect of taking part in a spontaneous project involving just a handful of climbers and praised Ward in the most extravagant terms for his inspirational initiative. It was, he said, something that "suddenly sprang up out of nothing through what Plato would have called a divine madness coming over you. . . . These are the sort of expeditions that are worth going on."[6]

Ward and Murray persuaded Cam Secord, the Canadian mountaineer, to join them. Secord had climbed in the Himalayas with Bill Tilman and another famous Everest veteran, Frank Smythe. As an economist in the Cabinet Office, he also had better establishment connections than either Ward or Murray. With his help, the committee was finally persuaded to seek permission for the reconnaissance and provide £600 toward the estimated costs of £1,800.[7]

Basil Goodfellow, honorary secretary of the committee and a leading member of the Alpine Club, approached the Foreign Office, stressing the committee's traditional sense of entitlement over Everest:

Through our long series of expeditions between 1921 and 1938 we have firmly established our leadership in attacking the greatest problem remaining outstanding in mountain exploration and adventure. Meanwhile the successes of other nationalities in the Himalayas have inevitably turned their interest in the direction of Everest. The Himalayan Committee feels it is essential to give expression to the continuing British interest in Mount Everest by sending a further expedition to Mount Everest as soon as possible.[8]

At first, this conventional appeal to national pride went down well with the Foreign Office. A telegram was sent to Mr. Summerhayes, the British ambassador in Kathmandu, asking him to apply for permission to attempt Everest and requesting as usual that "[s]hould the Nepalese decide against granting permission I trust it may be possible to ensure that permission is similarly refused to any other applications to prospect Everest this year?"[9]

A reassuring reply came from Summerhayes, affirming that permission for the reconnaissance had been granted, and that all similar "foreign" requests had been refused.[10]

At this point, Ward and Murray invited Tom Bourdillon, a popular and influential young climber, to join their expedition. He and Ward had helped set up the Alpine Climbing Group, an exclusive group composed of young mountaineers who wanted to improve standards and persuade British climbers, who were lagging behind their European counterparts, to be more daring and adventurous.[11] Bourdillon had inspired great admiration by climbing the north face of the spire-shaped Aiguille du Dru in Chamonix, which Ward described as "the first modern route . . . of a really classic Alpine calibre to be climbed by an Englishman."[12]

The preparations for the expedition were rushed, and Ward and Bourdillon, lacking previous Himalayan experience, were guided mainly by what they could find out from the reports of past expeditions. When Ward took charge of the medicine chest, Bourdillon said that his father wanted to advise on the contents. Bourdillon's father, R. B. Bourdillon, a founding member of the Oxford University Mountaineering Club, had been an enthusiastic Alpine climber in his youth until stopped by ill health.[13] Qualified in medicine and chemistry, he was the director of the Electro-Magnetic Research Unit of the Medical Research Council (MRC) in Stoke Mandeville, where Ward went to see him.

They soon fell into an animated discussion about the altitude problems on Everest. Both feared that the air pressure on the top of Everest—which had never been measured—would prove to be too low for human survival. Looking at the RAF altitude tables showing the relationship between altitude and air pressure, they found it hard to credit how men like Edward Norton could have climbed above 28,000 feet on Everest without using supplementary oxygen. Like most people—except meteorologists and physiologists—they did not appreciate that because Everest is geographically near the equator, the atmospheric pressure on the summit is actually higher than the pressure predicted by the simplified altitude tables used in international aviation. Nevertheless, the summit of Everest is still very near the limit of human survival.[14] The conversation ended with Bourdillon sending Ward to seek advice from Griffith Pugh, a distant work acquaintance of his who was known to have studied altitude and survival in the mountains.

After his first meeting with Pugh, when he found him in the icy bath, Ward went back to his Hampstead laboratory several times before leaving for the Himalayas, and they did some experiments together. The starting point was that nearly all the climbers who had tried using supplementary oxygen at high altitude complained that they had to expend so much energy in carrying the apparatus that it completely offset any benefit.

Pugh suggested that this common complaint might be well founded. The oxygen sets used on Everest between the wars had been adapted from equipment developed for high-altitude flying.[15] The supplementary oxygen was given to climbers at the same rates as to airmen—2 to 2.5 liters a minute. However, unlike pilots sitting in their cockpits, climbers had to carry the oxygen sets on their backs while also expending energy climbing. If pilots needed 2 liters a minute, everything suggested that climbers would need much more.

Pugh set up a simple experiment to measure how much energy was consumed by carrying oxygen equipment, with Michael Ward as the subject.

The results showed what climbers had always known for themselves—that carrying the equipment consumed a significant amount of energy in itself. Most of the benefit of the supplementary oxygen was being used up in this way. No wonder climbers felt the sets were no use.

To get positive benefits, Pugh suggested that climbers should be given oxygen at far higher rates—perhaps double the rate that had been tried thus far, or even more. It was a simple solution that did not seem to have occurred to anyone over the previous thirty years.

Nonetheless, neither Pugh nor Ward felt they could draw any conclusions from laboratory tests. They both thought that a physiologist should go to the mountains and carry out tests on acclimatized climbers at high altitude.

—◦—

About six weeks before Ward's team was due to depart for the Himalayas, legendary mountaineer Eric Shipton returned to England after spending two years as British consul at Kunming in China and agreed to take over leadership of the reconnaissance.[16] Shipton had been on all the Everest expeditions of the 1930s, and would bring invaluable experience to an otherwise inexperienced party. He was famously attractive, with a lithe figure, penetrating blue eyes, and a tanned complexion. Such was his impact on women that a frisson of excitement would run through the female staff at the RGS whenever the legendary climber-explorer was in the building. Last on Everest in 1935, he was now forty-four years old, but still fit and ready to have another go.

When Cam Secord dropped out, Shipton invited two extra climbers to join the trip: New Zealanders Edmund Hillary and Earle Riddiford.[17] Tom Bourdillon, suffering from the snobbery that was commonplace among Alpine Club members in the 1950s, was mildly surprised to find that he actually liked Hillary, despite the New Zealander not being a "gentleman." He confided to his wife: "I wish you could meet Ed. He is one of the best blokes I know. Earle is a good man—old N.Z. family, sheep farmer, soldier and now lawyer, 30, and he is a gentleman, which Ed is not, but I would as soon climb or talk with Ed as anyone I know . . ."[18]

They left England in early August, with Shipton protesting that they had "very little hope of success." He was wrong. They quickly discovered a viable route up the southern side of Everest, proving Ward's theory. Not equipped to try for the summit themselves, they realized that they should secure permission for a full-scale British expedition as soon as possible.

In mid-October 1951, while they continued to explore the environs of Everest, Shipton sent a message to Colonel Proud, first secretary at the British embassy in Kathmandu, asking him to apply at once for the following year. Unbeknownst to Shipton, Colonel Proud's boss, Ambassador Summerhayes, had already taken the precaution of asking the Maharajah of Nepal for a permit for a British expedition the following year, but had learned, to his consternation, that the Swiss already had verbal permission for 1952, precluding a British visit in the same year. The news sent shock waves through the British climbing establishment.

For almost half a century the Royal Geographical Society had labored under the illusion that it had exclusive rights of access to Everest. Since beginning life in 1830 as one of Britain's gentlemanly learned societies, the RGS had maneuvered itself to the forefront of mapping, measuring, and exploring the fringes of the known world, and had come to be regarded as "the spiritual home of British exploration." The Society had helped to organize and sponsor heroic pioneering expeditions such as Scott's and Shackleton's ventures in the Antarctic, ran courses on mapping and surveying that were heavily patronized by colonial civil servants, and was an important source of geographical information and advice for government departments, including the India Office.[19]

In the early part of the twentieth century, Mount Everest, as yet unexplored, unmapped, and unclimbed, presented the RGS with a perfect challenge. Many illustrious members of the society were sorely disappointed that Britain, the nation that controlled the largest empire the world had ever seen, had failed to be first to reach either the North Pole (claimed by American Robert Peary in 1909) or the South Pole, where Captain Scott (heavily sponsored by the RGS) lost out to Norwegian Roald Amundsen in 1911. Mount Everest was seen as "the Third Pole"; winning it would restore British honor. And in the glory days of the British Empire, it was tempting for the RGS to feel that Everest was their very own mountain of destiny.

The sense of ownership—"Dammit, it's *our* mountain!"—had been fully confirmed in 1921 when Tibet granted the first permit to climb Everest to the

British, represented by the RGS. The RGS immediately turned to Britain's premier climbing gentlemen's club, the Alpine Club. The Everest Committee representing both institutions was formed to organize and finance the expedition.

The British government invariably consulted the RGS about the suitability of proposed climbing expeditions to Everest, British and foreign alike, so the Everest Committee was able to influence their fate, and established an effective monopoly.

After the failure of the first three British expeditions in 1921, 1922, and 1924, a Swiss application in 1924 was dismissed as an "attempt to take advantage of the preliminary spade work which has been done and . . . snatch the final victory."[20] A German application in 1925 met with a similar fate, as did a further Swiss application in 1926 and an Italian application in 1928, and so it went on.

Officials at the India Office generally found it "impossible not to sympathise" with the committee's desire for exclusivity, though they worried that it was "not a sportsmanlike attitude." But having accepted that it was in Britain's interest to keep the competition at bay, British diplomats used three lines of defense against foreign expeditions. The first was to refuse to pass foreign applications for Everest on to Tibet, telling aspirants they had no chance of success due to the "sensitivities" of the political situation.

In cases where this tactic would be politically embarrassing, applications *were* passed on, but diplomats put pressure on the Tibetan government to refuse them in consideration of "favours" granted to Tibet, such as "the helpful attitude we took up when the Dalai Lama asked for arms and ammunition during the tension with China."[21] Britain's own requests for Everest were often refused, but the diplomats succeeded in ensuring that other countries were refused as well, guaranteeing that when permission *was* forthcoming, it was granted only to the Everest Committee.

This approach worked well until, in the mid-1930s, the Club Alpin Français was inspired to circumvent the British by asking the Chinese to pass along their Everest application to Tibet. The Chinese did so, and Tibet immediately granted permission.

Horrified, the British now resorted to a third line of defense made possible by the fact that all expeditions had to start in India and trek through Sikkim to reach Tibet. Carefully disguising the true reasons, the government of India refused the French team access to "facilities in India," and made sure they didn't obtain a permit to cross Sikkim.

Recognizing the British power of veto not just over Everest, but throughout the Himalayas, foreign teams understood they must tread carefully. Protests were muted, and applications were often dropped without fuss when Britain's displeasure became evident. Other countries became quite bitter: German climber Paul Bauer, who received permission to attempt Kanchenjunga in 1929, told the *Daily Telegraph* that he "originally hoped to attack Mount Everest," but his plan had been "thwarted by the jealousy of the English," who "flatly refused permission."[22]

Now, in mid-October 1951, after half a century of such politicking, the Swiss had seized their opportunity with Nepal, while, as they put it, "the British were asleep."

The British were particularly upset that the Swiss had not told them of their plans earlier on. The Swiss had received verbal permission in May 1951. Shipton only learned about it when he got back to Kathmandu after the reconnaissance. The ambassador telegraphed London: "Shipton thinks it can hardly be possible that the Swiss climbing people . . . would be planning an expedition without any word to our people, and with the idea of trying the route he has been testing."[23]

The Swiss were perhaps taking their revenge on Shipton, who had refused to allow top Swiss climber René Dittert to go with him on the reconnaissance, but then invited New Zealanders Hillary and Riddiford to join him. The Swiss reticence about their expedition was ominously reminiscent of Roald Amundsen's failure to tell Captain Scott that he intended to race him to the South Pole, even when Scott had visited him shortly before setting out. Scott made his plans and began his journey in June 1910, innocently unaware that he had competition, only to lose the race to Amundsen and perish with the rest of his team on the way home. RGS members comforted themselves by denigrating Amundsen as a cheat.

On December 11, 1951, Eric Shipton appeared in front of the Himalayan Committee and dropped the double bombshell: Everest could be climbed from the south, and the Swiss rather than the British had permission to attempt it by the new route in the following year. Adding insult to injury, a message from Ambassador Summerhayes put forward a most unwelcome suggestion: "It would seem a good solution if next year's expedition could be a combined one."[24] Hearing this for the first time, the committee could hardly believe it. Ten days later reality dawned, and Basil Goodfellow grudgingly went to Switzerland to discuss the possibility of joining in with the Swiss.

There proved to be several difficulties with a joint venture, but negotiations broke down over the issue of who would lead the expedition, with the British insisting that Shipton be appointed leader of any joint enterprise, and the Swiss advocating a joint leadership. But Basil Goodfellow privately admitted the other important reason to his Foreign Office contact (a certain Mr. R. H. Scott). Scott noted: "Mr. Goodfellow told me for my confidential information that another factor in the British decision was that the Alpine Club were not quite ready for a full-scale permission this year."[25]

The Foreign Office, who had been pursuing a policy of strategic cooperation with the Swiss in the Far East, was surprisingly unsympathetic to the committee's difficulties, pointing out: "The Swiss offer seemed worth looking at carefully; otherwise the Swiss might get up by themselves and beat us to it!"[26]

Another member of the Himalayan Committee, Laurence Kirwan, secretary and director of the RGS, met with a similar response from his contact in the South East Asia Office, who said, "We would deprecate making a political issue of climbing Everest and should like to avoid international bickering about it."[27]

Disappointed that the committee had rejected a joint Anglo-Swiss venture, the Foreign Office was less than enthusiastic about Goodfellow's alternative proposal. This was to send a British "training expedition" to Cho Oyu, another mountain in the Everest region, while the Swiss were on Everest, and, on the assumption that the Swiss would fail, to follow that up with an exclusively British attempt on Everest in 1953. Mr. Scott commented:

Goodfellow . . . was obviously hoping that I would endorse what had been done, but I refrained from doing so and instead left him in no doubt that I was very disappointed to hear this news. I warned him that the Alpine Club were taking a risk that the political atmosphere would be right for an expedition next year, and I warned him that the responsibility for this risk lay entirely with the Alpine Club.[28]

4

Turf Wars

In the years after the war, Eric Shipton had developed the habit of occasionally turning up uninvited at Griffith Pugh's laboratory in London to ask questions about the physiology of altitude. They had first met in Iran in 1942, when Shipton, on his way home from China, stopped off at the British consulate in Meshed, where Pugh was working as a doctor. They spent several days walking together in the hills. Pugh wrote home afterward that Shipton was "the strong silent type," a trait that "lent considerable charm to his rather stern appearance."[1]

Though not a great lover of science, Shipton was intrigued by news of some daring physiological experiments, entitled "Operation Everest," which had been carried out in America in 1946 by Charles Houston, working for the US Navy.[2] The experiments appeared to demonstrate that it was possible to survive on the summit of Everest without supplementary oxygen. Four young men had spent twenty-nine days in a pressure chamber, gradually acclimatizing to increasingly high altitudes. On the thirtieth day they were rushed from 22,500 feet to a simulated altitude roughly equivalent to the summit of Everest (29,029 feet). One dropped out on the way up; another asked for oxygen, but two remained unharmed without extra oxygen for 21 minutes.

Hearing of this in 1947, Shipton urged the Himalayan Committee to take an active interest: "I do hope something is going forward to coordinate physiological research regarding high altitudes, and I would be extremely interested to hear what is being done about this . . ."[3]

When he began visiting Pugh, Pugh reacted unenthusiastically. In his view laboratory experiments could be no substitute for studying men in the field. "Eric didn't get much useful information from me," he said. "You can't give really telling information from your laboratory chair." Pugh told Shipton, "If you want anything from me, I'll have to come with you."[4]

The Himalayan Committee was well aware that the war had brought substantial improvements in the oxygen equipment used by RAF fighter pilots, as well as in the design of protective equipment, clothing, and rations for soldiers operating in extreme conditions, all of which could be of use to climbers.[5] Three experienced men—Peter Lloyd, Dr. Raymond Greene, and Scott Russell (George Finch's son-in-law)—were delegated in 1947 to analyze the latest developments, but they had no more success than Shipton.[6]

Peter Lloyd, who took on the subject of oxygen, had the distinction of being the only Everest climber to come out strongly in favor of oxygen since Finch had done so in 1922. Lloyd was an engineer in his mid-forties, educated at public school and Cambridge. Once a powerful climber, and a former president of the Cambridge University Mountaineering Club, he was a member of the 1938 Everest expedition led by Bill Tilman.[7] On that expedition he had tried oxygen and found, "I was moving . . . much better . . . but the main difference was the absence of strain or fatigue."[8]

However, since many of the most revered climbers in the Alpine Club regarded the use of oxygen as cheating and unsportsmanlike, Lloyd could seldom bring himself to speak publicly in its support without first assuring his audience that he would far prefer to see Everest climbed without it.[9] Lloyd's ambivalence was symptomatic of the traditional values of the Alpine Club—values which originated in the "public-school amateur" sporting culture that a majority of Alpine Club and RGS members, and nearly all the Everest climbers, had been exposed to at school.[10]

As every public school–educated British gentleman knew, competing "well" was more important than winning. Amateur sport—that is to say, gentlemanly sport, for the words *amateur* and *gentleman* were interchangeable—was not supposed to be played primarily to win, but "for the love of the game." A British gentleman competed boldly, was not too worried about losing, and above all played by the rules. Elaborate preparation, training, and the use of scientific methods to boost performance were all viewed as a descent into professionalism, and were therefore "bad form" and ungentlemanly.[11]

In line with the public-school tradition, the British Everest quest was trumpeted to the world as an epic, elemental struggle between man and nature—a pure sporting challenge. As such, it was held to inhabit a superior moral sphere, above the grubby materialistic concerns of technology, science, politics, publicity, and international competition. British climbers wanted to climb Mount Everest, as Mallory so famously said, purely "because it is there." Getting to the summit, they claimed, was much less important than getting to the summit in a sporting way.

Writing in 1932, Noel Odell (who was on Everest with Mallory in 1924) abhorred the idea of climbers turning for help to engineers and scientists: "Both engineer and physiologist may be reminded that among many mountaineers the opinion prevails that if Mount Everest and other high Himalayan peaks are worth climbing at all, they should be ascended without such artificial aids as may reduce a sport to a mere laboratory experiment."[12] In 1948 the iconic Everest veteran Bill Tilman insisted: "If our end is just to plant a man on the top of the mountain then I suppose any means are justified, but if our end is mountaineering in the true sense, then we should stick by the rules."

The main enemy of true sport in Himalayan climbing was seen to be oxygen. The idea that, however much it might help them, only "rotters" would use oxygen remained a dominant view right up to World War II.[13] "It may be expedient to climb Mount Everest with oxygen apparatus," well-known climber Frank Smythe declared in 1942, "but speaking personally I would prefer to fail on that mountain without oxygen than I would to climb it with oxygen, for to my mind the whole charm of mountaineering lies in the employment of skill and energy with the minimum of artificial aid."[14] Tilman opined, witheringly, "When a man has to start inhaling oxygen, his spirit has already been conquered by the mountain and the limit of his capacity has been very clearly defined."[15]

Meanwhile, the repeated British failures on Everest were not mourned, but celebrated as "gallant failures," revealing the manly spirit that had made the Empire. "Everest cannot add to her height; but the spirit of man heightens with each repulse," declared Lieutenant Colonel Younghusband, the first president of the Everest Committee.[16] "Man reels back again and again, but again and again he returns to the onslaught."[17]

Mallory and Irvine, who died on Everest in 1924, were honored and mythologized in heroic imagery. Mallory was commemorated in the stained-glass windows of his local parish church alongside three great icons of impeccable saintliness and courtly chivalry—St. George, King Arthur, and Sir Galahad. In the pages of *Mountain Craft*, Geoffrey Young, doyen of British mountaineering circles, reminded aspiring young climbers of their duty to live up to this "glorious" tradition. "It lies with those who are now beginning, to keep the game a good one," Young urged, "to play it in a generous spirit according to the highest sporting tradition . . . to be observant of its rules." Furthermore, he opined, no right-thinking British mountaineer would harbor ambitions to compete with other countries: "The hills are our opponents, not other climbers, or even other nations . . . In the mountain game, no feelings are depressed if we win, no one triumphs by our defeat." Climbing, he insisted, should be above such petty concerns:

> *Every climber owes it to the great mountain past, to which he is heir, to keep climbing . . . free from international rivalries, from unsporting competitiveness, from publicity stunting, and from the fatal crowd infection of rating results above the spirit and manner of the doing.*[18]

As long as other countries could be kept away from Everest, the British Everest quest could be celebrated as a noble, romantic struggle with nature, and British climbers could continue to boast about their great sporting principles. The Everest Committee could continue to send ill-prepared, amateurish expeditions to Everest (particularly the later expeditions of 1935 and 1938, under leaders like Tilman and Shipton) and remain content to wait for the skill, talent, and indomitable courage of gentlemen-climbers to carry a British team to the summit . . . eventually.

But now, in December 1951, the Himalayan Committee faced competition for the first time. After seven British failures on Everest, it was galling to contemplate that the Swiss might succeed in their first attempt. It would be profoundly embarrassing to the committee and a major blow to British prestige if they did.

If, on the other hand, the Swiss failed, the British would probably only get one more chance to be first to the top. Other countries had begun to jostle for their turns. France, Germany, and Russia, all rumored to be about to request permission, did not suffer from British inhibitions about seeking professional scientific advice, nor did they exclude professional climbers from their teams. If the British failed in 1953, a foreign team would almost certainly succeed.

At this moment the British "sporting" morality began to crumble. There was no more talk of heroics. The three dynamic members of the committee, Laurence Kirwan, Basil Goodfellow, and Peter Lloyd, were galvanized into action. Even Eric Shipton was heard calling for oxygen meetings and scientific advice.[19]

Urgent preparations for the putative joint expedition with the Swiss began even before Goodfellow left for Switzerland to "clarify" the situation. Since the Swiss had had their own physiologists design climbing oxygen for their team, Britain's oxygen needs suddenly became a top priority. Peter Lloyd, who had always had trouble getting his fellow climbers to listen to him on the subject, now moved center stage.

Lloyd quickly convened a meeting to plan the British oxygen strategy. The RAF had been an important source of help and advice since Finch's day, and Group Captain Stewart and Wing Commander Roxburgh, of the Institute of Aviation Medicine at Farnborough, now agreed to lend a hand.[20] Lloyd also approached R. B. Bourdillon, who had been following the Everest problems for several months.

Two different oxygen systems were available: the "open-circuit" system, which Finch had used in 1922, and the "closed-circuit" system, which had been developed for mining rescue and firefighting, and adapted for climbing in 1936. The open-circuit was so called because the climber, using a mask, breathed in normal air from the atmosphere, supplemented by a small proportion of oxygen piped from the cylinders on his back and breathed out directly back into the atmosphere.[21] If he did not want to wear a mask, he could breathe in the oxygen through a simple tube held in his mouth, which he closed by clenching his teeth when breathing out so as not to waste the oxygen.

With the closed-circuit the climber wore a more-elaborate, airtight mask through which he was fed virtually 100 percent oxygen. He had no contact at all with the outside air. His exhaled breath was piped through a canister of soda-lime powder strapped to his body, which absorbed the carbon dioxide and recycled the remaining unused oxygen back to him. This was topped up with oxygen from the cylinders on his back.[22]

A few sets of both types had been sent on the last three Everest expeditions, but without definitive evidence to show which system worked best, the arguments between exponents of the respective systems were often as heated as those between pro- and anti-oxygen protagonists.

Peter Lloyd had tried both systems on Everest in 1938 and had found the closed-circuit suffocating and "unusable." However, R. B. Bourdillon was convinced that the closed-circuit system was far superior to the open-circuit, and just needed a little further development, which he and his son were planning to undertake in time for 1953.[23]

Given the time constraint, Lloyd was determined to stick to one type of apparatus only: the simple, reliable, tried-and-tested open-circuit sets developed from standard RAF equipment. "I am despondent about the oxygen situation," he confided to Laurence Kirwan. "Time is so desperately short; and industry is so fantastically bunged up with rearmament orders."[24]

Basil Goodfellow's negotiations with the Swiss soon broke down, and the committee decided to go ahead with the training expedition to Cho Oyu, an unconquered mountain of 26,906 feet, the sixth-highest in the world and 25 miles to the west of Everest, chosen mainly because two pairs of climbers on Shipton's Everest reconnaissance thought they had spotted a feasible route to the summit.[25]

Preparations now swung into action. Laurence Kirwan, the forceful director of the RGS, was the driving force. Kirwan had spent most of World War II as a staff officer in the Cabinet Office and the Ministry of Defense. He was an energetic fixer, renowned for his "shrewd knowledge of people, their potentialities, and how they might best be employed," and at six-foot-six, he had an air of "magisterial authority."[26]

Kirwan knew from Goodfellow that the Swiss had taken expert advice about oxygen, diet, and equipment, and he was also aware, as he admitted to Lloyd, that the Himalayan Committee had achieved "precisely nothing" on any of these topics since the war.[27] So he was in a receptive mood when R. B. Bourdillon contacted him to talk about getting professional help.

At Lloyd's oxygen meeting, Bourdillon had proposed a working party to study the use of oxygen at high altitude, as well as high-altitude deterioration, diet, clothing, and equipment. And he had suggested that Griffith Pugh and his boss Otto Edholm be asked to advise.[28] By lobbying Kirwan directly, he now sought to ensure that there would be no loss of momentum.[29]

Kirwan was won over, and he, Bourdillon, Shipton, Scott Russell, Michael Ward, and Robert McCance—a Cambridge professor who was a world expert on nutrition—met and made a snap decision to send a physiologist out to Cho Oyu with Shipton.[30] With Kirwan behind it, this idea became a top priority.

Faced with the problem of funding, Kirwan made an informal application to the Royal Society for a grant, and found he was pushing at an open door.[31] However, there were precious few specialists in the rarefied field of altitude physiology, and even fewer with direct experience working in the mountains, so for the third time Bourdillon suggested the only suitable candidate he could think of: Griffith Pugh of the Medical Research Council.[32]

Pugh had been mulling over the Everest problems since first meeting Michael Ward seven months earlier, and now an extraordinary opportunity was about to fall into his lap. Within days the training expedition received the Himalayan Committee's formal approval. The fact that the Nepalese had not yet given permission was ignored. On January 25, 1952, Shipton rang Pugh and formally invited him to join. He accepted at once.

The Royal Society asked Professor Bryan Matthews to review the Himalayan Committee's grant application, which had been written by Bourdillon.[33] Matthews, who had advised Everest expeditions since the early 1930s, was the head of a highly successful physiology department at Cambridge University. He had gained world renown as an altitude physiologist during the war when he took charge of the RAF physiological laboratory at Farnborough, transforming it into the internationally acclaimed RAF School of Aviation Medicine. He left to return to Cambridge in 1946, but remained the institute's influential "chief consultant."

Matthews was regarded as a highly practical leader—the type who quickly saw what had to be done and produced the simplest and quickest solution. This was combined with a fearsome reputation for impatience with bureaucracy, and for "banging heads together."[34] He was not optimistic about the prospect of obtaining useful information on Cho Oyu, writing: "It is unfortunate that time will be so short that little provision [for oxygen research] will be possible." However, because he thought the research project essential if there was to be "a serious attempt to climb Mount Everest next year," he gave his support. Of Pugh he wrote: "I am afraid I know rather little of him so cannot give support or otherwise to him personally; but I would support most strongly that someone with the necessary capacities should be attached to the expedition."[35]

The task facing Pugh was huge: There was little time to assemble the necessary equipment and devise experiments from scratch. He had limited contact with Matthews, and received no guidance from Shipton or Lloyd. Most of his equipment had to be ready by April 27, several days before the climbers would embark on the three-week boat trip to India. Rather than traveling by ship, Pugh wanted to fly out, thereby gaining three extra weeks to prepare.

This proved unpopular. It had been one thing for Kirwan to network among the Nobel Prize winners of the Royal Society for a grant to pay for a physiologist. It was quite another to sympathize with the difficulties facing the scientist chosen for the job, particularly when he had the temerity to expect to be flown to India, a privilege normally accorded only to the expedition leader.

After failing to persuade the MRC that Pugh should pay for his own fare, Kirwan grudgingly agreed to cover the cost of the journey.

5

In the Mountains of Lebanon

Michael Ward had come away from his first meeting with Griffith Pugh doubting whether he would learn much from the shambolic, forgetful, slightly crazy physiologist who fitted so perfectly the stereotype of the absentminded scientist. However, on his second visit, while chasing Pugh around Hampstead Heath, he became convinced that he had found the ideal person to help him tackle the problems climbers had been wrestling with on Everest. Pugh had gained the skills and experience during the war that made him the best man for the job.

British soldiers had suffered badly from cold, frostbite, and hypothermia while fighting the Axis powers in the mountains of Norway, Greece, and Italy. Pugh had seen it for himself when he was stationed in Greece in 1941. Later in his wartime career he was posted to a mountain-warfare training school in Lebanon, where he carried out the research that won him a reputation in senior British and American military and medical circles for being "someone who knows about cold."

In 1950 when the Medical Research Council—faced with the prospect of a war in Korea, where the British army might have to fight in mountainous conditions again—created a research unit to address the problems faced by soldiers in extreme environments, Pugh was one of the first recruits.

Poached from his postwar job as a medical registrar at Hammersmith Hospital in London, Pugh joined the newly formed "Division of Human Physiology," a division of the National Institute for Medical Research, the largest of the MRC's network of research institutes and units. The division had strong army backing and was generously funded and lavishly equipped with a wind tunnel and an expensive cold chamber. Professor Otto Edholm, an expert on survival, was brought over from Canada to be the director because no specialist in "applied human physiology" of sufficient seniority could be found at home. Pugh himself was too junior to become the director, but had recommended Edholm.

Pugh had qualified in medicine in 1938, and entered the war as a junior doctor—a captain in the Royal Army Medical Corps. He spent the first part of the war with a "mobile military hospital unit" in the Middle East Theater, stationed at hospital camps in Jerusalem and Greece, where he became an expert on syphilis, treating VD in soldiers and prostitutes in and around Athens. When the Germans invaded Greece, he cared for wounded Allied and enemy soldiers; in late 1941 after Greece fell and the Allied armies were evacuated, he worked in hospital camps in Bombay, Iraq, and Iran. The autumn of 1942 found him in northeast Iran, looking after Polish families—many of whom were suffering from typhus—evacuated from Russian labor camps after Stalin joined the Allies.

Life in the strategic backwater of Meshed was comfortable for Pugh. He enjoyed being his own boss in charge of the medical center. He was billeted at the luxurious British consulate, where the food was excellent. In his spare time he went walking and duck-shooting with the consul and his wife. And yet he was frustrated by what he regarded as the latest in a series of dead-end medical jobs.

For months he had been making fruitless efforts to be transferred to an army commando unit where the work would be more exciting, attempting to sell himself to headquarters on the basis of being a strong skier and mountaineer. He had kept himself extremely fit and had seized every opportunity to climb, first in Greece and later in the Alborz Mountains above Tehran.

But his efforts to impress General Headquarters (GHQ) were flatly ignored, and he often lamented his fate in his diary. After spending two months at Shuaiba Hospital Camp in the Iraqi desert outside Basra in 1941, he wrote:

> *How I wish I could go to the mountains in the north when there is snow or to Syria. But how to set about it? I have drafted a letter stating my experience of mountains & skiing, but to whom should I send it? Usual channels only lead to backwaters. I have not heard that there are any ski troops & doubt if the idea has yet occurred to the authorities.*[1]

A year later, in Meshed, his wishes were answered when, out of the blue, he was ordered to go to Lebanon for what seemed like a dream job as a ski instructor.

The summons came from an old school friend, James Riddell, chief instructor of the recently established mountain-warfare training school at the resort of Cedars in the mountains above Beirut. By sheer luck Riddell was looking for ski instructors to fill an acute shortage at the school. As he searched through the lists of British army officers at Middle East Command, Pugh's name leapt out at him. They had been in the same house at Harrow, and Riddell had been vice-captain of the 1936 Olympic ski team, of which Pugh was a member.

Pugh had learned to ski, ski-mountaineer, and climb in his early teens. His colonial family, based in Calcutta, often found it convenient to send him to Switzerland during the school holidays rather than transport him back to India. He stayed regularly at a small pension called Haldengütli in the resort of Engelberg, where he was taught to ski and climb by the son of the household, Lothar Hauthal, an expert skier and guide. Haldengütli became a home away from home for Pugh, who was a bit of a lost soul without a permanent residence in England. Returning for skiing holidays year after year and becoming a close friend of the Hauthal family, he developed into an excellent skier. He skied for the Oxford University ski team, competed for Britain in the World Championships at Innsbruck in 1935 and in Engelberg in 1937, and was selected to ski in the cross-country event in the 1936 Winter Olympic Games at Garmisch-Partenkirchen. He was given time off from his medical studies to prepare, but a back injury at the last minute prevented him from taking part.

Pugh's biggest passion, however, was ski-mountaineering: traveling on skis in small groups through the high Alps from mountain hut to mountain hut for several days at a time. The long Oxford summer vacations were often spent climbing in the Alps, too, giving him still more experience navigating in the mountains.

The idea for the Mountain Warfare Ski Unit at Cedars had arisen in the summer of 1941, when it dawned on the British Army that they might have to confront the Axis powers in the mountains of the Middle East, the Balkans, and Bavaria.[2] Allied troops had already suffered "bitter lessons" fighting in the mountains of Norway and northern Greece. Pugh had seen some of the casualties of the Greek conflict at Kephissia, outside Athens, in 1941, writing home to his mother:

> *The Greeks are doing wonderful things in the Albanian mountains; almost every day bells are ringing for the capture of another village. I am afraid they have suffered terribly from the cold, and the hospitals are full of frostbite casualties. Frostbite is worse than bullet wounds as it leads to the loss of whole limbs. The Italians, judging by the prisoners, must have suffered terribly too. They come back, poor things, hobbling on dead feet still encased in the boots they were wearing when captured.*[3]

Determined not to repeat past failures, GHQ made a snap decision to create a mountain-warfare training school in the Middle East. Riddell was chosen to set it up because he had been an Olympic skier. His less than impressive prewar background as a writer who had dropped out of Cambridge without finishing his modern languages degree proved to be no obstacle.[4] He was extracted from his position as British political agent at Homs in western Syria, promoted from captain to major, and given carte blanche.[5]

The resort of Cedars, near Bcharre in the Lebanese mountains, was a large, bowl-shaped plateau at a height of 5,741 feet, distinguished by its single isolated copse of magnificent ancient cedar trees. It was surrounded on three sides by mountains of 9,843 feet; the fourth side gave a view down to the Mediterranean, 30 miles away.

On his first morning, Pugh woke up unable to believe his luck. The posting of his dreams had dropped into his lap. He wrote to his wife: "When I woke this morning & looked out of my window a marvellous view greeted my eyes. Wonderful snow peaks all round rising 8,000 feet above the hotel. It was perfect Alpine scenery. The early sun shone on glistening white snow fields."[6]

The school was based in the only building, the large, rambling, unoccupied Hôtel des Cedres. Riddell and the commander, Lieutenant Colonel Henry (Bunny) Nugent Head, chose to keep army bureaucracy to a minimum, yet presided over a highly disciplined organization, relying on the natural authority of their brilliance at skiing to impress and enthuse the men. Head was an excellent skier, and Pugh used to say that Jimmie Riddell was one of the most talented and graceful skiers ever to come out of Britain.

Having always disliked army hierarchy and bureaucracy, Pugh found the relaxed atmosphere as delightful as the job of teaching skiing. Within a week he was writing ecstatic letters home to his wife: "It's wonderful to be skiing again . . . ," he told her, repeating in another letter, "I keep thinking how lucky I am to be here . . . I've just had a perfect day . . ."

Naturally inclined to question the status quo, Pugh immediately began to think about how the training and selection of the ski troops might be improved. The trainees were expected to do seven and a half hours of skiing every day from the day of their arrival, which Pugh considered extremely taxing: "The men were exhausted when we returned in the evening & there wasn't a sound to be heard from their quarters after nine o'clock."[7]

After three weeks, the trainees took a formal test. Seeing that only half of them passed, Pugh concluded: "Tired men lose their appetite for skiing and make no progress. The accident rate rises. Some even strain their hearts and have to be returned to their units."[8]

Realizing the schedule was too onerous, he convinced Riddell and Head to try reducing it by half. The new intakes were given three hours of skiing a day in the first week, increasing to six hours by the third. Ninety percent of the men on the new regime passed the test, having skied only half as much as the earlier groups. The accident rate was cut in half.[9] With that problem solved, Pugh went on to address the high dropout rates among recruits, many of whom proved "unsuitable" for mountain training. He persuaded the medical officer to help him collect data on each intake and observe the men during their training, with a view toward identifying selection criteria. He was taking the first steps to becoming a full-time physiologist.

The urge to experiment was in Pugh's nature. He had been an insatiably curious child, consumed by what Emmanuel Kant described as "the restless need to make sense of things," but in his most formative years he had lacked anyone to help him find answers to his many questions, and he often had to rely on his own resources.

In 1914, at the age of four, he had been left for five years isolated with his three-year-old sister on a Welsh country estate in the care of a nanny.

During that time he had no formal schooling, practically no discipline, and little contact with the outside world, and he spent most of his time playing outside in almost complete freedom. It was then, in his hungry search for knowledge, that Pugh was first stimulated to conduct homespun experiments. The instinct to try to get to the root of a problem by creating his own experiments remained with him for the rest of his life.

Later, as a medical student at Oxford, Pugh attended some classes on experimental physiology given by Professor Claude Gordon Douglas, a close friend and colleague of J. S. Haldane, the eminent scientist of the so-called "Oxford School" of physiology.[10] Haldane invented one of the most important tools in the applied physiologist's armory—the Haldane gas analyzer, used for measuring the proportions of oxygen and carbon dioxide in samples of breath. Douglas invented the Douglas bag, a rubberized canvas bag (later plastic) in which exhaled breath could be collected for analysis. Gas analyzers and Douglas bags were to become Pugh's trusty companions throughout his career. Douglas was semiretired when he taught Pugh, but earlier in his career he had taken part in what is generally accepted to have been the first major *scientific* high-altitude expedition, to Tenerife in 1910.[11]

In Switzerland Pugh began doing physiological experiments on his fellow guests at Haldengütli, subjecting them to all kinds of tests when they arrived and again a week later, to measure the changes in their fitness and acclimatization. Their ski trips were interrupted for sessions of breath-holding and pulse-taking. The same urge to experiment took hold of Pugh as soon as he arrived at Cedars.

When, just six weeks after Pugh's arrival, Middle East High Command ordered Cedars to start carrying out detailed research, Pugh found himself ahead of their game plan. GHQ was concerned that the British Army lacked any understanding of how to select, train, or equip troops for mountain warfare, and knew even less about efficient troop mobility in mountainous terrain. There was a complete dearth of army manuals on these subjects. Therefore, a "most important" directive emanated from Cairo, ordering that in addition to teaching soldiers to ski, the ski wing must now also start to train them to "act as long-range mountain patrols." They wanted research into all aspects of "fighting in the snow," including "equipment and the maintenance of the human body in fighting trim in such conditions." The experience was to be used "to formulate a doctrine for the training of troops in this kind of warfare."[12]

At this point, Pugh must have seemed a godsend to Riddell and Head. He was given full responsibility for the physiological research and the training of the long-range patrols. Ten days later he wrote to his wife:

> *I am handling all the advanced training as well as the medical scheme for finding out the best way of picking men for this kind of work . . . Everything has to be built up from the beginning & all the equipment worked out. It is all tremendously interesting & already results are beginning to show themselves. Being a doctor is a great help in finding the best training methods.*[13]

Pugh's career in physiology took off at that moment. He had an almost unlimited supply of experimental subjects, about 60 miles of varied terrain at between 4,600 and 9,800 feet, a wide variety of weather conditions, and the freedom and authority to research whatever he wanted. He responded by throwing himself, with huge energy, into the study of almost every aspect of "man in the mountain environment."

He read up on physiology, statistical methods, and theories on experimental design from textbooks obtained from the American Library in Beirut, which also gave him access to the limited academic papers that had been written on topics like adaptation to altitude, the physiology of exercise, and the effects of cold stress on physical performance. He had to be extremely adaptable, devising his own experiments with hardly any specialist equipment.

Pugh was given a free hand to form his own commando unit of elite "guinea pigs" who served as subjects for many of his experiments. He claimed they needed at least three months' fitness training to prepare them for his grueling six- to eight-day, long-range patrols. The patrols—designed to be entirely self-sufficient—covered as many as 120 miles on skis and climbed around 22,000 vertical feet, carrying loads of around 55 pounds, containing all their food and equipment.

"I love these long-range patrols," Pugh wrote home to his wife, "particularly the ones that end up by the sea."[14]

Nothing escaped his eye. He tested the army ski suits, originally designed for troops in the Arctic, and pronounced them "quite unsuitable" for the mountains of southern Europe. He designed an experimental suit made of a lightweight double-layered fabric, incorporating practical details such as air vents in the trousers to keep sweating to a minimum (previous solutions had been "opening fly buttons and rolling up trousers"). Deeming the ski boots equally unsuitable, he designed a flexible boot specifically for ski-mountaineering. He studied load-carrying and worked out how much weight mountain troops could carry without becoming exhausted or compromising their speed. He modified the rucksacks to distribute the weight more efficiently. He researched dietary requirements and devised ration scales for mountain exercises, applying the principle that men taking strenuous exercise at altitude tend to have faddish appetites and will not eat if they do not like the food. In addition to providing adequate nutrition, the rations had to suit individual tastes.

He examined fluid intakes and concluded that while on patrol, his commandos needed to drink approximately eight pints of water a day. The Primus stoves took an extremely long time to melt water from snow, so he designed a more efficient stove which the army adopted.[15] He modified the ski bindings to make them safer. The army's tents were heavy and inefficient, so he designed a lightweight, double-skinned tent for long-range patrols. He worked out how to construct snow holes and igloos in the unusually powdery Lebanese snow, and occasionally chose to sleep in his own snow hole rather than in a tent. He also made recommendations about safety, hygiene, navigation, snow craft, and survival in extreme conditions.

Jimmie Riddell wrote that Pugh became the "ambient, free-ranging central pivot around which this physically arduous school revolved. . . . Every man-jack whose path he crossed came to regard him both with respect and admiration—affection even—and yet with no little apprehension for whatever tests he next might have in mind! Everyone knew full well he never would ask for any effort he was not always ready to undertake himself . . ."[16]

Pugh's own letters home radiated a sense of comradeship and belonging:

I am afraid I am getting awfully bad at writing. We have such a busy time and I have a lot of lecturing & writing to do in the evenings.

I should really give up my game of chess after dinner & write letters instead, but the Colonel won't hear of it. It is such fun sitting in his room playing chess with the door leading to Jimmie's room open & the sound of the wireless coming through. One can always hear good music here, usually from Italian or German stations. Chess & skiing make a good combination. Do you remember Lotto & me playing almost every evening at Haldengütli?[17]

At the end of Pugh's first season, Head and Riddell were summoned back to London to report to an elite army committee headed by General Sir Alexander Hood and General Godwin-Austen.[18] Much of their report had been written by Pugh.[19] It was extremely well received, and Riddell and Head both spoke so highly of Pugh that he too was summoned to the War Office.[20]

His moment of glory was delayed, however, because in July 1943 he was recalled by the Royal Army Medical Corps and sent to take part in the Allied invasion of Sicily.[21] Genuinely pleased to be in the thick of battle at last, he tried to explain how he felt to his wife by quoting Ernest Hemingway: "War is the most exciting as well as the most terrible thing men can do to one another."[22] He never spoke much about the experience afterward, except to say that he had "seen and felt an awful lot," and that the survival rate for men in his regiment was only six weeks. "I was very lucky I came out of there without a scratch."

The Sicilian Campaign ended successfully in mid-August, and in September Pugh went to London. The War Office Committee on Mountain Warfare was sufficiently impressed to send him back to Cedars to carry out an expanded program of research for a new British manual of mountain warfare. He was promoted to the rank of "acting major," and given the title of Military Physiologist to the Mountain Warfare Training Unit.

He was excited but not a little apprehensive. In November, after meeting up with Riddell on his way back to Cedars, he wrote to his wife: "Jimmie & I have just had dinner in the officers' club [in Tripoli] over a bottle of Champagne. We drank to our new experience. I am secretly rather overawed by the importance that is being attached to [the work], & I hope I shall do justice to my share of it."[23]

Now considerably larger, the school inevitably became "much more military and formal, though not in an unpleasant way." Riddell was still chief instructor, but Bunny Nugent Head had been sent to America to liaise with the military authorities there, and was "missed dreadfully." Pugh was left alone to get on with his work.

As the expert on "selection," he often went down to Cairo to vet whole regiments of men and select candidates for training. His view of the mental qualities required in mountain-warfare troops was strikingly close to the manly ideals cherished by the Everest pioneers: "Mental qualities are at least as important as physical . . . The chief required qualities are intelligence, willpower, courage, adaptability, and enterprise."[24]

One particular group of trainees stood head and shoulders above all the others—the Gurkhas, born and raised in the Nepalese mountains: "Their courage, their good disposition and discipline, their intense determination and pride in achievement and their remarkable powers of endurance render them splendid material for mountaineer troops."[25]

The Gurkhas achieved a 75 percent success rate in the training course compared with only half of the men selected from lowland countries. New Zealand and Australian soldiers also achieved good results, but for Pugh the worst were British soldiers, whose physical condition often shocked him. After one selection mission he commented: "This morning I examined two hundred soldiers, many from Glasgow. Poor undernourished bodies, twisted feet, crooked legs, cross eyes. Men from the slums who never had a chance when they were young . . ."[26]

Colonel Head, meanwhile, did the rounds of American institutions, undertaking similar research to Pugh's, such as the Harvard Fatigue Laboratory, of which the highly respected physiologist Bruce Dill was the unofficial director.[27] Many of Pugh's ideas were incorporated into the design of clothing and equipment for American mountain troops, and, from Dill, Pugh received a flattering offer of "a job at Harvard as soon as I am free."

"I am amazed," he wrote, "at the effects of those hundred pages of typescript written in a hurry last spring in the mountains."[28]

At the end of the 1944 winter season, Cedars was closed down and the school and most of its staff transferred to Canada. Jimmie Riddell and several influential figures, including Dr. E. Arnold Carmichael of the Medical

Research Council in London, tried to persuade the Royal Army Medical Corps to send Pugh to Canada, too, but the RAMC refused. From Canada Riddell wrote to Pugh, saying that his new commander was "all steamed up about it."[29] Carmichael thought that the RAMC's refusal was "beyond understanding," and when the highly respected head of the Medical Research Council, Sir Edward Mellanby, tried to intervene, the RAMC still refused.[30]

There seemed no chance of Pugh being allowed to go to Harvard either. Pugh's past was catching up with him. As far as the RAMC was concerned, he had a blemished record. Used to making his own decisions from an early age, he had, at times, had difficulty in obeying orders if he didn't accept the reasoning behind them. On one occasion it had gotten him into serious trouble.

Hitler had invaded Greece on April 6, 1941, and the situation in the hospital camp at Kephissia, where Pugh was stationed, changed radically.[31] All the existing patients and most of the senior medical staff were evacuated, leaving behind just a handful of junior doctors. It was clear that Athens would soon be captured. Allied soldiers wounded in rear guard actions were being evacuated out of Greece rather than sent to Kephissia, leaving the doctors with no patients, but with the certain prospect, as noncombatants, of being taken as prisoners of war.

On the night before the German Army overran the hospital, Pugh took it upon himself to escape. He had convinced himself that he could be of more use to his country as a doctor on the front lines than as a prisoner of war. Several of his colleagues agreed with him but did not feel able to leave without formal orders. Pugh had prepared himself in advance with supplies of bully beef and chocolate and a suit of civilian clothes. Ready to live rough until he found a means of getting out of Greece, he eventually secured a place on an evacuation ship headed for Crete, which was also invaded shortly after he arrived there. He got out of Crete in the nick of time on another evacuation ship that was bombed by the Germans, and finished up in Cairo about two weeks later.

Reporting for duty at army headquarters, he found himself accused of desertion. Pugh claimed that he was not court-martialed because, in advance of leaving Kephissia, he had obtained a written order from a sympathetic senior officer to go into Athens on a medical errand. Athens was captured by

6

Excess Baggage

Seven years later, the invitation to carry out research on Cho Oyu was a huge challenge for Pugh. He may not have realized it, but he was following in the footsteps of an earlier pioneer called Alexander Kellas.[1] Kellas was the only person before Pugh to have tried to measure systematically the impact of supplementary oxygen on mountaineers at very high altitudes. A chemist from Middlesex Hospital Medical School, he studied altitude sickness and the effects of oxygen during eight trips to the Himalayas between 1907 and 1921. He was invited to take part in the first Everest expedition in 1921 and took a supply of oxygen with him, but died on the trek-in and the oxygen was not used. After his death the prescient academic paper in which he had described his latest findings and methods vanished into the bowels of the RGS without being published in Britain. It was not rediscovered until the 1980s.[2]

In the absence of a blueprint, Pugh immediately became immersed in planning experiments and choosing the equipment he would need. After a month of fevered preparations, he took advantage of a previously booked Swiss holiday at his usual haunt in Engelberg to practice with his instruments in mountain conditions.[3] Once in his favorite bedroom at the Haldengütli guesthouse, he set up the complicated glass instrument—the gas analyzer—that would be his constant companion in the Himalayas.

This essential tool for measuring the proportions of oxygen and carbon dioxide in samples of exhaled breath was fiddly and awkward to operate. Skill and concentration were needed, and he had to practice working with it in differing conditions. Pugh climbed Engelberg's highest mountain—the Titlis (10,623 feet)—and collected samples of his breath on the summit to take back and analyze. Later he took the gas analyzer itself to the top of the mountain.

Eric Shipton's preparations for Cho Oyu were somewhat relaxed. One concession to the newly competitive situation was to recruit what for him was a large team of nine climbers, three of whom—Tom Bourdillon, Earle Riddiford, and Edmund Hillary—had been with him on the reconnaissance the year before, together with Charles Evans, Ray Colledge, Alf Gregory, Cam Secord, and New Zealander George Lowe. Michael Ward was invited but could not get leave from his job. Shipton also agreed to incorporate Pugh and his physiology project into the expedition, and agreed to take along the oxygen equipment assembled by Peter Lloyd.

Despite these arrangements, Shipton was still not fully in tune with what he was supposed to be doing. In the first of a series of dispatches for *The Times*, he emphasized that his overriding aim was to conquer the unclimbed summit of Cho Oyu.[4] The training of climbers for Everest, the physiology, and the practice with oxygen equipment were only "important secondary aims." He freely acknowledged the urgent need for research, conceding: "We still know lamentably little about the reactions of the human body to great altitudes and still less about the reasons for those reactions." He also admitted that there were questions about oxygen that needed answering, such as: "From what altitude should it be used?" and "What is the correct oxygen flow at various altitudes?"

Nevertheless, he argued that this type of research should *not* be undertaken on a mountaineering expedition, but by "an expedition of qualified scientists whose sole purpose would be physiological research." While he had led Laurence Kirwan to believe that he was in favor of Pugh's project, he now seemed to be implying that it had been pushed upon him.

Shipton could not shake off his aversion to large-scale expeditions. However, even as he complained about the "grossly unwieldy and inconvenient" size of the expedition, he also bragged about how easy it was to organize, and how little time he had spent on it: "The organisation was not difficult . . . Lack of funds enforced both extreme economy and simplicity, and only the bare necessities could be taken. A single afternoon sufficed for drawing up a list of all our requirements in the matter of food and equipment."[5]

In practice, this meant that Shipton actually planned very little and left everything to others. It was New Zealander Earle Riddiford, already in London, who came to the rescue. His friend Norman Hardie described the situation:

Earle Riddiford visited the Royal Geographical Society office in Kens-
ington and he was horrified to find that there was virtually no action
being taken on the gigantic tasks involved in preparations for Cho Oyu.
Earle then unofficially took over the tasks of ordering and shipping
the considerable amounts of food and equipment which had to be for-
warded to Nepal. Shipton, the leader, was hard to locate, and he was
most reluctant to make decisions on a number of the planning matters
. . . Each morning Earle kept me informed of the frustrations he was
encountering. It did not look like a good start for the project.[6]

On February 18, less than three weeks before the date of departure,
Riddiford, who had no medical knowledge and had only been to the Himalayas once before, pleaded with Charles Evans, the expedition doctor, to
take charge of the medicine chest: "Dear Evans: I am afraid I will have to
ask you to get the medical stores yourself, as unless I farm out some of these
jobs I won't be able to get through everything before leaving . . . Would you
please instruct the firm supplying the goods . . . within a week?"[7] Despite the
rush, everything fell into place. Riddiford managed to marshal the necessary
equipment and supplies, Peter Lloyd assembled the "trial" oxygen equipment, and Pugh's supply of oxygen for his experiments arrived from the
Ministry of Supply in time for the departure of the main team by boat on
March 7.

Pugh and Shipton left by plane two weeks later, on March 24. Their flight
to India crossed directly over Cedars in Lebanon, where Pugh looked down
on "the whole of the plateau we used to patrol." He noticed that "[t]here
was still snow down as far as Basharri [Bcharre] at 5,000 feet." His only comment about Shipton was: "Shipton in trouble with burst eardrums."

In Delhi, Shipton gave a lecture at the Himalayan Club. Pugh, who
had had no opportunity to discuss his project with him before the expedition or during the flight, attended the lecture, hoping to learn something.
Shipton spoke about the difficulties climbers faced at altitudes above 23,000
feet—the inability to eat fatty foods, the drastic loss of weight, the mental
lethargy, the "sheer physical tiredness"—and described how on the 1933
Everest expedition he and other climbers remained above 23,000 feet for
nearly a month, coming down afterward "like skeletons."[8]

The next day Pugh and Shipton discussed the research program for the first time. It had been agreed with Bryan Matthews, Laurence Kirwan, and the Royal Geographical Society that Pugh would study the effects of supplementary oxygen on acclimatized men at high altitude and investigate acclimatization, nutrition, and protection against cold. But Shipton now unexpectedly suggested that "the most important research is to study high-altitude deterioration." The mixed signals were confusing.

Shipton and Pugh parted company, and Pugh traveled on alone from Delhi to Jainagar (near the Nepalese border), where the team was gathering. It was quite a challenge for the absentminded Pugh to keep track of his copious luggage during the forty-eight-hour journey, which involved several train changes. He had already lost his wallet and traveler's checks while sightseeing in Delhi and assumed they had been stolen, later discovering that he had left them in a shop where he bought a thermometer. His absentmindedness had been a constant worry to him as he prepared for the expedition. Making list after list, he frequently woke in the night worrying about things he had overlooked, and it was already clear that he had left several pieces of equipment behind.

Pugh reached Jainagar at midday on March 30, the last member of the expedition to arrive. Shipton was already there. From the outset Pugh felt like an outsider. He was joining a group of climbers who had spent nearly three weeks bonding with each other on the trip out to India, and, at age forty-one, he was a good ten years older than most of them. The climbers were all members of the English Alpine Club or the New Zealand Alpine Club (which was run along the same lines) and, to a greater or lesser extent, shared the traditional skepticism about bringing a scientist on a mountaineering expedition. They admired their leader, who was their guru of mountaineering, and were strongly attracted to his romantic ideals of traveling light and living off the land. Like him they were instinctively repulsed by lengthy baggage trains and elaborate equipment. Perhaps in the back of their minds was the knowledge that it was Shipton who would choose the Everest team the following year.

Into this group Pugh now came with his ten bulky pieces of luggage. As soon as he stepped off the train he started to feel harassed and on a different wavelength from the rest of the team:

*Coolies seized my baggage and carried it away on their heads—I fol-
lowing. They led me to a stone building where I found the rest of the
expedition and all its baggage stacked in piles on the veranda. . . .
Everyone was in a bustle breaking down the baggage into loads and I
was told to have my physiological stuff ready to move off by 5 a.m. next
morning. Result—rearranged my stuff hurriedly and now no longer
know where anything is.*[9]

The expedition set out early the next morning with six Sherpas and
six bullock carts. In his report for *The Times*, Shipton, who was clearly irritated by the burden imposed by Pugh, stressed that 15 of the "90 loads of
60lbs each" in the baggage train consisted of the oxygen and physiological
equipment.[10]

The trek to Namche Bazar took seventeen days. The first two were spent
crossing the flat, sandy countryside between Jainagar and the Himalayan
foothills, the Swallicks, dotted with small villages, mango plantations, and
fig trees in full bloom. On the third day the bullock carts were replaced by
porters recruited at Chisapani, and the next six days took them across hilly
countryside, seldom rising above 2,500 feet, to the village of Okhaldhunga
at 6,000 feet. From then on the countryside was dramatic and beautiful, the
ascents and descents more challenging, rising and falling between 6,000 and
12,000 feet.

While the team walked in groups of two or three, Pugh walked mostly
alone, occasionally keeping company with Cam Secord. The weather was
intensely hot and the sun very strong. In Jainagar, Shipton had sent everyone
to buy umbrellas for shade, but only he and Pugh, who had both spent time
living in hot countries in Asia, wore thin cotton pajamas to keep the sun
from their legs. The others found the pajamas eccentric and chose to wear
shorts, and thus suffered badly from sunburn.

Having had no time to gather physiological benchmarks at Jainagar,
Pugh threw himself into his research from the first day. He weighed the
climbers, estimated their body fat with calipers, and recorded their pulse
rates. He took blood samples to chart the increases in hemoglobin that occur
at altitude. He noted what the men ate, and began a study of drinking habits
and hydration, recording his own fluid intake and going around at the end

of each day asking how much everyone had drunk and how many times they had urinated. He also kept records of the climate, measuring temperatures, humidity, and wind speeds at regular intervals.

Pugh soon discovered that Shipton had not told the climbers they were supposed to participate in the physiology project, nor had he explained what Pugh's research was about. Least of all had he told them that Laurence Kirwan, the Royal Society, and important figures in the Whitehall medical establishment expected Pugh's research to make an important contribution to the forthcoming Everest expedition. Most of the climbers were tolerant of Pugh, but they were skeptical too.

Shipton portrayed him as a bizarre figure indefatigably going about his work while the rest of the team enjoyed the trek: "For Dr. Pugh . . . it was a busy time . . . He marched with his rucksack bristling with test tubes and glass retorts, and coiled about with lengths of plastic tubing. With tireless application he counted our heartbeats, measured our haemoglobin and recorded our liquid intake . . ."[11]

The expedition doctor, Charles Evans, reported that the Sherpas mistook Pugh for a holy man: "Griff Pugh strode along in pale blue pyjamas, a startling figure with red hair, in his left hand an aluminium measure, and in his right a whirling hydrometer, which the Sherpas mistook for the latest thing in prayer wheels. They whirled it for him intoning 'om ma pade hum' and looking on Pugh himself, at first, as a lama."[12]

If the climbers were amused by Pugh's single-minded application, there were also tensions, particularly over hygiene. On the day he arrived at the campsite at Jainagar, Pugh had already seen the climbers behaving in ways he strongly disagreed with: "At first two meals was shocked to find complete disregard for hygiene. Water from shallow village well being drunk unboiled and flies crawling all over tea mugs—no fly protection at all. Doctor doing nothing about it." Although it was not his role, he lost no time in protesting, causing Charles Evans to note in his diary, "Pugh bellyaching about water supply."

Pugh had spent a good part of the war looking after the health of soldiers in the Iraqi desert and in the Lebanese mountains. He had written army leaflets on hygiene. He worked in a hospital camp in Tehran, coping with a raging epidemic of lice-borne typhus. The dangers of drinking water from shallow, dirty wells, eating meals "covered in flies," and sleeping in flea- and lice-infested village houses were all too obvious to him. One day, as they passed a village that had recently suffered an epidemic of plague, Pugh noticed the villagers "putting the corpses in the river." Such were the dangers of drinking unboiled water from streams and wells that Pugh felt impelled to try to improve the situation. It was obvious that lack of hygiene would lead to illness, weakening the climbers and undermining their chances on Cho Oyu.

On the first day of the trek, when the climbers could not buy any tea at a village, he had tried to persuade them not to drink dirty water: "Argument as to whether water from shallow drinking well drinkable. Heat untrue and some drank it [the water] in spite of obvious dirt."[13]

Five days into the trek, having made little impression on the climbers or the doctor, Pugh urged Shipton to intervene. But Shipton, with his Himalayan experience, would not accept that Pugh's understanding of hygiene was superior to his own. Pugh noted:

> *Discussion today about need for measures against flies and water contamination. I argue that . . . we should cover the milk and sugar and look after our own mugs and boil the water. This should reduce [the] risk by 50 percent. S[hipton] think[s] only by 10 percent, therefore not worthwhile bothering about flies, but water should be boiled. On the whole there is gross ignorance and neglect of simple principles of hygiene . . . We shall see over the next few days.*[14]

And, just as he feared, most of the team soon developed stomach upsets and throat infections. Pugh himself caught tropical sprue, an intestinal infection. It became a chronic malaise which he did not manage to throw off until long after he returned home.

If Pugh had read Dr. Raymond Greene's account of the trek to Everest in 1933, he would have known that neglect of hygiene, and reluctance to listen to the advice of the doctor, were the norm for British Everest expeditions. Greene battled, often unsuccessfully, to persuade his fellow climbers not to camp in local villages, "surrounded by the accumulated filth of an oriental [bazar]," or in a spot where the water supply was "polluted by . . . unsanitary buildings on the hill above."[15] The popular Dr. Greene shrank from confrontation and limited himself to mild remonstrations: "Sickened by the sight of such ineptitude I stated firmly, but kindly, my complete refusal of all responsibility, kindly because Hugh [Ruttledge, expedition leader in 1933] already had enough to bother him."[16]

Pugh, however, was more forthright, and complained constantly to anyone who would listen. Naturally, this began to grate on the team, and the view began to form that Pugh was a "difficult" character; a view that only grew with each new clash.

Disputes aside, Pugh was enjoying the trek. He was as susceptible as the most romantic of the climbers to the dramatic beauty of the mountain landscapes, and he shared the awe and reverence that such beauty can inspire. On the evening of April 6, he wrote: "Last night it was very beautiful. Hills rising steeply all round softly illuminated in varying shades by 3/4 moon overhead, sound of rushing stream, dying campfires, fireflies, inevitably lead to talk of religion . . ."[17]

He derived huge pleasure from the physical sensations of trekking, the excitement of climbing over a pass and seeing the view on the other side, the delight of sitting in the umbrella shade of a banyan tree eating a meal when very hungry. He loved the "delicious bathes," the magnolia trees blooming in forests "heavy with scent." He listened to the crickets and the nightingales, and was always on the lookout for unfamiliar animals, birds, and plants, such as "a kind of rose the leaves of which close immediately when you touch them." His words reveal an irrepressible excitement at each new experience, and above all an immense curiosity about everything around him.

At one moment he was riveted by the sight of a woman "with the largest goitre I have ever seen. Her neck was as wide as her face. Goitres are common at all ages in these valleys, but I have not seen a child with one."[18] At another he was feeling thrilled at his first view of the high Himalayas.[19] Constantly fascinated by the local people, he described their living conditions and farming methods in great detail in his diary.

At the village of Chisapani he thought the local cooking techniques were "far more efficient than our own," and drew a diagram of the contraption the people were using for heating up water, the first of a series of annotated sketches of local tools and devices that impressed him. A few days later it was children who captured his attention: "I began to play at ball with them, and was surprised to find they had no idea how to catch a ball. After about an hour, however, they were getting the idea quite well, particularly a small boy of about eight who put out his tongue at each attempt."[20]

Pugh did not identify with the members of Shipton's team. He treated them not so much as comrades, but as objects of observation, like everything else. He did not even tell them he was a climber, although he had as much experience as most of them, if not more. He knew his knowledge of climbing was vital to his work, yet he allowed the team to think that he was a complete novice.

Shipton's failure to stress that there was important research to be done meant that the climbers did not make themselves available to Pugh as often as he wanted. Recognizing the need to avoid antagonizing them, Pugh turned his enquiring mind to the Sherpas and the porters.

The Sherpa people, who originally migrated from Tibet and settled in the high Solu-Khumbu district of Nepal, did the high-altitude load-carrying for climbing expeditions. They also did the cooking, looked after the climbers, and helped to recruit and manage the porters. The gangs of porters were Nepalese. They were recruited from villages along the way, usually only worked for certain stages of the trek, and did not go above base camps. The porters carried 80- or 90-pound loads, as well as their own sleeping mats, blankets, and food, weighing another 20 pounds. Several carried loads as heavy as themselves; five strong men hefted 120 pounds each. Pugh noticed that some of the older porters "did not seem very fit." There had been some hard bargaining, and he thought they might have undertaken the job "from economic pressure." "There are three children carrying loads," he also noted. "Must get ages and weights."[21]

The porters supported their loads on headbands across their foreheads, which, Pugh realized, channeled the weight down through the spine toward the pelvis so it did not fall mainly on the shoulders. When he measured how fast the porters climbed, he found that, while the "most able" men "climbed extremely fast," their average climbing rate was a moderate 1,600 feet per hour, because they rested every few minutes, propping their wicker baskets on sticks to ease the weight on the headbands. In one place the cavalcade had to ford a twisting river more than twenty times. Pugh had difficulty staying upright in the water and found it "amazing how surefooted" the porters were, even with their heavy loads.[22]

In their camps at night, he watched the Sherpa Sirdar, who "sits under his umbrella and directs operations." The sirdar and his assistant had air-beds to sleep on, whereas the ordinary porters, "in groups of 2–6," slept on "clothes spread out on the ground" around "a dozen small campfires . . . Some have cotton cloaks, others sleep almost naked." Pugh worried that their skimpy clothing and the increasing cold of the nights were adding to their fatigue.

When, one day, the porters resisted pressure to extend a long march to reach the next watering place, Pugh noted that they had already climbed 2,000 feet, which, "for men with loads of 80–120lbs working at an altitude of 9,400ft (2,865m), is almost a full day."[23] The porters agreed to continue, but arrived at the evening campsite long after the unencumbered climbers. Pugh wrote: "We were in serious danger today of over-reaching the porters and having to spend the night without our sleeping bags." A couple of days later he observed: "Porters getting increasingly slow. Probably cumulative fatigue. First day 3000ft up, 4000ft down and about 8 miles at 10,000ft was too much for them."[24]

Shipton and his climbers were heirs to a British tradition that viewed low-altitude porters as beasts of burden, carrying the maximum load for the minimum price. Their welfare was not a matter of great concern.[25] There was greater respect for the Sherpas, but they too were viewed by many as inferior beings. In the eyes of John Hunt, the soon-to-be-appointed leader of the 1953 Everest expedition, the Sherpa was "a faithful follower, who brings [the European climber] his tea in the morning, lays out his sleeping bags at night, helps to carry his personal belongings, and generally spoils his sahib." He added: "This Hindu word [sahib], denoting superior status, was used between us on the expedition, to distinguish between members of the party and their Sherpas."[26]

When Pugh made his recommendations for the 1953 expedition he argued that the Sherpas should be given the same quality of clothing and equipment as the climbers, and should also be provided with the same high-altitude oxygen sets. He warned of the adverse effect upon morale of their being allocated inferior equipment.[27]

On April 15, after just over two weeks of trekking, Shipton's team arrived at the gorge of the Dudh Khosi River. The scenery had become "increasingly wild and rugged, the river a roaring milky green torrent, the heads of the valleys dominated by snow peaks."[28]

The next day they made the steep climb up to Namche Bazar. The constant roar of the river grew fainter as they arrived at the Sherpa capital, a cluster of some sixty stone houses with wooden roofs, built in semicircular rows up the hillside. The Swiss had left for Everest only the day before, and their fears about competition with the British for porters and food had been well founded. Many of the local Sherpas had waited for Shipton rather than joining the less-well-known Swiss team. Furthermore, the Swiss couldn't get eggs, whereas Shipton's team had two eggs a day each throughout the trek.

Prudent about hygiene, the Swiss had chosen to camp "in tents outside the village" rather than sleep in Sherpa houses and expose themselves to the lice, fleas, smoky atmosphere, and endemic local infections. Shipton's climbers moved insouciantly into a Sherpa house. Before long the DDT powder Pugh had bought in Delhi was in great demand. Soon he noticed with amusement that they had moved out:

The potato patch outside the house now has four tents pitched on it. Climbers unable to tolerate lice and fleas any longer. Many have upper respiratory infections . . . factors probably responsible are mica dust raised by wind, smoke in Sherpa dwellings, and close contact with Sherpas among whom running noses, purulent sputum are prevalent, and who spit indiscriminately.[29]

Pugh later met two scientists from the Swiss expedition who told him that they had consistently avoided staying in native houses and suffered from none of the throat infections that plagued the British team.

It was in Namche Bazar, at 11,286 feet, that Pugh first began to notice the impact of the altitude—headaches, fatigue, irritability. Gathering blood samples suddenly seemed exhausting to him. The climbers who had previously been quite equable were tetchy with him. "Whereas until now I have not heard a harsh word spoken," he complained, "after arrival here [have] heard outbursts of irritability from R[ay] C[olledge], C[am] S[ecord],

G[reg], self included."[30] The words *self included* referred to an "outburst of irritability" on Pugh's part for which he would pay a heavy price. His mistake was to criticize the wife of the most popular climber in the team apart from Shipton—Tom Bourdillon.

Having worked with his father on the closed-circuit oxygen sets, Tom Bourdillon was one of the few climbers genuinely interested in Pugh's research. At the same time he was a terrific climber who commanded universal respect and affection from his fellow climbers. He was probably the only man on the expedition who had the charisma and motivation to persuade the skeptical men to cooperate with Pugh.

Bourdillon was newly married. The previous year, he had gone on Shipton's reconnaissance shortly after his wedding. This year his wife, Jennifer, had decided to come with him to Nepal.[31] They had trekked from Kathmandu, catching up with Shipton's team just before Namche Bazar. Jennifer was intending to travel around Nepal while her husband was on the mountain. Even so, the climbers were not keen to have a woman in the vicinity of their expedition, and Pugh apparently shared their disapproval. When he found that the tent he had brought along specifically for his experiments was taken without his permission and given to Bourdillon and his wife, he lost his temper. Already irritable from the altitude, all the frustrations of the march channeled themselves into his treatment of this young woman.[32] He retrieved his tent after only one night, but not before telling Jennifer bluntly that she was a fool. She should never have come to Nepal, and would get ill and become a burden to the expedition.

Sensitive and considerate, Jennifer Bourdillon was already acutely aware that she must avoid causing any disruption to the expedition. She found Pugh's harsh words hurtful. At age twenty-three, and totally inexperienced, she was intending to travel alone with a Sherpa to parts of Nepal never before visited by Europeans, with no expedition doctor to look after her if she fell ill. In the event, her trip passed without mishap, although she did catch typhus while trekking back to Kathmandu with her husband afterward, and was lucky to survive. Nonetheless, Pugh's blunt behavior offended Bourdillon, and risked depriving Pugh of his only effective ally on the expedition.

7

Miserable Failure

The Cho Oyu team stayed in Namche Bazar for two days before continuing their upward journey, but Pugh, who was exhausted and finding it difficult to keep accurate records, decided to wait until he was better acclimatized before going any higher. He remained at Namche Bazar for another four days, setting up his gas analyzer for the first time and practicing some of the exercise tests he was intending to use.

Physiology apart, he spent most of his time observing the local people.[1] Da Tenzing, the Sherpa who was to accompany him on the final part of the trek, took him to the top of the 1,000-foot ridge above Namche where there was a view of Everest. Pugh had great difficulty keeping up with him. Despite the warm weather the Sherpa was wearing the arctic clothing that had been issued to him by Shipton—one of the perks, Pugh thought, that drew Sherpas to European expeditions.

Tenzing invited Pugh to his home in the nearby village of Khumjung. Pugh watched, fascinated, as the Sherpa's wife prepared tea for him "after careful cleaning of the best china with a precious cake of soap." The tea was proffered with salt and some "very hard, dry fruits." Afterward, Tenzing took him to the Buddhist temple which had four magnificent brightly painted Buddhas. The walls inside had rows of pigeonholes containing packets of paper which Pugh thought must be prayers.

Pugh left Namche Bazar on April 24 with Da Tenzing, the Sherpa's fourteen-year-old son Mingma, and four porters. Passing "lovely dwarf irises" and red, pink, and mauve rhododendrons in full flower, they walked up the valley of the Bothe Khosi river toward the 19,050-foot Nangpa La (*La* meaning "pass"), an important trading route between Nepal and Tibet, near Cho Oyu. In three days they reached Lunak, the small settlement at 17,500 feet below the Nangpa La, where Shipton had established his base camp. Later that day, the climbers came back from reconnoitering possible routes up Cho Oyu, bringing disastrous news.

There appeared to be only one feasible route up Cho Oyu, on the western side, which had to be approached from the Tibetan side of the Nangpa La. This meant that at least one camp would have to be placed in Chinese-occupied Tibet. Without the camp they would not be able to make a full-scale assault on the summit.

Shipton was unwilling to establish a camp in Tibet. He had witnessed the Chinese Revolution of 1950 when he was British consul general in Kunming, the southernmost province of China, and had seen people shot in the back of the head or thrust indiscriminately into prison. Having escaped from China only with great difficulty, he was convinced that the Chinese would regard a group of British men camping on Tibetan territory as spies. Not wanting to risk them all being arrested, he was strongly against putting in a full camp on the Tibetan side of the Nangpa La. Instead he proposed to create an advanced base camp on the Nepalese side, just below the pass, at Jasamba, at 18,500 feet, and to send a much-reduced assault team to attempt Cho Oyu straight from there.[2]

If this plan was followed, Pugh would not be able to do any physiological work on Cho Oyu, but Shipton promised him what seemed like a very acceptable alternative: "Shipton wants to defer physiology to second half of the month after return to Namche & to devote 14 days to it in Everest region."[3]

For the next ten days not much happened. Most of the climbers had infections and were suffering from the altitude. Pugh wrote: "Shipton and Bourdillon have pharyngitis, and Secord has a severe paroxysmal cough. Riddiford still has diarrhoea. Hillary had 2 days' fever at Chule. Colledge sleeps much of the day . . ."[4] Shipton and Tom Bourdillon had such bad throat infections that Pugh urged them to go down to recuperate for a couple of days. They left for Thame (12,300 feet)—a village on the path back to Namche Bazar—on April 30.

Shipton had brought his team, already suffering from altitude symptoms, too quickly up to the 17,500-foot base camp. He had then sent them immediately to reconnoiter Cho Oyu, which meant, Pugh noted disapprovingly, that they "will have gone as high as 20,000 feet." The accepted modern rule of thumb for acclimatization is to allow one day for each rise of 1,000 feet, with a day off every third day and no upward movement if there is any sign of altitude sickness. Shipton had come up 10,000 feet in just three days.

Pugh saw that the climbers' faces and hands were bluish, and, whereas they had always been talkative in camp during the trek, there was now a "striking reduction in conversation, gaiety, and general activity"—indeed, a subdued silence. He interpreted these as signs and symptoms of exhaustion and "the depressant effect of oxygen lack." The poor health hampering the expedition—due in part to the slack hygiene—was being compounded by a lack of acclimatization. Pugh was not adapting well himself. Despite the care he had taken, he was still battling with disturbed breathing and a sense of overwhelming lethargy: "Apart from physiological work for 2–3 hours a day I spend nearly all the time sleeping or eating. Sleep at least 12 hours a day."[5]

It had already occurred to Pugh that, when Everest was approached through Tibet, climbers would have to undertake a six-week trek across the Tibetan high plains at altitudes of 13,000 to 17,500 feet. This acclimatized them to intermediate altitudes before they reached the mountain. But the trek through Nepal was only seventeen days, and the passes were only 3,000 to 10,000 feet, so climbing teams were arriving at the high mountains far less acclimatized than when they came in through Tibet, without apparently recognizing the difference.

Eric Shipton had spent so much time at high altitude that he acclimatized exceptionally quickly himself and was insensitive to the problem.[6] But the danger was obvious to discerning prewar observers. Dr. Charles Warren (Everest doctor in 1935, 1936, and 1938) wrote in 1939:

To reach Mount Everest from India it is necessary to go into Tibet and approach from the north. No doubt a quicker way would be through the native state of Nepal . . . but . . . it seems doubtful whether the shorter route would prove a real advantage, for one of the essential factors in bringing about acclimatisation is a certain length of time spent living at high altitude, and what could be better for such a purpose than the long march through Tibet?[7]

Another major advantage of the walk through Tibet was that it presented an opportunity to get fit. The British amateur climber rarely trained for an expedition. Taking fitness too seriously carried the stigma of professionalism. In *Mountain Craft*, Geoffrey Young recommended a little skipping and, possibly, a little swimming, but "above all, the morning cold bath."[8] The first time Shipton went into serious training for an expedition was not until 1959, when he furtively carried a 70-pound sack of pig nuts up and down a hill in Shropshire, apparently hoping he wouldn't be noticed.[9] Appalled at the general lack of fitness in Shipton's team, Pugh reported that the Sherpas were much fitter and stronger than the climbers: "Only Hillary had a performance in any way comparable with theirs."[10]

Pugh developed a cough and walked down to a lower altitude to recuperate shortly after Shipton and Bourdillon. He was not at Lunak when they returned, a few days later, still not fully recovered, to find the rest of the team in a state of fractious dissent about Shipton's decision to abandon the full assault on Cho Oyu.

Shipton, being a consensual leader who liked to talk over issues rather than hand out orders, tried to persuade his climbers that it was right not to establish a camp in Tibet. But Edmund Hillary wanted to put a camp on the Tibetan side and make a full assault despite the risks. The unity of the team had degenerated so far that when Cam Secord and Earle Riddiford took the same view as Hillary, Hillary claimed they did so "not because of any urgent desire to climb Cho Oyu," but "because of their intense reluctance to accept any of Eric's ideas on principle."[11] Criticism of Shipton was only acceptable to Hillary if he himself was doing the criticizing. "Eric handled the situation badly," he wrote afterwards. "By arguing all afternoon . . . he demoralised all of us . . . he should have made a firm decision." Secord was said to have protested, "This is no good, Eric; you can't fly an aeroplane by having a debate."[12]

In public, Hillary would always remain one of Eric Shipton's most stalwart supporters and admirers, yet later in the expedition, in the privacy of his diary, he was positively scathing about the quality of Shipton's leadership: "In my opinion Eric is now quite unsuitable as an Everest leader, as instead of a powerful combining and shaping factor in the expedition he disturbs people's confidence, saps their enthusiasm, and fills them with doubts entirely because he has now little or no confidence himself and is jealous of positive judgements of others."[13]

Riddiford eventually became so frustrated with Shipton that he went from tent to tent trying to persuade the climbers to let him take over and lead a full assault himself, but he failed to drum up any support. Despite everything, Shipton's plan was confirmed, and the team moved up and established the advanced base camp at Jasamba, just below the Nangpa La, ready to begin their assault.[14]

Pugh, still coughing and very tired, rejoined the expedition at Jasamba on May 7, only to find that the assault team consisting of Evans, Hillary, Lowe, Gregory, Secord, and Bourdillon had set out for Cho Oyu the previous day. Shipton was too ill to go with them. Riddiford was crippled by severe sciatica. Colledge was still very unwell. The trial oxygen equipment Peter Lloyd had worked so hard to get ready had been brought up to Jasamba, but they did not take it with them, wasting what would prove to be their last opportunity to try it out in realistic conditions. Nor did they take enough food.

The assault party crossed the Nangpa La and started up the lower slopes of Cho Oyu, making a camp at 19,500 feet. The next day they pushed up over slopes of shale and snow to a desolate ridge at 21,500 feet, where they put in another camp. There was a lot of snow on the mountain for the time of year. The weather was appalling; the visibility was bad, and they made little progress over the next two days. Evans, who had laryngitis, was getting worse, coughing all night. On the third day he was forced to descend, escorted by Secord and a Sherpa, leaving the remaining four climbers, in Hillary's words, "short of food and demoralised." At around 22,500 feet, an ice cliff that was 1,500 feet high barred the way forward. Hillary and Lowe, being the superior ice climbers, led the way up, followed by the other two.

Down at Jasamba, Shipton was finding Pugh's presence a burden. On May 8 he wrote to his friend Pamela Freston: "Pugh is another problem. In the circumstances I can't send him up onto the mountain to do his physiological work, and there is nothing much for him to do here—it's a difficult period."[15]

Pugh had brought most of his equipment up to Jasamba, but his diarrhea was so bad by this time that he felt incapable of doing any experiments or attempting to go higher. He did not worry because he was expecting to get fourteen days with the climbers in the Everest area to accomplish his project. He had no idea that Shipton was already thinking of going back on this promise.

Despite their poor health, Shipton and Riddiford now decided to go up and join the assault. Pugh commented: "Seems mad to me to attempt to climb under these circs." But they were too late anyway; the assault team had already given up.

On the ice cliff, Bourdillon and Gregory had become concerned that the snow conditions were dangerous, and had called to Hillary and Lowe to turn around. They complied, but afterward Hillary bitterly regretted giving up so soon: "Nothing could wipe away our sense of complete failure on Cho Oyu . . . in retrospect it would have been better to have abandoned Cho Oyu before dissension divided the group, and gone off to attempt one of the many other great virgin peaks in the area."[16]

Having failed to get to within 5,000 feet of the summit of Cho Oyu, and having thrown in the towel at a far lower altitude than most of the pre-war Everest teams, the climbers limped back to Jasamba, not happy at all. Apart from Hillary and Lowe, all of them were suffering from infections.[17]

Shipton now decided to abandon the attempt on Cho Oyu. Perhaps a little obtusely, Pugh imagined that the climbers might be willing to remain at Jasamba for a few days and allow him to carry out some experiments with them. He was sitting in his tent after lunch when he realized they were about to go down. He rushed out and "managed to persuade people to be weighed before leaving. . . . We suspended the spring balance from the roof of the croft tent. Most of us had lost weight."[18] Then he packed up and followed them down. When they got to Lunak they discovered they had brought down "practically no food." The Sherpas had to return to Jasamba to fetch food and equipment but came down with the wrong things. Their sugar ran out on the May 13. It was a shambles.

Quite apart from Pugh's physiological project, another of the "important secondary goals" of the expedition was to test Lloyd's trial oxygen equipment. This was Shipton's responsibility. Hillary and some of the others clearly knew about it, but they were no more enthusiastic about oxygen trials than they were about Pugh's project. Shipton did not insist that they participate in it either. Hillary wrote: "Some tests were to be carried out on oxygen equipment but Shipton agreed that George and I should head off on a trip by ourselves—I think he realised we weren't very happy about our Cho Oyu efforts."[19] Not long afterward, the entire supply of trial oxygen would be lost without having been used once.

Back in London, Laurence Kirwan had received a telegram from Dunlop, the manufacturers of the oxygen cylinders, warning that a cylinder had exploded at the Dunlop factory, killing an operative.[20] The Cho Oyu cylinders were not the same type, but the telegram warned that to be sure of safety, the pressure in them should be slightly reduced.

Kirwan had cabled this message to Kathmandu and it was sent on by wireless, and finally, by runner. Instead of slightly reducing the pressure in the cylinders, however, Shipton's team emptied them completely. All the trial oxygen was lost. Peter Lloyd would never forgive Shipton for this. Whether the climbers would have engaged in any "oxygen training" if the oxygen had *not* been lost remains an open question.

Without oxygen Pugh could not have carried out the most important part of his research. He escaped disaster only because his separate supply of oxygen (obtained for him by Kirwan from the Ministry of Supply) was still at Namche Bazar. As each day went by, however, it was becoming more difficult to get the climbers to cooperate. Morale was extremely low. There was talk of going home, and they were hardly in a mood to give themselves up to the tedium of stepping on and off boxes. Shipton, whom Pugh described as "very depressed and not feeling well," gave him no support. "Eric didn't go in much for the science side," Hillary told me later.

Now, instead of keeping his promise to take a group of climbers to a suitable venue for Pugh to carry out his high-altitude work, Shipton encouraged his men to disband and go off climbing. There was no attempt to ensure that Pugh would have enough experimental subjects for his project, and no question of Shipton setting an example by taking part himself. Tom Bourdillon complained to his wife that he found himself single-handedly trying to prevent Pugh's project from disintegrating entirely.

Only Bourdillon, Cam Secord, and Ray Colledge agreed to remain with Pugh. Bourdillon felt very torn; he would have loved to have gone climbing, but he also wanted to find out more about oxygen.[21] Secord for his part had become friendly with Pugh and was increasingly impressed with his ideas.

Shipton immediately disappeared with Gregory and Evans to visit an unexplored part of the nearby Menlung area, taking with him, as Pugh complained furiously in his diary, "my Sherpa Da Tenzing & my RGS compass & the bungalow tent which I was hoping to get for the physiology."[22] In pain from sciatica, Riddiford left the expedition in disgust at Shipton's failures of leadership. One small compensation was that Hillary and Lowe agreed to keep detailed records for Pugh of everything they drank and the amount they urinated during their weeklong jaunt on the Tibetan side of the Nup La, a pass to the east of Cho Oyu.

Pugh, Secord, and Colledge descended as far as Chule at 15,500 feet, where Pugh unpacked and set up his respiratory apparatus. It was much warmer now, and Pugh realized that he was, at last, becoming reasonably well acclimatized: "The contrast between my condition now & last time three weeks ago is striking. I can now do a full day's mental work and climb as well, whereas on April 27th when I first visited Chule, I sat for three hours after arriving, doing nothing at all, with my mind more or less blank. The others noticed similar effects."[23]

Pugh only saw Shipton once more, for an hour, when he passed through Chule on his way back from the Menlung La. It was only then that he finally told Pugh of the drastically curtailed facilities he was prepared to provide for the physiology. Pugh wrote in frustration: "I am being given only a week for my physiological work instead of the 10–14 days Shipton promised me. The pass leading to the plateau we are going to turns out to be difficult, so I am having to cut down my equipment drastically."[24]

The site on the Menlung Glacier that Shipton had chosen lay at 20,000 feet—2,000 feet lower than Pugh had originally been promised. The promised two weeks in the Everest area, with a full complement of ten climbers as experimental subjects, was never mentioned again. Instead of staying to help Pugh, Shipton was planning to take Evans, Hillary, and Lowe on a trip to the Barun Valley. He led them off with "practically no clothes and a tossed together heap of food."[25] Eventually the four men and their Sherpas ran out of food and were reduced to climbing trees to look for fungi.

On the face of it, things looked pretty disastrous for Pugh; frustrated, let down, yet under pressure to produce results, he was left with less than a week to complete his program. But he was nothing if not flexible and ready to make the best of things. He also now had a sympathetic companion in Secord with whom to let off steam. However disappointed he was, once he began experimenting, the thrill of discovery took over, and he became immersed in his work. Waiting at Chule while Bourdillon collected food and the physiological oxygen from Namche Bazar, he wrote: "I am employing the time doing physiology. . . . I am getting surprisingly consistent results. . . . It is a pleasant place and life seems very good."[26]

On May 21, Pugh's small party packed up and set off for the Menlung Glacier. From May 24–28, he, Bourdillon, Secord, and Colledge worked intensively—particularly Pugh, who had to analyze the results as well as manage and take part in the experiments. His diary records that on successive days he spent eleven hours doing physiology, retiring to bed exhausted at five o'clock in the evening. Later, when his boss Otto Edholm saw how exacting this work must have been, he commented to Kirwan at the RGS: "I have been most impressed . . . I think it is most unlikely that any other man would have been able to gather so much information in the time available, and that he must have been working well up to the limits of his ability."[27]

One of the most important things Pugh hoped to find out was what difference the heavy oxygen apparatus really made to the speed of climbing. The tests were done using a measured track on a steep snow slope, which the men had to climb as fast as they could at a steady pace, timed with a stopwatch.[28] They ascended the track without loads or oxygen to provide a benchmark. They did the same ascent with 23-pound loads (the weight of an oxygen set) but not using oxygen, to measure how much they were slowed down just by carrying the apparatus. Finally, they did the climb wearing the 23-pound open-circuit sets with masks, receiving supplementary oxygen at 2 liters a minute, 4 liters a minute, and finally, 10 liters a minute.

The tests showed that on oxygen at 2 liters a minute, the men climbed at the same speed as they climbed without oxygen. This confirmed what climbers themselves had been saying for years—carrying the sets consumed so much energy that it canceled out any positive benefits. Oxygen at 4 liters and 10 liters a minute *did* increase the speed of climbing, but still only slightly, because of the weight of the equipment. What was strikingly different, however, was that the climbers felt much better during and after the ascent. They were able to breathe more easily and panted less violently, their limbs seemed less heavy, and they recovered from their exertion more quickly.

Pugh reasoned that if climbers used oxygen at these rates for climbing at high altitude, they would have to stop and rest less often. If they didn't have to stop and pant every few steps, they might be able to climb twice as fast as they could without oxygen. Ten liters of oxygen a minute produced faster climbing speeds than 4 liters, but would also require climbers to carry greater quantities of oxygen. Pugh did not judge the improvement to be sufficient to justify the difficulties, so he recommended that 4 liters of oxygen a minute, delivered through open-circuit sets, should be provided for the 1953 expedition.

Climbers working at peak effort at high altitude may be breathing 120 liters of air a minute, or even more; one of Pugh's subjects climbing without oxygen reached 171 liters a minute. In this context a mere 4 liters of supplementary oxygen a minute seems rather small.[29] However, Pugh reckoned that men climbing at extreme altitudes were so near the limits of human endurance that a tiny proportion of extra oxygen could make a big difference. If oxygen made a noticeable difference at 20,000 feet, it would have far more impact higher up, where the difficulties for climbers were proportionately greater.

Skeptical about the open-circuit, Bourdillon and Secord were both more attracted to the closed-circuit system, which supplied climbers with 100 percent oxygen—that is oxygen at a higher pressure than the normal pressure at sea level.[30] This meant they should be able to climb much faster than with the open-circuit. Bourdillon's father had not managed to get any trial closed-circuit oxygen sets ready for Cho Oyu, but even without the sets, Pugh investigated the impact of 100 percent oxygen by having his subjects ascend the test slope while breathing pure oxygen carried in specially adapted Douglas bags.[31] Bourdillon and Secord felt so wonderful on 100 percent oxygen that they both became convinced that the closed-circuit was the only system worth pursuing, and should definitely be used on Everest. However, the closed-circuit suffered from a series of well-known technical problems that Bourdillon and his father were hoping to solve in time for the 1953 expedition.

At the end of the week, Bourdillon and Colledge left on a climbing trip, and Secord and Pugh, having done all they could, trekked back to Kathmandu by the Tesi Lapcha route.[32] They marched long distances each day and got back to Kathmandu at 9 p.m. on June 7, where they were received—Pugh in his grubby marching pajamas—by the ambassador, Mr. Summerhayes, a man who "dressed for dinner" every night of his adult life. Later Shipton would accuse them of having packed up and left the expedition prematurely without his permission.

Secord and Pugh broke their flight home at Zurich and went to Engelberg to convalesce for a few days, before arriving in London on July 3 to find themselves summoned to appear in front of the Himalayan Committee the very next day.

8

An Infusion of Strong Blood

While Pugh and Secord were trekking back to Kathmandu, Bourdillon and Colledge finished their climbing trip and rejoined the rest of the Cho Oyu team, who had congregated at Thyangboche, the beautiful monastery village on the route between Namche Bazar and Everest. Shortly afterward the Swiss passed through on their way back from Everest, bringing the news that they had not reached the summit, but that two of their team—Swiss guide Raymond Lambert and Sherpa Tenzing Norgay—had climbed to 28,220 feet, breaking the British altitude record that had held for twenty-eight years.

Despite their ultimate failure, the Swiss had put in a magnificent performance which cast the British debacle on Cho Oyu in a most unflattering light. This provoked a strong reaction from Tom Bourdillon, who drafted an uncompromising letter in Shipton's name to the Himalayan Committee in London.[1] The letter spoke of "dismay in the party" at the way in which "this and last year's British Everest expeditions had been run," insisting that if there was to be a "serious" attempt on Everest next year, an "entirely different" approach was needed. "Really urgent and extensive work" to improve the oxygen equipment must begin immediately, he said; there must be action to improve hygiene and prevent respiratory infections; and equipment must be improved. If next year's expedition was "to stand any real chance of success," all this work must begin "without delay." Bourdillon was Shipton's loyal friend and great admirer, and was evidently attempting to support him by calling for a drastic overhaul of the committee's organizational approach.

Nonetheless, on the face of it, the letter looked like a condemnation of the way Shipton had run the Cho Oyu expedition and an endorsement of the views of Griffith Pugh. Bourdillon was very much admired as a climber, but history does not record how he managed to persuade Shipton—and indeed, all the other climbers—to put their names to a document that was so critical of the conduct of their expedition.

If Pugh had influenced Bourdillon, Bourdillon certainly did not admit it. He had just spent nearly a week helping Pugh with his experiments, but neither Pugh's name nor his research project were mentioned in the letter. It was a glaring omission, as if Bourdillon considered Pugh entirely irrelevant to the formidable list of tasks he was asking the committee to carry out forthwith.

The Himalayan Committee responded to Bourdillon's imperative letter by calling a crisis meeting on July 4. Bourdillon and Shipton were still not back, but Pugh and Secord, who had only arrived home the day before, were summoned to give an account of the expedition. Pugh was still feeling very unwell from the diarrhea he contracted early in the expedition.[2]

By now it was common knowledge that the attempt on Cho Oyu had been an abject failure, while the Swiss had put in a record-breaking performance on Everest. There were murmurs of discontent on the committee. Doubts were expressed about Shipton's competence. Questions were asked about why he was not intending to come home immediately.[3]

The Swiss had permission to try Everest again that autumn, but the weather was likely to be against them so there was a fair chance they might not succeed, thus handing the British one more opportunity to be first to the top. Public interest was rising; other countries were clamoring for their turns, and it was apparent that if the British got another chance and failed yet again, it would be a serious blow to national prestige.

Cam Secord (whom Laurence Kirwan referred to privately as "the abominable snowman") was the first to speak at the crisis meeting. He had not been party to the letter written by Tom Bourdillon, but had sent the committee a letter of his own, making the same points as Bourdillon, just as forcefully. Like Bourdillon he condemned the casual way in which Everest expeditions had traditionally been organized, giving them "no solid chance of success." Like Bourdillon he called for a far more professional approach. "Either we must take it really seriously," he urged, or "leave it to others."[4]

Now, in his booming voice, Secord told the committee that the equipment on Cho Oyu had been "haphazard," elementary hygiene had been neglected, the British climbers had been unfit, the expedition had lacked resolve and determination, useful opportunities for research had been wasted, and the mistakes of the past had been repeated.

Pugh reinforced Secord's criticisms, pointing out that the Swiss had remained in good health on Everest, whereas the high rates of illness suffered by the British on Cho Oyu—the result of slack attitudes toward hygiene— had contributed to the failure of the expedition.[5] Shipton had made a bad situation worse by failing to give proper attention to acclimatization. The British climbers were so much less fit, less skilled, and less experienced than the Swiss team of elite professionals that only the very *best* oxygen equipment would enable the British to improve on the Swiss performance. What's more, Shipton had failed to support his research.[6]

Despite their trenchant criticisms, Secord and Pugh both reassured the committee that it would be possible to prepare adequately for a successful expedition in 1953 if the lessons from Cho Oyu were acted upon and work began immediately.

But where was the man who ought to be taking charge? Kirwan sent a message to Kathmandu through the Foreign Office, urging Shipton's immediate return. Shipton still did not come back to England for another couple of weeks,[7] and soon after his return, he left again for a two-week holiday in Norway.

Meanwhile, the newspapers were full of reports about where the Swiss had gone wrong. The slopes of Everest were "not of exceptional difficulty," the Swiss climbers told journalists. Nor had they failed because of a defect in strategy or organization. They had failed, they said, purely because of their "inadequate oxygen equipment" and the physiological problems of climbing at high altitude—the shortness of breath, the exhaustion, the blunted perceptions, the cold, the wind.[8] It all sounded very familiar.

In Shipton's continuing absence, Laurence Kirwan, Basil Goodfellow, and Peter Lloyd—the three committee members who had arranged the Cho Oyu expedition—now took on the task of getting the Everest preparations under way.[9] As before, it was the professional administrator, Kirwan, director of the RGS, who took the lead.

A few days after the crisis meeting, Kirwan summoned Pugh to the RGS for an informal chat about his research, which they conducted while strolling round Kensington Gardens. Kirwan came away convinced that it was essential to get Pugh working on the preparations as soon as possible. He wrote at once to Sir Harold Himsworth, the head of the Medical Research Council, pleading for Pugh to be seconded full-time to the Everest effort, because "the key to success lies in a solution to the physiology and oxygen problem."[10] If they couldn't have Pugh, he insisted, they might as well abandon Everest altogether and hand it over to another country.

Kirwan also asked the Royal Society to encourage the MRC to accede to his request, telling them:

> . . . *Pugh's help will be quite invaluable in planning the British Everest attempt next year. In fact, his discoveries have, I think, at last opened the eyes of some of our more die-hard colleagues in the mountaineering world to the need for a scientific method in tackling a problem like Everest . . . without this any hopes of reaching the summit of Everest are virtually nil.*[11]

Networking was one of Kirwan's greatest strengths. His next move was to engage in a whirlwind of lobbying in Whitehall to gain support and equipment from the armed services, taking Pugh along to his meetings with particularly important figures. He wrote urgent letters to the key men beforehand. To Lord Rennell of Rodd, Secretary of State for Air, he wrote: "I personally am quite convinced that unless we can produce a satisfactory oxygen equipment it really is a sheer waste of time trying to raise money and organising this expedition."[12]

At the subsequent meeting he asked Rennell to put pressure on Lord Cherwell—head of the Air Ministry—to allow the RAF institute at Farnborough to work on the oxygen equipment. Farnborough was busy with rearmament and might otherwise have refused to help. Pugh was instructed to tell Rennell that the Cho Oyu research and the Swiss experience showed that "if any country were to conquer Everest it must have a proper oxygen set," and to assert in the baldest terms that: "For our part it would probably be better to forego our concession for 1953 rather than undertake the job with inadequate scientific equipment, the failure of which would undoubtedly do much damage to our prestige."[13]

By the time Shipton came home on July 17, Kirwan had the task well in hand. The Air Ministry appeared willing to make laboratory space available at Farnborough, and they were ready to lend vital oxygen equipment to the expedition. The head of the MRC had agreed to second Pugh for Everest work. Pugh was to be supported by a committee headed by Sir Bryan Matthews, who had advised on Cho Oyu and had now agreed to do the same for Everest.[14] Kirwan had also persuaded the army to second the Sandhurst-educated Gurkha officer Charles Wylie to become the expedition's "secretary-organiser," who would undertake the daunting task of ordering, packing, and shipping the equipment and supplies.

On July 28, 1952, the Himalayan Committee met to decide on the issue of the Everest leadership. The names of other potential leaders had already been raised at the crisis meeting of July 4, when it was thought that Shipton might drop out voluntarily. Three names had been "noted"—John Hunt, Charles Wylie, and Major James Roberts. Hunt's name was put forward by Basil Goodfellow, who seriously doubted Shipton's leadership qualities. Goodfellow had met Hunt in 1951 in Saas-Fee in Switzerland, when Hunt was on leave from a posting in Germany. A professional soldier who served in India between 1931 and 1940, he had Himalayan climbing experience and had been considered for the Everest team of 1936.[15] Goodfellow spent a few days climbing with him, and found him just the type of highly organized, strongly motivated, "thrusting" character he felt was needed for Everest.

Appearing in front of the committee Shipton put on a show of diffidence, offering to back down if they wanted a fresh leader, but also making it quite clear that he was not prepared to relinquish his presumptive claim to the leadership voluntarily.[16] If they wanted to replace him, they would have to ask him to stand down.

Kirwan played the key role in what followed. He was convinced that Shipton's vast Himalayan experience and moral claim to the leadership made him the only possible choice of leader. Indeed, only a few months earlier, the Himalayan Committee had broken off negotiations with the Swiss over this very issue. It would be embarrassing to dump Shipton now and appear to acknowledge that the Swiss had been right to reject him. Kirwan was well aware of Shipton's ambivalence toward the use of oxygen and his tendency to be disorganized, but in his view the steps he was taking to provide Shipton with sound physiological support and administrative backup would be enough to counteract these weaknesses. Arguing strongly, he swung support behind Shipton, who was formally appointed leader.[17]

What Kirwan and the rest of the committee could not have foreseen was that Shipton's position was about to be seriously undermined by Griffith Pugh's frank reports to his senior scientific colleagues, in which he vehemently criticized the management of the Cho Oyu expedition as, at best, lackadaisical and wasteful, and at worst, "catastrophic." The committee might have been inclined to forgive Shipton his failings, but the scientific establishment was not.

The first sign of trouble appeared two days later in a letter from a "rather worried" Sir Bryan Matthews, who had just presided over a meeting in Cambridge at which Pugh had described Shipton's conduct of the Cho Oyu expedition. Matthews made it clear in a rather sarcastic tone that before committing himself to help the Himalayan Committee, he wanted to clarify with Kirwan whether "it was intended to run an expedition to get to the top of Mount Everest, making such plans and taking such personnel as will be needed." Or was it merely intended to indulge in one more "venture in mountaineering, taking some oxygen apparatus but hoping it will be unnecessary to use it?"[18]

After another meeting with Pugh a couple of days later, Matthews was no longer just worried. He was threatening to pull out. Shipton's cavalier treatment of the Cho Oyu scientific project had been a disaster, he thundered. "After great effort by many people to assist in oxygen equipment and provision for scientific observation, the chance of obtaining major scientific results was wasted . . . To those concerned with assisting, this waste of effort appears a catastrophe," wrote Matthews.[19]

Support for the coming expedition could only be justified "if there was a complete change of plan," he continued. "Oxygen equipment . . . is the primary requisite for success." Its use at high altitude on Everest must be "the main preoccupation of the plan." "Trained personnel" must be included in the Everest team "to ensure its proper use." So far there was "no suggestion" that anything of the kind was happening. If the committee was not prepared to change, they could go ahead with the 1953 expedition "as they wished, with or without oxygen, using the so far untried equipment from 1952"—in other words, without the scientists.[20]

For an establishment figure like Matthews to take such an extreme position, Pugh's criticisms must have been very harsh indeed. Later Matthews would confess to Sir Harry Himsworth of the MRC that his memo had been "almost one of despair," a last-ditch attempt to jolt the Himalayan Committee into getting their act together before it was too late.

After hearing from Pugh directly, Himsworth was also having "serious doubts" about whether "the plans being made for the expedition [were] such as to ensure it reaching high altitude in anything like the state of efficiency which would be needed."[21] The shortcomings of Shipton's regime had been conveyed to him "with such force and evidence that I feel your society should know of them whilst there is still time to take the appropriate measures." Without a change of approach the expedition had "little chance of success," and, furthermore, Himsworth was not prepared to "commit personnel of the MRC to spend time on the project" unless he received "assurances" that change would be implemented.

If the committee did make the necessary changes, the MRC would consider setting up its own panel of experts to supervise the high-altitude preparations. Pugh could be released to work on the Everest preparations, but only provided that he was subsequently taken on the expedition.

Kirwan's initial reaction to Matthews had been to try and smooth things over by assuring the eminent scientist that his concerns were groundless. The Himalayan Committee was in fact "wholeheartedly in favour of doing everything possible to get the most efficient oxygen equipment," he wrote. Shipton was also implacably in favor of oxygen. But Kirwan was careful to warn Matthews that Shipton was "unwilling to commit himself to taking a physiologist on the expedition . . . until we know what funds are available."

What Kirwan did not divulge was that he had sent Matthews's note to Shipton, who had returned it with his riposte scrawled on the back, repudiating all criticism. He laid all the blame squarely on Pugh for not being sufficiently assertive or asking for greater participation. Pugh had agreed to the research site on the Menlung La, he insisted. If Pugh had asked for a higher site, or for more experimental subjects, they would have been provided.

Furthermore, he accused Pugh and Secord of deserting the Menlung La unnecessarily early, abandoning their work without his permission.[22]

When Kirwan subsequently found that Himsworth, as well as Matthews, was threatening to withdraw, he realized that something had to be done. If he didn't win back the cooperation of these two, the consequences for the expedition could be disastrous. Both had close connections with the armed services and with Farnborough. If they thought the expedition was hopeless, the help and the equipment Kirwan was relying on might cease to be available.

In the hope that he, Shipton, and Goodfellow would be able to change the MRC chief's mind, he hastily set up a discreet meeting with Himsworth at the Army and Navy Club on August 12, 1952. Clearly, by then Shipton was fully apprised of the gravity of the situation, for he had changed his tune. Himsworth found that all three were, as he put it, "prepared to go to very great lengths to have our [the MRC's] cooperation." They professed to have fully adopted the scientists' advice:

> *Kirwan and Shipton commenced by both emphatically stating that the expedition had no chance of reaching the summit of Mount Everest unless all the relevant physiological knowledge were utilised and they had the full help of Physiologists. Furthermore they admitted that hygiene and elementary medical precautions had been grossly inadequate on this year's expedition, and that unless these are attended to and appropriate rules enforced, they might well bring next year's expedition to nothing.*[23]

One of their main concessions was to agree to include Pugh in the 1953 expedition as a quid pro quo for the MRC seconding him to work on the preparations.[24] They also agreed to Himsworth's proposal that a new "Medical Research Council High-Altitude Committee" be created with the power to determine the oxygen policy of the expedition and advise on all other matters to do with altitude. This would give ultimate control to the MRC rather than the Himalayan Committee, and thus ensure that Pugh's recommendations would be acted upon and not ignored.[25] Bryan Matthews later agreed to head the new panel.

Goodfellow was as convinced as Kirwan himself of the need for scientific support and improved oxygen, but he also had severe doubts about whether Shipton, whom he regarded as "far too gentle, far too vague on organisation and detail," possessed the organizational and leadership qualities required for success. By mid-August, having seen that Shipton was still failing to get to grips with the issues, he was sure, as he explained to John Hunt, that without "an infusion of strong blood," the new expedition was fated to become "another damp squib."[26]

Goodfellow had missed the leadership meeting of July 28 and had not been able to promote Hunt's candidacy over Shipton's. Just before that key meeting, John Hunt had made an effort to promote his own cause, dispatching a letter to the chairman of the committee, declaring that should he be "called upon to lead the Everest expedition" or serve in any other capacity, he "would spare no effort to encourage and assist in getting a British pair to the top."[27] It made no difference. Shipton was appointed anyway.

Goodfellow hoped that even if Hunt were not made the leader, he would be invited to join the expedition as deputy leader or secretary-organizer. But once appointed, Shipton firmly refused to take on Hunt in either role, and would accept him onto the expedition only as an ordinary climber.

With the new secretary-organizer Charles Wylie not filling his post until the beginning of September, Goodfellow, busy with his job at ICI, felt harassed by the continuing demands on his time imposed by Everest work, and became more and more frustrated at the prospect of Shipton remaining in charge. Admitting how anxious he felt—"my whole heart is in getting this show right"—but fearing the worst, he continued to lobby his fellow committee members to get Hunt included on the expedition roster in some kind of organizational capacity.

Hunt also had the support of Peter Lloyd, whose confidence in Shipton had been destroyed by the way the trial oxygen had been abandoned, unused, on Cho Oyu. Like Goodfellow, Lloyd had missed the meeting at which Shipton's appointment was confirmed. He regarded himself as the expedition's oxygen expert, and was miffed at the way the MRC High-Altitude Committee had been given control of the expedition's oxygen strategy. Lloyd thought he might recapture his former influence if Hunt, a fellow climber with whom he was already friendly, became the leader. In mid-August he wrote to Hunt, complaining about the way "the physiologists" were gaining too much influence, and encouraging Hunt to try for the leadership: "I very much hope you are going to take on Everest next year as it seems to me you are the obvious choice for it . . . the Cho Oyu fiasco makes it necessary to face things and to put our house in order."[28]

Matters might have remained in that state, but for the fact that the papers for the next meeting of the Himalayan Committee, due to take place on September 11, included copies of the forceful and extremely critical communications from both Himsworth and Matthews, predicting almost certain failure for the forthcoming expedition under Shipton's leadership and the present regime.

Goodfellow finally had his chance. "Now that I have read my papers and contacted others," he wrote, "I find that feeling is running very high on the question of weakness in the Everest leadership."[29] Before the meeting he, Lloyd, and several other members of the committee met privately at the Alpine Club and decided that they must take decisive action to save the expedition.[30]

While Kirwan was on vacation, the committee took advantage of his absence and sprang on Shipton the idea that John Hunt should be appointed joint leader of the expedition, equal to him in status. Faced with such a shattering turnaround, without any prior warning, Shipton was taken completely by surprise and offered to resign. His resignation was accepted, and Hunt was designated leader in his place.[31]

9

Warts and All

After the Cho Oyu expedition, in the midst of all the shenanigans behind the scenes, R. B. Bourdillon sent a letter to Eric Shipton apologizing for Griffith Pugh's difficult character.

> *I am very glad to find that in spite of unduly hurried preparations and his own ill health, Pugh was able to bring back some useful data. I hope that their value to future expeditions will outweigh the difficulties which* his equipment *and personality must have caused. I felt very guilty for having put forward his name on his skiing record without any knowledge of his personal characteristics.*[1] *[Emphasis added]*

A scientist himself, Tom Bourdillon's father was acknowledging that Pugh had collected "useful data" on the expedition, yet here he was apologizing to Shipton not simply for Pugh's "personal characteristics," but also for his scientific equipment.

Without his equipment, Pugh could not have undertaken his research. Nevertheless, he had irritated the Cho Oyu climbers in many different ways. They didn't like complainers. They didn't like being told by an outsider how to do their job. They didn't like anyone criticizing their revered leader. Pugh had been outspoken, he had criticized Shipton, he had shown his disapproval of many of the things they did, and, rather than enjoying the expedition primarily as an adventure, he had been obsessed about getting his work done. At times he was strident; occasionally he was downright rude.

I was not surprised to learn this about my father. Since my teenage years I had regarded him as selfish, egocentric, completely preoccupied with his own interests: a man with no time for everyday life, no interest in other people's needs, and no time for his children. Griffith was away on expeditions for much of my youth. On top of that he still went on his own skiing holidays in Switzerland every year, never allowing his children or his wife to go with him. He was an Olympic skier, but I, personally, never saw him on skis. Remote and uninvolved with me and my two brothers when we were young, Griffith rarely played with us, never read to us, and appeared to take little interest in our lives. Very occasionally, when he arrived home from an expedition, I remember him scooping us up and whirling us around, provoking shrieks of delight, but that was unusual. Once, when I was about ten years old, my mother asked him to help me with some math homework. He fired off a rapid, incomprehensible explanation and responded to my blank look by exclaiming loudly: "Oh Christ, I didn't realise just how stupid you really were!"

As I grew older, I felt increasingly that my father treated my mother badly, taking her for granted and expecting her to be at his beck and call at all times. When he came home from work, which was always quite late, he invariably went straight to his study, pausing just long enough to collect a large tumbler of whiskey and a cigar. There, sitting at the table, hardly visible through a thick fog of tobacco smoke, he would soon be surrounded by screwed-up pieces of paper, angrily cast off as he struggled with the unfinished draft of the article he was attempting to write. Being dyslexic, he wrote very slowly and with difficulty. After a while, he would decide that his anger was not caused by his writing, but by his supper being late. Tempted to have another whiskey, he would roar at the top of his voice: "Where's my supper? Your mother's turning me into an alcoholic!"

When supper was served, he ate it at once, very fast, sometimes finishing and leaving the table to sit by the fire in another room before my mother even sat down. He expected her to undertake tasks that most Englishmen would have felt guilty about leaving to their wives. It wasn't just that he never washed the dishes or carved the Sunday roast; neither did he carry the wood or the heavy buckets of coal into the house for the open fires. He left this to my mother, along with all the other heavy jobs in the house. On vacation she, rather than my father, carried the suitcases and drove the children. If he came with us at all, he traveled separately in his own sports car. During their fifty-four-year marriage he never treated my mother to a meal in a restaurant, because—he claimed—he preferred "home cooking." Worse still, he undermined my mother's confidence by frequently calling her stupid.

Intellectually he lacked respect for women. He would often say to my mother and me, "I can't talk to you women; you are so illogical, I have to say everything ten times." His frankness with regard to other people's personal characteristics could be upsetting too. I remember being profoundly embarrassed when I introduced him to a teenage friend of mine and he greeted her with the words: "Hello. You're too fat." Equally embarrassing was his unsolicited comment to a cousin, a girl in her mid-twenties, of whom he was supposed to be fond: "Your legs are like tree trunks."

I can well imagine the hurtful tirade he launched upon Jennifer, the wife of R. B. Bourdillon's son Tom, at Namche Bazar during the Cho Oyu expedition. He often said hurtful things to me too—deliberately, I thought. When I was unhappy, such as when my pet dog died, it seemed an invitation for him to utter an unkind remark, aimed—I was convinced—at increasing my misery. His behavior did not go unnoticed outside the family. One woman, who sometimes helped my mother with the cooking, told me: "I thought he was a worm." Some people were so badly hurt by his brutally direct remarks that they had difficulty ever forgiving him. A former colleague at the Medical Research Council commented, "I wonder if Griffith realized how much some people hated him."

Once asked to provide a testimonial on behalf of a colleague whose intellect he did not admire, Griffith inscribed the colleague's name in capital letters at the top of a blank sheet of paper and wrote just two words underneath: DEAD WOOD. To my mind such cruelty was typical of him.

- - -

Born in 1909, Lewis Griffith Cresswell Evans Pugh was the son of Lewis Pugh, a Welsh colonial barrister at the Calcutta Bar in India. His mother, Adah (née Chaplin), was the daughter of an English doctor of modest origins, who rose to prominence working for a charitable mission in Jerusalem. Griffith was the only boy, with five sisters. Lewis had built up a relatively lucrative legal practice in Calcutta, but the exigencies of providing for his family in a manner pleasing to his socially ambitious wife left him constantly stretched financially.

Griffith spent most of his childhood separated from his parents receiving an English public-school education at Harrow, followed by Oxford University. As a child, Griffith had suffered emotional disruption and deprivation, abandoned in the care of the nanny on the rented estate in Wales, but as a young man he led a charmed, indulged, carefree, irresponsible life, financed by his doting, if distant, parents. He passed ten leisurely years at Oxford, studying for degrees in law and then medicine, taking advantage of the long university vacations—five months a year—to pursue his sporting passions. His winters were spent skiing while the summers were filled with travel, climbing trips, and sailing jaunts—often undertaken with his greatest friend from school, James Cassel, who owned a substantial boat, and whose younger sister Josephine, Griffith would eventually marry.

In 1939, having only recently qualified as a doctor at the age of twenty-nine, Griffith had just begun his very first proper job—a low-paid junior post at Lambeth Hospital in London—when the outbreak of war prompted him to marry in haste for fear of what the future might bring. He had known the twenty-three-year-old Josephine since she was a child. She was a lovely girl—very pretty, bright, and effervescent, with an exquisite willowy figure—but she was exceptionally innocent, having led a sheltered, sequestered life at the home of her wealthy, protective parents. She was six months pregnant when, in 1940, Griffith embarked on a long wartime tour of duty as an army doctor in the Middle East.

For him the war did not prove to be a great trial. He traveled to some wonderful places and spent the latter part of the war doing the thing he loved most, skiing at Cedars in the Lebanese mountains. Pressed by Josephine in her letters to tell her what kind of career he hoped to pursue after the war, his replies displayed a complete insouciance about the future: "I am a great lover of contrast," he told her in one letter, "& for that reason may find it difficult to settle down to a job if it is monotonous." And in another he insisted, "It is impossible to tell what the future is going to be like, so why worry?"

Griffith returned from the war to a very different life than the one he had gotten used to. He had to take on a regular job and the responsibilities of a family man, which were all the heavier because his son, David, born in his absence, was mentally handicapped. Having led an entirely self-involved life, pursuing his own interests and pleasures until the age of thirty-six, this was an adjustment he found hard to make. It was in this period that his characteristic self-absorption, irascibility, and impatience began to come to the fore.

He and Josephine settled near Harpenden, in a house bought for them by Josephine's wealthy father, and had two more children in quick succession—my brother Simon, born in 1945, and me, Harriet, born in 1946. On the strength of his wartime research Griffith soon secured his research job at Hammersmith Hospital, moving on to the MRC five years later. He had been at the MRC for about eighteen months when he joined the Cho Oyu expedition.

It was largely my antipathy toward my father that held me back from beginning to research his life. Ten years had passed since the Everest anniversary lecture at the RGS before I sought out Dr. Michael Ward and had my first conversation about Griffith with a man who, I believed, had known him well. I still knew practically nothing about my father's personal background, and even less about his work.

In mid-2003, having just watched the BBC film *The Race for Everest*, celebrating the fiftieth anniversary of the ascent of Everest, I wrote a brief letter to Ward. I told him how his speech in praise of my father at the RGS ten years earlier had made such a deep impression on me that I hoped, one day, to try to write about his life. Ward replied immediately, full of encouragement, saying he thought it an "excellent idea."

Still postponing the day when I would have to begin my project, I did not get around to visiting Ward at his home, near Petworth in West Sussex, for several months. By then I had begun to realize to my dismay that I had left the search for former friends and colleagues of my father very late indeed. Many were already dead. Some were very old and had lost their memories. Had my father lived, he would have been almost ninety-four. Kicking myself for not having begun sooner, I decided to give first priority to meeting people who had known him, leaving other forms of information-gathering until later.

With my scant knowledge of my father's background, and only a few books about Everest under my belt, including one written by Ward himself, when I went to meet Ward I had not even thought about beginning the daunting task of delving into the major archives covering Griffith's life and career. These included the two large Everest archives at the RGS and the Alpine Club in London; the records of Griffith's employer, the Medical Research Council, which were kept at the National Archives in Kew; and his pension file at the MRC's headquarters in Regent's Park, London. Nor had I yet found and scrutinized his army records or discovered anything about his early youth. There were also the India Office files in the British Library, covering the diplomatic background to the prewar Everest expeditions, together with many other sources that I needed to consult before I could draft my book. Worst of all, despite my mother's pleas I had failed to prevent my father's own personal collection of papers from being taken abroad. Naturally these included a fair amount of technical, scientific material that I would have difficulty understanding, but there were also personal diaries from all his expeditions and many letters that might help to illuminate the man.

Shortly after Griffith's death in 1994, my mother had offered to donate his papers to the archives of the RGS and the Alpine Club. Both institutions refused them. They had no particular interest in Griffith Pugh—and why should they? He was practically unknown. The papers were kept in a shed at our house at Hatching Green, the home of the Pugh family since 1955. Stored in rusting filing cabinets and overflowing cardboard boxes, they were under attack from mice and damp and did not have long to survive. In the nick of time, one of Griffith's former colleagues, John West, an eminent professor of respiratory physiology at the University of California at San Diego, transported them safely to America, where they were placed in a special archive of high-altitude medicine he had established in the university library. It took two professional archivists a year to catalog Griffith's papers, which now occupy ninety-four pale-gray archive boxes. The sad truth was that I now had to travel to California before I could begin to read my own father's diaries and personal correspondence.

It was a fine day when I drove to Petworth to be welcomed by Michael Ward at the front door of his large house. Ten years earlier, from my seat near the back of the auditorium at the RGS, he had struck me as a distinguished-looking man. Noted for having been extremely handsome in his youth, he was still good-looking, with exceptionally high cheekbones, dark-brown, deep-set eyes, an olive complexion, and a tall graceful, athletic figure, with elegant, well-proportioned hands and feet—visible in his slippers. Looking and sounding much younger than his seventy-eight years, he led me into a pleasant, book-lined sitting room with a view over the garden and fields beyond. A few moments later his wife, Jane, followed us in with a tray of coffee and cakes, and treated me to some stories of my father at his most eccentric.

Jane remembered Griffith arriving at a big private party at the famous Café Royal in London, announcing that he could not stay long because he had "something very important to do." He then fell deep into conversation. Half an hour passed before someone remarked, "Griff, I thought you couldn't stay!" "Oh Christ!" he exclaimed, running a guilty hand through his unruly red hair. "I'd better go! Josephine's in the car, and she's in labor!" It was the summer of 1955, and my father had been driving my mother to St. Thomas's Hospital to give birth to their fourth child, Oliver. The Café Royal in Regent Street happened to be en route to the hospital, so he had left her in the car outside, popped into the party to make his excuses, and promptly forgot about her.

After a few more tales of that ilk, Jane left me to question Michael about his own memories of my father. Our conversation lasted for almost the whole day, with a short break for lunch. Speaking animatedly and fluently, he described their first meeting, when he had helped to rescue my father from the ice-cold bath in his laboratory. He told me about their early experiments, emphasizing that Griffith was probably "the only person in England" at the time with the necessary skills to tackle the perennial problems faced by climbers attempting Everest. Michael spoke of the "extreme" difficulties he experienced at first in "getting on the same wavelength" as Griffith. There was a "vast intellectual gulf" between them, Griffith being "at the cutting edge of his subject," while Michael, the younger man, had only a "basic" understanding. Patiently, he attempted to convey to me how my father's skills were able to contribute to the solution of the Everest problems.

He and Griffith had both appreciated that the early Everest pioneers were "excellent observers," describing their experiences in such graphic detail that it was possible to build a preliminary "pathological story of cold and altitude." Seeing many reports of Everest climbers feeling desperately thirsty and drinking fifteen or more cups of tea after climbing at high altitude, they both saw that "[i]t was perfectly obvious that everybody was terribly dehydrated." Griffith knew from his research at Cedars that dehydration could be an urgent problem. He and Michael had contacted early Everesters Charles Warren and Raymond Greene, who recalled rarely passing urine at high altitude, and that it had been dark and concentrated when they did urinate—obvious signs of dehydration.

"Whereas I could make the observation," Michael explained, "Griff could quantify. He could work out how much water you lost from your lungs each minute, and from that you could work out how much fluid you needed each day to stop getting dehydrated."[2]

As I would later learn from his expedition diary, this crucial issue was one that Griffith took up and studied on Cho Oyu, and his ideas about how to resolve it would be a central plank of his recommendations for success on Everest.

While Michael did not go to Cho Oyu, he recounted stories of other expeditions he had shared with Griffith, and much else besides. As he spoke, his eyes occasionally flashed, and I realized he was deeply passionate about climbing, and medicine. His memory for the details of events that had happened long ago seemed extraordinary. I came away with an audio recording that was 13,000 words long, packed with information.

After hearing Michael's factual history of his adventures with Griffith, I took the opportunity to explore more-personal territory. "What was Griffith like to work with?" I ventured.

"I found him absolutely fine to work with," Michael replied. "I had no trouble with him at all. He was pretty obsessional about his work, but you have to be. To get anywhere, you have to be obsessional."

My father was indeed obsessive about his work, yet without such a single-minded, determined approach, and without the intellectual rigor and meticulous attention to detail he brought to it, he could never have carried out successful pioneering research in the hostile and difficult conditions he faced high on the Menlung La on the Cho Oyu expedition.

From this point on, however, Michael's description of my father's work persona became less and less flattering. Griffith, he said, was quite capable of working in a group as long as he was the dominant figure: "He was a team player, providing it was a small team and he was in charge."

"Did he listen to other people's views?" I asked.

"He was quite happy to have suggestions—all sorts of suggestions—but he would brush them aside . . . he would brush people aside if he felt they were talking nonsense . . . I have come across people who found [that] very putting off."

Yet Michael insisted that he personally had not been intimidated by Griffith's intolerance: "I didn't mind at all, (a) because I have a thick skin, and (b) because I knew that he had the answers to my questions, and it was just a question of plugging on and getting them. I was prepared to do this, and he accepted me."

Emboldened, I tried being even more direct. "I thought my father was sometimes rather cruel," I said, somewhat tentatively.

"I am sure he was," Michael answered with perceptible relish. "He was totally self-obsessed, but that didn't trouble men as much as it does women. It certainly didn't trouble me. I accepted he was like that . . . When he wasn't interested, he wasn't interested. As a teacher he was terrible. I would have thought as a father he would have been dreadful."

He went on to reiterate that Griffith was "totally selfish" and "completely self-obsessed," concluding, "I would have thought he would have been absolutely dreadful to have been married to. I don't know how your mother survived."

All this was meat and drink to me. It seemed to validate the hostility toward my father that had prevented me from beginning my project, his comments coming as they did without my having disclosed anything about my own difficult relationship with Griffith. Michael just seemed intuitively to have sensed it. At the end of our meeting, he encouraged me to write about my father's failings as well as his achievements. His final words were: "If you are doing something like this, you want to do it, warts and all."

It was only when I transcribed the interview that a remark Michael had made during our conversation struck me forcibly, though at the time it had passed me by. "Apart from sharing your work interests, did you find Griffith good company?" I had asked him, to which he had replied: "That didn't really come up. I mean, I really knew very little about his life other than what he told me, and what we were involved with. It was extraordinarily difficult to get under his skin."

Though he had spoken at length about my father's negative qualities, here was an admission from Michael that revealed he did not understand my father as a person. And yet he had freely criticized his character to me—the questing daughter—in terms that most people would have regarded as positively damning.

I was sure that he meant well and had no intention of hurting my feelings. He clearly felt great admiration for Griffith, and had spent many years loyally trying to win public recognition for his achievements. But his blunt, emphatic way of communicating criticism was strangely reminiscent of Griffith's own forthright behavior, which seemed to pay no regard to the impact he might be having on the recipient of his message.

My first encounter with Michael confirmed my negative views of my father's dismissive and self-centered character. When, later, I saw how he had annoyed Shipton and the other climbers on Cho Oyu, and heard from Jennifer Bourdillon of the insensitive way he had treated her, I was only further convinced that he had been a difficult and unpleasant person. And yet, as I was soon to discover, the personal diaries he kept over many years told a rather different story.

10

"It's a Wonderful Life"

It was Griffith's personal Cho Oyu diary that delivered the first serious challenge to my settled view of my father, for it revealed far more breadth and depth of human sympathy than I had ever given him credit for. His romantic enjoyment of nature, his thoughtfulness about the Sherpas and porters, the fine-grained, sympathetic observations of the local people, just did not fit with my image of his character. Not everyone on a Himalayan approach march would bother to record that he had "noticed a man who I thought was delousing his friend's hair; on closer inspection it turned out he was removing grey hairs." Nor would many hardened climbers have taken quite such a sentimental view of the mother of a young Sherpani, "pulling her daughter's head cloth straight and fixing the slides holding her plaits & generally fussing over her just like an English mamma and her debutante daughter."

Griffith's diaries are full of charming encounters with Sherpa women who were seemingly very attracted to his striking red hair and often gave him gifts. On his way up to rejoin Shipton after his extended stay in Namche Bazar, Pugh sat down to rest under a wall in a grove of yew trees near the village of Thame. Soon: "A party of women appeared and gave me enough boiled potatoes to make a good lunch. They expressed interest in my red hair and beard; they then went back to their own lunch sitting in a ring round their basket of potatoes in the middle of the adjacent field which they had been hoeing and dunging."[1]

Further on: "We fell in with the peasants carrying an enormous upright bundle of cattle fodder. Several groups of people passed . . . mostly carrying potatoes. One woman had her baby slung crosswise on her back in a wicker cradle. The baby was completely covered by a cloth. The woman let me lift up a corner and have a peep."

Apart from his constant outward-looking desire to understand local people, I had never realised that my father also had a particular fondness for animals; his expedition diaries were punctuated with detailed observations about animals, both wild and domestic. The very quaintness of his observations was another puzzling quality I had not encountered before. When he was beginning his oxygen experiments at the village of Chule, he was particularly taken with the villagers' yaks: "The yak are very handsome beasts with long black fur hanging down below their bellies & round their hooves. They are very agile and graceful in their movements and seem strangely sensitive, as though they understand human speech. In fact they seem almost human. They remind me of ladies in fur coats."[2]

When, a while later, I read my father's war diaries and letters home to his wife, sisters, and mother in England, these only served to strengthen my awareness that I had not understood his character.[3] One of his palpable qualities, which elicited a sneaking admiration from me, was the sheer enthusiasm for life they revealed. The diaries and letters alike were so full of comments—like "I am having a splendid time here," and "It's a wonderful life"; and there were so many stories of "delightful interludes" and "entirely unexpected adventures"—that I found it impossible not to respond, a little, to such abundant joie de vivre.

Griffith's war diaries, written when he was in his early thirties, revealed an easygoing, outward-looking young man, the type who can strike up a conversation with people on trains and end up being told their entire family history. Here was someone who made friends easily and always had a group of special "cronies" to keep him company—a man who threw himself into things, grasping every opportunity and extracting every possible ounce of pleasure from every new experience.

At one end of the spectrum of his delight in simple pleasures was a picnic in the summer of 1942. Griffith described sitting with a group of friends on a shaded marble seat in a beautiful garden in the foothills of the Alborz Mountains, just north of Tehran. Water from a limpid pool cascaded down over rocks into a lily pond against a backdrop of snowcapped mountains sparkling in the sun. It was "a truly romantic scene," he enthused, and proceeded to tell my mother in England, where food was strictly rationed, exactly what they ate: "We had an excellent lunch with chicken & ham, Russian salad, peaches & cream, cherries, white wine & beer . . . After lunch I went climbing."[4] The Alborz Mountains struck him as being "just like the Alps . . . cool air, rushing torrents, green trees, precipitous crags." His letter ended with the words: "Truly life is good."

But it wasn't only the obviously pleasant places that called forth a positive response. At the other end of the spectrum, in October 1941, Griffith was at Shuaiba Hospital Camp in the desert outside Basra—an "out of the way place where nothing happens, there is nowhere to go and only the desert to look at."[5] "Beset by flies" and consigned to a tent that had recently suffered a plague of scorpions, he was longing for the mountains. He did not have enough medical work to keep him busy, and was fed up with his dead-end job.

Yet before long he was regularly duck-shooting with friends at Lake Hawr al-Hammar, 90 miles northwest of the camp, going for long walks in search of archaeological remains, learning Farsi, undertaking a daily routine of ballet exercises adapted into his own special fitness program, and avidly reading from the parcels of books sent by his wife, Josephine. On top of all of his activities, he made strenuous efforts to ensure that his living quarters were as comfortable as possible, and was now claiming that living in a tent was really so enjoyable that he preferred it to being indoors:

> Our tent is so comfortable now that I should hate to leave it for a building . . . The cement floor is covered with a blue & yellow mat & I have a lovely Turkmen rug as well. The walls are yellow & the ceiling white. When the cold weather came I had to get a rug for my camp bed, so I bought a black & white goat hair one, which is very decorative. In the evening we have two hurricane lamps and a table lamp burning. A large pan of glowing charcoal called a sigaree is placed in the centre of the tent & is wonderfully warm to sit by.[6]

Not being well read in the literary classics, Griffith used the opportunity of the war to catch up, although even the most compelling Shakespearean tragedy failed to overwhelm his abiding medical instincts: "Finished

Othello—Desdemona's death is all wrong medically. If she [was] unconscious after asphyxia, she would undoubtedly have lived."[7]

Griffith's zest for life was not merely reserved for leisure activities, but applied to work as well. When he arrived at a 600-bed reception center in Tehran to help with a typhus epidemic among Polish evacuees from Russian labor camps, who were being transported through Tehran on their way south, Pugh was immediately put in charge of an isolation unit with 208 patients.[8] The hospital, which had been opened only ten days before Griffith arrived, was overwhelmed. Two-thirds of the patients were lying on the ground, still in their own clothes. Dressed in white overalls and gum boots, Griffith set about applying what he described as "simple general principles" of care, "securing beds, clothing, basic nursing and the essentials of treatment." He clearly derived great satisfaction from the feeling that he was making a difference, his enthusiasm spilling over into his letters home: "It is marvellous how lives can be saved by the simple measures of providing food, care & comfort. I am losing very few cases now . . . do get hold of a book called *Rats, Lice and History* by Hans Zinser . . ."[9]

So stimulating was this experience that, on his own initiative, he carried out a systematic study of his patients, comparing different treatments, and wrote a paper to provide guidance for future epidemics. It was read by the consultant physician to the forces and led to Griffith being put in charge of establishing a new medical center at Meshed.

Griffith was always eager to share his enthusiasms, however mundane or prosaic. Briefly posted to Bombay, staying in digs infested with bedbugs, he kept the bugs off his camp bed by standing each leg in a tobacco tin full of paraffin. A letter giving chapter and verse went straight back to Josephine, who replied: "Thanks a million for letter about bedbugs, perspiration & lavatories . . . I couldn't help laughing at your choice of subject. Still the letter was in keeping as a whole."[10]

There were clearly moments when Griffith proved to be a little too independent-minded for the army, as demonstrated by his escape from the Nazi occupation of Greece, undertaken not because he had orders to escape, but because he considered it to be the right thing to do. A close shave with a court-martial on that occasion had no lasting effect on his response to orders he disagreed with. Forbidden to take a gun with him on the journey between

Tehran and his new posting in Meshed, he flatly ignored his chief officer's instructions: "I saw fit to disregard his order—after all, it is not him that is going on this 600-mile journey across the wildest country."[11]

Rereading my father's Cho Oyu diary with an open mind, I no longer felt convinced that all the difficulties Griffith had faced on Shipton's expedition could be explained away simply by the defects in his personality. Many of his criticisms, welcome or not, seemed perfectly reasonable and proved well-founded. Taken together, my father's diaries simply did not square with the self-centered, antisocial, one-track person I believed him to be. I consulted my brother Simon, who had transcribed the diaries from Griffith's illegible handwriting, and found that he had responded in the same way as I had. The gregarious and life-loving man of the diaries seemed an entirely different person from the father we both knew.

11

All Possible Steps

John Hunt was released from his army job in Germany and began work in the Everest office at the RGS on October 9, 1952. The office was housed in the "Polar Room," where the walls were covered with photographs of Captain Scott's failed expedition to the South Pole in 1910–12. The preparations were already well under way. Charles Wylie, the secretary-organizer, was busy buying and shipping equipment and supplies, closely advised by Griffith Pugh; Peter Lloyd was assembling the oxygen apparatus; and Tom Bourdillon had been released from his scientific job to work with his father on improving the closed-circuit oxygen sets.

The new Everest leader was tall, wiry, and tough, with sandy-brown hair, a firm chin, a neatly trimmed mustache, and the typical clipped, upper-class accent of the Sandhurst army officer. Hunt wore his role as leader lightly. His manner was friendly and unassuming, and he had the habit of listening politely and attentively to people who wanted to advise him, looking directly into their eyes as he thanked them gravely for their help, even when he intended to ignore them.[1]

In the months before taking up his post, Hunt had been concerned that he was joining the expedition "very late in the day." Although he had climbed in the Himalayas, he admitted to Basil Goodfellow that he was "not familiar with the problem of Everest," which "will be a great handicap."[2] Before leaving Germany he had bombarded Wylie with requests for maps and texts about Everest as he attempted to get "quickly into the saddle."

He freely admitted that he had no "scientific background" and knew little about the problems of climbing at extreme altitude, and nothing about oxygen. Unaware that the MRC had agreed to act as the scientific advisers, he wrote in September asking the Himalayan Committee to set up "one single scientific authority" to decide on the oxygen policy and other altitude issues.[3] Wylie reassured him that "the MRC has taken on all our scientific problems," and informed him—as did Goodfellow—of the commitment to take Pugh on the expedition.[4]

Pugh had been hard at work for over three months when Hunt finally arrived in London. One of his most important tasks had been to draw together all his Cho Oyu research findings into a final report—"The British Himalayan Expedition to Cho Oyu, 1952"—which would be central to the planning of the expedition.[5]

Before Hunt arrived, Pugh had received discreet support from Laurence Kirwan. Pugh wanted to supplement his analysis of the clothing and protective gear from Cho Oyu with a questionnaire completed by the climbers. Kirwan, realizing that his protégé might not have sufficient clout with the climbers to get a rapid response, arranged to send the questionnaire out under his own name.[6] Kirwan also helped to arrange for Pugh to visit the Swiss.

When Kirwan first approached them, the Swiss reacted coolly, refusing to agree to a meeting. But in September they relented and Pugh made a four-day visit to Geneva, where his old-established contacts and his command of French and German helped win their cooperation.[7] In exchange for sight of his Cho Oyu research, the Swiss gave Pugh detailed inventories of their clothing, equipment, and diet, along with written accounts of their experiences.[8] This was extraordinarily generous in view of the years of frustration they had suffered while the British conspired to prevent them from attempting Everest.

An induction program had been arranged for Hunt's first week in London, which left no room for doubt that the Himalayan Committee expected him to rely heavily on scientific advice. His first meeting was with Kirwan, who made clear his belief that it would be better not to go to Everest at all than to do so without decent oxygen equipment and full physiological support. Goodfellow had already warned Hunt of the importance of aligning himself with Kirwan's priorities: "Kirwan needs careful handling . . . He is exceedingly competent in expedition organising matters and knows his way about high quarters in London. An ally you cannot do without."[9]

Next, Hunt was to meet Sir Harold Himsworth of the MRC. Himsworth came away convinced that Hunt "was quite clear that unless serious attention was paid to the physiological and medical considerations involved, the expedition had no chance of reaching the summit." He was also confident that Hunt had accepted that the expedition "had to justify itself by providing opportunities for scientific work."[10] To Himsworth this meant not only that Pugh would go to Everest with the team, but also that Hunt—unlike Shipton—would ensure that he had the facilities to carry out his research. Himsworth even tried to persuade Hunt to accept a second physiologist in addition to Pugh.

The following day, Hunt spent several hours with Pugh, and two days later he went to Cambridge for his first meeting with Bryan Matthews's MRC High-Altitude Committee (HAC), which was officially in "control" of the expedition's oxygen policy, and official adviser on "the physiological aspects of equipment and rations."[11] Matthews did not intend to allow Hunt any room to deviate from the committee's plans for oxygen, and wanted him to declare immediately that he fully accepted the committee's oxygen strategy. Hunt complained afterward about being asked to commit himself at such an early stage.

Hunt selected his thirteen-strong team very quickly—a provisional list was ready by October 28. At its core were the Cho Oyu climbers: Tom Bourdillon, Charles Evans, Alf Gregory, Ed Hillary, and George Lowe. One man who did not get chosen as a "full climbing member" was Michael Ward. Ward had played a vital role in finding the route up Everest and in instigating the reconnaissance. He possessed previous Himalayan experience, was well liked, and was, by common consent, one of Britain's top climbers, but Hunt had made him the expedition doctor. Perhaps he had expressed a little too much enthusiasm for physiology in his selection interview.[12]

Apart from Alf Gregory and New Zealand climbers Ed Hillary and George Lowe, the rest of Hunt's team met the traditional British criteria of having been educated at public school and either Oxbridge or Sandhurst. Three—Hunt, Wylie, and Ward—were from the same school, Marlborough College.

The tradition of ensuring that Alpine Club members were not exposed to the "wrong" sort of people went back a long way. Since its inception in the mid-nineteenth century, the Alpine Club had always endeavored to maintain a "gentlemanly," "socially harmonious" character. Until 1938, the year of the seventh Everest expedition, would-be members of the club had to meet a set of "mountaineering" entry criteria, but they also had to survive a members' ballot, in which the practice of "blackballing" allowed for socially undesirable candidates to be quietly excluded.

The Alpine Club shared its social exclusivity not only with most other gentlemen's clubs of the era, but also with many of the amateur sporting clubs and associations. The Amateur Athletics Club, formed in 1866, denied membership to "mechanics, artisans and labourers"; and the Amateur Rowing Association, formed in 1878, excluded anyone who was or had been "by trade or employment for wages, a mechanic, artisan or labourer."[13] Some of these class-based restrictions were not abandoned until after World War II.

Blackballing—the voting practice in which each "black" negative ballot cast against a prospective Alpine Club member canceled out five votes in his favor—was a more subtle method of vetting prospective members because it did not require the qualities of "a good chap" to be explicitly stated. Shortly after being admitted to the Alpine Club in 1935, Scott Russell was taken aside by one of the club's vice presidents and told: "I hope your proposers told you that in addition to being the oldest club in the world, the Alpine Club is a unique one—a club for gentlemen who also climb."[14] Russell's mentor illustrated his point by pointing at a street sweeper outside the window and explaining, "I mean, we would never elect that fellow even if he were the finest climber in the world."

Blackballing initially prevented one of the greatest climbers of his era, Alfred Mummery, from being accepted into the Alpine Club, on suspicion that he owned a shop in Dover and was therefore tainted by his association with "trade."[15] It was finally abandoned in 1938, the year of the last prewar Everest expedition.

Establishment secrecy and public deference being the norm in the 1950s, news of the preparations for Everest in 1953 was carefully managed. The key decisions were made behind closed doors. Pugh's advice to the expedition was kept out of the public domain. His preliminary paper setting out the basic guidelines for the Himalayan Committee was never published, nor was his subsequent report on the Cho Oyu expedition. Only eight copies were produced, and the report was not shown to the climbing team (except for Michael Ward). Apart from Hunt and Wylie, few of the climbers knew how much work Pugh was doing for the expedition.

Three weeks after arriving in London, John Hunt produced a draft plan for the expedition that bore the hallmarks of Pugh's influence on almost every page.[16] As Pugh had advised, Hunt stipulated that open-circuit oxygen, delivered at a rate of 4 liters a minute, should be provided for the climbers and their Sherpas above 23,000 feet, and should be available at lower rates for climbing down and also for sleeping at high altitude.

In his report Pugh had explained why he felt oxygen should be provided for descent as well as ascent: "It must be emphasised that the descent from high mountains, owing to the cumulative effect of cold and fatigue, may be more dangerous than the ascent."[17]

The use of oxygen for sleeping at high altitudes had a longer history. When in 1922 George Finch found himself pinned down for two nights at 25,500 feet, in a flimsy tent in appalling weather, he found that breathing small quantities of oxygen during the night was a "heaven-sent" lifesaver. George Mallory may also have tried it in 1924, but it had not been used again for sleeping until Pugh tested its effects on Cho Oyu. He found that it helped the climbers sleep better, and had a very beneficial effect on their ability to keep warm and recover from fatigue. Equally important, it did not significantly impair acclimatization to altitude, as many people had feared. Pugh recommended its use at 1 liter a minute, with a mask on, in camps above 23,000 feet.

There had been a lot of talk in the High-Altitude Committee—not just about oxygen-flow rates and night oxygen, but also about which type of oxygen set to use: open-circuit or closed-circuit. The open-circuit might be reliable, but it was also wasteful of oxygen; any oxygen not taken up by the climber's lungs was lost into the atmosphere when he breathed out. Some people, particularly Tom Bourdillon and his father—encouraged by Tom's experiences with 100 percent oxygen on Cho Oyu—seriously doubted whether a mere 4 liters of supplementary oxygen, the maximum Pugh felt was practical to supply using the open-circuit system, would be enough to get climbers up Everest.

With the closed-circuit system the unused oxygen in the climber's exhaled breath was filtered and recycled back to him. This was so much more economical that it permitted virtually 100 percent oxygen to be fed to the climber without requiring him to carry an impractically large load of oxygen on his back. And as Bourdillon and Secord had discovered on Cho Oyu, breathing 100 percent oxygen felt very good indeed. Even better, it enabled them to climb much faster.

On the other hand, the closed-circuit system was plagued by problems of its own. The soda-lime powder filter increased resistance to breathing; the filtering process gave off heat and water, which bubbled in the tubes and tended to freeze the valves; channels and gaps sometimes formed in the soda lime, allowing carbon dioxide to flow through and escape back to the climber; and the system required a completely airtight mask, which had not yet been satisfactorily developed. Whether the Bourdillons would succeed in solving these problems remained an open question.

Like the Bourdillons, Pugh and Bryan Matthews were very impressed with the closed-circuit. It was only because the system was blighted by technical difficulties—and the Bourdillons' modified version was not even finished, let alone proven at high altitude—that they decided to give firm priority to the tried-and-tested open-circuit. Pugh had written in his Cho Oyu report: "It would be highly desirable to have closed-circuit sets available for trial on the next Everest expedition, but quite unsafe to rely on them as the sole method of applying oxygen."[18] Hunt, in turn, was persuaded that some closed-circuit equipment "should be prepared now for eventual experiment in the field" by the two Bourdillons.

Pugh's recommendations on acclimatization were also central to the planning of the expedition. On Cho Oyu, Shipton had blithely taken his climbers from 12,000 feet to 21,000 feet with barely a pause along the way, and the Swiss had made the same mistake on Everest. As a result, Pugh believed, both teams had deteriorated more rapidly and profoundly at the assault stage of their expeditions than they would have done if better acclimatized. His advice was that a period of roughly four weeks should be allowed for acclimatization. This would have the added benefit of giving the

British climbers, whose lack of fitness had shocked Pugh on Cho Oyu, a chance to improve their physical condition.

To ensure that acclimatization helped to improve fitness and stamina, Pugh suggested three guiding principles: The climbers should feel well at all times; they must not lose their appetites; and they must not suffer from altitude sickness. All the climbers should sleep at altitudes of approximately 12,000 to 13,000 feet for the first fourteen days, followed by another fourteen days no higher than 15,500 feet. During this time the climbers could climb as high as they liked during the day but should sleep at the recommended altitudes, which Pugh expected to be "comfortably within their tolerances." If, in the third fortnight, camps up to 20,000 feet were established, the climbers should only stay there for two or three days, followed by a rest at a comfortable altitude before going higher.

Recognizing that there were wide variations in responses to altitude, and that illness might slow down acclimatization, Pugh emphasized that his recommendations were guiding principles rather than rigid rules.[19] Clearly following Pugh's advice, John Hunt's plan underscored "the absolute need for a period of acclimatization" of "up to four weeks."

Another of Pugh's defining contributions was his policy on fluid intake. Historically, high-altitude climbers of all nationalities consumed far too little fluid. In the spring of 1952 the first Swiss assault team—Tenzing Norgay and Raymond Lambert—only had a candle to melt snow for drinking water and became desperately dehydrated.[20] The autumn assault team, which failed partly because of bad weather, spent three days on the South Col, drinking only half a liter of liquid a day each, and eating very little. This left them so weakened that they were in no fit state to go higher, whatever the weather.

Nobody before Pugh had fully understood that dehydration, which causes the blood to become thicker and more viscous, also makes the blood less efficient at transporting oxygen around the body, leaving the climber increasingly debilitated. He insisted that the climbers must drink between 3 and 4 liters of water a day to avoid dehydration, and ensured they had the means to do so.

Previous expeditions had tended to drink too little partly because the stoves they used for melting snow were slow and inefficient, and they often ran short of fuel. Pugh had already designed a more efficient, lightweight stove for his commandos in Lebanon, and the same design was used for the 1953 expedition.[21] Two sizes were provided: a larger stove for the lower camps, and a small one for high altitudes, where weight was a vital factor. Pugh worked out precisely how much kerosene was needed to melt enough snow per climber, per day, and calculated the energy cost of carrying the kerosene; all the calculations were factored into the planning of supplies.[22]

Already the official adviser on acclimatization, fluid intake, and the strategic use of oxygen, Pugh also became deeply involved in modifying the expedition's clothing and equipment, and had already planned the expedition's diet when, curiously, he received a letter from John Hunt, saying: "I would very much like you to take on responsibility for the whole diet problem. I very much hope you will be willing to agree to this."[23]

On Cho Oyu, Pugh had observed the climbers' eating habits and preferences for certain foods. He weighed the food they ate and analyzed its caloric content. He measured the energy they expended on the approach march and in the climbing phases, and showed that the food provided on Cho Oyu did not match the outlay of energy. He noticed, too, that the lack of acclimatization caused appetites to fail even at relatively moderate altitudes. Furthermore, the "bulky and strange" local Nepalese diet had caused digestive problems and stomach upsets.[24] It was hardly surprising that climbers had suffered drastic losses in weight and condition at altitude.

Pugh's diet plan contained sufficient calories to meet the climbers' needs and was more like a normal European diet than the rations on earlier expeditions. Different prepacked menus were provided for each day of the week, and were to be supplemented with local foods such as eggs, rice, and potatoes. There were special "twenty-four-hour, vacuum-packed assault rations" for the climbers going to high altitude and those taking part in attempts on the summit. They consisted of a basic meal—from which the climbers could reject items they felt unable to eat—supplemented by luxury items they themselves had selected before the expedition. In this way they were able to cater to the picky appetites of men at high altitude.[25] George Finch had suggested prepacked high-altitude rations as early as 1924, but until 1953, no one provided them.

In November 1952, long after all the main decisions on diet had been made, John Hunt assigned George Band, the youngest climber in the team, to assist Pugh with the rations. Band was rather disdainful about Pugh's dietary plans, as he made clear to Edmund Hillary: "Dear Ed . . . the assault ration seems frightful. It was composed by Pugh on last year's experience, when, I gather, most people were never truly acclimatised. Thus it will be unsatisfactory for a fit team. Unfortunately it is too late to alter it now . . ."[26] However, a recent review of Pugh's diet for the expedition came to the opposite conclusion—that Pugh's "approaches are still ascribed to today, fifty years later."[27]

Pugh had been withering about Shipton's attitude toward hygiene on Cho Oyu. With Michael Ward, he prepared a careful hygiene and health plan which Hunt echoed in a homily to the team, telling them they would not be able to indulge in "the same liberties as a private party," but must take "all possible steps . . . to ensure that the health and strength of the party are preserved." They would not be allowed to sleep in local houses, and their campsites would be sited away from villages. Pugh also provided Hunt with briefings on specific issues, such as diseases encountered during Himalayan trips and treatments for them.[28]

Pugh had to work extremely hard in the run-up to the expedition, spending long hours toiling flat out in his laboratory at Hampstead, as well as traveling to different parts of the country. He went to Snowdonia in north Wales with the climbers to test oxygen equipment and masks; to the Royal Aircraft Establishment at Farnborough to test equipment in the wind tunnel; to Cambridge for the meetings of the High-Altitude Committee; and to the Oxford School of Physiology to consult with experts on respiration. In addition, he was developing a program of experiments to conduct on Everest and assembling his experimental equipment, modifying items that had not worked well on Cho Oyu. There was precious little time for home life or leisure.

Very little of the climbers' equipment that went to Everest escaped Pugh's attention. He was particularly interested in high-altitude footwear. The Swiss had used lightweight boots made of reindeer skin for high-altitude climbing. They were excellent, but too expensive for the British, so Pugh collaborated with the British Boot and Shoe Association to develop a cheaper, lightweight boot for use above 20,000 feet.[29] Having designed a prototype boot for ski-mountaineering, he was very conscious of the Harvard Fatigue

Laboratory's wartime finding that 1 pound of weight carried on the feet is equivalent to 4 pounds on the back. Testing samples of rubber for the soles at the MRC, he decided that microcellular rubber would be lightest and provide the best insulation.[30] The finished soles had half the density and three times the insulation of the cleated Vibram soles of conventional mountain boots.

As the boots had to cope with temperatures as low as −40°F, the uppers had three layers: an inner waterproof layer and an outer leather layer enclosing a kapok insulation filling, with a further rubberized waterproof outer layer, to protect from melting snow; the inner waterproof layer prevented sweat from the foot from compromising the insulation. Pugh insisted the boots have large eyelets so the laces could be easily adjusted, and at each stage in the production process he had the boots tested in the cold chambers at Farnborough.

On Cho Oyu, Pugh had made a detailed survey of the climate and weather conditions and used the results—combined with the limited information available from previous expeditions—to predict the likely conditions at high altitude on Everest. He then subjected the Cho Oyu clothing and equipment to systematic analysis, using the thermal insulation ("clo values") system for measuring the insulation values of clothing, supplemented by the questionnaires filled in by the climbers themselves.[31]

His conclusion was that a better fabric was needed for tents and windproof clothing, so, together with academics at Farnborough, he tested nine different fabrics, ultimately choosing a new cotton-nylon fabric called "Wyncol" for the Everest tents and climbing suits.[32] It was an exceptionally windproof, "breathable," lightweight fabric, highly resistant to tearing. The windproof smocks and trousers that he designed were modified from arctic clothing. Many of the features were typical of his attention to detail, such as the black taffeta inner linings for the outer garments—a slippery material that made them easy to pull on over the inner insulating layers—and an adjustable hood, to which he added a wire-stiffened visor for protection against the wind and snow. Crucially, Pugh made strenuous efforts to ensure the Everest clothing was properly fitted, unlike the clothes for the climbers on Cho Oyu. He also added extra pockets and loops and had the clothes fitted with zips rather than buttons.

Having recorded temperatures and conditions inside the tents on Cho Oyu, Pugh proposed several modifications: strong, sewn-in, tear-resistant groundsheets; adequate ventilation; economy of weight; and sleeve entrances to keep out snow and drafts. The sleeping bags used on Cho Oyu had also proven inadequate, so he studied their thermal properties and specified the amount of down needed to give protection for temperatures as low as −40°F. He stipulated that the sleeping bags must be long enough to pull over the head and wide enough to allow a man to turn over inside, assisted by a slippery inside lining.

At Cedars, he had concluded that air mattresses ("Lilos") were superior to the more-conventional camping mattresses, so he recommended that they be used on the expedition.[33] He also helped to design an innovative double-layered airbed with improved insulation and increased comfort. In addition, he insisted that items like sunscreen, which had not been officially supplied on Cho Oyu, must be provided for Everest, and that the goggles should be darker-tinted than those used on Cho Oyu.

By the time the expedition set off from England, Pugh's analytical and creative skills had been applied to a seemingly endless list of topics. However, he did not find himself being treated like the guru who held the key to success on Everest. The few people in the climbing world who knew anything about what he was doing found it hard to credit that, as a scientist, he was capable of making a useful contribution. Far from treating him as worthy of their respect, they regarded him as an object of skepticism and suspicion, and even, in some quarters, scorn and derision.

12

Opposition and Suspicion

John Hunt was told in advance to expect "hostility" when he arrived in England in October. His appointment as the new Everest leader was greeted with a storm of protests from the climbing world. So vociferous was the outcry that the Himalayan Committee met at the Alpine Club on September 24 to reconsider its decision and vote again. Tom Bourdillon, who had been promised a place on the Everest team by the now-ousted Shipton, appeared at the meeting and read aloud an indignant letter of resignation. Laurence Kirwan, who believed that Shipton was the best choice of leader, voted against Hunt.

Hunt's appointment was confirmed by six votes to two, but Basil Good-fellow sent a letter to Germany, forewarning Hunt of "the difficulty of your position."[1] The Cho Oyu climbers were "intensely loyal to Shipton," he cautioned, and were having "profound doubts" as to whether they would "join an Everest party under any leader but Shipton." He also warned of "nervousness that the expedition will become a military operation, not in the British mountaineering tradition."

Hunt reassured Goodfellow that he was "quite prepared" to encounter "opposition and suspicion."[2] Once in England, he embarked on a charm offensive to win the support of the doubting climbers, insisting that he too was a climber in the romantic tradition. He shared their values and disliked having to adopt a professional approach as much as they did. But it was, he insisted, a necessary evil: "The fact must be faced that we are inevitably involved in the competition for Everest, and that our opportunity in 1953 should be exploited while it lasts. It would be surprising if either the French in 1954 or the Swiss in 1955 failed to reap the advantage if we let it slip past."[3]

When Edmund Hillary wrote to him expressing dismay at the burgeoning size of the expedition, Hunt replied: "Your remarks on the size and weight of the expedition are very fully sympathised with! . . . You and I enjoy climbing mountains in quite a different way [from this], but we are caught up in the symbolic significance of this show and the consequent importance of succeeding by all reasonable means."[4]

In his letter from Thyangboche of June 8, Tom Bourdillon had used the same rationale to justify his support for a large-scale, highly organized, professional approach to the Everest project, and had made it clear that he too was setting aside his preference for the kind of climbing he enjoyed, purely out of patriotism: "Everest attempts have become an international competition in which . . . the pleasure of the climber takes second place to national prestige."[5]

Nonetheless, assuming a competitive stance toward any climbing project, even the climbing of Everest, and organizing a military-style expedition making use of professional scientific advice, as Hunt intended to do, was in direct conflict with the traditional values of the Alpine Club. This conflict between Hunt's professed romantic climbing credo and his need for technological and scientific support was at the heart of what would soon be a difficult relationship between himself and Griffith Pugh.

The climbing community's antipathy toward militaristic expeditions had its roots in a fundamental difference of outlook between the Alpine Club and the Royal Geographical Society, which had caused many stormy arguments between the two world wars. The RGS was a learned society founded to promote knowledge. It had always been committed to the principle that it would only support expeditions that had scientific as well as exploratory or sporting aims, and the society never doubted that the heroic and the scientific could march happily side by side. In 1921, Lieutenant Colonel Francis Younghusband, president of the RGS, waxed lyrical about the heroic sporting goal of the first Everest expedition, yet was equally enthusiastic that a geodesist, a glaciologist, geographers, and a gentleman physiologist would accompany the climbers.[6]

The Alpine Club, with its amateur sporting ideals, was less well disposed toward science. As the revered Leslie Stephen (onetime club president and editor of the *Alpine Journal*) told members in 1924: "True alpine travellers loved the mountains for their own sake and considered scientific intruders with their barometers and their theorising to be a simple nuisance."[7]

By the 1930s an influential contingent had become convinced that the huge size and mixed objectives of the early Everest expeditions, with all the scientists and their equipment, were largely to blame for the repeated failures. The other problem, in their eyes, was that several of the early expeditions were led by army officers rather than climbers, as a consequence of RGS influence.

In the mid-1930s the Alpine Club view gained the ascendancy, fiercely advocated by iconic Everest veterans like Frank Smythe, Bill Tilman, and Eric Shipton. The RGS's scientific aspirations were set aside; the juggernaut missions of the past were supplanted by small, flexible expeditions far more enjoyable for the climbers and more consistent with their sporting principles.

After World War II, the ideas associated with Shipton and Tilman—that only climbers could understand the needs of other climbers, and that small, casual expeditions were the only type worth going on—remained articles of faith. The casual approach was in perfect harmony with the public-school sporting ethos of "untutored brilliance," the so-called "Corinthian Spirit" by which gentlemen sportsmen achieved effortless success without really trying. Only the mundane professional—an altogether lower order of person—would stoop to engage in elaborate preparations and heavy training, or feel the need for scientific advice.

As for involving scientists in mountaineering expeditions, not only was it unpleasant, but in Bill Tilman's view, it was also dangerous: "The frenzy of the scientist readily extinguishes the common sense of the mountaineer and raises a very ugly head indeed. As the Spanish proverb says, 'Science is madness if good sense does not cure it.'"[8]

Goodfellow and the other beleaguered members of the Himalayan Committee felt enormous relief once they began to see the great competence and vigor that Hunt brought to the Everest enterprise. As organization charts and planning and selection documents started to appear with amazing alacrity, they were happy to resume a passive, supportive role. Over at the MRC, Sir Harold Himsworth was delighted too. And even Laurence Kirwan concluded that Hunt had been "the right decision, taken in the wrong way."[9]

Behind the scenes at the Alpine Club, however, resentment ran deep. Geoffrey Winthrop Young, doyen of the club's old guard, spoke for many when he regretted that the Everest quest had been turned into a "soulless and vulgar" exercise in "peak bagging," "an international dogfight and stunt . . . invaded with all the clamour of competition."[10] As Hunt had astutely anticipated, however, the prospective climbers found the challenge of Everest irresistible, and none of them refused his invitation to join. Even Tom Bourdillon came back into the fold once he saw the chance of persuading Hunt to try out his father's closed-circuit oxygen on the expedition.

Despite the negative undercurrents, everyone wanted the expedition to succeed. As news of Hunt's plans filtered through, many of the older climbers hastened to come forward with their own views on how to handle the ascent. This was especially true of the Everest veterans who had firsthand experience of high-altitude climbing.

What really worried them was that Hunt appeared to be so much under the sway of non-climbing scientists. They were particularly concerned about his plans for using oxygen. Edward Norton, whose twenty-eight-year altitude record had only just been broken by the Swiss, was appalled that Hunt had become so committed to oxygen: "As I see it your plan . . . depends in its present form on the efficiency of oxygen . . . all previous experience warns against relying on it."[11]

Despite being a scientist himself, George Finch, who brought the first modified RAF oxygen sets to Everest in 1922, was quite certain that Hunt was intending to use oxygen from too low an altitude. He was also extremely critical of Hunt's decision to take closed-circuit as well as open-circuit oxygen equipment on the expedition. Finch's son-in-law, Scott Russell, joined in. "This naturally discredits the simple open system which is the choice of the only two men who have the necessary qualifications to form a real judgement, namely Finch and Peter Lloyd [who both had firsthand experience of using oxygen sets on Everest]," he stormed.[12] Russell sent Hunt an exceedingly derogatory letter on Finch's behalf, suggesting that Pugh and the other scientists advising Hunt did not have the respect of elite scientists:

Discussion on the use of oxygen on Everest in the past seems to have gone wrong largely because people with insufficient judgement to form sound opinions and insufficient experience have shouted loudly. What alarms me at the moment is the view, which is not endorsed in the highest scientific quarters, that the physiologists are now in a position to make a much better theoretical assessment than they were a few years ago.[13]

So strong was this tendency to believe that the climbers had a better understanding of the problems than the scientists that Russell felt able to put forward this view in complete ignorance of Pugh's recent research. Later, he had the grace to apologize and admit to Pugh that his father-in-law was "not in the picture."

Peter Lloyd, who had the huge job of procuring all the oxygen equipment for the expedition, was one of Pugh's most dedicated critics. Lloyd had never been happy about Pugh muscling in on the oxygen, and was even less happy about the amount of power that had been conceded to the High-Altitude Committee. He had hoped initially to become Hunt's "executive adviser" on oxygen himself, but as Charles Wylie reported to Hunt early on, he had failed to get his way. "The MRC have been appointed and all Lloyd can hope to be is a member of Professor Matthews' Committee . . . The best scientists on oxygen are on the committee. Lloyd has a lot of experience of practical application of oxygen apparatus, but is neither a physiologist nor an oxygen scientist."[14]

Hunt, however, was sympathetic toward Lloyd. Lloyd had been a staunch supporter of his bid for the leadership and was a personal friend. To make Lloyd feel better, Hunt came up with a plan to give him direct responsibility for the closed-circuit oxygen work being carried out by the Bourdillons.[15]

When Sir Bryan Matthews found out, he hit the roof. He demanded an explicit letter from the chairman of the Himalayan Committee confirming that Lloyd's role was to carry out the recommendations of the High-Altitude Committee, not to give advice or make decisions himself. Kirwan had to send a memo to Hunt headed "Oxygen Organization," explaining this to him.[16] But Lloyd was not to be silenced and became messianic in his efforts to influence the expedition's oxygen strategy.

One of Lloyd's biggest complaints was that Pugh was causing far too much oxygen to be shipped to Everest. The amount needed depended partly on the oxygen-flow rates and partly on how fast the climbers would climb with oxygen. Using his Cho Oyu findings to calculate the requirements, Pugh wanted the British team to take far more oxygen to Everest than had ever been taken before—nearly ten times more than the Swiss had taken the previous autumn.[17] The High-Altitude Committee backed his recommendations.

Brushing aside Pugh's estimates, Lloyd produced his own, purely theoretical calculations, which purported to show that the climbers would in fact ascend much faster than Pugh thought, so they would need far less oxygen than Pugh imagined.[18] He also disagreed with Pugh's view that oxygen should be available for descent as well as ascent. He tried to convince the Himalayan Committee that the proposed amount was "too expansive," and that it would be impossible to transport; most of it would be wasted.[19] He badgered John Hunt—ultimately without success—with insistent messages urging him to reduce the quantities. In the end, however, it would prove profoundly fortunate that Hunt ignored Lloyd and deferred to the greater authority of the High-Altitude Committee.[20]

Oxygen masks were yet another bone of contention. Lloyd and George Finch both believed fervently that climbers would never be able to tolerate them. Both had tried the prewar oxygen masks—Finch on Everest in 1922, and Lloyd in 1938—and had found them suffocating. In their view, the only feasible way of delivering oxygen to climbers was the alternative system designed by Finch in 1922, where the climber breathed the oxygen in through a wide-bore tube and closed the tube with his teeth when breathing out.

Wing Commander H. L. Roxburgh of Farnborough had published a paper in 1947 explaining why the prewar masks had been unsuitable for climbing. The masks, tubes, and valves were designed for use by seated pilots and were too small to cope with the much greater quantities of air breathed in by climbers in the midst of vigorous exercise. The solution was to fit the masks with bigger tubes and larger, more-sensitive valves.

But the message failed to get through to Lloyd or to Finch, or indeed, to the Swiss Everest team in 1952. The Swiss oxygen sets developed suffocating resistance to breathing when the climbers panted and could only be used comfortably when they were sitting down and breathing normally.[21] Consequently the Swiss had to attempt Everest effectively without climbing oxygen.

The Farnborough scientists who had helped Lloyd in early 1952, before the Cho Oyu expedition, had brought in a young colleague named John Cotes to adapt the RAF oxygen apparatus—including the masks—for climbing. Cotes tried to persuade Lloyd that he could modify the masks very effectively, but made no headway. "They were so fixed in their idea that they had to have an oxygen tube," he recalled. "It seemed a monstrous suggestion. I was absolutely appalled. This was a hopeless way of going about things, and I reckoned that we could do much better!"[22] Instead, Lloyd ordered Cotes to ignore the masks and work on improving the Finch-style tubes.

It was only when Sir Bryan Matthews came on the scene to help with the preparations for Cho Oyu that Lloyd's instructions to Cotes were changed, and he was able to adapt the masks, widening the tubes connected to the mask and making the valves more sensitive as suggested by Roxburgh, and also creating a special latex cowl to fit over the front, to prevent freezing. Pugh carried out some trials on Cho Oyu and suggested a few modifications. He also compared the performances of the masks and the tubes and found that the climbers far preferred the masks.[23]

Cotes was persuaded to continue working on the masks for Everest, but Finch and Lloyd remained hostile, Finch announcing in a lecture to the Royal Society in December 1952 that the high-altitude climber—being "particularly prone to claustrophobia"—would simply "not be able to tolerate a close-fitting mask," and Lloyd insisting that a consignment of wide-bore tubes be sent to Everest, where—in the end—they would not be used.[24]

The fearsome Sir Bryan clearly found his encounters with Lloyd and Hunt frustrating at times. After his initial contretemps with them, Matthews made a special point of protesting every time Hunt or Lloyd missed a meeting of the HAC.[25] Then in late January, when it looked as if Lloyd would fail to have all the oxygen cylinders ready to be shipped out to India with the main Everest party, Matthews sent Hunt a caustic letter, complaining about the "slow progress of the production of oxygen" made by "your oxygen controller," and criticizing the Himalayan Committee:

The main responsibility for any deficiency rests with the Himalayan Committee who have never been prepared to make or support any long-term plan by which proper climbing oxygen equipment can be evolved.

I am only sorry that the Himalayan Committee did not regard oxygen as essential to the success of the expedition from an earlier date.[26]

Hunt passed the letter to Lloyd, who returned it having scrawled on the bottom, "Sorry, any comments are unprintable." The oxygen was not ready in time and had to be flown out to India separately.

Although John Hunt relied heavily on Pugh, they were slow in getting to know one another personally. They were very different characters with different cultural outlooks. Pugh was blunt and straightforward; he was capable of keeping his thoughts to himself, but when he spoke he said what he meant. Hunt was far more subtle and elusive. As befitted his army background, he was a consummate manager who laid great stress on planning and team-building, showing firm though motivational and inspiring leadership. Pugh respected Hunt's management and organizational skills, which he considered essential if the expedition was to have a reasonable chance of success. Unlike many of the climbers—among them Hillary, Lowe, Gregory, Wylie, and Ward—Pugh never thought Shipton capable of meeting the organizational challenge of Everest: "Shipton was a very dreamy sort of man—he never would have managed it—never would have managed to get the oxygen organized. Hunt was forceful and he kept the momentum going."[27] It was some time, however, before Pugh came to understand that he and Hunt were on very different wavelengths.

Pugh's first chance to get to know Hunt outside the context of formal meetings came in early December when he traveled with Hunt, Wylie, and Gregory to the Jungfraujoch above Grindelwald in Switzerland. They took great quantities of equipment with them, including twenty-two different types of climbing boots, five types of tents, and assorted cookers, sleeping bags, gloves, and goggles. Pugh was expecting to conduct systematic trials to establish which were the best. However, things did not go to plan. Hunt regarded himself as an expert on climbing equipment, and he was not prepared to waste good climbing time on what he regarded as unnecessary and pedantic scientific trials. The result was that the choices were not made in the systematic way Pugh would have liked. He hid his dissatisfaction, but he was very disappointed.

Back in London, as Christmas drew near, Eric Shipton gave a talk about the Cho Oyu expedition at the Royal Geographical Society. Pugh was invited to say a few words about "the physiological problems connected with the climbing of Mount Everest."[28] He took his assignment literally and, with his usual blunt forthrightness, delivered a doom-laden lecture that conveyed all too accurately the doubts about the oxygen equipment that were being discussed behind the scenes—particularly about the logistics of transporting enough oxygen cylinders to the highest camps.

We shall be putting our faith in an old-fashioned open-circuit system because we know that it will work. The unfortunate part is that because nine-tenths of the oxygen is wasted, it is necessary to take with us a large number of oxygen cylinders, and it is doubtful whether it is possible to take enough up to the South Col [of Everest] to supply the climbers with sufficient oxygen.

Pugh wasn't all that hopeful that the Bourdillons would successfully modify the closed-circuit system either, saying, "We are trying to develop an improved apparatus, but I'm not sure it will work." As for a summit assault in poor weather without oxygen? That, too, was fraught with problems: "Even if the climbers reach the summit they might well sit down on their way back from the summit and die of cold." Honest as it was, this was most definitely not the kind of talk that Hunt wanted the public or his climbers to hear. A week later, he sent Pugh a letter, tactfully but firmly asking for greater circumspection. "A contented and confident party is one of the basic needs for success and will be my very personal concern," Hunt explained. "It may not be easy, at times, to preserve amity, and confidence is easily shaken, particularly by a scientific 'slant' in the mind of the 'layman.'" If Pugh held "strong opinions," he should share them with Hunt himself "rather than [with] other members of the team."[29]

So irritated was Hunt that he was moved to give Pugh a salutary reminder of the strength of feeling within the climbing community against mixing science with mountaineering. "Scientific research combined with Everest has in the past been the subject of some controversy and, I suspect, the cause of a certain amount of friction. Views have been strongly expressed and renewed to myself in recent weeks that the two objectives are better pursued separately on different mountains." And he emphasized that it was only because he, Hunt, had stood up against their objections that Pugh had a place on the expedition.

I do not agree with this view which is the principal reason why I have agreed all along with the Himalayan Committee's proposal to accept the MRC's offer (or request) to send out 1–2 physiologists with the party, hence your inclusion. It is my firm belief that the two interests <u>can</u> live side by side and <u>can</u> be mutually beneficial during the course of an expedition.

In truth, because of the prior commitment made to the MRC, it would have been difficult for Hunt to have left Pugh behind. If he had excluded Pugh, he might have put the committee in the embarrassing position of being asked to return the £600 Royal Society grant for Pugh's research that they themselves had applied for and gratefully received.[30]

Though he professed himself to be in favor of science in private, in public Hunt tended to associate himself with the antiscience camp, and to dwell on his fears that Pugh's involvement with the expedition might get in the way of the overriding objective. "One of the lessons learned from the past is that science and mountaineering do not readily mix," he would later write. "I was always sure that we must concentrate single-mindedly on the main purpose of getting up."[31]

Pugh, however, was just as keen as Hunt for the expedition to succeed. He did his best to reassure Hunt, sending him a letter emphasizing that he regarded his research project as secondary to the overriding aim of the expedition, and that in his view, "The physiology should in no way interfere with the general plan, and should be as unobtrusive as possible."[32] He assured Hunt that his program of experiments "looks more formidable on paper than it really is," and also pointed out that the main purpose of the research was to find practical ways of helping high-altitude climbers to achieve their goals: namely, "to get information which will enable the maximum benefit to be obtained from the oxygen," and "to find the best methods of getting acclimatised and of preventing high-altitude deterioration."

Try as he might, however, Pugh did not find Hunt wholly supportive in the run-up to the expedition. Having rebuffed Lloyd's efforts to get him to cut down on the oxygen being sent to Everest, Hunt decided to assuage Lloyd's feelings by cutting most of the fifteen oxygen cylinders allocated to Pugh for his experiments.

Pugh also wanted a new and better tent for his Everest research. The pyramid tent he had used on Cho Oyu was too dark, too low for his apparatus, and had reached extraordinarily high temperatures when the sun was out. Hunt refused, and did not respond to Pugh's subsequent letters. On the other hand, when he discovered that Pugh had sent his gun to Nepal, he wrote at once: "I really was taken aback to learn that you have put your .22 rifle in the ship despite the decision which Major Wylie passed on to you from me that we could not accept it."[33]

None of this dissonance behind the scenes delayed the preparations. All those involved worked extremely hard, and most of the equipment and supplies (except for the oxygen) were ready to be shipped out on February 12. Pugh, Hunt, Bourdillon, and the two New Zealanders made their way separately. Pugh flew out at the beginning of March, having gained almost three weeks extra for his preparations. Admittedly, he used two of those weeks to visit Engelberg, to "try out experiments" and derive sustenance from the place he loved most, leaving his wife and children at home as usual.

Pugh flew alone from London to Kathmandu, with four changes of plane in Zurich, Beirut, Delhi, and Patna, carrying with him several "precious cases" of equipment. At Beirut airport, he tore his coat rushing to rescue them from some porters, who appeared to be making off with them. On March 5 he finally arrived, slightly disheveled, in Kathmandu, where he took the airport bus into town and went directly to the British embassy, to look for the rest of the expedition.

13

The Trek from Kathmandu

Griffith Pugh found John Hunt, most of the climbers, and twenty Sherpas at the British embassy. The Sherpas had walked from Darjeeling, led by Tenzing Norgay. Many had brought along their wives, who were being photographed on the embassy lawn, dressed in colorful traditional costumes. Pugh was delighted to find that the British team was being put up in luxury, either in the embassy or one of the bungalows on the embassy grounds. His own bedroom was in the embassy itself, next door to John Hunt.

But it soon became clear that Tenzing and his fellow Sherpas were not at all pleased that they had been billeted in the garages, formerly the stables, at the back of the building, without beds, toilets, or washing facilities. Tenzing himself was offered a room in a hotel but refused to leave his team.[1] Indian independence was still recent, and sensitivities about colonial attitudes were very near the surface. The next morning, the Sherpas expressed their displeasure by standing in a row and ceremoniously urinating on the road in front of the embassy building.

They were given a severe reprimand by John Hunt. It was not well received, and relations between the Sherpas and their British employers were strained during the early part of the expedition.[2] Nevertheless, Tenzing's knowledge of Everest promised to be of great value, and Hunt sought to diffuse any bad feelings by following the Swiss example of formally inviting him to become a full "climbing member" of the British team, in addition to his role as expedition Sirdar. This honor failed to allay Tenzing's resentment and, to the consternation of the British, just before leaving Kathmandu, he expressed his feelings publicly in an interview with Ralph Izzard, a British journalist from the *Daily Mail*.

Tenzing had not signed the confidentiality agreement preventing the rest of the team from talking to the press. The agreement was designed to ensure that the expedition's chief sponsor, *The Times*, could maintain exclusive control over all the news emanating from the expedition. Like all the other journalists (except for James Morris of *The Times*), Izzard was having a hard time covering the expedition. Lacking any other story, he was relieved to get the interview with Tenzing, who spoke fulsomely about how much he preferred working with the Swiss and the French to the British.[3] Izzard was thoroughly patriotic and enjoyed nothing better than writing heroic articles in rousing purple prose about British valor, but he now resorted to framing a controversial story about Tenzing's tense relationship with his British employers. The resulting article, which was syndicated to a prominent Indian newspaper, led to Izzard being branded an "enemy" of the expedition.[4]

Hunt decided to split his large and unwieldy expedition into two groups for the trek to Thyangboche, the village near Everest that had been chosen as the base for the extended acclimatization period Pugh had recommended. They set off from the medieval town of Bhadgaon, 10 miles east of Kathmandu, where their eight tons of luggage had been laid out in orderly piles on the Nepalese army's parade ground. The first convoy left on March 10. It consisted of Hunt; the climbers: George Band, Tom Bourdillon, Charles Evans, Alf Gregory, Wilfred Noyce, Mike Westmacott, and New Zealanders Ed Hillary and George Lowe; cameraman Tom Stobart; 45 Sherpas; and 150 porters. Pugh and Ward were relegated to the second convoy with the one remaining climber, Charles Wylie. They departed the following day with 11 Sherpas and 210 porters.

For the second time in his career Pugh faced the prospect of having to live and work for several months with men who, quite apart from any personal feelings toward him, were instinctively hostile to the presence of a scientist on their expedition. Hunt could have made life easier for Pugh by telling the climbers about the huge contribution he had made before the expedition, and the fact that he had relied heavily on Pugh's recommendations. However, addressing the team shortly before departure, he signally failed to do so; instead, he was deliberately dismissive.

Pugh appreciated that Hunt was preoccupied with the formidable logistical challenge of steering his team up Everest, yet he could not help but find

Hunt's attitude disturbing. "I was very worried by two pep talks Hunt gave at Kathmandu," he reported to Otto Edholm back in London, "in which he went out of his way to stress the minor importance of physiology to the expedition."[5] And he confided to his wife, Josephine: "I'm afraid I'm in for a difficult time with Hunt, who turns out to be extremely pompous and quite out of reach as far as I am concerned. There is nothing for it but to be patient and say nothing and get on with my own job."[6]

Pugh had already tried to reassure Hunt that his main ambition was to help put the climbers in the best possible position to succeed. He regarded his research as secondary and intended to carry it out unobtrusively, taking the greatest care not to interfere with the climbing. But this did not mean it was insignificant. It was specifically designed to gather information that would help climbers perform better at high altitude in the future. It was in the climbers' interests to cooperate.

However, Hunt's words about the "minor importance" of Pugh's role fell on receptive ears. The majority of the climbers subscribed to the view that science had no place in mountaineering, and that most scientists had no understanding of climbing. To them Pugh was "a boffin [scientist], with his head way up in the clouds."[7] They certainly didn't want to waste time participating in his experiments. "To some of us," Noyce wrote, revealing an almost visceral aversion to the prospect of being drawn into scientific experiments, ". . . the idea of taking a physiologist was repugnant . . . I myself fully imagined a kind of vampire, lurking at Camp III in readiness to absorb our blood and deflate our lungs as we weaved wearily over the icefall."[8]

Pugh felt isolated by the cultural divide separating him from most of the team. This struck him forcefully on the first evening of the trek as he gazed at a beautiful mountain view that had caught his attention the year before. Reminded of having felt equally cut off from the climbers on Cho Oyu, he found himself wishing that he could simply "go to sleep and wake up three months later to find the whole Everest expedition over."

After mentioning these insecure thoughts in a letter to Josephine, however, he dismissed them in the next paragraph as a mere product of oxygen shortage. He was not the type to dwell on negative issues. In any case, there were things to look forward to. On Cho Oyu he had mostly trekked alone, but he now had a like-minded and enthusiastic companion: "Ward is in his element," he wrote to Josephine, "and I think we shall get on very well together."

Michael Ward was similar to Tom Bourdillon in having one foot in the climbing camp and the other in the science camp. He was admired as a climber and was popular among his peers. Ed Hillary wrote approvingly of his "raffish grin" and "easy tempestuous nature," and Wilfred Noyce stressed how much he enjoyed climbing with Ward. At the same time, Ward was completely won over by Pugh's physiological prescriptions and quite sure that his mentor would soon be shown to have solved the key problems of altitude, cold, and dehydration that had bedeviled previous expeditions. Pugh was also quietly hopeful that his ideas were about to revolutionize high-altitude mountaineering.

The two doctors soon shrugged off any doubts they had about being segregated from the main party and settled down to enjoy the trek. The path took them across the grain of the hilly countryside, descending steeply into river valleys, climbing out again across "well tilled" terraced hillsides and "fields of green wheat and early potatoes" and upward to the rhododendron forests, where the "mossy trunks of the trees were twisted in fantastic shapes."

The only other European in the second convoy was Charles Wylie, who regarded science as a foreign language for which he had no personal aptitude or interest. Educated at public school and Sandhurst like John Hunt, Wylie was a Gurkha officer, fluent in Nepalese. He had been put in charge (with Tenzing) of hiring the porters for the march-in, and had volunteered to join the second convoy, to act as a "tail end Charlie," sweeping up stragglers and making sure all the baggage arrived safely at its destination. He felt bored and excluded by what he described as the "seventeen-day conversation" about physiology going on between the two doctors. They, on the contrary, regarded it as a "great advantage" to be in his company, because he presided over a satisfyingly comfortable regime, spoke the language well, and was "good at organising the Sherpas and coolies."[9]

Under Wylie's supervision, they dined every evening in front of their tents with two Sherpas standing attentively behind them, fulfilling their every wish. "We all get on very well together and our arrangements are less Spartan than those of the earlier party," Pugh confided happily to Josephine.[10]

Some of the great Everest veterans, such as Bill Tilman and Eric Shipton, regarded any such luxury as "sissy," but Pugh was dedicated in his opposition to the fashion for "Spartan" regimes in the mountains. In his view, the human body already had enough to contend with at high altitude without being subjected to unnecessary stress, so he had set out to ensure that all reasonable comforts were provided for the team. Comfort at night was a priority, hence his attention to the detailed design of the sleeping bags and air mattresses. "Toughness, if it implies neglecting to take measures to reduce fatigue and strain, has no place in Himalayan planning," he said.[11] A decent cup of coffee for breakfast in the morning was important to him, so he had brought his own tins of good-quality ground coffee and a coffee strainer. Knowing how uncomfortable it could be to crouch in front of a gas analyzer, he was the only member of the Everest team to take a chair to base camp. The chair seemed a stroke of genius to cameraman Tom Stobart, whose lanky body was always uncomfortable reclining on the ground. At base camp he frequently sneaked into Pugh's tent to snatch a few restful moments sitting on it.[12]

A few days into the trek, Hunt wrote home that he regretted having had to split the two medical men off from the main party: "It's a pity we are not all in one party, particularly as I wanted to get to know Mike Ward better, and for 'Pug' [Pugh] to settle in with the rest; he is the only peculiar one, and it would be good to let people get used to him and for him to be used to being laughed at."[13]

In his mountaineering bible, *Mountain Craft*, which Hunt had almost certainly read, Geoffrey Young emphasized that having a person in a mountaineering party whom all the others could "laugh with or at" had a beneficial, unifying impact on "the collective good humour" of the group.[14] Hunt consciously seemed to intend this role for Pugh, who, with his absent-minded ways and distracted air, was a natural candidate.

Wylie also took the view that laughing at Pugh fulfilled a useful, morale-boosting function: "I liked him yes, very much—I think everybody liked him, loved him, they really did. But they could pull his leg . . . We laughed at him for his absentmindedness. And that was a very good thing that we had somebody on the expedition whom the others could talk about and laugh about."[15]

Hunt's deliberately jokey stance toward Pugh was evident in his description of the moment halfway through the trek, when he and Hillary left the lead convoy and went to check on how the second convoy was faring, only to discover that "there had been sacrifices to science" in the latter. Hunt and Hillary left immediately, to avoid getting roped in.

Pugh had taken baseline measurements—blood samples, body weights, pulse rates, and the like—from all the team and most of the Sherpas in Kathmandu. Now he and Ward had begun doing exercise tests to measure the changes in their maximum exercise rates as they gradually acclimatized and grew fitter.[16] Far from finding them burdensome, Pugh and Ward thought the tests were improving their fitness, and enjoyed competing with each another.

Betraying not a hint that it was experiments like this that had underpinned the entire planning of the expedition, Hunt wrote in a typically jocular tone:

> *Griff Pugh had subjected the party [actually only himself and Ward] to a fearful ordeal known as the "maximum work test," which consisted of rushing uphill at best possible speed until the lungs were bursting and then expiring air into an enormous bag until it swelled out like a balloon . . . It was satisfactory to learn that Griff . . . had not spared himself the tortures he inflicted on his guinea-pigs.*[17]

The outfit Pugh wore for the trek—sky-blue pajamas (which soon became gray), a hat, and an umbrella to shade his fair skin from the sun—was also seen as immensely eccentric and comical. Surprisingly indifferent to the strong sun, Hunt and the other climbers remained impervious to the fact that Pugh's pajamas were vastly more practical than the shorts they chose to wear, even when they suffered painful sunburn as a result. In an effort to keep cool, Charles Wylie went so far as having his hair cut with "short back and sides." Pugh was quick to record the painful consequences: "Wiley [*sic*] had the back of his neck shaved halfway up to the crown of his head at Banepa; as a result he has second-degree sunburn, and the back of his head is all swollen and blistered."[18]

Another of Pugh's practical measures that Hunt treated as a tremendous joke was a huge, lightweight aluminum box weighing only 13 pounds into which Pugh had packed 100 pounds of his physiological equipment. He was exceedingly proud of his weight-efficient box, but Hunt ridiculed it as a "formidable monster," "a coffin [that provoked] protests and jests on all sides." Pugh delighted in pointing out that the boxes Hunt was using to transport the expedition's oxygen weighed more than the equipment carried inside them.

When they were together as a group the climbers often laughed at Pugh, but individually most of them found him very good company. Evans wrote in his diary that Pugh was "[a]musing, vague, irascible and likeable—takes ten times as long as everyone else to get packed—except Tom S[tobart]—5 times as long as me." His best remark, Evans thought, was: "The thing is to avoid this awful up at 9 (to London, that is) back at 6 life."[19] Hillary reported that Pugh "kept us amused with his sardonic, absentminded humour."[20] Noyce enjoyed his "wealth of stories told in the slow academic voice . . . usually ending on a note of startling frivolity."[21]

The second convoy arrived at the small settlement of Thyangboche on March 27. Pugh described this little village, situated at 12,000 feet amidst lush green vegetation, with the dramatic Everest cirque of mountains rising all around, as "the most beautiful place I have ever seen."

Pugh and Ward had insisted that higher standards of hygiene were essential to avoid ill health. Hunt had therefore placed the camp on a hill above the village, a safe distance from the local population with its endemic infections. Pugh and Ward arrived to find tents already pitched and a scene of industrious unpacking and rearranging of equipment.

Not long after their arrival, tensions flared when the first consignment of oxygen was brought into camp and it emerged that a third of the forty-eight cylinders for the training program were empty, having leaked in transit. Since Hunt had already eliminated Pugh's fifteen cylinders, some of the oxygen intended for the assault would now have to be given over to training. Thereafter, shortage of oxygen remained an acute worry. Ward described the loss as "a major catastrophe, as it meant that we would not be able to start using oxygen as low down as we had intended."[22] Pugh saw immediately that if Peter Lloyd had succeeded in persuading Hunt to bring less oxygen they would have had "a grossly inadequate supply."

The predictable reaction of the climbers was to feel that such oxygen as they had must not be wasted on physiological experiments. "Inevitably," Pugh noted, "this seriously curtailed the training and the research."[23] Hunt's refusal to provide him with his own supply of oxygen had come back to haunt him.

The climbers now embarked on their formal acclimatization program. Pugh had recommended that this should be carried out away from Everest itself, so the team would remain fresh and interested. Hunt split the climbers into three groups and sent them off on five-day acclimatization trips, giving them opportunities to practice using the oxygen equipment and improve their fitness. Each group visited a different area, exploring and climbing some of the unconquered local peaks, which they greatly enjoyed.

One person for whom this period was particularly stressful was Tom Bourdillon. The onus was on him to show that the closed-circuit sets passionately championed by himself and his father really did work. They had toiled for many months to resolve the technical problems; now it was time to find out if they had succeeded.

Pugh stayed mainly at Thyangboche with Stobart, the cameraman. Tall and slim with tousled, sun-bleached hair, Stobart looked much younger than his thirty-nine years. He was rather unfit but exceptionally charming. Charles Evans described him as an "attractive vagabond" who kept everyone amused with thrilling tales of his travels in Antarctica and his adventures photographing wild game in Africa. Recognizing him as a kindred spirit, Pugh had made friends with him in Kathmandu, and the two men had bonded well. Stobart wrote of Pugh that he combined "the two traditional qualities of the professor—clear-sighted intelligence and absentmindedness. . . . He had that sort of speculative curiosity, wonder and originality of thought possessed by all the scientific elite. He never became dull and we never ran out of topics for conversation."[24]

Stobart also liked Pugh's attitude toward comfort, describing himself and the physiologist as "the most sybaritic members of the team." Together they undertook their own three-day acclimatization trip, after which they each resumed work at Thyangboche—Stobart with his camera, Pugh taking detailed records from the climbers as they returned from their excursions. He reported to Edholm:

It turns out that each party had camped one or more nights at about 18,000 feet and had worked probably harder than was good for them.

However, recovery was quick and I got the impression that there was less trouble with altitude symptoms than last year, even among the "new boys." Of course there is a good deal of competition between the climbers and they tend to push themselves pretty hard. This applies particularly to John Hunt.[25]

At the beginning of the expedition, most of the climbers were still skeptical about oxygen. Charles Evans and Ed Hillary both secretly hoped to have a shot at the summit without it. But attitudes were becoming more positive. Pugh was gratified when they reported finding the oxygen helpful even as low as 19,000 feet.[26]

George Lowe was one of many who started out believing that the oxygen could not compensate for the weight of the 35 pounds of equipment. But during his acclimatization trip with Tenzing, when he had been feeling lethargic, off-color, and had a bad headache, breathing oxygen had been a revelation. "We fitted on the mask, checked the bottles and flow rates, connected up and set off . . . adding to our natural intake three litres of oxygen every minute. Instead of puffing and panting I breathed deeply without the feeling of fatigue that one has before being acclimatised."[27] When he turned up the flow rate to 6 liters a minute: "I felt like running and could climb at sea level pace."

As they came and went, a few of the climbers agreed to participate in the exercise tests that Hunt and Hillary had studiously avoided on the march-in. When Hillary—always looking to show his mettle—realized the tests could be seen as a measure of his fitness and strength, he threw himself into them. Tenzing and a few other Sherpas also did the tests, but Pugh remarked ruefully that he was unable to persuade the Sherpas to "exert themselves as much as Ed Hillary."

Hillary was the kind of man who never felt that men walking alongside him were merely keeping pace with him in a companionable way. Instead, he *always* assumed that they were racing him and invariably responded with a "surge of speed" designed to put them in their place. Only once his primacy had been established could normal walking be resumed. His description of Hunt on the Everest march-in is typical:

Hunt drove himself with incredible determination and I always felt he was out to prove himself the physical equal of any member—even though most of us were a good deal younger than himself. I can remember on the third day's march pounding up the long steep hill from Dologhat and catching up with John and the way he shot ahead, absolutely determined not to be passed—the sort of challenge I could not then resist. I surged past with a burst of speed, cheerfully revelling in the contest, and was astonished to see John's face white and drawn as he threw every bit of his strength into the effort. There was an impression of desperation because he wasn't quite fast enough. What was he trying to prove, I wondered?[28]

Pugh also noticed that Hunt was so competitive that he often pushed himself almost to the point of compromising his health: "I wonder if he will stand the pace. He always likes to go faster and further and carry more than anyone else, and although he is very strong he gets very exhausted."[29]

In the second phase of the acclimatization period, an advance party consisting of Hillary, Lowe, Westmacott, and Band, plus six Sherpas and thirty-eight porters, went ahead to lay the foundations of the base camp at 17,900 feet and start to form a route up the fearsome Khumbu Icefall. Pugh and Stobart went with them. One of the six major glaciers on the slopes of Everest, the Khumbu Glacier flows gently down the mountain until it arrives at a height of 19,500 feet, where the slope steepens and it tips over the edge and is transformed into a vast waterfall of ice. This tumbling frozen torrent of chaotic jumbled ice-pillars, cliffs, and chasms shifts, groans, and cracks its way downward for 2,000 feet before giving way to a rocky terminal moraine where the base camp was to be established. Finding and preparing a relatively safe route up the dangerous icefall, negotiating the cliffs and visible crevasses, and avoiding the still more treacherous hidden chasms was the first major climbing hurdle the expedition had to overcome.

On the way to the base camp site, some of the low-altitude porters began to suffer from snow blindness. Dark goggles had been provided for the Sherpas but not for them. Pugh's diary tells how he and Stobart made "improvised goggles for about twenty porters" using cardboard and yellow Perspex, bound together with Stobart's black photographic tape. The story seems to have improved in Stobart's memory; the number of goggles multiplied. In his book *Adventurer's Eye* he recalled: "Soon we had sixty pairs of goggles made and fitted."[30]

The last part of the route was rough, stony, and uneven, and some of the porters slipped under their 60-pound loads. One girl porter fell down with her load pressing her head into the ground, causing the supporting strap to catch around her neck. Pugh went forward to help and was touched that she averted her face as he released her. He supposed that "she was ashamed at having fallen" and did not want him to see who she was. Offered the chance to leave the expedition and go home on full pay, on the grounds that the load was too much for her, she was most indignant. He tried to pay off another girl who was "almost snow blind," but she too "refused to take the money and insisted on going on." Several such incidents moved Westmacott to note that Pugh "was very caring."

Once base camp had been established on the bleak gray stones and boulders of the icefall's terminal moraine, the vanguard climbers began to pioneer the route upward. George Lowe, who was "on his back with diarrhoea," was the only climber unable to go with them.[31] Pugh and the cameraman, Stobart, made their own excursion up the icefall. Climbing a third of the way up, constantly threatened by yawning crevasses and tottering ice seracs, "which seemed about to fall on us," Pugh was gratified that his alpine "glacier technique" was coming back to him.

Returning to base camp, he and Stobart found an unexpected visitor sitting on a stone just above the tents: journalist Ralph Izzard of the *Daily Mail*, apparently looking for a scoop. Izzard had walked from Kathmandu to Thyangboche alone and then struggled to base camp in three days, without proper equipment or even a decent tent. Determined not to arrive looking down on his luck, he was clean-shaven, his hair neatly brushed, and he was dressed in a sporty jacket and silk cravat. He seemed quite unaware that his lips were blue and his eyes terribly inflamed. He appeared to Stobart to be in severe danger of "rapidly becoming snow blind."[32]

George Lowe was the only person in camp when Izzard arrived, and because Hunt had designated Izzard an "enemy of the expedition," Lowe had steadfastly ignored him for three hours. However, Pugh found the situation highly amusing, and Stobart was amused by Pugh's amusement: "'Awkward!'

said Griff, in a way I knew meant, 'How lovely—what a lovely situation,'" Stobart recalled. "Griff was a tolerant man filled with secret amusement about many things, and liable to poke fun."[33]

Disregarding Hunt's orders to have nothing to do with him, Pugh took pleasure in inviting Izzard to tea. "Pugh greeted me in a very kindly fashion," the journalist remembered, "and led me to a tent where I met George Lowe and Tom Stobart."[34] After tea Izzard set off back down the mountain. Concerned for his safety, Stobart remarked to Pugh: "I hope he makes it," and enjoyed Pugh's response: "'He'll make it,' said Griff, mentally rubbing his hands. 'But what a lovely case of anoxia! Absolutely classic symptoms.'"[35]

14

The Triumphant Ascent

The expedition's main stores arrived at base camp two weeks after the advance party. Pugh noticed the expressions of intense gratification on the faces of the porters as they signed off and collected their pay.[1] The push to climb the mountain would soon begin. Camp Three was already being put in above the icefall, and teams of Sherpas working in relays were about to start ferrying supplies up the mountain as each new camp was established.

Base camp was now very crowded, and Pugh did his best to ensure that the hygiene rules he and Ward had prescribed were properly observed. He told the Sherpanis (the female Sherpas) and some "boy porters with streaming noses" not to go into the cookhouse, and persuaded Tenzing to lecture the cooks yet again about boiling the utensils and washing their hands.

Amid all the activities, Pugh had been anxiously sounding out the climbers and the Sherpas about how well his dietary innovations and new equipment were performing in the field. Earlier, after a violent storm on the march-in, he had noted happily in his diary: "I was glad to find the tent material completely waterproof."[2] He was relieved that the rations seemed to be "proving a success," and that the clothing and airbeds appeared to be going down well too: "All are very pleased with their windproofs and down clothing, tents, and especially their double-level inflatable sleeping mats."[3]

But the same could not be said for the Lawrie climbing boots intended for intermediate altitudes, which had been chosen by Hunt after the trip to the Jungfraujoch. Pugh asked the Sherpas for their views. Dawa Tenzing volunteered the opinion: "Well, they are cold boots, but I expect they will be alright during the warm months of the year."[4] Everyone agreed that the boots were not warm enough.

The high-altitude boots were different. Pugh himself had been closely involved in their design and was eager to try them out, though he had trouble obtaining a pair. "We haven't tried the high-altitude boots yet—I am annoyed to find that Wiley did not order a pair for me, although I expressly asked him to do so. This was because they were originally intended to use only on the Lhotse Face and above. In fact, they will be needed all the way above the Ice Fall."[5]

When he got his hands on some, he wore them for a whole day, finding to his satisfaction that they gripped the snow as well as the conventional Lawrie boots, and were warm and comfortable. "Sitting in the mess tent after supper I had warm feet for the first time," he noted in his diary.[6]

He was also delighted to find that the open-circuit oxygen equipment was working well, even over extended periods: "Oxygen has been tried for 4–5 hour periods at 18–19,000 feet. Most people have succeeded in sleeping in their masks, no back pressure [i.e., no resistance to breathing] during work."

Asked for their views on the oxygen, the Sherpas told him: "You don't have to breathe so fast & you don't have to breathe so deeply; and going uphill is like walking on the level." These he regarded as deeply insightful observations.[7]

However, when Alf Gregory's air mattress proved to be faulty, Pugh was frustrated to find there were no spares: "Greg's Lilo is defective and there are no spares! I begged Hunt & Wiley to order 1/2 doz. spares before we left UK but they didn't do it. Now someone has to suffer for it."[8]

But he kept his opinions to himself, only revealing in his diary and in his letters to his MRC boss, Edholm, that he considered Hunt and Wylie incompetent in matters of equipment: "I am afraid wherever Wiley and Hunt were left to themselves they have made a mess of things viz. the Lawrie boots, snow goggles [not provided for porters], and knickknacks."[9]

Despite the problems, frustrations, stresses, strains, and jokes, with the expedition well under way, Pugh felt able to tell Edholm that a breakthrough had occurred: "Now, after a month, I am fairly satisfied that physiological thought has somehow permeated and influenced the minds of what we call the 'O group,' consisting of Hunt, Hillary, and Evans, who do the planning . . ."[10]

There had been a secretly triumphant moment at Lobuje—the team's pleasant recuperation camp below base camp—when Pugh had listened in to Hillary, Gregory, Westmacott, and Noyce having an animated conversation about how, in ideal circumstances, they thought oxygen ought to be used for the final assault. None of them had been favorably disposed toward oxygen at the start of the expedition, but now, Pugh noted with amusement, "The party thinks that the assault should be made on open-circuit . . . breathing oxygen all the way from base camp!" Clearly they had completely come round to the oxygen.[11]

Hunt had given Bourdillon, rather than Pugh, the task of teaching the climbers about altitude. Pugh had to "listen to Tom Bourdillon holding forth at base camp about the effects of anoxia and the use of oxygen at high altitude." But his pleasure and relief that the ideas were being disseminated far outweighed any irritation he may have felt at being usurped as the altitude expert.

Pugh's first attempt to carry out experiments above the icefall ended in a fiasco. Setting out on his own with a few Sherpas, he climbed to Camp Three, just above the top of the icefall, intending to set up a makeshift laboratory. His equipment, packed in a ration box, was carried up by Sherpas. When it was opened, it turned out to be full of bottles of mango chutney.

Mango chutney was Pugh's favorite relish, brought along on his express instructions as one of the expedition's luxury foods. He was convinced the climbers had deliberately swapped the boxes. When he arrived back at base camp, he found them helpless with laughter, and described the incident in his diary as "a tiresome and time wasting joke which caused much merriment."[12] A practical joke it may have been, but there was a lingering suspicion that, without the tacit approval of Hunt, the climbers would not have tricked Pugh and the Sherpas carrying his gear into making a pointless five-hour climb up the dangerous and unstable icefall.

Above Camp Three, the Western Cwm (pronounced *coom*, Welsh for "bowl-shaped valley")—a wide valley with sloping sides and a crevassed glacial floor—rose gently for about 3 miles to the foot of the 4,000-foot Lhotse Face.

Camp Four, the advanced base camp and command center from which the assault on the summit was to be directed, was created near the top of the

Western Cwm, at 21,200 feet, on May 1. From here, the route led up the steep Lhotse Face—a wall of hard-packed snow, ice, and rock—to the South Col, where the main assault camp would be established at 26,000 feet, still 3,000 feet below the summit. The route had to be reconnoitered, steps cut, fixed ropes placed, and camps put in before the Sherpas could safely ferry their loads of equipment and oxygen up to the South Col.

Pugh remained at base camp during this period, conducting experiments on water loss from the lungs, analyzing samples, monitoring the physical condition of the climbers coming down from the Western Cwm and the Lhotse Face, and taking copious notes on how their oxygen sets had performed. He reported to Edholm:

> *The anti-fatigue effect of O2 is very striking. Hillary and Tenzing went from here (base) to Camp Four—22,000 feet—on 4 litres a minute O2 in 5 hours (including half an hour's rest) without fatigue, and returned the same evening in a snowstorm. They did not use O2 on the descent, but they say they would never have risked the descent under the conditions prevailing, had they not felt remarkably fresh.*[13]

The preparation of the route up the Lhotse Face was hindered by bad weather. Band and Westmacott, both Himalayan novices allocated to the task, became sick and had to go down.[14] George Lowe and one Sherpa, "doing a climber's job," were left to prepare much of the path on their own, without oxygen, which was being carefully conserved. Others went up to help, only to retreat back down, cold and exhausted. Hunt had allocated only four days to the task; it took eleven. Lowe spent such a long time without oxygen at altitudes above 23,000 feet that Pugh began to fear he might suffer brain damage and remonstrated with Hunt.[15]

When, after seven days of hard work, the route up the Lhotse Face was still unfinished, Hunt felt compelled to drive forward regardless. Calling the team together at base camp on May 7, he announced his plan for the assault on the summit. The atmosphere became electric as he told them there were to be two summit assaults. The first, by Bourdillon and Evans, using closed-circuit oxygen, would be undertaken directly from the South Col with no intervening camp on the way up. The second, by Hillary and Tenzing, with open-circuit oxygen, would have an overnight stop at a high camp roughly two-thirds of the way up to the summit from the Col.

Pugh was not surprised by Hunt's choice of climbers. Evans was the deputy leader; Bourdillon and his father had developed the closed-circuit oxygen. Hillary's fitness, strength, and speed had already impressed Pugh on Cho Oyu; Tenzing had unique experience of the route, gained with the Swiss the previous year. The strategy of providing a high camp between the South Col and the summit for the open-circuit team, but not for the closed-circuit team, was no surprise either. Bourdillon and Evans, breathing virtually pure oxygen with the closed-circuit equipment, were expected to be able to climb fast enough to go all the way to the summit and return to the South Col in one day. Hillary and Tenzing, receiving much less supplementary oxygen through their open-circuit sets, would climb more slowly and would therefore need to spend an extra night high on the mountain in the high camp, where they would pick up fresh supplies of oxygen.

The decision not to provide a high camp for the closed-circuit pair proved very contentious. Ward and Gregory both argued strongly against it. Back in London many months earlier, Pugh and Bryan Matthews had both been adamant that the open-circuit oxygen sets must take priority on the expedition, but they had never been entirely confident that it would prove possible to carry enough oxygen cylinders up to extreme altitude to supply the wasteful open-circuit sets even for one summit attempt, let alone two. This was an important reason why the High-Altitude Committee had encouraged Hunt to take some of the Bourdillons' relatively unproven closed-circuit sets to try out as well.[16]

Tom Bourdillon and his father had been arguing this case since the previous autumn.[17] In October 1952, encouraged by the MRC, Bourdillon senior had secured a private meeting with Hunt at which he contended that since every summit attempt with open-circuit oxygen would need the support of a very high camp, and since Hunt would only have sufficient men and resources to supply one such camp, the only way to have two summit attempts would be for one of them to start out directly from the South Col without a high camp using closed-circuit oxygen.[18] When they criticized Hunt's summit plan, Ward and Gregory did not know that the Bourdillons themselves had done their best to convince Hunt that this was the only viable strategy. Nor did they know that Charles Evans, the deputy leader, Hillary, and Hunt had discussed the oxygen-supply problem interminably throughout the expedition, and had concluded regretfully that it would not be possible to carry enough cylinders up to very high altitude to supply two successive high camps.[19]

Pugh still doubted whether the Bourdillons had resolved all of the problems with the closed-circuit sets, but he did not criticize Hunt's decision to try it for one of the summit attempts. A letter written by Charles Wylie on May 9 gives the considered view of most of the team, including Pugh:

> *Chas and Tom are being given first crack at the top direct from the S Col on CC oxy. I don't think John [Hunt] (or anyone else) thinks they will make it, for he has described them as a scouting pair for our big guns—Tensing and Ed Hillary—who will follow one day later on open-circuit from as high a camp as we can carry on the Sth ridge. I think they have a good chance.*[20]

Shortly after the assault plans were announced, Pugh went up to Camp Three for a second time. Setting up his equipment, he did exercise tests on himself, took blood samples, and gathered samples of air from the bottom of the lungs of any willing climbers and Sherpas who were coming and going, transporting supplies up to Camp Four. Hunt had been driving himself relentlessly up and down the Western Cwm. Pugh gave him sleeping oxygen for the first time, which afforded him "a really restful night and pleasant dreams."[21]

The preparation of the route up the Lhotse Face was so slow that the atmosphere at Camp Four (advanced base camp) became very tense. Eventually, feeling he could wait no longer, Hunt dispatched the first party of Sherpas with supplies for the South Col up the face before the last part of the steep slope had been climbed, let alone the route prepared. Most of the climbers had assembled at Camp Four by then, including Pugh. It was the highest camp he reached on the expedition because he did not adapt well to the altitude.

Pugh admired Hunt's decision to press on without delay, regarding it as pivotal to the ultimate success of the expedition. Noyce climbed the Lhotse

Face using oxygen and found it very useful: "A taste or breath of metallic new life seemed to slip through the mouth to the lungs, mocking every disadvantage and making life seem good once again."[22] But the Sherpas who accompanied him, carrying loads of about 50 pounds, struggled without it. After stopping for the night at Camp Seven, halfway up the Lhotse Face, only one of the eight Sherpas was willing to continue the next morning.[23] He and Noyce went on alone, both using oxygen, and finally made it to the South Col. This was a great breakthrough.

Hunt sent up a second team of Sherpas with additional loads, led by Charles Wylie. But when they arrived at Camp Seven, they too refused to go higher, maintaining they felt too unwell. The camp had now become very crowded. Unless the Sherpas could be persuaded to continue, it would not be possible to establish the assault camp on the South Col. Hunt was so worried about the logjam that he dispatched his two star climbers—whom he had planned to keep fresh for their impending summit attempt—up to Camp Seven in hopes they might convince the Sherpas to resume their climb. Using oxygen, Hillary and Tenzing did the climb and, together with Wylie, succeeded in pressuring the Sherpas to make it to the South Col so the assault camp could at last be established.

But then there were further problems. Only two of the chosen team of elite high-altitude Sherpas were well enough to go above the South Col as planned.[24] Pugh thought this was because they had not been given sleeping oxygen, and therefore had difficulty in recuperating from climbing up the Lhotse Face without oxygen. Similarly, if Hillary and Tenzing had made their unscheduled climb up the Lhotse Face *without* oxygen, it would have taken an enormous toll on their energy just before their summit attempt. Even with the use of oxygen, Hunt had been reluctant to allow them to undertake the climb; without it, the entire expedition might have stalled on the Lhotse Face.[25]

Two days later, Bourdillon and Evans made the first attempt on the summit.[26] As Pugh had feared, one of their closed-circuit oxygen sets malfunctioned, and they were forced to give up at 28,720 feet, returning to the col completely exhausted, with Bourdillon in a state of collapse.

In his Cho Oyu report Pugh had recommended that the high camp for the open-circuit summit attempt be placed at roughly 28,000 feet. Oxygen and supplies had to be carried up in advance. Hunt was so determined to be at the center of the action that, rather than giving this important job to one of the younger, fitter climbers, he had awarded it to himself. When he announced this, Ward was extremely critical, spitting out his words, journalist James Morris remembered, "with a vehemence that nearly knocked me off my packing case."[27] Ward later told his wife that his main fear was that if Hunt had an accident—which in his view was quite likely, because of his tired, overwrought condition—the expedition would be brought to a halt and might have to be abandoned.

As Bourdillon and Evans set off for the summit, Hunt, ignoring Ward's strictures, embarked on the 2,000-foot, high-altitude "carry" with Sherpa Namgyal. Both were using open-circuit oxygen—Hunt at 4 liters a minute, the Sherpa at 2. Disaster struck when Hunt's set malfunctioned, forcing him to stop 700 feet short of the destination.[28] He became so exhausted while climbing back down without oxygen that he lost control of his bodily functions, suffered "spasms of collapse," and was lucky not to have a serious accident. "Gasping and moaning for breath was an experience I'll never forget," he confided in his diary. "Self-control vanished . . . never have I been put to such physical strain."[29]

Having finally arrived back on the col, Hunt failed to realize the seriousness of his condition and still wanted to remain at the heart of the action. His gait, according to Pugh, "resembled drunkenness," and he was so debilitated that he had "the voice and appearance of an aged man."[30] Eventually he had to be forced by the younger climbers to give up his place in the assault camp to a fitter man and return to advanced base camp below the Lhotse Face.

Hillary and Tenzing began their two-stage summit assault with open-circuit oxygen on May 28 with Lowe, Gregory, and Sherpa Ang Nyima carrying a second load of oxygen and equipment for the high camp. All five men used open-circuit oxygen. When they picked up the additional loads dumped by Hunt and Namgyal two days earlier, they turned their oxygen up above 4 liters a minute to help them cope with the extra weight. This reduced the amount of oxygen available for the summit assault the next day.

The day's work complete, Gregory, Lowe, and Ang Nyima returned to the South Col leaving Hillary and Tenzing alone in their high camp. That evening, sheltered by a tent made of the fabric chosen by Pugh, they started up their cooker (made to Pugh's specifications) and, finding it "worked like a charm," brewed "large amounts of lemon juice and sugar." After consuming what Hillary described as a "satisfying meal out of our store of delicacies"— recommended by Pugh—they retired for the night using sleeping oxygen (courtesy of Pugh),[31] resting on air mattresses also developed by Pugh.

Throughout the expedition Pugh had continually stressed to the climbers the vital importance of drinking plenty of liquid, even if they did not feel thirsty, and told them to observe how often they urinated, to check if they were getting dehydrated.[32] Rising at 4:00 a.m. the next day, Hillary and Tenzing reignited their cooker and drank huge quantities of liquid in a "determined effort to prevent the weaknesses arising from dehydration."[33] Then, having donned their protective clothing (designed by Pugh) and their oxygen sets, they set out for the summit of Everest at 6:30 a.m.[34] They dealt with the shortage of oxygen by using an average of 3 (rather than 4) liters a minute. This was an eventuality Pugh had contemplated in the Cho Oyu report. "Unless the efficiency of the oxygen cylinders can be improved," he had written, "a flow rate of less than 4 liters per minute [might] have to be accepted, at any rate for part of the time."[35] Both men were extremely fit and very well acclimatized, and Pugh regarded them as exceptionally tolerant of oxygen lack.

What happened next on Everest has been described countless times. The route did not prove technically difficult except for a short section near the top, which later became known as the "Hillary Step." After just five hours, Hillary, quickly followed by Tenzing, stepped onto the summit of Mount Everest and made history. On reaching the summit, Hillary found he had "no choice but to urinate on it."

Two days before the final summit assault, Pugh, who had been up at Camp Four with the rest of the team for the previous two weeks, went down to base camp where he spent an evening "drinking and talking" with James Morris, who wrote afterwards:

On the evening of the 28th [he probably meant May 27] I had as my companion at base camp, Pugh, the physiologist, and we sat late beside the fire drinking and talking, while he puffed at an odd angular French pipe. I always enjoyed his company. He was full of peculiar knowledge and passed it on at surprising moments in a hesitating, slow spoken, pipe puffing manner; as if some gentle country parson, settling down for a quiet scriptural chat with his parishioners, were suddenly to present some theories about Kafka, the dipping hem line, or space travel. That night, I remember, we did in fact discuss religion, or at least those activities such as Yoga and Moral Rearmament, which leap and linger around the fringes of it.[36]

Morris was frightened that press competitors might infiltrate the base camp and steal his story, and was loath to leave his position next to the radio transmitter. Pugh disagreed. "I think you're wrong," he told Morris. "I think you ought to be up in the Cwm when they come back from the assault. What if somebody does arrive here? You'll be bringing the news down yourself, so they can hardly get hold of it before you do."

They set off together the next morning. On the way up, an avalanche rolled by on a parallel course. They threw themselves onto the ground but it swept past them "imperiously," without touching them. Spending the night at Camp Three, they went on up to Camp Four the next morning, arriving at 11:30 a.m.

The conquest of Everest on May 29, 1953, was a triumph for every member of the Everest team, most of all for the leader and the two men who first stepped onto the summit. But for Pugh in particular, it was a truly magnificent personal achievement, a validation of his ideas and his indefatigable work before the expedition. Yet his Everest diary contains only the deadpan words—"2pm, Hillary and Tenzing arrive back"—then ceases altogether. He immediately became completely preoccupied with examining the climbers and Sherpas as they came down from the South Col. All proved to be in "surprisingly good condition," including Hillary and Tenzing, who had no trace of frostbite and were in far better health than any previous Everest summit-assault pair.

15

A Gulf of Mutual Incomprehension

"Griff, this was a damn boring expedition; nothing went wrong," Tom Stobart remarked to Pugh as they retreated down the mountain together after the Everest conquest.[1] Stobart's initial delight at the successful ascent had swiftly been replaced by a consuming worry that his film of the expedition would not prove up to scratch. There had been no "desperate ventures" of the kind that made good images; the climbers looked such "ordinary fellows"—hardly the heroes of successful film drama.

"Don't worry," Pugh replied. "You'll see—the myth will grow."

John Hunt had wept for joy at the news of Hillary and Tenzing's triumphant climb, but Stobart was not alone in having mixed feelings. "Our first feelings in success," Michael Ward wrote, "were those of relief. No member of the party was particularly elated."[2] "Don't imagine our band . . . rolling and rollicking in an ecstasy brought on by victory," George Lowe told his family.[3]

In his diary Tom Bourdillon had written, nobly, "Hillary and Tenzing have made it. Very pleasing." But then he confessed to being beset by regrets. If only he had managed his own summit attempt a little differently: "I could have done it—very miserable."[4]

Wilf Noyce, who was up on the South Col while Hillary and Tenzing were climbing to the summit, was unable to suppress his disappointment that there would be no third summit attempt in which he might have participated. Earlier, at advanced base camp, he had reacted angrily to the sight of Griffith Pugh experimenting and, in his view, wasting "a precious oxygen cylinder" that might be needed for that third attempt.[5] Pugh had seized the moment, while the assaults were taking place and the rest of the climbers were waiting around, to put Stobart and Band through a series of exercise tests with and without oxygen.

Irritated though he was, Noyce was generous enough to acknowledge that he owed a debt of gratitude to Griff Pugh. The main reason he was able to entertain such ambitious thoughts at the rarefied height of the South Col was because "my body was plastered with the aids of modern science and technology . . . On the South Col I was breathing and appreciating and even feeling a certain inspiration—because I was wearing an oxygen mask and my feet were encased in special boots. Without the mask, away goes the enjoyment . . . I was feeling well partly because I had been told [by Pugh] to drink some six pints of liquid a day."[6]

Pugh himself had been extremely busy since Bourdillon and Evans had returned to advanced base camp after the first summit attempt. The Swiss had warned him in 1952 that discrepancies had emerged between the stories told on the spot by their climbers and the accounts they gave later at home. So he had been making strenuous efforts to examine the climbers and Sherpas as soon as they came off the Lhotse Face, questioning them closely about their experiences. He was interested in every detail: how well they slept, what they ate and drank for breakfast, how much oxygen they used, and how they felt at each stage of the climb. All the men were tired and thin, but they were far healthier and much less exhausted than the climbers of prewar expeditions, or, indeed, the Swiss, who had come off the mountain as haggard, ghostly shadows of their former selves.

In some ways the success of the expedition was a disappointment even for Pugh, who had been unable to carry out as much research as he would have liked: "The scope of the physiological work accomplished was . . . limited by the fact that the expedition met with no setbacks, and members of the party were usually too fully occupied in other directions to concern themselves with the physiological experiments. On all occasions, however, they collaborated as far as could reasonably be expected."[7]

Vistas of unanswered questions about "man and altitude" were calling, like siren songs, to the scientist in Pugh, and he was already thinking about trying to organize his own high-altitude scientific expedition—one that would give him the freedom to do the kind of work he wanted to do. Far from being an end in itself, the ascent of Everest had merely opened the door to what Michael Ward would later describe as "this cornucopia of science."

Once it was clear that there would be no further attempts on the summit, none of the climbers could wait to get back to civilization, and the exodus from the mountain was extremely fast. They were all down at base camp by June 2, the day of the coronation of the new Queen, Elizabeth II, when the news of their triumph was announced in London. They walked into Kathmandu on June 20. Hunt had already begun to think about their achievement in somewhat numinous terms, writing home to his wife on June 1, "I've felt very sure . . . of the final outcome all along, as though guided along a pre-destined track, a curious sensation of confidence answering to faith."[8] Few of the climbers, except for Hunt himself, had any concept of the avalanche of publicity that was about to engulf them.

The team arrived back in England on July 6 to a tumultuous welcome, and was immediately swept into a bewildering whirl of champagne receptions, lunches, dinners, and royal garden parties. There was much joyous speech-making and congratulation. They were feted everywhere they went; they met the Queen and the Duke of Edinburgh, and were summoned to Buckingham Palace to be presented with special Everest medals. The spotlight was naturally on John Hunt and the climbers, but even Pugh became a bit of a celebrity, attending over forty Everest receptions and parties in the first couple of months after arriving home.

The two most important vehicles for promoting the expedition to a wider audience and raising money for future expeditions were to be the film based on Tom Stobart's cinematography and the official expedition book by John Hunt. Both were to be brought out quickly to take full advantage of the public excitement. Three weeks after returning to England, Hunt absented himself from the parties and the razzmatazz and retired to the country to write his book in seclusion. The rest of the team was asked to send him interesting snippets of information, diary extracts, and funny stories. Five of them were also asked to contribute appendices, which would provide specialist information. Pugh was to write two: one on diet with George Band, another on physiology and medicine with Michael Ward.[9] Bourdillon was to write on oxygen and Wylie on equipment and clothing. The deadline was the end of August.

The film, *The Conquest of Everest*, came out first. Made by Countryman Films, with a commentary written by Irish poet Louis MacNeice, it had a glittering London premiere at the Warner Cinema, Leicester Square, on October 21. This was such an important national event that it merited the presence of the Queen, the Duke of Edinburgh, and several other members of the Royal Family. Naturally Hunt and the Everest team and the Himalayan Committee were there too, accompanied by their wives, all bursting with pride.

The film was widely praised for its "astonishingly vivid" photography. Stobart had brilliantly captured the vulnerability of the climbers as they grappled with the monumental chaos of the icefall, or cowered in their tiny tents on the Western Cwm, battered and threatened by screaming winds and blinding snow. Always on the watch for the human aspect of the drama, his perceptive photographer's eye had spotted and recorded the rising tension in Hunt's face as he waited at advanced base camp, taut as a wire, to find out if his team had succeeded in climbing the Lhotse Face.

With the help of Stobart's stunning images, the commentary, spoken in eager, carefully enunciated tones by the well-known Welsh film actor, Meredith Edwards, emphasized the magnitude of the challenge. This was Everest, "aloof, inviolate, murderous." High on its vast, brutal slopes the men of Hunt's team would do battle with "the terrible problems of altitude, the unbelievably treacherous weather and, most of all, with the terrifying lack of oxygen." As the drama of the fight for the summit unfolded, it was accompanied by a musical score of positively epic grandeur, with suites of soaring trumpets and clashing cymbals at every turn.[10]

The film rapidly became a huge box office success all around the world. It was named one of the ten best films of the year by both *Time* magazine and the *New York Times*, and received a coveted British Academy Award for best documentary. The academy also gave Tom Stobart a Certificate of Merit for the photography (although all the filming above advanced base camp had been undertaken by George Lowe, because Stobart could not cope with the altitude).

The following June, Stobart was made a Commander of the British Empire for his services to the film industry. Bosley Crowther, the famous film critic of the *New York Times*, admitted to having been transported into a state of "indescribable awe and thrill" by the sight and sound of "the great Everest massif, where the wind howls with banshee terror and the soul of man is naked and alone."[11] Back in London, a reviewer from *The Times* wrote, more prosaically, that he thought the commentary "strove a little too much for effect," and complained that Arthur Benjamin's dramatic musical score had introduced every shot of Everest "as if the mountain was a cross between King Kong and Frankenstein."[12]

Pugh's wife Josephine was with him at the royal premiere. Still pretty and slim at the age of thirty-six, she wore an exquisite blue-green floaty chiffon ball gown that she had salvaged from earlier days. Pugh must have felt very proud of her, for he told me and my brother Simon afterward, "Your mother was still the most beautiful woman in the room." It was so unusual for him to express personal feelings, especially complimentary feelings about our mother, that neither of us has ever forgotten it.

The film gave Josephine her first chance to see how the Everest expedition would be presented to the public. The photography was wonderful and the story exciting, but the footage of her husband was far from flattering, and there was no mention of the expedition's new strategies for coping with altitude. Nor was there any hint that Pugh had been involved in the preparations; in fact, his research project during the expedition was dismissed as an inconvenience and a burden to the climbers.

All the scientific preparations for the expedition were presented as if John Hunt alone had been responsible for them. The first image of Hunt, just called over from Germany to take charge of the Everest challenge, was of a tall, straight-backed man, dressed in a well-cut suit, the very model of a heroic leader, striding purposefully into the Alpine Club to begin planning his Everest conquest. "A project like this needs a vast amount of planning and testing," the commentary explained. Hunt had to equip his team "with the very best possible equipment." Most important of all was "oxygen"—"for no apparatus hitherto had fitted the bill upon Everest." The high-altitude boots were shown being hand-made. There was footage of the vacuum-packed rations; and the fabric for the expedition tents and clothing was pictured being tested in wind tunnels at Farnborough. "Everything had to be thought of," the narrator said, as the spotlight returned to Hunt, lacing up his Lawrie boots with a look of purposeful determination. "He will have to climb a long way in them," the narrator declaimed, a little portentously.

In sharp contrast, the first image of Pugh was a huge, uncomplimentary close-up of his head. His eyes were closed and he was twitching and jerking unnaturally as if he was having a fit. Josephine was far from pleased. This, the narrator explained, was "Pugh, a research doctor" starved of oxygen, "using himself as a specimen in a pressure chamber." The air pressure in the chamber had been lowered to demonstrate the impact of oxygen lack on the brain. But the impression given was deceptive. John Cotes, not Pugh, had organized the demonstration, and most of the team was involved. The others had reacted similarly to Pugh, though he was the only one shown.

Later in the film, Pugh appeared again, supposedly at base camp when the expedition was at its busiest. He was conducting an experiment on "the unfortunate George Band." "Pugh's experiments were not very popular," the narrator explained pointedly. "When someone came into camp after a hard day on the icefall, Pugh would harness them into a contraption of glass and rubber and then make them work until they were exhausted." The film footage showed Band stepping monotonously on and off a box while Pugh hovered next to him with a stopwatch. Cruelly, this was exactly the kind of obstructive behavior that Pugh had been at pains to avoid. Worse still, the experiment shown in the film had not been carried out at base camp when the climbers were busy, but a month later at advanced base camp, when they had nothing to do but wait for the outcome of the summit assaults. When challenged, John Taylor, the producer at Countryman Films who put the film together, admitted rather flippantly that he had "made the story up to provide light relief."

Josephine reacted badly. In her own way she had invested a lot of effort in the Everest campaign, coping with her husband's long absences from home, making few demands on him, and caring for the family like a single parent. If the film had acknowledged Pugh's contribution in any way, however briefly, she would have felt validated and rewarded. As it was, she felt that her husband had been belittled and his work passed over without mention.

Coping on her own had been quite an ordeal for Josephine. Her father had been very wealthy, and her pampered upbringing in a grand house surrounded by servants had not prepared her for the hard work she faced as Pugh's wife. When she first married, she had no idea how to boil an egg, and described herself as "hazy" on the subject of housework. In marrying Pugh, a penniless junior doctor, she had taken a significant step down the social ladder. Soon after their marriage, Pugh went off to the Middle East for almost five years of war service. She was six months pregnant when he left. Their son David, born in September 1940, proved to be a victim of the rubella Josephine had contracted early in the pregnancy. He was two years old before she fully realized that he was deaf and mute.

With two more children born shortly after the war, life was hard for Josephine. David suffered from bouts of frustrated rage and would often physically attack his younger siblings, so he had to be watched constantly when he was near them. Weakened by the two recent pregnancies, and by looking after the three children on her own, on a tight budget, Josephine became exhausted. In 1948 she contracted tuberculosis, affecting both her lungs, and nearly died. After six months in the hospital she recovered slowly, but never fully regained her strength.

Despite this, she had a strong sense of duty and wanted terribly to be a good wife and mother. When Pugh became utterly absorbed in his Everest work, she did her best to support him, though it was often a struggle. For nearly eighteen months Pugh had been away in the Himalayas, traveling around England, or working extremely long hours in his laboratory. That he should now be depicted as a foolish, useless scientist who had contributed nothing to the expedition struck Josephine as an insult not only to the work he had done, but also to her own efforts to support him.

Pugh was also irritated, although he refused to be provoked. He and Josephine were content to wait for John Hunt's book to put things right by telling the true story. But when the book appeared three weeks later, it did not do so.

Written in only a month, *The Ascent of Everest* was published on November 12, 1953. It was an instant success, soon becoming a classic, translated into thirty different languages and outselling any previous book on mountaineering. Like the film, it portrayed the Everest quest as a military-style campaign, carefully planned with great attention to detail. But, above all, the book was a rousing tale of heroism and derring-do.

John Hunt was a profoundly religious man imbued with a Words-worthian reverence for the mountains. Holidaying in Kashmir in 1931 he confided in his journal: "It is enchanting after living in surroundings that are inimical to turn back to the mountain scene, to find oneself once again face to face with the power of nature, wherein the mountaineer finds Faith."[13]

On the trek to Everest in 1953 Wilf Noyce observed that Hunt ". . . believed immensely in the inspiration of Everest to the world . . . behind this was a deep religious sense. John once said round a camp-fire at Thyang-boche: 'I don't mind admitting that the mountains make me pray.'"[14]

Hunt told his wife that on Everest he had carried with him a feeling that the hand of God was guiding him toward his goal. This sense of being cho-sen by God colored the way he framed the official history of the expedition, and it became clear that his view had set the tone of the film.

Recognizing the inspirational potential of the Everest triumph, Hunt wanted to convey what he described as a "deeper and more lasting message . . . than the mere ephemeral sensation of a physical feat." His was to be a story of adventure and teamwork of the highest order. It was to be a beacon of inspiration capable of stimulating young people all over the world to go out and find "Everests" of their own, through which, Hunt believed, they could reach their moral, physical, and spiritual potential as human beings.

The Ascent of Everest was punctuated with reverential passages convey-ing the moral earnestness with which the author approached his subject: "For us who took part in the venture . . . we have shared a high endeavour; we have witnessed scenes of beauty and grandeur; we have built up lasting comradeship among ourselves and have seen the fruits of comradeship ripen into achievement. We shall not forget those moments of great living upon that mountain."[15]

In 1921, Francis Younghusband, chairman of the first Everest Commit-tee, had expressed the grand expectation that "the man who first stands on the summit of Mount Everest will have raised the spirit of countless others for generations to come."[16] Hunt wanted to consummate Younghusband's prediction. Echoing Younghusband's words, the final sentence of his book proclaimed: "There is no height, no depth that the spirit of man, guided by a higher spirit, cannot attain."[17]

The unfortunate casualty of this high-flown rhetoric was Griffith Pugh. For, unlike Lieutenant Colonel Younghusband, who thought that science and heroism could march hand in hand, Hunt was convinced that the potency of the Everest conquest's romantic heroism would be damaged if too much attention was given to the role played by science. If it were admitted that physiological breakthroughs had made the key difference, the achievement of the climbers would appear less glorious and less significant. "No one will want to hear about the science," he insisted to Charles Wylie shortly after the expedition. "The spotlight must be firmly on the human aspects of the achievement."

The book must concentrate, he said, on feats such as Edmund Hillary's courageous decision to climb the challenging "Hillary Step" just below the summit of Everest. In this ice chimney, the snow cornice on one side might have given way, causing Hillary and Tenzing to fall thousands of feet to their death. Yet they bravely ignored the danger.

While he did not deny that he had received technical and scientific support, the overriding message Hunt wanted to convey was that it is not science but "man who climbs the mountain," and he does so by drawing "on the resources of the human spirit." Everest had been conquered, he wanted people to see, by the human qualities of courage, skill, fortitude, teamwork, and persistence in adversity, just as Eric Shipton, Bill Tilman, Geoffrey Winthrop Young, and many other stalwarts of the Alpine Club had always hoped that it would be.

The readers of Hunt's book were treated to an even more thorough and detailed account of the elaborate preparations for the expedition than the audience of the film. As in the film they were given the impression that everything had been done under the direction of Hunt alone. The clothing, the tents, the high-altitude boots, even the double-layered air mattresses were all described in detail. But, as in the film, there was no mention of the role Griffith Pugh played in their design. There was no hint that Pugh had influenced the way the expedition was planned, or that he had brought to the table any creative thinking on its use of oxygen, its policies on acclimatization, or the consumption of fluids. The only concrete contribution Hunt attributed to Pugh was the planning of the expedition's diet.

What particularly stirred Josephine was that Hunt did not pass over the Everest preparations without naming names. If no one else had been given credit, then Hunt's failure to mention Pugh's contributions might not have troubled her. But the reverse was true. Hunt went out of his way to acknowledge the work other people had done. When he explained his team's approach to the use of oxygen, he spoke of choosing to rely on open-circuit "partly in recognition of the advocacy of Professor George Finch." He divulged that the experimental closed-circuit oxygen had been "constructed by Dr. R. B. Bourdillon and his son Tom," adding that Tom "had experimented with the use of oxygen" on Eric Shipton's Cho Oyu expedition. The readers were told about the "wise and able" Peter Lloyd, who was in charge of the "development and provision" of the open-circuit oxygen and liaising with the "High-Altitude Committee under the Chairmanship of Sir Bryan Matthews."

The readers learned of the "immense energy and fixity of purpose" brought to bear on the packing and shipping of the oxygen by Hunt's "old climbing companion," the "exceptional" Alfred Bridge: "The addition of Bridge to our helpers was a great event in the history of the expedition."[18] They were told the names of Mr. Mensforth, the head of Normalair, and Sir Robert Davis, the head of Siebe Gorman, the firms that manufactured the oxygen apparatus. They were told about John Cotes's work on the oxygen masks. Only one person's name was missing from the long roll call of oxygen honors, and it was the name of Griffith Pugh.

Hunt heaped elaborate praise on so many people: the "generosity and selflessness" of Emylin Jones, who briefly stood in as organizing secretary; the "most important" work of that "Himalayan mountaineer of renown," C. R. Cook, who "invented" the novel new design of the mountain stoves; the "capable hands" of Stuart Bain, who organized the shipping of equipment to India; the "fine job of work" done by Peter Fitt, who adapted some oxygen cylinders; the "splendid assistance given us by our Secretaries Ann Debenham and Elizabeth Johnson"; the "conscientious" work of the treasurer, R. W. Lloyd; the "indefatigable labours" of the committee on packing, "the wonderful work done by my wife and Mrs. Mowbrey Green in sewing many hundreds of name tapes onto our garments"; and so on and so on and so on.[19]

Having received little credit for his contribution, Pugh was treated as the book's main source of light relief, just as he had been in the film. His unpopular experiments, his dirty pajamas, his coffin box, and his mango chutney were all given suitable prominence. The image of "Griff Pugh, a horrifying sight; so short of oxygen that his tongue was hanging out" in the pressure chamber at Farnborough was highlighted once again.[20]

Many years later Hunt admitted in his autobiography, *Life is Meeting*, that he had failed to give due credit to Pugh for his "great contribution." He also confessed that he had a deep distaste for science. But in *The Ascent of Everest* he did not express this distaste. He merely emphasized that he didn't approve of conducting scientific research on a mountaineering expedition, and highlighted the reluctance he had felt about including Pugh in his expedition.

Most significantly, while Hunt was willing to admit that oxygen had played a vital role in the Everest success, he gave no clue that his team had benefited from the *new* ways of using oxygen suggested by Pugh. Nor did he admit that they had also benefited from a new approach to acclimatization, fluid intake, and diet. These innovations were simply not mentioned in his main text. The lay reader was given no sense that, apart from some basic improvements in equipment, there were any essential differences between the techniques used in 1953 and those available to the climbers who had gone before.

The science in Hunt's book was relegated to the specialist appendices, where again Pugh's contribution was downplayed. Writing the appendix on the expedition's use of oxygen, Tom Bourdillon did not mention Pugh, or the fact that oxygen was used differently from before.[21] Pugh's appendix on physiology and medicine was placed near the back of the appendices, where it was unlikely to be seen by the general reader.

To rub salt in the wound, Pugh's appendices were scornfully dismissed as worthless by Bill Tilman. Reviewing *The Ascent of Everest* in *Time and Tide*, he wrote that he had found all the appendices very interesting except for the two "irksome" articles by Pugh, which were notable only for their "questionable assumptions, platitudes and complacency."[22] Tilman was clearly angered because Pugh had included some trenchant criticisms of the regressive attitudes of prewar Everesters—criticisms aimed straight at iconic figures like Tilman himself—whose "futile controversy over the ethics of using oxygen" and "failure to accept the findings of the pioneers in its application" had "handicapped for more than thirty years the introduction of a method which promises to revolutionise high-altitude mountaineering."[23] This was not an observation that was likely to find merit with one of the most famous anti-science, anti-oxygen exponents of his day.

At the time, no one spoke up for Pugh. Most of the Everest climbers were either unaware that Hunt had downplayed Pugh's contribution, or they turned a blind eye. Michael Ward had become immersed in medical exams as soon as he got home. Wilfred Noyce was the one exception. He was the least technically minded member of the team, but in his book *South Col*, published a few months after the *Ascent of Everest*, he wrote:

> *It is not generally known to what extent our expedition built on the physiological knowledge [Pugh] gained on Cho Oyu; much was learned about food, drink and the effects of oxygen, to mention only these. Without this knowledge Everest might never have been climbed at all. But climbers are notoriously lazy people. They accept the tools of their trade from the workshop, grumble at the inconveniences imposed by scientific gadgets and think they are getting up entirely under their own steam.*[24]

Hunt remained convinced for the rest of his life that the human spirit must be protected from the scientific Frankenstein. "Man's inventions would seem to bid fair to take over from Man himself!" he warned in a new introduction written in 1993 for the reissue of *The Ascent of Everest*, to mark the fortieth anniversary. "But what of us humans and the spirit which moves us? The inspiration . . . rests still, I believe, on a higher plane. People everywhere appear to feel uplifted by deeds of daring."

It was to that "higher plane" that he had aimed *The Ascent of Everest*. His distaste for technological advance and his decision to downplay its role on Everest reflected a view endemic in British society since the nineteenth century—that science was soulless, materialistic, and amoral.

Hunt—and Pugh—had been educated in an age when British public schools had an aversion to science. Geared to producing administrators and army officers to run the Empire, most took the view that only an education in the humanities—especially the classics—could cultivate the leadership qualities, moral sense, and breadth of vision required by the elite of society. The sciences were considered to be vocational subjects, more suitable for the "training" of the socially inferior than for the "education" of the gentleman-leader. Pugh had come up against this problem after Harrow when his father had refused to allow him to study chemistry at Oxford, insisting that he read for a degree in the respectable subject of law instead.

The Nobel Prize–winning scientist Peter Medawar—later the head of the MRC institute where Pugh worked—remembered how the biology teacher at Marlborough, where he and John Hunt were both educated, "was sneered at and looked down on by all the other masters." He was, Medawar said, "a rough and coarsely spoken man . . . appointed, as public-school science teachers sometimes were, to bring science into discredit and turn the boys rather to the study of other subjects."[25] There was, accordingly, an element of snobbery in the Everest climbers' choice of words like *repugnant* to describe Pugh's experiments, and in the sneering, dismissive attitudes toward him displayed by the likes of Bill Tilman.

Alpine Club members were inspired in their dislike of science by the nineteenth-century Romantic Movement, which had been so influential in the public schools. Indeed some of the key Romantic thinkers—including Matthew Arnold and John Ruskin—were also members of the Alpine Club. The Romantics bemoaned the poverty and squalor of the new industrial cities and the cruel inhumanity of modern methods of production; and men like Thomas Carlyle, Arnold, and Ruskin questioned the Victorian Age's faith in the "mechanistic," "scientific," "objective" modes of thought that underpinned the industrialization of Britain. In the eyes of many, Charles Darwin's *On the Origin of Species*, published in 1859—a classic scientific text—made things worse by challenging the biblical account of creation, threatening belief in God and undermining organized religion.

John Hunt's wish to inspire heroic achievement had its roots in Ruskin's nostalgia for the chivalric, Christian ideals of preindustrial medieval society and in Carlyle's call for heroes to lead and guide the populace. Hunt shared the Romantic poets' deeply emotional responses to the grandeur of magnificent landscapes, believing—like Wordsworth—that nature at its grandest and fiercest cleanses the soul and uplifts the human spirit.[26] For Hunt and many mountaineers, this emphasis on subjective experience, intense emotion, and spiritual growth went hand in hand with a strong antipathy toward the materialistic, dispassionate values of science and technology.

During World War II, Hunt and Pugh both worked as instructors for mountain-warfare training units—Pugh in Lebanon, and Hunt at Braemar in Scotland, where Frank Smythe, the prewar Everest climber famous for his commitment to small-expedition ideals and his opposition to oxygen, was the chief instructor. At Braemar Hunt focused his training regime largely on character development and motivation, and came away with a lifelong belief that arduous and exciting adventure training could morally elevate the characters of young people. Pugh, on the other hand, focused on improving the practical aspects of the training: better selection of candidates, systematic development of fitness, better protective clothing, better boots, and so on. He was unmoved by what he considered to be woolly, abstract concepts of character development through high endeavor at the expense of the practicalities of the task at hand.

Hunt's and Pugh's contrasting approaches were illustrative of what a member of the War Cabinet identified as early as 1941 as a fundamental problem in the British approach to the war as a whole. The establishment, Sir Stafford Cripps said, had failed to realize "sufficiently early" that the war would not be won "merely by the physical ascendancy of our race." It was a "truly scientific war" that could only be won by "the ingenuity of those who have been trained in our schools, technical colleges and universities."[27]

Hunt and Pugh were on opposite sides of this divide. They were on the cusp of a cultural shift, with Hunt representing a traditionally educated elite raised on the old heroic ideals associated with the past glories of the British Empire, and Pugh representing a future dominated by scientific and technological progress, professionalism, and meritocracy. C. P. Snow famously identified a destructive lack of empathy between these "two cultures"—a "gulf of mutual incomprehension," characterized by "hostility and dislike but most of all lack of understanding."[28] An element of this distrust and lack of understanding lay at the heart of Hunt's relationship with Pugh.

16

The Golden Age

Griffith Pugh's wife Josephine had never attended school and knew nothing about science. Educated entirely at home by a succession of governesses, she was well read in literature and the arts, could speak French and German fluently, knew all Shakespeare's sonnets by heart, and was a very perceptive literary critic. Modest and unassuming, she was also a very loyal wife. Feeling that her husband had been made to look foolish and his achievements deliberately underplayed, or even suppressed, it was she rather than Pugh who was furious about the film and the book.

I have a distant memory of sitting as a young child with my brother Simon in the back of our ancient Ford Popular car, on the way home from seeing *The Conquest of Everest* at the theater. Our mother was clearly upset. "The film was disgraceful," she was saying, "frightful . . . so unfair about Griffith." Neither of us could understand what she meant.

By the time John Hunt's book was published, the Everest film was being shown to packed theater audiences throughout the country, and Josephine was being showered with telephone calls and messages from friends and family commiserating with her about the way her husband was portrayed. Wherever she went, people teased and joked about her husband's "brutal" behavior toward the exhausted climbers on Everest. Hunt's book was the last straw. She was furious that Hunt had failed to acknowledge most of Pugh's work, instead claiming much of the credit for himself. That streak of determination which normally lay buried far below the surface of Josephine's gentle personality now came to the fore. Her dander was up, and she started to egg on her unwilling husband to do something to set the record straight.

Pugh, however, belonged to a generation brought up never to blow your own horn. He wanted to ignore the film and the book, and get on with his work. But since Josephine was so upset, he agreed to take the small step of protesting about the factual error in the film—the accusation that he had imposed his experiments on busy climbers at base camp as they struggled to find a route up the icefall. Josephine regarded this scene as particularly damaging because it gave the impression that his one and only role on the expedition had been to make unreasonable demands on the climbers and get in their way.[1]

Pugh wrote to Countryman Films asking them to cut out the offending scene. "The commentary is, in fact, completely untrue," he explained. "I have received so many adverse comments . . . that I believe my reputation is being damaged."[2] But with the film already in circulation, the producers, while not denying the falsehood, refused—knowing that Pugh could do nothing about it.

Turning to the chairman of the Himalayan Committee, Sir Edwin Herbert, Pugh wrote, "I was not very pleased at being shown in this light as the story was untrue and it created the wrong impression."[3] So embarrassed was he that he felt it necessary to point out—and reiterate—in his letter that it was really his wife who was upset: "I forgot about it until my wife came to me . . . saying that all sorts of people had mentioned it to her, asking whether her husband was really such a brute." Herbert wrote back saying he would do his best. Not surprisingly, nothing came of it.[4]

Pugh went on trying to get the offending scene cut out, writing in January to Sir Arthur Landsborough Thomson—Harold Himsworth's deputy at the Medical Research Council—again blaming his objections to the film mainly on his wife.[5] Landsborough Thomson replied, "It seemed to me that the commentator's remark was rather silly, slightly irritating, but not really harmful." At last Pugh let the issue drop. Yet he was frequently reminded that most people were completely unaware of his contribution to the Everest success. Indeed, the film made them feel rather scornful about the inept behavior of the scientist on the mountain. One of the worst instances of this came from Alfred Bridge.

In preparing a report for the MRC about the expedition's use of oxygen, Pugh wanted to quote the total weight of the oxygen equipment sent to

Everest and requested this information from the shippers. They passed his request on to Alfred Bridge, Hunt's friend, who had been responsible for packing the Everest oxygen. Bridge's response was scornful and dismissive: "I am really sorry Dr. Pugh is asking you for information about the gross weight of the oxygen equipment . . . for the life of me I cannot see what this has to do with Dr. Pugh."[6]

The shippers forwarded Bridge's reply directly to Pugh, who, stung by the disrespectful tone, wrote to tell Bridge in no uncertain terms that without the help given by the MRC—"which had extended over two years"—the expedition would have had "no effective [oxygen] apparatus and no adequate supply of oxygen." The Medical Research Council's High-Altitude Committee had had "a hard fight to get the necessary amount accepted."[7]

It was hurtful that a loyal friend of Hunt's should have formed such a disparaging view of Pugh, and also, that he did not seem to realize that Pugh had had any legitimate role in organizing the expedition's oxygen.

Meeting this kind of curt, dismissive treatment again and again, Pugh became increasingly touchy. He was sufficiently irritated by an article in the *Lancet*—which said that "the [1953 Everest] expedition differed from its predecessors in having a physiologist who was not a mountaineer"—to fire back a letter of protest, insisting that: "The physiologist had, in fact, as much mountaineering experience as most of the climbers . . . the scientific contribution to the success of the expedition was made possible by the survey of the physiological problems carried out on Cho Oyu the previous year. This would not have been done by a physiologist who was not a mountaineer."[8]

Pugh was not petty and would not usually have bothered about such things, but now he fumed. When asked by Laurence Kirwan and Sir James Wordie, the new president of the Royal Geographical Society and a veteran of Ernest Shackleton's *Endurance* expedition of 1914–17, to comment on a letter to the *Geographical Journal* from Professor Noel Odell, denying the existence of high-altitude deterioration, Pugh lost patience completely.

Odell was an exponent of the old-guard view that "physiologists" like Pugh had no understanding of climbing and had got all their ideas wrong. "In the opinion of many who have climbed high," Odell had written pointedly, "so-called deterioration . . . can be regarded as unproven and is probably fictitious."[9] Pugh had seen with his own eyes the effects of high-altitude deterioration—the drastic loss of weight suffered by the Cho Oyu team, and the thin, exhausted Swiss climbers just back from Everest, whom he had met in Kathmandu after the Cho Oyu expedition. That Kirwan and Wordie expected him to dignify Odell's letter with a serious response annoyed him intensely, and he retorted in a curt note to Wordie: "I think Odell's letter . . . is too stupid to be worth replying [to] in detail."[10] The final draft of his reply began with the words: "Professor Odell is completely out of touch with modern thought on the subject of high-altitude deterioration and, in addition, has got his facts wrong . . ."[11]

But, however annoyed he was, the opinions of the old-guard climbing community and the general public did not matter to Pugh nearly as much as the views of his peers in the medical world. And in medical and scientific circles he was receiving acclaim for his Everest work. He had become a bit of a star at the MRC, where he was felt to have brought credit to Otto Edholm's division and to the MRC as a whole. Invitations to speak at prestigious institutions like the Royal Society, the Royal College of Physicians, and the Physiological Society, and to give papers at academic symposia at home and abroad, were coming in thick and fast. For a scientist of Pugh's relatively junior status, this newfound celebrity was highly flattering.

Pugh could have enhanced his reputation by writing his own book. Wilfred Noyce and Michael Ward both expected him to do so. In 1954, commenting on the Everest climbers' failure to acknowledge Pugh's contribution, Noyce wrote: "I know Griff will publish something to expose the real case, and our human weakness."[12]

In November 1953, the Hutchinson & Co. publishing firm invited Pugh to write a book about the Everest science, but he declined, saying he was too busy. He also refused an offer from Penguin to write a book popularizing altitude medicine, to be called *Man and Oxygen*. A couple of years later he told Hutchinson he was now ready, and even signed a contract, but never finished the book because of "pressure of work."

Ward, who was even more troubled than Noyce by Hunt's failure to credit the role of science in the Everest success—"Let's put it like this: I trusted John Hunt to tell the true story!"—was perplexed and frustrated by Pugh's apparent lack of concern:

He seemed to have no concept of PR . . . It didn't seem to worry him, or perhaps he felt he was above it, but he had absolutely no concept of pushing himself . . . if he had been a different chap, during the post-Everest period he would have made it absolutely certain what actually happened. I couldn't do it because I couldn't do it intellectually, because he had done all the work and it was not appropriate.[13]

However, Pugh was far less interested in publicizing his own name and achievements than he was in pursuing his ideas. And, when he said he was too busy to write a book, he meant it. In the period immediately after Everest he was overwhelmed by his work, and at the same time his health was deteriorating.

By the end of 1953, he had been toiling flat out on the Everest project for almost two years without a proper vacation. The two exacting Himalayan expeditions had taken a toll on his health, and he had failed to throw off the stomach infection he had contracted on Cho Oyu. He was spending a great deal of time traveling around the country, giving lectures and speaking about Everest at conferences and seminars, and also felt under pressure to get his Himalayan research written up in academic papers—quite a different thing from "pushing himself" in a popular book. Writing was a struggle for him, however, and he could not do it quickly. At the same time he felt an urgent need to get back to his research into Channel swimmers and hypothermia. On top of everything else he was being drawn into a time-consuming study group investigating respiratory failure in polio victims.[14]

By the end of December 1953, Pugh's colleagues were beginning to notice that he was perpetually exhausted and becoming increasingly grumpy, irritable, and cantankerous. Previously, he had typically been outspoken, blunt, even sometimes strident or tactless, but only rarely intentionally rude. The MRC instructed Pugh to cut down drastically on his lecturing. Things came to such a pass that Sir Richard Bayliss, physician to the Queen, who was at a lecture Pugh gave at the Royal Postgraduate Medical School at Hammersmith, wrote to warn Edholm that Pugh had seemed "extremely tired and overwrought." He "looks as if he is heading for a breakdown," Bayliss wrote, and should be given sick leave to "prevent him suffering the same troubles as other members of the expedition"—a reference to John

Hunt, who had been overwhelmed by stress after Everest.[15] Pugh was given four weeks' leave of absence from his job. He went to scientific meetings in Holland and Germany and undertook a short lecture tour in Austria before taking a month's vacation in Switzerland. As ever Josephine was left behind, looking after the children.

Returning home at the end of March, Pugh regained his equilibrium. A number of things boosted his spirits. Most importantly he was gratified by the growing evidence that his ideas were having an extraordinary impact on high-altitude climbing.

While Pugh's role in the Everest success did not enter the public mind, knowledge of the way Hunt's expedition had addressed the problems of altitude did spread quickly to those with special interest. Pugh's lectures and appearances at conferences at home and abroad played a part in this, as did the six articles he published in academic journals in the year after Everest. Laurence Kirwan arranged for two further articles to appear in the *Geographical Journal*, telling Pugh, "This sort of thing should be recorded in a journal read by expedition people so that they may see the contribution made by science to an expedition of this kind."[16] An article by Pugh entitled "Oxygen Apparatus on the Mountain" was printed in the *Alpine Journal*, and the Swiss Foundation for Alpine Research published an extract from the Cho Oyu Report, which Pugh had given to them in 1952.[17] Also Pugh occasionally welcomed climbers to his laboratory; for instance, in 1954 he was visited by the French team, who subsequently succeeded on Makalu, the fifth-highest of the Himalayan peaks. But, oddly enough, probably the single most important vehicle for disseminating Pugh's ideas within the small world of high-altitude climbing was Hunt's book.

A best-seller in many countries, Hunt's book told the high-altitude climbing teams who followed on from the Everest success most of what they needed to know about how to cope with high altitude. This was particularly true of Pugh's appendices, which had so irritated old-school climbers like Bill Tilman.

Written in the tone of a dispassionate commentator, Pugh's appendices explained the physiological impact of high altitude in simple layman's terms, and went on to describe the key methods for overcoming the problems. Acclimatization, hydration, oxygen-flow rates, coping with the cold—it was all there. Some of the information was extremely detailed; there were tables giving the precise daily rations, diagrams of the closed- and open-circuit oxygen sets. Pugh did not, however, mention that he was the originator of the recommendations, or give any indication that they were based on his own research.

After Everest, Pugh's methods became a template for virtually all high-altitude expeditions, and over the next few years the changes in climbers' fortunes were dramatic and immediate. Before 1953, only one of the fourteen mountains in the world above 8,000 meters (26,250 feet) had been climbed. This was Annapurna, which is only 246 feet higher than Everest's South Col, and was summited in 1950 by French climbers Maurice Herzog and Louis Lachenal, resulting in the loss of all their toes and nearly all their fingers. Both men were lucky to be rescued by their fellow climbers and escape with their lives. Many of the other top Himalayan peaks had been attempted, but had consistently confounded the best efforts of the greatest climbers in the world, often with tragic loss of life or serious injury. But now, high mountain summit after high mountain summit suddenly began to fall with amazing speed.

Within only three years the world's six highest mountains had all been climbed—K2, the second-highest, and Cho Oyu, the sixth-highest, were climbed in 1954; Kanchenjunga, the third-highest, and Makalu, the fifth-highest, were climbed in 1955; and so on. Five years after Everest, only two peaks above 26,250 feet remained unclimbed, one of which was inaccessible. This was certainly what has been dubbed "the golden age of Himalayan climbing." Today, the successes are usually attributed to a sudden blossoming of skill, courage, and fortitude among the legendary mountaineers of the mid-1950s, their hearts and spirits inspired, so it is often said, by the noble British example on Everest.

However, the great Swiss climber Jürg Marmet, who, together with Ernst Schmied, made the second ascent of Everest in 1956, remembered being influenced by Pugh's recommendations on oxygen consumption for climbing and sleeping, and on acclimatization. He also told me that the results of Pugh's tests on clothing, equipment, food intake, and energy balances "were incorporated into our planning for 1956," and "they are still valid today." Four climbers on his expedition reached the summit. They also made the first ascent of Lhotse—27,940 feet—the world's fourth-highest mountain.

The American climber-physiologist, Tom Hornbein, who in 1963 made the first ascent of Everest up the difficult West Ridge route, remembered Pugh's altitude policies as being the accepted rules of high-altitude climbing, "a bit of gospel with the attribution lost along the way."

Looking back on the early 1950s, the Austrian climber-physiologist Oswald Oelz reflected, "The Swiss would have climbed Everest in 1952 if they had had a scientist like G. Pugh." Oelz was with the expedition in 1978 on which—twenty-five years after the first ascent—Peter Habeler and Reinhold Messner made the first ascent without oxygen. As they did so, one of Pugh's dictums was constantly on their minds. Every spare minute when they were not climbing was spent brewing sweetened lemonade and telling themselves: "We must drink. We must drink."

Writing in 2004, the famous physiologist John Severinghaus commented on Pugh's recommendations for Everest: "What was good fifty years ago is still good today . . . Pugh's emphasis on adequate energy- and fluid-intake at altitude is as sound today as it was then."[18]

Soon after Pugh returned to work in the spring of 1954, he began to receive invitations from fellow members of the 1953 Everest team to join their future expeditions. In April, Alf Gregory invited him onto an expedition to the Himalayan Karakorum—a mountain range that bestrides the Indian and Pakistani sectors of Kashmir—and sought his advice on tents, boots, and cooking stoves. Shortly afterward, Charles Evans—in Pugh's eyes, now fully converted to sensible physiological thinking on Everest—asked him to help with preparations for the attempt on Kanchenjunga that Evans was to lead in 1955. Kanchenjunga, at 28,169 feet, is the world's third-highest mountain, and a far more serious climbing challenge than Everest. Evans asked Pugh to advise on oxygen and plan the low-altitude diet.[19] Later, Norman Hardie, to whom Evans had given the job of organizing the high-altitude diet, begged for Pugh's help with the high-altitude food boxes too.[20]

The MRC forbade Pugh to take part in any more mountaineering expeditions, though he was able to give Evans's team the advice they needed. The oxygen was being supplied by the firm Normalair, of Yeovil in Somerset, which had provided some of the oxygen equipment for Everest. Sir Eric Mensforth, the head of Normalair, who had not met Pugh before, heard him contributing to a seminar on oxygen in October 1954, and was so impressed that he immediately invited him to become his firm's "consulting physiologist."[21] Pugh drove to Yeovil every week for a couple of months to work with Tom Bourdillon, Charles Evans, and Norman Hardie on the expedition's oxygen. Evans subsequently led his team to triumphant success on Kanchenjunga. Four climbers—George Band, Joe Brown, Norman Hardie, and Tony Streather—all reached the summit.[22]

Although Pugh was extremely interested in altitude and its problems, he was still fretting about his Channel-swimming studies, which had been in their infancy when Michael Ward dragged him out of the cold bath in his laboratory in the spring of 1951. The studies were an important branch of research into hypothermia. He had continued with them in the months after Ward's visit, before having to drop them altogether in January 1952, when he gave himself over to the preparations for Cho Oyu. None of his early findings had yet been written up, and Pugh was afraid that if he didn't get back to them quickly, other members of his department would be only too ready to step into his place.

17

Braving the Cold

The perfect opportunity for Pugh to continue his Channel-swimming studies presented itself when, after a three-year hiatus, the international cross-Channel swimming race from France to Britain was revived in the summer of 1954 by Billy Butlin, the irrepressible founder of Butlin's holiday camps. The work Pugh did in this field was part of a long-running engagement with the subject of hypothermia which had begun during the war at Cedars and continued until the end of his career.

Pugh's first research project at the MRC was a commission from the Royal Navy to study hypothermia and survival at sea. Survival at sea was an immense problem for all shipwrecked sailors.[1] Some sailors drowned, but more died from hypothermia, which, if it did not kill directly, often caused them to drown when they became unconscious or lost the ability to swim because of it. Given enough time in the water, these unfortunate victims would doubtless have died of hypothermia anyway.

Hypothermia wasn't only a serious problem for the world's navies—it was the curse of all the armed services. When the Russians invaded Finland in World War II, they lost 200,000 soldiers, many from starvation and exposure to cold. Catastrophic numbers of German soldiers died of exposure in the icy Russian winter of 1941–42 during Hitler's invasion of Russia. And when in 1943 the Americans launched an offensive in the north Pacific to retake the island of Attu from the Japanese, for every soldier who died of his injuries, another died of cold.

But nowhere was the problem worse than in the water. The German U-boat crews in World War II had the highest mortality and casualty rates of any service, and most of the 28,000 crewmen who died, died of hypothermia, or of drowning caused by hypothermia. Hypothermia had an equally devastating effect on the Royal Navy. Two-thirds of all fatal naval casualties in World War II died of drowning or hypothermia, and of the 30,000 men who lost their lives in this way, the great majority did so from hypothermia.

This huge problem led many countries to embark on research programs. The Japanese carried out secret cold experiments on American and Chinese prisoners of war in Manchuria during the war. Highly unethical hypothermia experiments were conducted at the German concentration camp at Dachau, where naked prisoners were immersed in cold water while their body temperatures were measured until they died. Although some scientific progress was made, five years after the war, hypothermia was still not fully understood, and the best methods of avoidance and treatment had not yet been established. Even the Royal Navy's traditional advice to shipwreck victims was being called into question.

The advice at that time was to avoid struggling or striking out for the shore and to concentrate on staying afloat by clinging to a lifebelt or a piece of wreckage. However, in 1950, E. M. Glaser, a physiologist writing in the academic journal *Nature*, claimed that his research had demonstrated that this was the wrong advice, and that lives had been lost as a result: "Fit men who are in danger . . . in cold water might be advised to swim or struggle as hard as they can for as long as they can. If they try to preserve their strength by clinging to wreckage or floating on their lifebelts, they will die from cold. Perhaps more lives would have been saved in the past if this had been understood."[2]

In 1949, Pugh spent a month at the behest of the MRC on an Arctic cruise aboard HMS *Vengeance*, studying the impact of cold on naval personnel on board ship. Afterward, he roundly criticized the Royal Navy's duffel coats, which buttoned down the front, and pronounced their waterproof oversuits for use in the lifeboats to be "grossly inadequate."[3]

Reviewing previous research into the relationship between body fat and insulation from cold, Pugh saw that in the late 1930s some American researchers claimed to have "exploded" the popular idea that fat people, insulated by their layers of subcutaneous fat, were better able to survive in cold water and felt the cold less than thin people.[4] The Americans had compared the insulating properties of beef fat and beef muscle and had apparently identified hardly any difference between them.

Pugh decided to test their findings by comparing the insulating properties not of beef muscle and fat, but of *human* muscle and fat. Using samples of human fat obtained from the morgue at Hammersmith Hospital, he and a colleague demonstrated for the first time that human fat did indeed have nearly double the insulating properties of human muscle.[5] The fat study led to an idea that was to become the hallmark of Pugh's career. On joining the MRC he decided not to study survival at sea by gathering data on a large number of people, but instead to focus on a few extreme examples of men who survived in cold water—namely, marathon swimmers. "If you want to study some extreme subject like intense cold," he announced, "go and find somebody who is good at it."

The idea came to him when an international swimming race across the British Channel, sponsored by the *Daily Mail* in 1950, made him aware that long-distance swimmers, who were mostly very fat indeed, were able to survive in relatively cold water for many hours, whereas the victims of shipwrecks normally died of hypothermia within a few hours in water of similar temperatures.[6]

The competitors in the *Daily Mail* cross-Channel swim started out from northern France and swam across to England, landing wherever they could along a 10-mile strip of the Kent coastline.[7] The English Channel was particularly challenging, not merely because of the distance of 21 miles, but also because of the relatively cold summer conditions—the average temperature of the water was around 60.4 degrees Fahrenheit—the changeable weather, and the fierce currents and tides. The tides were capable of delaying even the strongest swimmers for many hours, preventing them from reaching the shore and sometimes forcing them to swim up to 50 or 60 miles to complete the crossing.

When the race was repeated the following year, Pugh rushed to Folkestone and made friends with one of the competitors, Jason Zirganos, a cheerful, ebullient, gold-toothed major in the Greek army. Zirganos took 16 hours, 19 minutes to complete the crossing, coming in seventh, beating his time of the previous year. He embodied the classic characteristics of the marathon swimmer in being short, stocky, and very fat, with a gargantuan appetite. During his career as a long-distance swimmer, he competed in most of the recognized marathon swims throughout the world, eventually swimming the English Channel four times. He and Pugh got along so well that he agreed to be studied while swimming in Lake Windermere, where he intended to challenge the record of seven hours for swimming the length of the lake. The average temperature of the water in Windermere is the same as in the English Channel.

After nearly two weeks of training at Windermere with Pugh experimenting on him, Zirganos made his attempt on the record. Amazingly he undertook this not-inconsiderable challenge with a thermometer inserted five inches into his rectum and wearing a mouthpiece from which a tube ran under his body to a Douglas bag attached to a pole. The pole was fixed to the dinghy that Pugh rowed along beside him.[8] Samples of Zirganos's exhaled breath were collected in the bag and subsequently analyzed to find out how much energy Zirganos was expending at different stages of the swim.

Zirganos swam for over six hours without apparently feeling the cold. Afterward, having beaten the record, he ran up the beach and stood in the open air for a further half an hour without shivering, while Pugh finished his experiments. However, when Pugh (who was very much thinner than Zirganos) embarked on the same swim to compare his reactions with those of Zirganos, he collapsed in less than half an hour. Pulled helpless from the water, he flopped onto the floor of the rescue dinghy and lay shivering violently for 20 minutes.

Later Zirganos became a regular sight in the pool in the basement of the Lansdowne Club in Mayfair, patiently swimming up and down, wearing a mask with a tube attached to the ubiquitous Douglas bag which was tied onto a fishing line carried by Pugh, who trotted along the poolside next to him. Zirganos also went to Pugh's laboratory in Hampstead for a series of comparative experiments in a bath of cold water the same temperature as the lake. Pugh had been in the midst of the same bath experiments when Michael Ward first visited him before the Everest expedition.

Although Pugh's experiments appeared crude, his early work with marathon swimmers was to have lasting implications. The results were well ahead of their time and proved seminal. Pugh was the first person to demonstrate properly that the fatter someone is, the better insulated they will be from the cold, and the better their bodies will tolerate the stress of exposure to cold.[9]

At the same time, comparing the results of his experiments at Windermere with those in the bath at Hampstead, Pugh found that he lost heat more slowly while lying *still* in the bath than he had done while *swimming* in water of the same temperature in Lake Windermere.[10] This suggested that it was more advantageous to remain still in the water and conserve energy than it was to try to keep warm by swimming. Swimming and thrashing about increases the flow of cold water over the warm skin, causing further heat loss and using up vital energy. Replicated many times with larger numbers of subjects, Pugh's findings were proved right, and the navy's original recommendations for survival at sea proved to be correct all along.[11] Many lives were saved as a result. The accepted strategy for survival in cold water—keep still and conserve energy—remains the same today.

In 1954, when Pugh discovered that the Channel-swimming competition was to be revived, he got in touch with the sponsor, Billy Butlin, and begged permission to make observations on the competitors before and during the swim.[12] The project raised so many interesting issues that he asked Butlin for increased access the following year. Declaring himself a staunch supporter of science, Butlin agreed. To that end Pugh recruited a small team of researchers from the MRC and persuaded the navy to provide a fast, lightweight motorboat so they could monitor the swimmers in the water and examine competitors who had to give up.

Just as he was finalizing these arrangements, his boss Otto Edholm decided to step in. As head of Pugh's department, he was entitled to take a closer interest. Naturally the naval officials and Mr. Butlin's secretary now began to defer to the senior man, so Pugh suddenly found himself the junior partner in his own project. I have distant memories of my mother trying to persuade—perhaps even goad—my father into doing something about Edholm "stealing" his ideas, and my father replying, "Oh, never mind—I've got plenty more ideas."

Nonetheless, he was clearly resentful of Edholm's intrusion, and his suppressed frustration about his Everest work played its part. From that moment his relationship with Edholm began to deteriorate. Talking about his Channel-swimming studies on camera thirty years later, Pugh suddenly abandoned all decorum and burst out: "Then Edholm got in the act and . . . took the whole thing over, and my name was forgotten and he didn't do anything at all."[13]

In the midst of these problems, Pugh went off to the United States for a two-week trip, all expenses paid by the US Navy. The invitation came from Dr. Orr Reynolds, head of the US Office of Naval Research in Washington, who would later join NASA and involve Pugh in secret research projects connected with space travel.[14]

Pugh's first stop in America was a prestigious symposium at the University of California at Berkeley, where he gave a paper on Everest.[15] Later he was taken on a trip to the newly built White Mountain High-Altitude Research Station—a series of research huts with living quarters at between 10,050 feet and 14,250 feet—which had just been created with navy money in the Sierra Nevada.[16] It was one of the highest research stations in the world, and Pugh was impressed by the well-appointed prefabricated huts which allowed the scientists to carry out their work in comfort.[17]

Pugh struck up an excellent relationship with two of his hosts, Nello Pace and Will Siri, who were both employed at Berkeley. Siri, a biophysicist from the famous Donner Laboratory ("the birthplace of nuclear medicine"), had led the American attempt on Makalu the year before, with Pace as the chief scientist carrying out high-altitude research similar to Pugh's on Cho Oyu. Later, in 1963, Siri would become deputy leader and chief scientist on the first American expedition to conquer Everest.[18] Pace had close links with the US Navy and had been the driving force behind the setting up of the White Mountain Station.

Pugh spent his second week in California being shown around the science laboratories at Berkeley and Stanford universities, lost in wonder at what he described in his diary as the "beautiful experiments" being performed there. At Stanford he spoke about his altitude research to an appreciative audience of elite physiologists, who asked so many questions that the session lasted for nearly three hours. Pugh responded to the respect being shown him by revealing a very different persona from the irascible, intolerant character he was becoming at Hampstead. In California he was sociable, outgoing, appreciative, and considerate. He went to parties every night and seemed to find everyone he met—indeed, everything about America, even the sight of people gambling on slot machines in Reno—interesting and stimulating. His diaries give the distinct impression that he might have been happier and more fulfilled if he had made his career not in England but among the more relaxed and appreciative academics in the United States.

Later in the year Siri and Pace joined Pugh's Channel-swimming project at Folkestone. The Channel-swimming studies resulted in several acclaimed publications—albeit with Pugh's boss Edholm as joint author—and Pugh developed great respect and affection for Zirganos and his fellow swimmers.[19] He estimated that Zirganos expended between 9,000 and 15,000 calories crossing the English Channel, making Channel swimming "possibly the greatest feat of endurance in the world of sport."[20] But the story of Jason Zirganos ended sadly four years later, when at the age of forty-nine he died during an attempted marathon swim between Scotland and Ireland.

Pugh was told by an Irish doctor that Zirganos had been pulled out of the water nearly seven hours into his swim, after he had been lying on his back for some time. Saddened, Pugh asked for postmortem results, but was told there had been no postmortem, and the authorities had been unable to trace any relatives of Zirganos in Greece. Still, Pugh did not let the subject drop. He wrote a tribute to Zirganos and tried to persuade the *Lancet* to publish it, but they refused.

Pugh's visit to the White Mountain Station in the Sierra Nevada had prompted him to suggest to Will Siri and Nello Pace the idea of jointly organizing an Anglo-American high-altitude expedition to the Himalayas. Both men expressed great enthusiasm, but before the idea got off the ground, they invited Pugh to join their own expedition to Antarctica in 1957–58.

18

"Your Natures Are So Completely Different"

Griff Pugh may have been received with open arms in America—he was enjoying a degree of celebrity in Britain, too—but, beneath the surface, things were not going quite so well. Pugh's lack of postgraduate qualifications was already beginning to prove an obstacle to advancement.

The notoriously difficult examinations leading to Membership of the Royal College of Physicians (MRCP) were the key to becoming a senior doctor or consultant in the UK. Without this qualification, and without a PhD or an MD, the medical equivalent, Pugh's chances of heading a department of his own or becoming a university professor would be seriously curtailed. Nor would he ever be accepted into the inner circles of the Physiological Society, of which he was elected a member in 1955.

The MRC, being a paternalistic employer, was very conscious of such issues. Successive directors had wanted the institute to be "rather a nursery for future professors than an asylum for research workers who had failed to secure academic advancement."[1] Talented young researchers who lacked the qualifications necessary to move onward and upward were encouraged to earn them and given every assistance to do so. When Pugh joined in 1950, he was awarded six months' paid leave to prepare for his MRCP. He took the money and the leave, but inexplicably, when the time came, he walked out of the exam room without writing a word.

After Everest, two senior figures at the MRC encouraged him to retake the MRCP exams and get a partial exemption by submitting a thesis on his Everest and Cho Oyu research.[2] Pugh said he would, but did nothing, nor did he attempt to use his Everest work to gain a PhD or an MD.

It might have mattered less had he been, like John Hunt, politically astute, a good communicator, and an energetic networker, but he was none of these things. He always approached life with the optimistic view that "something will come up," and wonderful opportunities always had come up, usually with little effort on his part. Greatly indulged by his absent parents as a young man, and never having had to struggle for his life chances, he lacked the motivation to struggle now. It was his work that interested him, not his career.

Perhaps the most important reason for his insouciant attitude was the change in his financial circumstances after the death of Josephine's father in February 1953.

The loss was traumatic for Josephine, finally cutting her off from the life she had known in her youth. Her mother had died in 1947, but her father's house and his reassuring presence had always offered sanctuary if things got too difficult. She coped with her grief and her sense of loss with little support from Griffith, who was preoccupied with his Everest work and would soon depart for the Himalayas.

Felix Cassel left his daughter a legacy that lifted her out of her dependence on her husband. Immediately Pugh stopped feeling any need to provide for his family. He had been giving Josephine a reasonable allowance of £500 a year. It continued, but he didn't increase it for the rest of his life, leaving Josephine to support the family and pay for the children's education. He became a kept man, using his salary for his own pleasures, treating himself to sports cars—the first, a silver-gray Austin-Healey convertible, shortly after Everest—and everyday luxuries like expensive cigars.

Being forced to be the breadwinner might have driven him to improve his prospects, but once his earning power ceased to be essential, he lost the will to climb the career ladder and focused all his energy on research. Loathing committees and finding administration intensely boring, he left these things to other people and projected himself as a latter-day gentleman scientist motivated only by the love of knowledge. Despite these positives, he was already beginning to resent his junior status, finding he lacked influence and had difficulty in getting his voice heard.

It was during the three years after Everest, when Pugh was extremely busy, that he started to display the outrageous absentmindedness that became an endless source of amusement to all who knew him. When Hillary and Lowe came to stay at Hatching Green in 1953, Pugh, in a rare effort to relieve the burden on Josephine, agreed to take me and Simon off her hands for a day. He drove us to his laboratory in Hampstead where I remember the panoramic view over London from the windows, the chemical smell, and the mysterious cold chamber.

That day, when he was summoned to MRC head office in central London, we had to go with him, and he left us locked in the car while he went to his meeting. Afterward, lost in thought, he walked out of the building and caught the tube back to Hampstead. A couple of hours later, ready to go home, he went to the parking lot. Finding his car missing, he stormed back inside, angrily demanding of his colleagues, "Where's my bloody car?" Only when Jim Adam, an army doctor seconded to Pugh's department, reminded him that he had driven it to the head office did it dawn on Pugh that he had left the car parked in Old Queen Street with his children locked inside.

Within a year, he did it again. Agreeing to take us to the dentist, he left us in Harley Street and went off to the Lansdowne Club to do some experiments in the swimming pool, then drove home having forgotten all about us. Simon and I waited at the dentist's. At closing time we were still waiting. At last someone rang Josephine and an hour later our somewhat chastened father arrived to pick us up.

Josephine had quite a lot to put up with. When, in the spring of 1954, Griffith took off for his four weeks' convalescence in Engelberg, she was left looking after the children, having not had a vacation herself for several years. In August 1955, he really excelled himself on that fabled occasion when he left his pregnant wife sitting in the car, in labor, while he "popped into" an Everest reunion party at the Café Royal in Regent Street and promptly forgot about her. This was his most famous misdemeanor—laughed about by all the Everesters. But they didn't realize the seriousness of Pugh's behavior.

This was Josephine's third pregnancy since she had had TB. The first two were terminated on medical advice, but she refused to have a third abortion. Yet her doctor husband displayed scant concern when he left her languishing in the car. Nor was his behavior particularly surprising. Josephine knew before she married him that this irrepressible young man was unlikely to be the most solicitous of husbands.

Josephine Cassel had first met Griffith Pugh in the mid-1920s, through her brother James, his best friend at Harrow. James Cassel, "the inkiest boy at Harrow," was an extremely clever scholar who went on to get a first in physics at New College, Oxford, where Pugh managed only a poor third in law.

The source of the family's money was Josephine's great-uncle Sir Ernest Cassel, who had been one of Edward VII's so-called "Jewish circle" of rich friends, which included Nathaniel Rothschild and Baron Maurice de Hirsch.[3] Josephine's father Felix, who married Lady Helen Grimston, daughter of the Earl of Verulam, inherited a portion of his uncle's great wealth.

Brought up in the sumptuous Cassel family home near Luton in Bedfordshire, Josephine had a "handmaiden" to look after her every need from the age of six, and grew up mistakenly believing that she was rather tidy. The five Cassel children all had large allowances, wonderful clothes, luxurious holidays, and chauffeurs to drive them about. The food was exquisite, and the houseguests were fascinating. Often at loose ends during school vacations, Griffith Pugh became a frequent visitor, sometimes going with the Cassels in the summer to a villa rented by Felix each year at Cap Ferrat.

Josephine, known to all as Doey, was infatuated with Griffith by the time she was twelve. Indeed, in their own ways all the Cassel children became infatuated with him. Bold, forceful, vigorous—he was everything they were not. Entranced by his athleticism, his free-spirited nature, his adventurous optimism, they regularly followed him to Haldengütli in Switzerland where Doey idolized him as her lion-haired skiing hero.

Griffith began sleeping with Doey when she was nineteen and he was twenty-six, though he was never faithful to her. Like everyone else, he was charmed by her lovely looks and her childlike sweetness. Long-legged and delicate, like a gazelle or an exotic flower, she was a warm, gentle, yet effervescent character. More importantly, she was available, and he was a man who took his opportunities where he found them. He had already tried and failed to bed her elder sister, Hermione. "Mione never would," he used to say to my brothers, never quite finishing the sentence, "but your mother . . ."

Griffith married Doey hastily a few days after the outbreak of war. In the summer of 1939, with war imminent, Doey's twin brother Harold had been called up. Griffith was outside the age range of the call-up, but Harold—who was quite as enthralled by Griffith as his sister—volunteered him to serve as a doctor in his Bedfordshire Regiment. Two weeks before reporting for duty, the two young men hitchhiked down to Cap Ferrat to join the rest of the family at the marble-floored Villa Prima Vera.

There, sitting on the rocky private beach below the villa on a balmy Mediterranean evening, the air full of the scent of wild rosemary and the singing of cicadas, Griffith and Harold were filled with foreboding. Watching the sunset they discussed the generation of fine British men who had died in World War I, many without siring any offspring. Betraying the pervasive influence of eugenics, Griffith argued that strong, healthy men like themselves must not allow it to happen again. They must "leave something behind." They made a pact that, in the event of war, they would marry and make their wives pregnant as quickly as possible. Griffith and Doey married four days after war was declared. Shortly afterward Harold married too. In sharp contrast, six days after Harold's wedding, Doey's eldest brother James climbed a Welsh mountain and shot himself on the summit, leaving an incomprehensible suicide note saying, "Sorry Pip."

Doey became pregnant in 1940. An impecunious young man like Griffith could not, responsibly, have married a girl and made her pregnant before going off to war, leaving her with no means of support should something happen to him. But there was no such problem with Doey. In that sense, he married her because of her money. Much later, he admitted that his earnings as a junior doctor were not enough to support a wife, and in other circumstances he would not have married when he did.

Felix Cassel regarded Griffith as an "adventurer," but did not feel he could object to the marriage. He was not alone in thinking that Griffith and Doey were not well suited. Griffith's greatest enthusiasms—physically, scientifically, and intellectually—were the mountains and outdoor life. Exercise, however, made Doey feel ill. She loved art, literature, poetry, and music; with the exception of music, the arts were of marginal interest to her husband. Doey was beset by doubts about the frivolity of her existence, and longed to find a purpose in life, whereas Griffith's positive nature found little room for doubts about himself or his mission in life. His main confidante, the perceptive Elsa Hauthal, sister of Lotto who had taught him to ski, sounded a note of warning when the relationship began: "Doey is charming, but I am not sure she will understand you, Griffith. Your natures are so completely different."

When he was sent to the Middle East by the Royal Army Medical Corps, Griffith's early letters to Doey were full of advice about the coming baby. He thought that she should breast-feed for at least six months and give the baby regular doses of cod liver oil. When, in September 1940, he received the news that he had a son, David, he was overjoyed. However, as time went on, his letters varied. When he was having a bad time, he wrote long, encouraging letters full of tender remarks. When things were going well, his letters became few and far between and full of stories about the wonderful time he was having—the picnics, the climbing, the Persian stallions—and showed scant interest in David or Doey.

It was while Griffith was at Cedars that Doey was at last compelled to face the tragic reality that David was handicapped. The connection between rubella and handicapped babies was not generally understood in the early 1940s, so there had been nothing to alert her to the problem.[4] The truth dawned only gradually. David was her first baby, and it was tempting to cling to the idea that he was merely a slow developer. When she aired her doubts to Griffith, he brushed off her worries with optimistic comments—"Funny [that] D is so slow in beginning to speak. Gwladys [Pugh's elder sister] told me I was the same." His failure to ask questions gave Doey the impression that he did not want to learn anything negative about his son.

Two of Griffith's sisters added to the pressure by insisting that their brother's morale would be irretrievably damaged by the shock of hearing that David was mentally disabled. Doey was tormented with worry about whether to tell Griffith or not, and occasionally her doubts surfaced cryptically in her letters. In one she described a dream about a disembodied voice giving her a message: "Last night I dreamed about you . . . you said you were not happy . . . I said I would tell you about it in bed. Then a voice said very loud <u>don't tell him don't tell him,</u> on and on, until I woke up & I still heard it when I was awake. The silly thing is I can't for the life of me think what it was I was supposed to be telling you . . ."[5]

A different man might have recognized a cry for help—but not Griffith.

Halfway through Griffith's first season at Cedars, it had become inescapable that David was deaf and mute and his movements were jerky and unnatural. But Griffith, preoccupied with his ski patrols and his exciting research, was not disposed to worry about what was going on at home. Only when he was sent to take part in the Allied invasion of Sicily in the summer of 1943, finding himself in mortal danger with men dying all around him, did his attitude change.

With heightened emotions he resumed writing the kind of letters he had written to Doey when he had first left home. He had simply refused to focus on the problem. On August 29, 1943, he admitted: "I have been worrying a little bit about David lately & should be glad of more news about him."

But nothing prepared Griffith for the shock when, in September 1943, after an absence of three years, he saw David for the first time. He told my brother Simon, "I came home expecting to find my son and I found a creature quacking like a duck." Cruel as they were, those words accurately conveyed the impact of the shock.

Griffith's failure to respond to David was profoundly disappointing to Doey, who was fiercely protective of her son. David's handicap drove a corrosive wedge into the fragile structure of their already-tenuous relationship. Their reunion was ruined.

Griffith remained in England working at the War Office for just a few weeks before being posted back to Cedars. There, once again, he was able to set aside the problem of his disabled son and resume his life of sport, adventure, and research. It was not until nine months later, in June 1944, that he acknowledged there were problems in a letter to Doey: "How different our experiences these four years, when we should have been sharing life together . . . I am afraid I wasn't really very well when I was home in September & it must have been rather a shock to you to find me so vague. Next time it will be different."[6]

But his words of apology were themselves "rather vague," and did not confront the fact that he had been horrified and repelled by the sight of his disabled son.

In the 1940s it was a source of shame to have a mentally disabled child. Doey and Griffith had grown up at a time when mental deficiencies were thought to be inherited, and it was believed that unless "mental defectives" were locked away, they would "infect" the rest of society. In 1929, a government report argued that the "racial disaster of mental deficiency" could only be prevented if the "feeble-minded" were segregated into asylums and the sexes were kept apart so they could not procreate.[7] It was not uncommon for families to commit their mentally or physically disabled children to asylums and keep their existence secret, to protect their other children from the stigma of association with a "defective" brother or sister. A disability like epilepsy was considered bad enough to merit such drastic treatment. Every specialist Doey consulted urged her to put David into an institution, but she was determined not to.

In the first few years after the war, Griffith had little time for home life. When in 1948 Doey was spirited away to the hospital with TB, he took on a nanny to look after Simon and me, but no nanny could be asked to look after our turbulent brother. The only solution that presented itself was the local mental hospital, Napsbury Asylum. Napsbury was a hangover from the past, full of poor souls, some mad, some with minor disabilities, who had been locked away and were likely to remain so for the rest of their lives.[8] It was exactly the kind of harsh, inhumane institution that Doey had dreaded. In her absence Griffith formally committed David to Napsbury.

When she came out of the hospital, Doey was horrified and rushed to visit David at the asylum. He clung to her with a look of sheer desperation in his eyes and had to be dragged off screaming and crying when she left. It was an experience that haunted her for the rest of her life.

Because David had been committed by his father, Doey had to battle bureaucratic red tape to bring him home. Beneath the soft, gentle personality was a vein of steel that seldom showed itself except in adversity.

Home at last, David showed clear signs of damage. He had developed a great variety of nervous twitches and phobias, most commonly at mealtimes, when he would become deeply agitated until he was given his portion, suggesting that he had sometimes gone short of food. Any sign of preparations for a trip away from home would fling him into paroxysms of screaming and crying.

As a young child David had been assessed as "unteachable" by a succession of experts, and very little effort had been made to educate him. When he was nine, Doey arranged for the retired headmaster of a local boys' school to come to our house every morning and engage in this apparently impossible task. Slowly and patiently, using his own methods, Mr. Watts taught David the rudimentary elements of reading and writing, partially releasing him from the prison of being unable to communicate or understand what was going on around him. Gradually, it became clear that he was very intelligent, though for many years he continued to be tempestuous and sometimes violent.

Looking after David and keeping her younger children safe from his violent outbursts were a formidable task for Doey, which she undertook stoically. Meanwhile, Griffith appeared to lack the emotional resources to cope with the situation and turned away, not just from David, but from family life as a whole. Taking no responsibility for David's welfare, he did not develop any kind of relationship with him. Least of all did he apply his problem-solving mind to the task of helping David to develop. Throwing himself into his work, and mostly ignoring his children, he behaved much as if he were still the carefree bachelor of his youth. And his Himalayan expeditions gave him the opportunity to return to the outdoor adventures he had always loved most.

Doey, being a self-effacing character, felt herself partly to blame for Griffith's poor reaction to David because of her failure to warn him in advance. She also felt a sense of guilt about marrying Griffith, despite knowing in her heart that she was not really his type, and knowing that he was marrying her mainly because of his ill-fated desire to father a son. Faced with the sad irony of the outcome, she, in sharp contrast to her husband, responded to her insecurities by dedicating her life to providing a good home for the family and looking after us as best she could. After all, for all his faults and failings, she still admired, loved, and respected her husband. And she sensed instinctively that, beneath the surface of Griffith's abrasive character, lay repressed emotional needs he was hardly aware of himself.

19

A Man in a Hurry

"Your mother—she was a sweetie," Sir Edmund Hillary told me when I visited him at his house in Auckland, New Zealand, in 2006. "Griff gave her a pretty rough time, I thought. He was very pleasant to me, but not so much to his family . . . He was a very complex person."

In the years immediately after Everest, Ed Hillary was an occasional visitor to our Harpenden home, sometimes staying for up to two weeks. I had not seen him since I was a child, though his handsome face had smiled jauntily at me from countless ski-resort posters in Switzerland and France over the years.

Now, at age eighty-seven, the famous Everest hero struck me as big, burly, and benign. Rising to greet me from his armchair in the center of a light, airy sitting room, he grinned down at me from his great height. It was a slightly lopsided grin. The formidable barrel chest that had seemed extraordinarily large to my six-year-old eyes was no longer so imposing, for he had become rather portly. There was humor in his voice and a twinkle in his eye, and I could see at once why so many people felt great affection for him.

It had taken several years to set up this meeting. At first I had felt hurt when my letters, e-mails, and faxes addressed to Sir Edmund at his home in Auckland had elicited no reply, only a blank silence. Hillary had been on four expeditions with my father and had co-led one of them with him, so I had hoped and imagined that he would respond in some way, even if he did not want to meet me. In 2006, having failed to get any reaction, I decided to travel to New Zealand anyway, thinking I would knock on his door and beard him in his lair. Only then did it occur to me to make contact with Hillary's second wife, June Mulgrew, who had met my father in England and in Nepal. His first wife had been killed in a plane crash with their daughter Belinda in 1975. Plucking up my courage, I rang Hillary's telephone number. Lady Hillary answered. I explained who I was and asked to be allowed to interview her, rather than her husband. A friendly conversation ensued, which culminated in an opportunity to meet both husband and wife.

When Hillary and I settled down to talk and I began to question him about Cho Oyu and Everest, he immediately diverted the conversation to his memories of my father's idiosyncrasies. Chuckling, he recounted a story about being driven to London in the 1950s in Griffith's sports car:

> *When I stayed in your home . . . [Griff] had this little sports car and he would drive me into town and drop me off. On one memorable occasion he drove at an appalling speed . . . we whipped down this straight and I could see that there was a truck turning onto it. I thought [in terror], "Here we go" . . . then Griff put on his brakes and we ended up with the front of Griff's car just under the back of the big truck. Another six inches and we would both have had it.*

Behind the wheel Griffith behaved like the daring ski-racer he was in his youth. His silver-gray Austin-Healey 100, bought in 1953, was his pride and joy. All the Everesters and most of their wives were pressed into terrifyingly fast demonstration rides in it. When it was a month old, he fell asleep at the wheel on the way home from a boozy Everest reception and wrote it off. A plaintive letter in his correspondence file apologized to a certain Sir Edward Penton—one of "the good and the great"—for having failed to turn up at a lunch party Penton had arranged at the Garrick Club to introduce my father to some eminent personages: "I am so very sorry about missing lunch today. I had to go out of London to see about my car which has been smashed up and so did not look at my engagement book until too late. I hope you will forgive me!"[1]

There are countless similar letters of contrition among Griffith's papers, covering innumerable car crashes and forgotten appointments. Many an Everest reunion party was enlivened by tales of "Griff's fast cars, his crashes and his lady friends."[2] If Hillary regarded Pugh as a terrifying driver, when it came to climbing expeditions the judgments were reversed. There were to be times in the years after Everest when Pugh found Hillary a disturbingly gung-ho expedition leader.

Hillary was instinctively attracted to small, flexible expeditions with the minimum of equipment and the maximum of spontaneity. He derived immense physical exhilaration from climbing, his enthusiasm frequently bursting forth in "exuberant shouts" and "wild New Zealand yells" of joy.[3]

Having ascended Everest helped by oxygen on the back of a large expedition, it was always likely that he would feel that he had not yet really proven himself. Few climbers were completely immune to that dismissive remark of Bill Tilman's: "When a man has to start inhaling oxygen, his spirit has already been conquered by the mountain and the limit of his capacity has been very clearly defined."

The Everest oxygen was one of the topics I wanted to broach with Hillary, but he seemed unwilling to dwell on it. "Griff didn't have much to do with the oxygen, I don't think," he said, dismissively. When I pointed out that Pugh had "set the flow rates," his only response was that he personally had used less oxygen than Pugh had recommended: "Griff decided that the correct amount of oxygen at altitude was four liters a minute, but I didn't use that. I used three and it worked very well. In actual fact four liters is what they use now."

This boast of his prowess only made me aware that there must have been times after Everest when Ed Hillary felt under pressure to affirm that he deserved his soaring reputation as a high-altitude climber. Everest 1953 had turned him into a worldwide celebrity. With his engaging, unpretentious manner, craggy good looks, and tall, lanky physique, this proved to be something he was very good at, though he always modestly claimed not to enjoy his fame. He traveled the world telling the Everest story to rapturous audiences, receiving medals and awards.[4] And, in the bright glow of the Everest spotlight, he came to be viewed as a high-altitude climber of unparalleled skill and courage, though in reality his experience of climbing at extreme altitude was still limited. Before 1951, all Hillary's climbing, with the exception of a brief trip to the European Alps in 1949, had been undertaken in the mountains of New Zealand, where Mount Cook, at 12,316 feet, is the highest peak.

Born in 1919, Hillary was one of three children of an independent-minded, forcefully moralistic man who once ran a small-time newspaper but later became a professional beekeeper. Hillary emerged from a strict, ascetic upbringing under his father's watchful eye, by his own account shy, unconfident, lacking in friends, and resentful of his uncompromising parent, though deeply fond of his gentler mother. A lackluster career at Auckland Grammar School, during which he felt persecuted and inferior, had been made bearable by reading and dreaming: "Books of adventure became my greatest support—Edgar Rice Burroughs, Rider Haggard, John Buchan . . . In my imagination I constantly re-enacted heroic episodes, and I was always the hero. I died dramatically on a score of battlefields and rescued a hundred lovely maidens."[5]

School was followed by "two notably unsuccessful years studying mathematics and science" at the University of Auckland before he dropped out to join the family beekeeping business. At the end of the 1930s he began trekking and climbing in the New Zealand mountains and at last found a milieu in which his physical prowess and limitless energy enabled him to excel: "I was . . . happy to carry any load, push anybody up hills, rush off on any reconnaissance, make any trail . . . I knew I had more physical energy than most and I revelled in driving myself to the utmost."[6]

After a spell in the New Zealand Air Force toward the end of the war, seeking out opportunities to climb in his spare time, Hillary returned to beekeeping, disappearing to the New Zealand Alps whenever he could get away. Through climbing he met a community of like-minded New Zealanders whom he described as "the first real friends I ever had." Taken under the wing of the renowned New Zealand guide Harry Ayres in the second half of the 1940s, he improved his skills as an ice climber, and learned "a little of that subtle science of snow- and ice-craft that only experience can really teach."[7] He was on his first trip to the Himalayas in 1951, when the invitation came from Eric Shipton to join the Everest reconnaissance. Neither Shipton's expedition of 1951 nor the Cho Oyu expedition of 1952 took Hillary above 23,000 feet, and this was the limit of his experience of extreme altitude, until the Everest triumph catapulted him into unexpected stardom as one of the greatest high-altitude climbers the world had ever seen.

The newspapers swooned about Hillary's "immense strength." He was "as tough as a plaited steel hawser," "as quick-witted as a champion fencer," "as fit as a highly trained Olympic athlete," "a born climber," "a man utterly without fear," "a hugely experienced mountaineer," "one of the most powerful climbers in the world." In Britain, Germany, America, South Africa—wherever he went—the one question on everyone's lips was "What next?" As a Welsh newspaper asked its readers, after Hillary had lectured to wildly enthusiastic audiences in Cardiff:

> *Had you climbed Everest, would you be satisfied?*
> *I think so!*
> *But not Sir Edmund Hillary, the man who made the ascent! His one thought is to continue climbing; to attempt Everest from the north col and also to lead an expedition to Makalu . . . This is the kind of spirit that has brought such fame to the modest bee-keeping New Zealander.*[8]

In March 1954, Hillary deserted the lecture rostrum to take on the leadership of his own Himalayan expedition for the first time. It then became evident that the Everest experience had failed to convince him of the importance of the acclimatization and hydration strategies devised by Pugh for climbing at high altitudes.

In a venture organized by the New Zealand Alpine Club—with sponsorship of Hillary from *The Times*—Hillary, with Charles Evans, Dr. Michael Ball, New Zealanders Norman Hardie and George Lowe, and five of their compatriots, set off for the Barun Valley, 15 miles from Everest, which Hillary had visited with Eric Shipton after the Cho Oyu expedition.

The plan was to bag some of the moderately high unclimbed peaks in the area and carry out a survey. But while they were there, they discovered a promising approach to Makalu, the world's fifth-highest mountain, which was then still unconquered. The 27,825-foot Makalu is more difficult than Everest and was not included in their original plan, but they could not resist the idea of rushing this formidable mountain.

The consequences for Hillary made this—in his own words—an "unbelievably stupid" decision. A few days earlier he had injured his ribs in a failed attempt to rescue a member of his team from a crevasse. He had tried to conduct the rescue by tying a rope around his waist and having five Sherpas lower him into the crevasse where Jim McFarlane was lying injured. But Hillary had failed to realize that his weight would cause the rope to rise up his body and crush his ribs—a symptom of his inexperience. (It was standard practice to wear a harness for such an exercise, or to loop the rope beneath the feet.) McFarlane, who was left in the crevasse overnight and successfully rescued the next day, lost half of each foot, both his little fingers, and all the outer tendons of the others to frostbite.[9]

Shortly afterward, despite his injured ribs and with scant regard for whether his team was properly acclimatized or equipped, Hillary hurled himself enthusiastically into the assault on Makalu, climbing to a height of 23,000 feet as fast as he could. "I couldn't bear to be left out," he later wrote, adding with relish: "Despite our lack of acclimatization we hacked our way up . . . we didn't have the equipment to go really high but the party threw itself into a vigorous reconnaissance."[10]

The ascent came to an abrupt end at 23,000 feet when Hillary collapsed and fell into a state of semiconsciousness. Since they had no oxygen for emergencies, he remained semiconscious for four days while he was carried down to a lower camp, suffering from "terrible hallucinations" and "a terrible feeling of suffocation and extreme dehydration."[11] Only then did he come around. Brian Wilkins, one of the New Zealand climbers, later claimed that Hillary had been in "indifferent health and not eating well" even before he "rushed the crevasse rescue." His life as an after-dinner speaker had probably "taken its toll on his fitness."

The previous year, John Hunt had made sure that all the climbers in the Everest team adhered to Pugh's altitude regime, but Norman Hardie remembered Hillary and George Lowe in early 1954 boasting that they themselves "had not taken Griff's advice very seriously."[12] Then Hillary threw caution to the winds, dashing up Makalu when he was neither fit nor acclimatized, and was clearly dehydrated.[13] He had performed exceptionally well on Everest, but after the Makalu incident he had difficulty tolerating high altitude for the rest of his life: "I believe my experience on Makalu started the deterioration of the ability to acclimatize I had shown on Everest," he reflected later.[14]

In 1955 Hillary joined the British and Commonwealth Trans-Antarctic Expedition (TAE), led by British geologist Vivian (Bunny) Fuchs. Antarctica is mountainous, but its highest peak is only 16,050 feet, offering little scope for high-altitude climbing. The aim of Fuchs's expedition was to make the first land crossing of the Antarctic continent.[15] This kept Hillary busy until the summer of 1958. By the time the project came to an end, nearly all the major Himalayan summits had been vanquished, and the world's elite mountaineers were already moving on to the challenges of climbing the highest mountains by the more difficult routes, and climbing them without oxygen.

Pugh also went to Antarctica in December 1957 with an American expedition led by Nello Pace and Will Siri, financed by the US Office of Naval Research. It was part of the "International Geophysical Year," when scientists from many different countries converged on Antarctica to carry out cooperative research.[16] Pugh was to study acclimatization to cold and had persuaded Vivian Fuchs to let him use the TAE as his chief source of experimental subjects.[17] Pugh and Jim Adam—an MRC colleague—pitched camp on Hut Point Peninsula near "Scott Base," the New Zealand station established by Hillary.[18]

In early January, Hillary returned to Scott Base after several months out on the frozen wastes, and was delighted to see Pugh again. He told me: "I said to Griffith, 'Why don't you come and stay with us?' And he did, like a shot . . . he carried [out] a lot of his experiments over at Scott Base, and he really in many ways became just part of our team. And he and I got on very well indeed."

Using Hillary's team as experimental subjects, Pugh found little evidence that people who spent long periods in cold conditions felt the cold less than new arrivals, nor did they need fewer clothes, as many people—including Vivian Fuchs—believed. With this research topic proving a dead end, Pugh's thoughts were straying to a subject that had been on his mind since Everest: the possibility of arranging his own scientific expedition to high altitude to continue the work begun on Cho Oyu and Everest. The sight of a great many Antarctic scientists hard at work in comfortable huts, similar to those Pugh had admired at the White Mountain Research Station in California, was an additional inspiration. His aim would be to find out how well lowlanders could acclimatize to altitude over the longer term. This had not been investigated in depth before, and Pugh felt that an attempt on Everest without oxygen would be a great way of testing how far his climber-subjects could adapt to altitude.

With his Antarctic venture nearing its end, Hillary had begun to contemplate an attempt on Everest without oxygen from the Tibetan side. This was an ambitious goal in light of his dreadful experience on Makalu, but Pugh, who had admired Hillary's performance on Everest, his "speed over the ground," and his exceptional tolerance of lack of oxygen, saw him as the ideal man to have a go. They made a tentative plan for a joint expedition.

Hillary's interest in a joint expedition with Pugh was nevertheless surprising, given his openly expressed skepticism about science. In his book *High Adventure*, written shortly after Everest, he had even gone so far as to highlight the moment when, as he put it, "my faith in science and scientists disappeared forever."[19]

In 1952, at base camp on Cho Oyu, Pugh had measured the level of hemoglobin in Hillary's blood, and had found a lower concentration than in most of the other climbers. The competitive Hillary thought that a high concentration of hemoglobin indicated fitness and good acclimatization. Believing himself to be the fittest member of the team, he was not impressed. Rather to my chagrin, I found he had repeated the story fifty-four years later in his autobiography, *View from the Summit*, where he again emphasized that his "confidence in this aspect of high-altitude science disappeared, never to return."[20]

This single blood test result, puzzling though it was to Hillary, struck me as a rather flimsy justification for losing all faith in science and scientists "forever." I asked Professor John B. West, one of the authors of the textbook *High Altitude Medicine and Physiology*, how much credence should be attached to it. "The single blood measurement means almost nothing," he replied, adding that, among other things, the result might have been affected by how much water Hillary had been drinking.[21]

Now, before I could broach the subject with Hillary, he started telling me the same story yet again. I had to restrain myself from protesting, "But Ed, you, of all people, benefited the most from Griff's science on Everest! You must know that! Why are you putting him down?"

Fortunately, I held my tongue and said nothing, because later Hillary went out of his way to acknowledge my father's contribution to Everest. "Griff was hammering away at us to drink all the time," he said. "In fact, his constant, almost boring, talk about drinking fluid did play, I think, a big part in our success."

> *He in a way made it possible for us to actually climb Everest because he emphasized that it was enormously important for us to drink lots of liquid—a thing that one hadn't thought about before. So I certainly drank a lot. I followed his advice and it seemed to have a very good effect . . . All expeditions now know they have to drink.*

He reiterated this point at least four times over the two hours of our meeting, though he was keen to temper his praise with an assertion that Pugh knew very little about "mountaineering."

> *We were all climbers and knew a great deal more about mountaineering than [Griff] did. But he had much more knowledge about the possible effects of altitude than we did . . . I always regarded Griff as a rather brave man, because even though he had a considerable lack of knowledge of what one does in the mountains, he would always give it a go. And he wouldn't let anything stop him, really.*

Griffith was less ignorant of the mountains than Hillary thought, but it was still a fulsome endorsement. Hillary also told me that he personally had been more helpful to Pugh on Cho Oyu and on Everest than any of the other climbers, partly because, coming from a New World country, he was less burdened with the prejudices of his British counterparts: "I did carry out his experiments . . . they didn't want to, but I was always agreeable to doing such things . . . I think I had more contact with him [on Everest] than anyone except perhaps Mike Ward . . . I was always ready to cooperate with Griff, and he put me into some very uncomfortable positions as a consequence."

The more Hillary spoke, the better he conveyed to me the tensions my father had to cope with on Cho Oyu and Everest as he sought to get the climbers to listen to his advice rather than simply laugh at him and write him off as the expedition fool:

> *Griff was a lonely soul. He didn't mix freely with the other members of the party. That's understandable, because the other members of the party were mountaineers. But he could be very quiet. I mean, I didn't know he was around at times, but then when he got a bee in his bonnet about something, he would speak up at considerable length. He had strong ideas. We didn't always accept what he said, but he would go on about it. He had a wide knowledge of altitude and he would inflict this knowledge on us too. But a lot of it was really good stuff.*

The contradictions in what Sir Edmund Hillary said to me about science made it clear that he was able to embrace more than one point of view. He recognized the value of Pugh's work, but when the climber in him had the upper hand, he ceased to be sure if he really believed in scientists and their ideas at all. He was a man who was always in a hurry, easily irritated by the perfectionism or meticulousness of the scientist. Without a scientific background, his impatient personality probably took precedence over everything else.

While Pugh was in Antarctica he witnessed Hillary behaving in a headstrong and, some would say, foolhardy way—disobeying the instructions of his expedition leader, and risking the lives of his teammates. Vivian Fuchs had set out to complete what the newspapers described as "the last great journey of the world," a journey first attempted by Ernest Shackleton's Imperial Trans-Antarctic Expedition in 1914–16. Shackleton's ship the *Endurance* was crushed by polar ice before he could even begin his trip across the Antarctic continent.

Hillary had had doubts about how well he could work with the imperialminded Fuchs early in their relationship, when it became clear that Fuchs did not intend the New Zealanders to accompany him across the continent, or even to the Pole, but merely to lay a chain of supply depots for the second half of Fuchs's journey. It was the British who were to get all the glory. Fuchs set out from the Weddell Sea on the far side of the Antarctic in late November 1957. A month earlier, five New Zealanders led by Hillary had left Scott Base to establish the depots on the New Zealand side, stopping 500 miles short of the Pole to await Fuchs's arrival, as instructed. Their only role thereafter was to guide the British team back to Scott Base.

As soon as Hillary realized that Fuchs was behind schedule, however, and still nowhere near the Pole, he put pressure on his companions to carry on to the Pole, deliberately creating the impression of a Scott Amundsen–style race. Fuchs, with his slow, expensive Sno-Cats costing £8,000 apiece, was the ponderous old imperial power.[22] The New Zealand team led by Hillary, driving ordinary farm tractors costing £700 each and cleverly adapted for polar travel, was the speedy little dominion opponent. Fuchs sent him furious messages telling him to stop. He ignored them all. "I just would read their messages and carry on."[23]

Hillary arrived at the Pole on January 3, long before Fuchs. "Sir Edmund Hillary, the conqueror of Mount Everest, and his dead-tired Polar Expedition reached the South Pole today," the *Chicago Daily News* announced. "They were winners of an Antarctic Race and the first men to trek to the pole in 46 years." Fuchs reached the Pole more than two weeks later, completely upstaged and made to appear foolish and slow, while Hillary basked in glory. Hillary's maverick behavior was played down by the deferential British press,[24] but it was reported in the foreign press and often criticized as an egocentric publicity stunt. Writing in *Paris Match*, well-known French journalist Raymond Cartier observed: "Few men have come into contact with [Hillary] without having reason to complain of his egocentricity . . . One knew he would want to go to the Pole and that he would be pushed into it by the chauvinistic clamour of his country."[25]

Fuchs eventually made it to Scott Base on March 2, having traveled the full 2,158 miles across the Antarctic continent.

Hillary admitted that he had been lucky to get away with his escapade. He arrived at the Pole with scarcely any fuel to spare. He had taken risks with his own life and those of his teammates when he dumped his emergency tents, camping gear, and ration boxes en route, to save weight.[26] If he had made even a minor navigational error, his petrol would have run out and he would have had to continue on foot across the icy wastes in the cruel polar weather, without the right equipment and without enough food. No doubt he could have summoned up air support if he had run into serious problems, but he was still sailing close to the wind. "I thought the race was great fun," he recalled later, "although I was scared stiff at the time."

Pugh followed the unfolding drama from the radio room at Scott Base. He had been critical of Fuchs himself, deploring his old-fashioned food supplies and clumsy scientific equipment. Far from being shocked by Hillary's behavior, he found it highly entertaining, and did not seem concerned that it was rather foolhardy and egotistical. His only criticism was that Hillary had "made mistakes in the difficult art of leadership and was not sufficiently frank about his intentions early on." Pugh was even prepared to overlook the fact that Hillary had upset the scientists in his team by requisitioning their tractors for his race to the Pole, preventing some of them from undertaking the once-in-a-lifetime research projects they had come out for.[27] He failed to spot any warning signs for his own planned collaboration with Hillary.

20

Everest without Oxygen

Hillary returned home from Antarctica in April 1958, "rather shaken" by the "violent" press criticism of his maverick race for the South Pole.[1] Stung by the thought that some people now considered him not a hero but a mere publicity seeker and opportunist, his first instinct was to give up his adventurous lifestyle, find a "responsible position in business or society," and transform himself into a "reliable family man." But he soon discovered, as he said, that "the ability to get a tractor to the South Pole didn't count for much in business." The "directorships and good government jobs" he hoped for did not materialize, and apart from lecturing and writing books, he was reduced to his former occupation—beekeeping. After a few months he began to get itchy feet.

In April of 1959, Griffith Pugh sent him an outline proposal for the joint expedition they had discussed the previous year. The very first sentence left no doubt about the eye-catching historic goal Pugh had in mind. "The primary mountaineering objective," he wrote, "would be to climb [Everest] without the use of oxygen equipment." And Pugh went on to emphasize, repeatedly, that he considered climbing Everest without oxygen to be a perfectly achievable goal: "I believe that with at least six months' preparation and personnel of proven ability to tolerate extreme altitude, the mountain could be climbed without oxygen equipment."[2]

The main scientific purpose behind this exercise was to test whether climbers, with six months of acclimatization, would become better adapted to altitude. This would mean staying at high altitude for most of the winter before attempting Everest the following spring, and it raised the obvious question of how to survive in the high mountains at the most inclement time of the year.

Pugh's proposed solution was to provide two huts for the team to live in—one at the foot of the Khumbu Glacier at around 18,000 feet, on the south side of Everest, and the other at 20,000 feet, on the Western Cwm just above the notorious Khumbu Icefall. The huts would be comfortably fitted out and—like the huts that had so impressed Pugh in Antarctica and at the White Mountain Station in the Sierra Nevada—would have all the facilities necessary for a reasonable standard of comfort and recreation.

The acclimatization program would begin with a three-month period in the autumn, living at "intermediate" altitudes of around 13,000 feet, near Sherpa villages. Over the winter the climbers and the scientists observing them would move higher up and spend a further three to four months alternating between the two high camps, attempting to achieve what Pugh described as "complete acclimatization" at 20,000 feet.

Toward the end of the program, a climbing party using supplementary oxygen would go ahead and forge a route all the way to the summit of Everest, putting in ropes and establishing and supplying the necessary high-altitude camps. Then, the star climbers would attempt the summit *without* oxygen, using the high camps and the prepared route.

Hillary seemed enthusiastic. But he was not prepared to return to the Nepalese side of Everest. Nor did he think he could raise the necessary funds: "I find the thought of returning to Everest from the South a rather dull one, and in any case I'm damned if I know if I could raise much cash for a large-scale expedition that would be required, seeing the thing's been done several times before. The same might also apply to Makalu . . . although I would quite like a crack at that mountain."[3] In late 1958, Hillary had applied to the Chinese for permission to attempt Everest from the north, though he and Pugh both knew that there was no real chance of his application succeeding.

Hillary's lack of enthusiasm for repeating the 1953 route was well known to Pugh. The Everest hero's fame as a high-altitude climber rested entirely on that one successful ascent. An attempt by the same route without oxygen—should it fail—would do his climbing reputation no favors. "It would have been difficult for Ed being in the public eye on Everest again," one of his close friends explained. "For one thing, the public would have expected him to get to the top."[4]

A joint expedition with Pugh to a different destination like Makalu did have its attractions, however. Sensitive about his perceived lack of gravitas, Hillary was tempted by the idea of associating himself with an expedition which, because it had serious scientific objectives, would not be dismissed as just another self-indulgent sporting adventure, and would confer respectability on all those involved.

At the same time, the other strand in Hillary's character—the part of him that loved unfussy, inexpensive, Shipton-style expeditions—was pulling him in a different direction. He was tempted to turn his back on the Himalayan giants, and opt instead for a cheaper climbing expedition with the New Zealand Alpine Club, to a lower, unclimbed Himalayan peak. "Would you be interested physiologically in an expedition to a 25,100-foot peak in 1961?" he asked Pugh.

None of this fitted with Pugh's adventurous concept, however, and he was single-minded in either flatly ignoring Hillary's demurrals or sweeping them aside as if they were irrelevant. He had his eyes firmly fixed on Everest. But, while his six-page plan gave the impression that the central aim of the expedition was to address one of the biggest challenges in mountaineering, in fact, the scientific side of the expedition was also hugely ambitious. If it came off, it promised to be the crowning achievement of his career.

The only people who had spent significant time at or above 20,000 feet were mountaineers who had shown that it was possible to remain relatively healthy at this height for as long as four to six weeks. On the other hand, most of the climbers who went above 23,000 feet and remained there for more than a few days found they deteriorated rapidly, with the deterioration increasing as they went higher. Whether these limits would remain the same if people spent longer at intermediate heights, adjusting to altitude, was not known. Pugh was determined to find out.

Mountaineers were not the only people who stood to benefit from a better understanding of the physiology of acclimatization. Pugh estimated that there were at least 10 million people working or living permanently at heights of 12,000 feet, mostly in South America and Tibet.[5] At sea level, too, there were compelling medical and scientific reasons for studying the impact of high altitude on the human body.

Lowland people suffering from chronic illnesses such as heart disease, bronchitis, and emphysema lived with long-term deprivation of oxygen. Lacking a comprehensive understanding of what happens to the healthy body when deprived of oxygen over a long period of time, it was hard for physicians to distinguish which of their symptoms were caused by their bodies adapting—"acclimatizing"—to the shortage of oxygen, and which were the direct result of their illnesses. Anesthetists handling patients in intensive care units also required a better understanding of the impact of oxygen lack on the healthy body, as did engineers designing pressurization and oxygen equipment for high-flying aircraft and space capsules.

There were crucial gaps in the scientific knowledge, and yet there had only been a handful of major scientific expeditions to high altitude in the first half of the twentieth century. Each of them had made important contributions, but none had lasted for more than a few weeks, and very little research had been carried out above 18,000 feet. Twenty-five years had elapsed since the last landmark expedition, which went to Aucanquilcha in the Chilean Andes in 1935, with Bruce Dill of the Harvard Fatigue Laboratory as the scientific director.[6] Dill's team spent several weeks studying their own responses to altitude, at heights up to 20,140 feet. But most of the research at their highest camp had to be carried out by the only two members of the team who felt well enough—Ancel Keys, a physiologist from Harvard, and the youthful Bryan Matthews, then a Cambridge undergraduate, who later became the redoubtable head of the Everest High-Altitude Committee. They stayed at the top camp for only ten days. Pugh had done his own studies at heights up to 21,200 feet on Cho Oyu and Everest, and the pioneering gentleman scientist Alexander Kellas had experimented for short periods at similar heights on the Himalayan mountain of Kamet in the early part of the century.

An intriguing part of the Andes expedition of 1935 was the interest the researchers took in the lives of a group of miners at the village of Quilcha, at 17,500 feet. The village was 1,500 feet below the sulphur mine where the miners worked. It took them one and a half hours to climb up on foot to go to work and 25 minutes to come down, yet they refused to accept accommodation at 18,500 feet, just below the mine. They preferred to expend all the extra time and effort getting to work, rather than living higher up where they suffered loss of weight and appetite and an inability to sleep. Many physiologists concluded from this evidence that a height of around 17,500 feet was the limit at which people could live permanently.

There were wonderful opportunities to do pioneering research, but Pugh's proposal relied heavily on finding sponsors interested in the prospect of the great Sir Edmund Hillary climbing Everest without oxygen. The largest sum Pugh had ever raised on his own account was £2,300.[7] But now he boldly suggested to Hillary that they should attempt to raise £50,000—the equivalent of roughly £900,000 today.[8] Hillary knew that would be difficult, and suggested introducing some popular theme, like a search for the Yeti.[9] However, as time went on, he appeared to lose interest, brushing Pugh off with the words: "Frankly, Griff, I haven't been very optimistic about financial backing for the Everest job, and my thoughts have been turning in a rather different direction."

Then, after a silence of over two months, Pugh received a letter from Hillary in the United States announcing, out of the blue, that he had raised the money from an American source—"£40,000 or more"—enough to "do some excellent physiological research, have a look for the Yeti, and do some damn good climbing."[10] And he wanted Pugh to join him. "The question is—If I get the finance for this trip will you come in with me on it? . . . YES or NO . . . If I get the money and you aren't interested, I'd like your advice anyway, but hope you'd be in it hammer and tongs!"

Pugh cabled an immediate response: ACCEPT ENTHUSIASTICALLY AND COUNT ON MRC SUPPORT.[11]

Hillary's sponsor was Field Enterprises Educational Corporation, wealthy American publishers of *World Book Encyclopedia*. Hillary had been in New York to receive an award when Field Enterprises had invited him to their headquarters in Chicago to take part in an educational television program. Dining one evening with the public relations director, John Dienhart, Hillary mentioned his "dream" of combining a serious study of acclimatization with a Yeti-hunting expedition in the Himalayas. Dienhart leapt at the idea.[12]

Hillary did not involve Pugh in the negotiations, which won him a grant of £42,000. Telling Pugh not to "worry too much about the details," he wrote his own expedition plan that was similar to Pugh's but with two key differences. Where Pugh had tried to sell the expedition as a climbing venture, Hillary hardly mentioned the climbing. His key objectives were the Yeti hunt, and the research into extended acclimatization, which he claimed to have been working on with "Dr. Griffith Pugh, the eminent research physiologist of the British Medical Research Council."[13]

The first mention of climbing appeared only at the bottom of the second page, in Hillary's description of the "Physiological Program," where he explained that the team would attempt an oxygen-free ascent of Makalu to test how well they had adapted to high altitude. He justified opting for Makalu, rather than Everest, by saying he thought it better to try out the theory that Everest could be climbed without oxygen "on a lesser giant before putting it to the ultimate test." But he did not adopt Pugh's plan to have climbers with oxygen prepare a route to the summit in advance of the attempt without oxygen. This was to be a completely oxygen-free attempt.

The subject that took real pride of place in Hillary's proposal, however, was the hunt for the Yeti, or "Abominable Snowman." Belief in the existence of this mythical, giant, hairy, man-like creature of the Himalayas was widespread among the Sherpas. There were numerous stories of Sherpa sightings of Yetis, but none of European sightings, although both Europeans and Sherpas had seen strange humanoid footprints in the snow, thought to be Yeti tracks, in remote mountainous areas. After the Everest reconnaissance in 1951, Michael Ward and Eric Shipton had taken some exceptionally clear photographs of "Yeti footprints" near the Rolwaling Valley, which had generated huge fascination in Europe and America.

There had already been several Yeti hunts, including one in 1954 by the Everest cameraman Tom Stobart and the *Daily Mail* journalist Ralph Izzard.[14] But Hillary promised that his Yeti hunt would be superior to all previous efforts, requiring "a far greater degree of mountaineering skill and ruggedness than the ordinary Yeti party, and probably a great deal more patience." Yeti hunting was just the kind of "publicity stunt" that Alpine Club members frowned upon. Michael Ward—the first person Pugh invited onto the expedition—was concerned about being associated with it.[15] Pugh, on the contrary, thought it was an inspired way of "inducing the climbers to spend a long time at altitude."

Pugh was worried, however, that Hillary might not fully appreciate the scale of his scientific ambition. He wanted his side of the expedition to be a world-class scientific venture. His worst fear was that it might degenerate into a repetition of Cho Oyu or Everest—"just another climbing expedition with a physiologist attached."[16] When Hillary came to England in October, Pugh made him promise that physiology would be a "primary objective," and that the climbers would be required to "collaborate in the physiological work throughout the expedition."[17]

Having raised the money, Hillary assumed the role of overall leader of the expedition, and Field Enterprises gave him carte blanche to choose the team, except for two experts—Marlin Perkins, the director of Chicago's Lincoln Park Zoo, and Dr. Larry Swann, a biologist from San Francisco State College—who were included to give the Yeti hunt some gravitas. As leader of the scientific side, Pugh was acutely aware of the need to recruit "a strong enough physiological team to do a first-class job." Hillary let him select his own three scientists, plus Michael Ward.

Pugh went for younger men, who would find it easier to tolerate a grueling winter at high altitude. Perhaps he also wanted to avoid facing any personal challenges from contemporaries with better paper qualifications. He did not advertise, and the process was very informal. Two of the three recruits simply heard about the expedition on the grapevine and volunteered themselves.

This was true of John West, a gifted twenty-nine-year-old Australian respiratory physiologist from Hammersmith Hospital Postgraduate Medical School. Pugh took him on after one interview despite his lack of either climbing or high-altitude experience. Dr. Jim Milledge, a registrar in respiratory medicine at Southampton Hospital, and a climber with Himalayan experience, also volunteered. The third scientist, Dr. Sukhamay Lahiri, was studying for a doctor of philosophy degree at the famous "Oxford School" of physiology, which had been doing research into the way the body controls breathing at high altitude ever since the heyday of Professor J. S. Haldane. The two leading lights of the department, Dan Cunningham and Bryan Lloyd (under whom Lahiri was studying), had developed sophisticated tools of analysis and had collaborated with Pugh before, lending him equipment, advising him on techniques, and analyzing samples he had brought home in sealed ampoules from the Himalayas.

Leading a group of young scientists on a complex project under testing conditions was a daunting prospect for a man who was not regarded as a team player. But Pugh's recruits turned out to be as ambitious and perfectionist as he was.

When, in July 1960, they gathered to train and to collect baseline data from the members of the expedition, Pugh expected them to keep up with him intellectually, even on unfamiliar territory. He would accept only the highest of standards, but they admired his rigor and matched it with their own. They teased him about his absentmindedness and reacted calmly to his outbursts of temper: "When he occasionally lost his temper," Milledge and Ward later recalled, "it was like a flash flood, overwhelming at first and then disappearing without trace."[18] John West thought him "a very lovable person"; Sukhamay Lahiri found him "gracious and considerate"; and Milledge remembered affectionately: "Fifteen months closely associated with Griff are among the happiest in my life."[19] Pugh, in turn, rose above the awkward side of his nature and became an inspirational leader and mentor.

In December 1959, Hillary had flown to Kathmandu and secured permission from the Nepalese government to attempt Makalu in the record time of four days.

Though it seemed contradictory to Pugh's plan, Hillary had decided not to remain at high altitude over the winter himself. He planned to lead the Yeti hunt in the autumn of 1960, establish the scientists and climbers in their winter quarters, and then return to New Zealand, rejoining the expedition with a team of fresh climbers in the spring. The performances of the fresh climbers could then be compared with those of the men who had been at high altitude all winter.

Like Pugh, Hillary was fascinated by the question of how to accommodate the winter team. The higher of the two high-altitude huts, where most of the scientific work would take place, would need to house a laboratory and provide comfortable living quarters for up to eight people. It would have to be strong enough to withstand violent winter storms, yet light enough for Sherpas to carry.

Hillary favored a wire-and-canvas structure, but Pugh maintained that good science could only be done properly at high altitude in comfortable surroundings.[20] He insisted on a prefabricated hut to be assembled on-site, and then worked for six months on the design with Ezra Levin, chief architect of the Timber Development Association.[21]

The result was a tunnel-shaped structure made up of about 100 component parts, each weighing roughly 46 pounds. The finished hut, made of 4-inch-thick plywood panels insulated with plastic foam, was nearly 23 feet long and 10 feet wide. The outside was painted silver to provide further insulation, and it soon became known as the Silver Hut. When Hillary came to London in May 1960, he, Pugh, and several other members of the team did a trial run of assembling it. True to character Hillary viewed it as a race, writing afterward that "the dour little foreman" had expected the job to take seventeen hours. "But he had underestimated the skills and resourcefulness of my party. In six hours of vigorous labour we had everything up, and a fine job it looked too."[22] Afterward they all went to tea with John Hunt at his house in Henley-on-Thames.

As overall leader, Hillary undertook the basic organization for the expedition, buying food, fuel, supplies, and equipment, and arranging for transport. Pugh was intensely busy planning the scientific program and assembling the huge amount of equipment required. He also designed the high-altitude rations for the assault on Makalu and procured oxygen equipment for research and emergency rescue.

The preparations were going well, until, in early August 1960, Pugh noticed newspaper reports about the expedition that touched a very raw nerve indeed. Hillary, it seemed, had been telling journalists that the scientific side of the expedition was his own concept, and that Pugh was merely his adviser—his "senior physiologist."

Pugh had entered into what he had understood to be a jointly conceived expedition. Hillary had secured the financial backing, but without Pugh he could not deliver the scientific program. It was Pugh's status as an acclaimed physiologist with unique experience of Himalayan research that had attracted first-rate scientists and won the collaboration of the MRC and the Oxford School. Now Pugh feared that he was about to be the victim of a replay of the Everest experience at the hands of John Hunt. In an indignant letter to Hillary he told him that he had found the newspaper reports "distressing," and threatened to resign if his status wasn't properly recognized.

So please send me assurance (a) that you will see that my position and work for the expedition are properly recognised, and (b) that I am referred to not as Senior Physiologist, which, so far as the press is concerned, means the oldest physiologist, but as Director of Medicine and Physiology for the expedition . . . I have come to feel that this is so important to the success of the physiological programme that I cannot allow any MRC equipment to be shipped until I get your answer.

Pugh also wanted the authority that went with the title. His experience on Cho Oyu had convinced him that he must have full control over everything that would impact on his work. Success depended on the proper management of the expedition as a whole—facilities, food, hygiene, discipline. Therefore, he wanted explicit acknowledgment that he would be overall leader during the winter while Hillary was away. "In your absence this can only be me," he wrote. "As you know, dear Ed," Pugh entreated, "I have always had the highest personal regard for you, and I feel sure you will understand my point of view."

In subsequent private correspondence Hillary reluctantly acknowledged Pugh as "Director of Physiology and Medical Services," but in public he repeatedly referred to him as "my senior physiologist." The issue of who would be in charge during Hillary's absence continued to fester until the expedition was well under way.

21

"Only If I Have Complete Control"

With less than a year to prepare for such a complex project, Pugh was overburdened with work in the months before his departure, and paid less attention to home life than ever. Throughout this time he received the usual devoted support from Doey, who understood how much the expedition—which promised to be the greatest achievement of his career—meant to him. She made no fuss about the length of the trip and fiercely backed him when he took issue with Hillary about leadership during the winter.

He did not get to Kathmandu until the main part of the expedition had already left. Hillary and his Yeti hunters, equipped with trip wires, tranquilizer guns, "mating horns," microphones, rifles, cameras, and telescopes, had set off for the remote Rolwaling Valley, 12 miles southwest of the Everest area. Norman Hardie, the experienced New Zealand climber, whom Hillary had persuaded to take on the logistics for Pugh's winter project, was on his way to the Mingbo Valley with a train of 310 porters. Hillary felt Pugh should have been in Kathmandu in time to supervise the arrangements for this complex carry, which included precious scientific equipment as well as the Silver Hut parts.[1]

When Pugh finally reached Kathmandu and started to prepare the second baggage train, he did not find everything to his liking. He wanted radio contact with Kathmandu during the winter, both for emergencies and for ordering spare parts from London, but Hillary had failed to get a permit for a shortwave radio transmitter. He also thought that the rations Hillary had procured were deficient, and wanted to establish a helicopter link between Kathmandu and Mingbo to deliver supplies of fresh food. The plastic jerry cans Hillary had used for storing the fuel supplies were leaky too. A despairing note in his diary records his reaction: "Disaster! . . . The plastic paraffin containers . . . will never stand up to winter conditions. Even gentle pressure on the seams is enough to split them. We shall have to get 84 ordinary tin 4 gall[on] containers to replace them . . . whenever shall I get away? . . . Cannot leave until this problem is solved as our hut will be untenable without fuel."[2]

By the time he had procured the cans, Pugh had made yet another exasperating discovery—Hillary's choice of down clothing did not match up to his own high standards: "Putting on my NZ down jacket for the first time I am horrified to find it has no hood, no down in the arms & open sleeves. [The] protection against great cold [it offers] may be adequate for men cutting steps but certainly not for light activity."[3] On top of being too lightweight, the outer jacket did not fit him properly: "The windproof outer garments are of poor quality & sleeves of mine much too short. The old mistake over 'sizing' which was a feature of the Cho Oyu expedition & completely avoided on Everest."

After shepherding his baggage train to Mingbo, Pugh finally caught up with Hillary once the Yeti hunt was over. There were several climbers in Hillary's eleven-man party, including Mike Gill, a New Zealand medical student; Tom Nevison, a US Air Force physiologist; and Hillary's great friends, Peter Mulgrew and George Lowe. Mulgrew had been with him on his dash to the Pole. The Yeti hunters had trekked back from the Rolwaling Valley over the Tesi Lapcha pass and were in the village of Khumjung near Namche Bazar to inspect a famous Yeti scalp.

The hunt had not produced any firm evidence of the existence of the Abominable Snowman. The most disappointing find had come when the hunters followed fox tracks over a ridge onto a sunny slope where they expanded into beautiful "Yeti footprints." As soon as the tracks passed into the shade on the other side of the slope, they shrank back into fox tracks. It was only the intense heat of the sun on the contours of the tracks that had melted them into what looked like Yeti footprints.

Refusing to be discouraged, they had collected various Yeti relics, including some supposed Yeti skins, one of which was judged to be similar to the skin of a blue bear. The Khumjung Yeti scalp, a prized possession of the village, promised to be the star relic, although the press officer, British-born journalist Desmond Doig, and Marlin Perkins, the naturalist from the Chicago Zoo, both suspected even this of being a man-made artifact.[4] Despite their doubts, Hillary was intending to take the scalp and the other relics on a whirlwind trip to be examined by experts in Chicago, New York, and London.

After a brief stay at Khumjung the full expedition moved over to Changmatang, near Thyangboche, where Hardie had established a low camp and store next to the path leading to the Mingbo Valley. On Hillary's instructions Hardie had also put in a base camp at the bottom of the Mingbo Valley, and built the lower of the two high-altitude huts further up the valley—a staging post for the route to the Silver Hut, which would be constructed at the head of the valley. Pugh approved of the low storage camp and was delighted with the high-altitude hut, but he was not at all happy with the base camp, which he considered to be "on a thoroughly bad site with no level ground." "I think I can make a success of my part of the expedition," he wrote to Doey, "but only if I have complete control."[5]

At the earliest opportunity, he tackled Hillary about the base camp, the helicopter, and radio, and crucially about the question of leadership in the winter, which had still not been resolved. Irritated perhaps by Pugh's late arrival, Hillary prevaricated. Pugh reported to Doey that he had achieved "inconclusive results all round."

Hillary was eager to press on with the work, and the largest remaining job was the erection of the Silver Hut. So he gathered together a handful of willing helpers and set off for the upper glacier without inviting Pugh to go with him. He was exhilarated at the prospect of heading up the mountain, and his companions had to struggle to keep up with him.[6]

A few weeks earlier, Hardie, charged with carrying the Silver Hut parts up to the 19,600-foot Mingbo La, the pass at the head of the valley where the hut was to be built, had immediately realized that the site was wholly unsuitable.[7] The access, up fluted ice-avalanche runnels, was steep and dangerous, and the pass itself was excessively windy and lacking in shelter. After one sleepless night on the pass, in a flapping tent during a howling gale, Hillary conceded they should look for an alternative.

The next morning they chose a less-exposed position on the Mingbo Glacier at 19,000 feet, "on a small snow field . . . protected from avalanche danger by a large open crevasse." By the end of the day they had created a platform for the hut; the next day they put together the hut's tubular outer shell.[8]

Pugh, having received, as he put it, "no encouragement to join [the] hut party and no information about intentions," had remained down at Changmatang with his nose a little out of joint.[9] In Hillary's absence he gossiped with Marlin Perkins and Desmond Doig about the New Zealander's leadership qualities (or lack of them), and confided in a letter to Doey that Hillary's habit of rushing off to do things without explaining his intentions was irritating the "older" members of the team: "He seems unable to delegate authority & yet does not communicate his plans so none of us know where we are."[10] Hillary, he complained, did not understand the needs of the "older and more experienced men" in the party—as opposed to the younger climbers.

The irritation led to unkind banter about Hillary's apparent brashness and boorishness.[11] Pugh quoted Doig saying that he was fed up with the low level of conversation permitted at Hillary's table: "Talk is entirely anecdotal and intensely boring, any attempt to introduce new topics being frowned upon." Pugh himself speculated, perhaps a little ungenerously, that Hillary was refusing to agree to the radio and helicopter links because he did not want the scientists to attract any attention to themselves during the winter by talking to journalists in Kathmandu. "I expect he feels ashamed secretly about going back [to New Zealand for the winter] and wants to keep things as dark as possible while he is away."[12] Suspecting Hillary of being more concerned with his public image than with the task at hand, he wrote: "Ed is a hopeless leader but good at forging on. He turns out to be much too small a man for an expedition like this."[13]

When the news came through that "Ed has abandoned the top camp site and is looking for a new one," Pugh determined to go up on his own and watch the hut being built. But as soon as he was high enough up the valley to get a view of the top of the glacier, he saw that "the hut had already been erected." He was furious that Hillary had changed the position without consulting him. To make matters worse, again without consulting Pugh, Hillary then ordered Jim Milledge—one of Pugh's young recruits—to take charge of fitting out the interior of the hut.

These were only two of many slights Pugh felt he suffered in the first two weeks. He and several others had contracted serious stomach upsets, which Pugh blamed on the "disgusting hygiene" Hillary was permitting in camp. When he pointed out that the cooking was being done in filthy surroundings with water from a dirty well, Hillary—echoing Shipton's reaction on Cho Oyu—snubbed him, and his suggestions for improvements were "met with disapproval."[14] Hillary also refused to plan the rations in the orderly way Pugh considered vital.

Pugh had spent weeks in London packing his complicated scientific equipment according to a meticulous system. Now, he complained, Hillary "has muddled up all my equipment in Kathmandu . . . destroying all the careful work which has gone into classifying it." Hillary had ordered Milledge and Nevison to repack the equipment into Sherpa loads, rather than asking Gill, who understood the system.[15] Then it emerged that the two delicate gas analyzers—Pugh's most vital instruments—had been accidentally smashed on the march to Mingbo.[16] Without them the physiology could not begin.

As tensions mounted, the atmosphere became "very sticky," particularly at mealtimes. "I have been repeatedly snubbed before the rest of the party," Pugh complained bitterly in his notes. "It seems I am not to be consulted in any way."[17]

Eventually, things came to a head. After many hours alone in his tent, drafting and redrafting what he wanted to say, Pugh squared up and told Hillary all his complaints—the plastic fuel containers, the food supplies, the clothing, the failure to consult him, the disgusting hygiene, the radio, the helicopter, and, worst of all, Hillary's refusal to acknowledge him as the scientific leader. Hillary must agree—in writing, Pugh insisted—that Pugh would have full control of the expedition in Hillary's absence, including the movement of men, work program, money, and news. If he refused, Pugh would pack up and take his scientists home. Warming to his subject, he then went further. Betraying one of the less-appealing aspects of his fiery temperament, he indulged in some wounding remarks about Hillary's leadership qualities.

His criticisms hit home hard enough to merit a place in Hillary's autobiography of 1975, where the New Zealander described the force of Pugh's attack: "Pugh approached me, opened his notebook, and reeled off a long and detailed list of my various weaknesses and inadequacies. My incompetence as a leader was beyond belief, but what could you expect from someone without a suitable background and education . . . it was a frightening declaration—like God summing up on judgement day."[18] Hillary added, "This was a most devastating criticism and I had been largely unaware of my transgressions."

Whether or not he was hurt by Pugh's tirade, Hillary refused to discuss it. Pugh's diary records only the briefest of composed but blunt responses to his litany of complaints: "Hillary listened patiently, and then told me I could go." Faced with an impasse, Pugh sidestepped by demanding that Hillary give him a "written release" from all his obligations to the expedition. But Hillary refused, saying: "Oh, I'm not such a mug as that."[19]

Pugh continued to press for a written release. They repaired to the quarters of Marlin Perkins and Desmond Doig—a walled shelter with a polythene tarpaulin roof and animal skins on the floor over a base of fir branches. There, hidden from view, diplomatic negotiations took place, conducted mainly by Perkins, with assistance from Doig. Both clearly sympathized with Pugh. The outcome was that Hillary agreed to all of Pugh's demands and, most importantly, promised to acknowledge explicitly that Pugh was in sole charge of the scientific program and would be acting leader of the expedition in his absence.

Hillary later admitted with disarming frankness: "When I examined the situation conscientiously I realised that Griff had some basis for his dissatisfaction. He had been closely involved in the designing of the Silver Hut but because he hadn't been up on the glacier with us I had not thought to consult him on its final location or its erection . . . I determined to give more consideration to his wishes and feelings."[20]

The negotiations in the tent were not altogether one-sided. Hillary refused to allow the base camp to be moved unless Pugh lent him the 800 rupees he needed to make up the deposit of 8,000 rupees which the villagers of Khumjung had demanded for the loan of their Yeti scalp.[21] According to Pugh's diary, the villagers' other condition was that Hillary should build them a school.[22]

Within hours of their confrontation, Pugh and Hillary had apparently recovered a perfectly amicable relationship, trekking up the valley together companionably to discuss the layout of the new base camp at 15,200 feet, at the summer village of Mingbo, two and a half hours' walk above Chang-matang. It was "a jewel of a place set in a hollow in the giant moraine round Ama Dablam," Pugh reported in his diary.

The village consisted of a few stone huts and about an acre of level pasture, divided by stone walls into small hay fields and protective enclosures. The expedition rented three of the huts, which were normally only used in the monsoon season, when the villagers from lower down the valley brought up their yaks to graze in the high pastures. Pugh wrote home that "relations with Ed [are on a] pretty good footing again."

Before Hillary left Mingbo, he publicly handed over the leadership to Pugh, and Pugh walked out to Thyangboche with him to say a final goodbye. Later, Hillary sent Pugh a friendly letter from Kathmandu reporting that he had had a positive meeting with a contact of Pugh's about the radio permit, and that he had arranged for the first helicopter visit. Arrangements had also been made for replacement gas analyzers to be brought out from England by two of Pugh's winter scientists, John West and Michael Ward, who were expected to arrive in mid-December. A gift of a bottle of whiskey accompanied the letter, and Hillary promised to send more in due course.

Now that he was in charge at last, the pall of anxiety lifted from Pugh's shoulders, and his natural optimism, love of his work, and pleasure in living outdoors in the mountains reasserted themselves. His letters and diary entries, no longer full of complaints, became infused with irrepressible delight in the way his project was taking shape, and in his "wonderfully beautiful" surroundings. He took daily two-hour walks, seeking out paths through the aromatic dwarf rhododendron scrub near Changmatang, finding "hidden valleys" with grassy pastures and birch woods with "long greenish-grey strands of lichen hanging from the branches"—"like an Arthur Rackham illustration from *Grimm's Fairy Tales*." He saw black musk deer, Thar goats, foxes, and many varieties of birds. There were splendid views of Everest and of the formidable Ama Dablam, a spectacular pointed peak overlooking the Mingbo Valley, which was shaped, Pugh wrote, "a little like the top part of the Matterhorn."

On November 25, Pugh moved into his new base camp with rented huts at tiny Mingbo Village. He treated Doey to an enthusiastic description of how climber Wally Romanes—recruited by Hillary partly because he was a skilled carpenter—had converted the huts into a kitchen, a store, and a mess, adding plastic sheeting to the flat stone and juniper-bough roofs, stopping up the chinks in the walls with mud, "brightening the inner walls with a pale grey wash," and, in one of them, installing a fireplace with a chimney made of petrol cans. The laboratory and most of the living quarters were accommodated in tents.[23] Romanes erected the laboratory tent—a yellow, twelve-man arctic dome tent—on top of a 2-foot stone wall, "so that there is plenty of headroom inside," and fitted it out with "two excellent work benches."

True to his axiom about the need for comfort at altitude, Pugh had brought along a special "caravan tent" for himself. This had separate compartments for living and sleeping, and he decorated it with hangings on the walls, a sheepskin rug on the floor, and a square of leopard skin, edged with red cloth, draped over the chair. At night the tent was lit with a propane lamp, and a charcoal brazier glowed cozily in the center of the floor, but it nearly gave Pugh carbon monoxide poisoning and had to be abandoned.[24]

Above Mingbo, an "energetic two- to three-hour pull" over rocky, stony ground took the climber up to the lower of the two high-altitude huts, known as the "Green Hut," on account of its green walls. Designed by Hillary and built by Wally Romanes, mostly with local materials, this wood-and-canvas structure stood in a stony trough next to a small lake. It was just below the snout of the Mingbo Glacier at 17,300 feet, and was mainly used as a transit camp on the way to and from the Silver Hut.

From the Green Hut it took the climbers another two and a half hours to wind their way up through the glacier icefall and climb the wide, sloping snowfield leading up to the Silver Hut. Curved and shiny in the bright mountain light, the Silver Hut was in a beautiful position on a crest at the edge of the snowfield, next to the exquisite fan-like cirque of steep fluted slopes which closed the head of the valley. Standing on jacks, it was firmly anchored down to its snowy knoll with wire guy ropes attached to ice-filled sacks countersunk 6 feet into the ground. Once Pugh had recovered from not being consulted about the site, he conceded it was in an excellent position.

After Hillary's departure, Pugh was left in the company of Jim Milledge, Wally Romanes, Mike Gill, Barry Bishop (a climber, photographer, and glaciologist employed by *National Geographic*), and Tom Nevison, the American physiologist recruited by Hillary—whom the others suspected of being sent by the Americans to spy on the Chinese.

Pugh's remaining three scientists, Michael Ward, John West, and Sukhamay Lahiri, arrived three weeks later on December 17, bearing the precious replacement gas analyzers. The winter team was completed by Captain Motwani, a doctor from the Indian army, which was concerned about the effects of altitude on their troops in Himalayan border posts. By this time most of the first group had already gone up to the Silver Hut, leaving Pugh at Mingbo, overseeing arrangements.

The Silver Hut was more comfortable than base camp. The entrance was sheltered by a porch, with interior and exterior doors to block out the wind and snow. Inside there were eight bunk beds fitted along the walls near the entrance, with the dining table extending down the center between them. The top bunks were set high enough to allow people to sit on the bottom bunks at the table in daytime. Each bunk was fitted with a comfortable foam mattress and an electric light so team members could read at night. The laboratory was at the far end, lit by a large window. Pugh had helped to design a special kerosene heater that would avoid any danger of carbon monoxide poisoning, and had searched out the best possible equipment to generate and store electricity—a wind generator erected on a 16-foot pole, plus a set of alkaline batteries.

The first time the whole team got together was on Christmas Day at the Silver Hut, which had been decked out with crimson and silver streamers. They spent the morning skiing on the snowfield and then returned to the hut for an elaborate Christmas lunch of mushroom soup, freeze-dried shrimp, roast lamb, fried yak, Christmas pudding, fresh oranges, and cherry brandy.[25]

Pugh produced Hillary's bottle of whiskey and presented the team with "a bulky green bag of mail." They did not know that he had mislaid a second bag which only turned up six weeks later. After lunch they toasted absent friends and sang songs. Pugh, who had limited tolerance for group jollity, left for the Green Hut long before it was over, having called an expedition meeting for the following morning at ten o'clock. There was to be no slacking on Boxing Day.

After Christmas the new arrivals returned with Pugh to base camp and spent three more weeks acclimatizing and finishing off the first phases of their research, before finally going up to live at the Silver Hut in mid-January. Pugh and Lahiri, who were both having difficulty adjusting to the altitude, did not join them until early February.

During the first weeks of the winter the temperature outside the hut was hardly ever colder than 5° Fahrenheit, and during the day the sun shone almost continuously. Even when clouds swelled and filled the Mingbo Valley in the afternoons, the sky high up usually remained clear. After the turn of the year it became steadily colder: Temperatures went down as low as –16°F, winds averaged 25 mph, and every month there would be a few days of stormy weather, with winds rising to 40 mph, gusting up to 75 mph, when the hut would rock like a train. One night, when Milledge and Gill were alone, the wind blew so hard they thought the guy ropes would rip loose and the hut would plunge down the glacier. The next day, they added extra guy ropes on all sides.

When Pugh and Lahiri finally went up to the hut, Pugh dug his own personal ice cave outside which he ventilated with a glass tube stuck through the roof. The cave remained at a constant temperature near freezing point, which he found more comfortable than the temperature inside the hut. He worked and skied happily with the team, but in the evenings he retired to his ice cave, leaving the others to their postprandial jollity and their games of bridge. They sensed that he preferred to keep himself slightly aloof but did not hold this against him. "I couldn't reiterate too strongly how happy a group we were in the Silver Hut through that winter," Mike Gill commented, and his view was enthusiastically endorsed by every scientist in Pugh's team.

Food supplies proved less of a problem than Pugh had feared. Their basic provisions included freeze-dried meat and vegetables, tinned foods, butter, chocolate, and cheese, which they kept cool in ice caves. In the autumn they had fresh mutton and yak meat, and fruit and vegetables brought up by local people. In the winter, fresh vegetables were occasionally flown in from Kathmandu after Hillary arranged for the winter party to build the Swiss Red Cross a makeshift airstrip at Mingbo. The Red Cross was in the area to help Tibetan refugees from Chinese Communist rule.

By December 28, Pugh, in full control and with his team settled in and working well together, had summed up progress in a letter to Josephine: "I am in full control here and am doing my best to keep everyone happy. So far everything is going smoothly and reasonably efficiently. Ed . . . has done everything possible to be helpful since we had that row in November, but I am afraid I shall never really trust him again. I don't think he ever really understood what a scientific expedition involves."[26]

22

Winter in the Silver Hut

One day toward the end of January, a strange man walked into base camp at Mingbo. A small, slight figure, he was wearing a red turban, a short black jacket, cotton trousers, and a shirt, and he was barefoot in spite of the cold and the snow. The man asked if he could stay for a month, promising he wouldn't need much food—only a small amount of meat and a little milk. Pugh was not prepared to allow him to remain since he had no warm clothing, sleeping bag, or shoes, and the temperatures at night were often as low as 14° Fahrenheit. Giving him a bar of dried meat and offering him some money, he told the man to go down and spend the night at the expedition's camp at Changmatang, where it would be warmer.

But the man refused to leave, instead turning his face westward and beginning to pray volubly. Surprisingly he was still at Mingbo the next morning, having spent the night in the Sherpas' hut. They had tried to make him go away, but he refused, telling them that they could kill him if they chose. The Sherpas suspected him of being a Chinese spy, one pointing to a bullet scar on the man's hand and some khaki clothing in his scant bundle. They were implacable that he could not remain at the camp, so in the end he left, but instead of going down he set off uphill toward the Mingbo Glacier. The next day he was seen by some of the Sherpas, wandering barefoot in the snow near the Green Hut. Still refusing to go down, he told them he had spent the night sheltering under a rock.

Three days later a violent snowstorm developed. The temperature inside the laboratory tent dipped below 14°F. That night, Pugh, lying in his warm sleeping bag listening to the harsh wind outside, felt so guilty that he couldn't sleep. At first light, fearing the man was already dead, he took two Sherpas, rushed up onto the glacier, and began a frantic search. After a miserable and fruitless day they returned to Mingbo only to find the man sitting by the cookhouse, looking perfectly healthy, having survived for several days on the glacier without food and only such water as he could get from eating snow. At night he had slept in the lee of a rock covered by his meager overcoat, yet he had no trace of frostbite. This astonishing feat of endurance entirely changed everyone's attitude toward him. The Sherpas recognized him as a holy pilgrim, and Pugh, seizing a research opportunity, agreed to let the man stay for two weeks on condition that he participate in some physiological tests.

Pugh was fascinated. His previous research had suggested that people were better able to survive exposure to cold if they were fat, yet this man was very thin. He turned out to be a Nepalese carpenter named Man Badhur, from a village a few valleys away. Blessed with a religious revelation the year before, he had been living ever since on a simple diet of fruit, raw meat, milk, and tea, until, only four weeks past, a second religious revelation had brought him to the Mingbo Valley on the present pilgrimage.

Pugh carried out a battery of experiments to find out how he survived the cold. He consumed only about 600 calories per day but had a curious habit of eating glass, showing a marked preference for microscope slides and pipettes, and eventually had to be restrained from devouring their precious supplies.

The tests did not reveal any magical ability to tolerate cold but rather what Pugh described as "an exceptionally fine adjustment of normal physiological processes" as compared with the "coarse" responses of most people. Exposed to intense cold, a person's usual reaction is a fivefold rise in metabolism, with violent bouts of shivering as the body tries to warm itself. Blood retreats to the trunk to protect the vital organs, predisposing the bloodless hands and feet to frostbite. Man Badhur's metabolism, however, increased only half as much as a normal person's, albeit enough to keep his body at a sustainable temperature, and his blood did not retreat from his extremities. This much more apt response to cold allowed him to sleep comfortably without the temperatures of his hands and feet falling to dangerous levels.[1]

Pugh's study of Man Badhur was an interesting diversion from the main research program, which had set out to establish the highest altitude to which people could become fully acclimatized, and to investigate how altitude affects the body over an extended period. The Silver Hut was only about 4,000 feet higher than the base camp at Mingbo, but the impact of this relatively small increase in altitude proved far greater than expected. Most of the young scientists adapted easily to the altitude at Mingbo, but all were "challenged" by living in the Silver Hut, where the pressure of oxygen in the air was about half what it is at sea level. They had to descend from time to time to recuperate. John West described what it felt like:

You are constantly aware of shortness of breath, and even a small effort such as sitting up in the bunk at night left you panting for breath for a couple of minutes. There was a marked loss of initiative so that it was always difficult to start new projects. Memory was poor and people made a lot of arithmetical and other errors. We found that we could carry out experiments if the protocol was clearly defined, especially if there was a checklist, but problem solving when there was an unexpected situation was slow and difficult.[2]

Everyone at the Silver Hut found their appetite was poor and they lost weight and muscle bulk relentlessly—at a rate of between 1 and 3 pounds a week. For that reason alone they probably could not have remained there indefinitely. Minor infections and injuries such as cuts were slow to heal. In the early days they suffered bouts of uneven breathing at night. West later wrote that it was like "having some sort of chronic, grumbling disease; nothing is really working as well as it should."[3]

No one had spent such long periods at high altitude before, and Pugh was acutely aware of the risk of his men suffering permanent damage. He was particularly concerned that they should not stay high without breaks for longer than was good for them, simply out of bravado. "The object is to produce the best results," he insisted, "not wear ourselves out by trying to exceed our tolerance."[4] An important safety measure was the "generous supply of oxygen" they took with them "for the treatment of sickness and for rescue operations in case of accident."[5]

The young scientists were well aware that if they went down to Mingbo, their mood and their appetite would improve and their weight would increase, but they were always keen to remain up at the Silver Hut, which was very comfortable compared with Mingbo. Also, as West and Jim Milledge both admitted, there was an element of competitive pressure not to go down.

Some coped better than others. Mike Gill, the youngest team member, felt he achieved a "sort of equilibrium" after a while. But Pugh and Lahiri both had difficulty all through the expedition, frequently having to leave the Silver Hut and retire down to the Green Hut for a rest. Even the expedition puppy, Rakpa, became listless and stopped growing. Nevertheless, the Silver Hut was continuously occupied from December 17 until the end of April the following year. All the members of the winter party spent at least 70 days at 19,000 feet, and two, Milledge and Gill, were at that height for 110 days.

Much of the research was devoted to exploring the impact of altitude on the oxygen transport system—the mechanisms by which oxygen is absorbed from the atmosphere and carried to the tissues. Continuing the work Pugh had begun on Cho Oyu and Everest, an important part of the program was devoted to measuring the body's responses to varying levels of exercise at high altitude.[6]

The old exercise tests, done by stepping on and off boxes and running up measured tracks, were replaced by two specially designed stationary bicycles—one at Mingbo and one at the Silver Hut—which Pugh had adapted from racing bicycles. To measure maximum exercise capability, the men took turns pedaling in time to the inexorable ticking of a metronome. While they pedaled, a brake was gradually applied to the wheel, making them feel as if they were cycling up an ever-steeper hill, until at the end they were totally exhausted and blue from lack of oxygen. Pugh was never happy unless they reached the point of virtual collapse and "practically fell off [the bicycle] semi-conscious."[7]

In the final minutes of the test the cyclist breathed through a mouthpiece which delivered his exhaled breath into a Douglas bag. This enabled breathing rates to be measured and samples of breath to be analyzed with the precious Haldane gas analyzers. The tests confirmed what Pugh had found on Everest: that even when they were fully acclimatized, the men's maximum work output at 19,000 feet was only about half what it was at sea level.

The scientists wanted to find out whether the same applied to Sherpas, but the Sherpas had never seen a bicycle before, and only Da Tenzing had the coordination to ride one (or was the only Sherpa foolish enough to admit he could handle it). The tests revealed that Da Tenzing's maximum capacity for exercise had declined far less than that of the sea-level scientists, suggesting that Sherpas, as might be expected, were better adapted to altitude. This was confirmed in many practical ways: The Sherpas regularly carried 60-pound loads up to the Silver Hut at the same speed as the acclimatized lowlanders could climb without loads. The comparisons broke new ground. It had not yet been recognized, for example, that athletes brought up at high altitude have superior oxygen-transport systems, which give them a built-in advantage over lowlanders in long-distance running.

On top of the tubes, mouthpieces, and Douglas bags, the stationary cyclist had a great many other devices and probes to put up with. He would have an oximeter attached to his ear, measuring the concentration of oxygen in his arterial blood. An electrocardiogram recorded the behavior of his heart. Blood samples were taken from a vein in the hand so the carbon dioxide and oxygen levels could be analyzed and the chemical changes in the blood charted. His blood pressure was taken, electrodes attached to his head measured brain activity, thermometers measured temperature, pulses were taken, and so on.

Benchmark data gathered at sea level was used for comparison. Data like this had never been obtained from men who were exceptionally well acclimatized, and Pugh hoped to go further, taking a stationary bicycle up onto Makalu to make the highest-ever observations.

The bicycle tests revealed that levels of oxygen in the subjects' arterial blood fell sharply with exercise. At sea level the arterial blood is usually around 95 percent saturated with oxygen, but even at rest in the Silver Hut, it averaged only about 67 percent. On the bicycle, however, as the cyclists neared exhaustion, the level occasionally dropped as low as 50 percent— below the level at which an unacclimatized person might lose consciousness. By comparison the cyclists only felt extremely breathless.

One of the factors that determines the level of oxygen in the arterial blood is how easily oxygen transfers from the lungs into the blood. John West studied the process to find whether, with acclimatization, changes occur in the lungs to allow oxygen to transfer more efficiently through the lung walls into the blood. He used a method which entailed giving his subjects small quantities of carbon monoxide to inhale to see how much they absorbed.

When he began analyzing their exhaled breath, however, he found to his horror that they were breathing out more carbon monoxide than he was giving them. This led to the discovery that they were all suffering from carbon monoxide poisoning from the fumes of the Primus stoves used for cooking in the hut. After that, all the cooking was done outside and everyone in the hut felt noticeably better.

The problem sorted out, West was able to establish that the lungs did not become more efficient with acclimatization. Under "conditions of extreme oxygen deprivation," he later wrote, "the lungs just do not have time to properly oxygenate the blood as it flows through them."[8] This was a groundbreaking discovery.

The shortage of oxygen at high altitude causes people to breathe faster than they do at sea level. Many also suffer bouts of uneven breathing at night. Breathing is regulated with the help of sensors in the body which respond to the levels of carbon dioxide and oxygen in the blood. Jim Milledge studied how this system is affected by altitude and acclimatization. Sukhamay Lahiri studied the gases in the blood. Pugh focused on the increases in red blood cells, and the impact of oxygen deprivation on the function of the heart. Mike Ward explored the effects of altitude on the kidneys and the endocrine glands. Mike Gill investigated the impact of oxygen deprivation on the senses, such as hearing and sight, and the mental functions of the brain, such as concentration and memory.[9] His psychometric tests, which included tasks like card sorting, were specially designed to avoid "invidious" comparisons between the highly competitive scientists in the hut who minded a great deal about their intellectual prowess.

Day in and day out, the scientists pedaled doggedly on the stationary bikes. With infinite patience they worked with fiddly instruments like the Haldane analyzers, which required steady hands, skill, and concentration—tasks which today would be done instantly with machines. There were no computers to record and process their results—everything had to be calculated and copied out by hand.[10] Demanding even at sea level, this work was harder still at altitude, where concentration, motivation, and intellectual sharpness were depressed by the lack of oxygen. It was Pugh's awareness of the challenges he and his team faced that led him to attach so much importance to providing a comfortable environment. No discomforts should distract them from maintaining the highest standards. The sheer range and quality of the research they carried out are illustrated by the thirty-six scientific articles, many published in top academic journals, which came out of the expedition, and none of their findings have been refuted.

Pugh looked forward, when the winter was over, to rejoining Hillary for the spring attempt on Makalu without oxygen. From a physiological viewpoint, Everest at 29,029 feet would have been a more-interesting climbing target than the 27,825-foot Makalu; eight men had already climbed as high as 28,000 feet on Everest without oxygen. But it would still be exciting to compare the performances of the climbers who were just back from sea level with those of the climber-scientists who had spent the winter at the Silver Hut.

Edmund Hillary visited the scientists once during the winter. Delayed by bad weather, he flew into Mingbo by Bell helicopter on January 5, having returned the Khumjung Yeti scalp to its home village on the last day before he would forfeit his 8,000-rupee deposit. Feeling "none the worse for his hectic round the world trip," he told them that the experts he visited in London, Chicago, and New York had pronounced the Khumjung Yeti scalp to be a man-made artifact, fashioned from the skin of the serow goat.[11] As promised, he brought with him the shortwave radio, which was now greatly needed for ordering spare parts for the scientific equipment. Hillary had said he would be staying for six days, but he flew out again after only twenty hours, having dropped a bombshell about his plans for the spring attempt on Makalu.

He told Pugh that, instead of the full-scale expedition, he now intended to mount a classic lightweight "lightning" assault on Makalu—a spontaneous, sparsely equipped, flexible, Shipton-style expedition. This meant that Pugh's physiological program would have to be dropped, though he and his climbing scientists could still join the climb. In the interests of keeping weight to the minimum, Hillary had also decided against taking any oxygen for rescue operations, though he would take a tiny supply for medical purposes. The 50,000 liters of rescue oxygen that Pugh had procured for the Makalu assault would be left behind in Kathmandu, where it was in storage.

Pugh was appalled. That Hillary wanted to ax the last phase of the physiological program was upsetting enough. But the idea that he was planning to attempt an oxygen-free ascent of the formidable Makalu without any rescue oxygen seemed crazy, and Pugh was not willing to allow the men of the winter team, for whom he felt personally responsible, to put themselves at such risk.[12] Twice now when he had disagreed with Hillary, Pugh had confronted him with "straight talk" and threats to resign. This time he was more circumspect, at least to begin with. Saying nothing to Hillary's face, he waited until after the New Zealander had flown out before drafting with the greatest care a letter that he hoped would persuade Hillary to change his mind. Sensing Hillary's desire to be seen as an expedition leader of substance, Pugh tried to offer him a tempting alternative.

Hillary could achieve his goal without abandoning the physiology, Pugh argued.[13] He could take a team of climbers to make their own "genuine non-oxygen attempt [on Makalu] unencumbered by physiologists." Pugh and a small science group with much reduced equipment would form an independent physiological camp nearby and finish the last phase of the research completely separately. The scientists would take the oxygen for their experiments. That way, "you would still have the safeguard of the rescue oxygen in the background," he said, and "you would have fulfilled your original programme to the letter, to the great satisfaction of us all."

To abandon the physiology would be "a breach of faith" with the MRC, the Wellcome Foundation, and all the physiologists at the Silver Hut, he added. The work on Makalu was to have been the crowning glory. "But for this part of the programme, it would not have been possible to obtain support for the physiological team in the first place . . . Mountains like Makalu will be climbed again one day, but it seems unlikely that it will ever again be possible to carry out physiological studies of the kind we are equipped to undertake."[14]

The calm tone of the letter belied the strength of Pugh's feeling. And when Hillary refused to budge, Pugh wrote to Edholm in London, asking the MRC's permission to withdraw from the expedition. He also wrote to the managing director of Field Enterprises, threatening to resign, and warning that Hillary was about to commit an act of "gross negligence."[15] Of Hillary's decision to abandon the physiology, he claimed: "This is a direct breach of the agreement with myself and the scientific party, [as well as] the Medical Research Council and all the other bodies who have supported the expedition." Of Hillary's refusal to take rescue oxygen to Makalu, he explained:

"Physiological and medical opinion today is strongly opposed to the idea of attempting to climb Himalayan peaks of 28,000 feet without oxygen, unless oxygen equipment is available for rescue purposes; and no responsible scientific body could possibly support such an expedition without it." He felt deeply unhappy about being part of such a venture: "Should an accident happen on Mt. Makalu, it will not be sufficient for me as scientific leader to shift the blame for the absence of rescue oxygen apparatus on to Sir Edmund. It will be said that I should have insisted on the original agreement being carried out. Sir Edmund Hillary himself would be considered guilty of gross negligence."

Assuring Field Enterprises that he was "doing his best" to get Hillary to change his mind, he told them that if Hillary would not alter his plans, the entire scientific team would be forced to retire from the expedition. Knowing that Field Enterprises was extremely protective of its public image, he added that, if Hillary returned to the original plan, "no more will be said about this matter."

Back in London, Edholm was horrified. From the outset, the MRC had been deeply concerned about the dangers of attempting high mountains without oxygen, and had only agreed to support the expedition on the express condition that oxygen equipment to mount a full rescue operation would be available for the Makalu assault. He quickly wrote back, reassuring Pugh that he was acting entirely correctly: "We are all unanimous that the [MRC] will back you to the hilt in your stand and that you should feel completely free to withdraw from the Makalu adventure if Hillary persists with his fantastic plans."[16]

At last, after sticking to his position for some seven weeks, Hillary changed his mind and went back to the original plan.[17] He did not explain his reasons, but, apart from any other considerations, he needed the climber-scientists from the Silver Hut team for his assault on Makalu. Pugh's panic was over. Again he had achieved what he wanted, though this was the third time that he had had to go to the brink to get it.

Pugh said nothing about these problems to the young scientists at the Silver Hut, since his main concern was to keep them happy and focused on their work. One of the things that sustained him throughout the winter was his awareness of how well his side of the expedition was going.

At the end of February, the research was so well advanced that Ward, Gill, Bishop, and Romanes—led by Ward—were able to take time off to make the first ascent of the technically difficult Ama Dablam (22,349 feet), which would not be climbed again for nineteen years.[18] While they were on Ama Dablam Hillary arrived back in Mingbo with six wives of members of the expedition. He had returned to Kathmandu in February with extra equipment, two fresh climbers—Leigh Ortenburger from California and New Zealander John Harrison—and his own wife, Louise. The ladies' trek, which left Kathmandu on March 2, was Hillary's own pet project, and Louise was in the forefront. Jim Milledge's wife Betty, Barry Bishop's wife Lila, Ortenburger's wife Irene, and Peter Mulgrew's wife June were also in the party.[19]

Pugh's wife Doey had been invited to join them, but she had declined. She wasn't strong enough. Nevertheless, Pugh had begged her to come out to Kathmandu so he could fly down on the Red Cross plane and spend a few days with her. His abiding awareness of her presence back in England, supporting him and understanding his point of view, had been a source of strength to him. Having repeatedly unburdened himself of his worries in his letters to her, he longed to see her in person.

Responding to her husband's entreaties, Doey organized a trip to Nepal with her elder sister Hermione. But after all her years of being left at home, she was not content merely to visit Griffith in Kathmandu. Arranging for the children to be taken care of, she had planned an expedition of her own—a grand tour of India, taking in all the major sights, and culminating in the holy city of Rishikesh in the foothills of the Himalayas, where she and Hermione would attend a course on transcendental meditation given by the Maharishi Mahesh Yogi. It was not the first time in her life that she failed to be completely open with her husband, neglecting to tell Griffith about her ambitious plans. Perhaps she did not want to worry him, or perhaps she felt he would oppose her visit to the Maharishi.

The Maharishi Mahesh Yogi was an Indian yogic guru who set out on a world tour in the late 1950s to introduce the technique of "transcendental meditation" and "the healing powers of cosmic consciousness" to potential followers. Appealing to people like Doey and Hermione, who were dissatisfied with conventional religion but still wanted to find spiritual meaning and purpose in life, he quickly attracted a substantial following in the UK. Doey and Hermione did not know it at the time, but they were at the vanguard of spiritual fashion. In 1968, the Maharishi would become world famous when the Beatles joined his movement and made the pilgrimage to the Maharishi's ashram in Rishikesh.

On March 19, while the rest of the Silver Hut team joined Hillary and the ladies at Changmatang, Pugh accompanied an injured Sherpa, Gumen Dorje, to Kathmandu on the Red Cross plane, where Pugh brought him to the hospital. Afterward, he met up with Doey and Hermione in the bar of the Royal Hotel in Kathmandu, drank a small glass of whiskey, and promptly passed out.

He felt "very slack and sleepy" throughout his three-day stay in the capital. Nevertheless, seeing Doey was an enormous relief, and, after flying back to Mingbo, he sent her an unusually warm, appreciative letter: "Seeing you for these 3 days has been simply wonderful. Please try to forgive all my grousing, but being able to talk over my difficulties with you has helped & supported me, and I think I shall be able to carry on now to the end in a good spirit."[20] He added that he thought she had been looking "very well and relaxed." "We must try and make sure you have proper holidays in future and don't go on working the way you do month after month without a change and a rest."

He had no idea that she was about to set off on a personal adventure of her own.

23

Disaster on Makalu

Makalu, which is roughly 30 miles from Mingbo, could be approached by two possible routes—a sixteen-day trek up the Arun Valley and the Barun Valley, or a much shorter high route which involved crossing the Mingbo La and two further 20,000-foot passes. Hillary had originally intended to send half his team to Makalu by the low route, but opted instead to take his entire party and all his equipment over the high route, which could be covered in four or five days. The disadvantage was that the fifty Sherpas he had employed would have to trek back and forth three or four times, chaperoned by the climbers. The carry would take almost as long as the low route, but would need fewer Sherpas and would therefore be cheaper.

Hillary's preparations for the trip were interrupted when an entirely unexpected political fracas blew up over the recent ascent of Ama Dablam, due, perhaps to a change of government. Delayed in Kathmandu for two weeks sorting it out, he finally landed back at Mingbo, tired, anxious, and unacclimatized, but determined to make up the time they had lost. By then the carry to Makalu was already well under way. Climbers had already cut ice steps and fixed ropes up the vertical fluted ice slopes leading to the Mingbo La.[1] Teams of Sherpas had ferried sixty loads to the top of the pass, and a camp had been established on the Hongu Glacier on the other side. Across the glacier, the second even higher and equally precipitous pass led to the high Barun Plateau, from which the final demanding pass gave access to the Barun Glacier, which drains the west face of Makalu.

Pugh himself was aware that he "would probably not be fit enough" to tackle the route to Makalu. Already, he wrote, he "could only just keep going steadily at 19,000 feet & cannot expect to do long days at 20,000 feet without risk."[2] The winter had taken a toll on his health, and the long days of working had been making him so tired that he was sometimes incapable of doing accurate analysis. Hillary responded sympathetically: "I was anxious for Pugh to cross the Barun if possible and supervise the scientific work [on Makalu], but his long period at high altitudes was undoubtedly affecting him (he was a good deal older than the rest of us), and he doubted if it would be wise for him to attempt the journey."[3]

After a few days at Mingbo adjusting to the altitude and checking supplies, Hillary rushed up the valley to take charge of the carry, paying scant regard to the fact that he felt "lethargic and unacclimatised," and had to drive himself "every inch of the way."[4] It wasn't particularly late in the climbing season, but in his desire to catch up with his timetable he minimized rest periods and urged his team to make the utmost haste across the passes: "We had imbued the Sherpas with our sense of urgency. Although I gave them rest days when I felt they needed them, I was loath to waste a working day."[5]

Reveling in the fact that the route was "probably more technically demanding than any other approach to . . . a really high mountain," Hillary suffered no qualms about imposing more than two weeks of "hard unceasing work over difficult country" on men who were just about to take on the challenge of ascending the world's fifth-highest mountain without oxygen. "We worked like demons," he reflected later. "It was a formidable route over which to take 200 loads of 60 lbs each, but I reckoned we had the men to do it."

John Harrison and Peter Mulgrew agreed about the scale of the challenge. Harrison described the carry as "a mammoth carrying task." Mulgrew called it "one of the most strenuous periods of the expedition."[6] But no one appears to have suggested that such exhausting activities at altitudes of around 20,000 feet might not be the best way to prepare for the task ahead.

The high route proved extremely arduous for the Sherpas and the climbers alike. Each of the three passes was steep, icy, and dangerous. Hundreds of steps had to be cut, and at least 600 feet of ropes fixed to enable the heavily laden Sherpas to cross them, which they did repeatedly. Blessed by reasonable weather, they made up all the lost time, and after two weeks of hard work the final loads arrived at Camp One on the Barun Glacier at the foot of Makalu on April 25. Hillary described struggling toward the top of the third pass:

> *A bitter wind was blowing. I found it cold and hard work. As we crept towards the crest of the pass the impression of exposure, of a terrific drop beneath, was overwhelming. But the fixed ropes gave even the laden Sherpas the confidence to push on upwards as hard as their aching muscles and gasping lungs would let them. I was glad to stagger over the top of the 20,300-foot col.[7]*

As if the carry itself wasn't exhausting enough, Hillary had added to his labors by twice trekking all the way back to Mingbo for discussions with Pugh and the press officer, Desmond Doig. Most of the scientists had been toiling at the Silver Hut, working twelve-hour days and occasionally staying up until midnight, to get their projects finished before moving on to Makalu. They were not involved in the carry. After Hillary's second visit, two of the scientists, John West and Jim Milledge, joined him for the return trek to Makalu. By now Hillary's exertions were beginning to tell on him, and he noticed that he couldn't keep up with the younger men. "These two were in fine form and seemed capable of going faster than I found comfortable."[8]

Concerned about the scientists' well-being, Pugh had arranged that, after their trek to Makalu, they would "spend 5 days recuperating at low altitude in the Barun Valley" before going up to start their scientific program.[9] In sharp contrast, Hillary rushed straight up the mountain to lead the vanguard of climbers preparing the route and establishing the camps.

Pugh complained later that, by opting for the high route, Hillary had "made it impossible for me to accompany him," but as the end of April drew near, he also realized that the extra time at the Silver Hut would be very useful.[10] Telling Hillary of his final decision over the radio, he asked his old Everest companion Michael Ward to take charge of the physiological team, commenting in his diary that evening, "If [Hillary] gives the physiologists a fair run, I am confident they will carry out our programme satisfactorily."[11]

Pugh was not the only one who chose to miss out on Makalu. Desmond Doig was due to trek over the high route a few days after the main party, but withdrew at the last minute, dissatisfied with Hillary's arrangements, explaining to Pugh in a note: "As usual [Hillary's] instructions are delightfully vague. I'm to wander across to Makalu taking days and days and carrying cooking pots, etc. So definitely NO GO!"[12] Instead, Doig stationed himself at the Silver Hut and took charge of the only radio link with Hillary, so he could control the news passed on to Kathmandu and the world's press.[13]

Despite the weather taking a turn for the worse, the push up Makalu progressed very well at first. By April 30, in constant winds and daily snow-falls, the climbers had succeeded in establishing and stocking Camp Two at 19,600 feet, and Camp Three at 21,000 feet. On May 1 and 2, Camp Four was put in at 23,000 feet, and on May 5, Michael Ward and New Zealander Mike Gill cut the final steps up the steep slopes leading to the exceedingly windy 24,400-foot Makalu Col.

Two days later Hillary and the climber-carpenter Wally Romanes were improving the ice steps and fixing ropes between Camps Three and Four when, on reaching 23,000 feet—just above the place where he had collapsed in 1954—Hillary developed a severe headache. Returning down to Camp Three, he did not recover overnight. Realizing he had been "grossly overdo-ing it," he descended to Camp Two, but the following morning he was still describing himself, in his understated way, as "not too happy." By the end of the day he was talking gibberish, unable to stand, seeing double, and had no feeling in his left side. He had suffered a high-altitude stroke.

Hillary was put straight onto oxygen, and the scientists, who all hap-pened to be at Camp Two at the time, took it in turns to keep an all-night vigil at his bedside. By the morning he had recovered "fumbling" powers of speech but not his normal vision, and he was still groggy, out of balance, and "shaky in hand."

Oxygen was also being used on a Sherpa with the potentially fatal condi-tion of high-altitude pulmonary edema, in which fluid leaks into and accu-mulates in the lungs, preventing normal breathing. West and Milledge had brought the Sherpa down from Camp Three. He collapsed halfway down and they were forced to go down to fetch some rescue oxygen before he could complete the descent. He remained on oxygen for a further twenty-four hours.

The attempt on Makalu was only just getting under way, and already Pugh's rescue oxygen had been needed by two men. But this was nothing compared with what was to come.

The two scientists, Ward and Milledge, who were both practicing doctors, ordered Hillary to go down to 15,000 feet or below, threatening all manner of dire consequences for his health if he returned above that height within a few months. He was unwilling to obey. Consulted over the radio, Pugh advised that the New Zealander should be collected immediately by helicopter and flown straight back to Kathmandu. Instead, Hillary decided to return on foot to Khumjung to build the schoolhouse he had promised the village. This meant walking down the Barun Valley along a low, safe route that did not rise above 15,000 feet—the route that he had decided against using for the in-going trek.

Ward and Milledge both felt that Hillary should not undertake the walk without a doctor, so Milledge gave up his role in the scientific program, together with his chances of reaching the summit of Makalu, to become Hillary's personal physician on his way down the Barun Valley. For Hillary it was a terrible wrench to have to give up and hand over control to someone else. Before leaving he asked Michael Ward to take over the leadership of the assault on Makalu.

Hillary would reach Khumjung without mishap and build his promised schoolhouse with the money he had raised in Chicago during his Christmas trip around the world. From then on, his career as a high-altitude climber all but finished, he would put his peerless ability as a fund-raiser to the service of the Sherpas of Nepal, setting up a network of hospitals and schools, and achieving many other good works in the Solu-Khumbu region. In the process, he would become known as New Zealand's "best loved citizen."

With Hillary gone, the full Makalu assault was launched on May 11, when the first assault team—consisting of Wally Romanes and Mike Gill from the winter group, and American Leigh Ortenburger, one of the fresh climbers—moved up to Camp Five on the Makalu Col, at 24,400 feet. A support party of climbers, Sherpas, and supplies came up with them, together with scientists Ward, West, and Tom Nevison, who brought with them the stationary bicycle and other scientific equipment. Nevison had left the winter party in early January and returned with Hillary in the spring. Mike Gill described the Makalu Col as "the most desolate place one could imagine."

Ward and West assembled the stationary bicycle and spent the next five days undertaking the final stage of their program of physiological experiments, with Ward heroically substituting for Jim Milledge, who had dropped out to help Hillary. Ward explained: "I thought if I took Milledge's place on the Makalu Col doing physiological work with West, we should still be able to complete our physiological programme as well as climb Makalu."[14] However, the maximum work exercises were taking their toll on Ward, and Hillary would later complain that he gave greater priority to the science than to the climbing, undermining his fitness by staying too long on the col.

Meanwhile, the first assault team, Romanes, Gill, and Ortenburger, continued up the mountain on May 12, hoping to establish two further camps on their way, and then make for the summit using the same route as the successful French team in 1955. The key difference was to be that while the French climbed with oxygen, they had none.

They established Camp Six at 25,800 feet, but the next day became so tired cutting steps across a stretch of glacier icefall that they failed to ascend high enough to put in Camp Seven. Gill described how stressed he felt: "The first few blows of the ice axe used all my tiny reserve of oxygen, leaving me fighting for breath. Another five steps and I would sink to a halt. A rest, recovery, and the struggle would go on."[15]

Dumping the equipment and supplies they had brought up for Camp Seven at a temporary depot at 26,300 feet, they started down for Camp Six with a blizzard "beating at our backs." On the way, Gill lost his footing, and he and Romanes, to whom he was roped, hurtled down the steep ice slope, desperately trying to save themselves with their ice axes, the Sherpas watching in dumb silence. Luckily they came to a natural halt 50 feet below, when they hit a patch of deep snow. Uninjured, but subdued, they staggered back to Camp Six.

When they awoke the next morning, the gale was still blowing full force, and Gill had a frostbitten nose and had lost all feeling in his fingers and toes. So they decided to give up and return down to the Makalu Col. All three men reached Camp Five exhausted. Wally Romanes felt so bad during the night that Ward, assuming the role of expedition doctor, gave him some medical oxygen to relieve him. Ward himself had been secretly resorting to the odd bout of oxygen at night as well. Mike Gill was mildly frostbitten and also suffering from the altitude. Ortenburger, Gill, and Romanes descended to Camp Three the following day.

The second assault party, consisting of the American climber-scientist Tom Nevison and Hillary's friend Peter Mulgrew, set off from the Makalu Col on May 16. Both men were fresh climbers, having only just returned to Nepal after several months away.

The first day of their assault passed without mishap, but the following day on the glacier between Camp Six and the proposed site of Camp Seven, one of their six Sherpas—who were all tied onto a single rope—slipped and fell backwards, pulling the others with him. Chaotically they crashed down the steep and treacherous ice slope toward a sheer drop of thousands of feet over the northern wall of the Makalu massif.[16] They looked certain to be killed. Miraculously the rope snagged, bringing them all to a halt. But one Sherpa broke his ankle, another cut his head, and a third—Annullu—cracked a rib, though he did not realize it at the time. All of them were badly shaken.

Nevison and Mulgrew sent the two obviously injured men back to Camp Six, and continued upward with the remaining Sherpas, Mulgrew shouldering the lion's share of the loads left by the injured men. He and Nevison established Camp Seven at just over 27,000 feet—only about 750 feet below the summit—and sent all the remaining Sherpas down, except for Annullu. Mulgrew described himself and Nevison as "desperately tired after the exertions of the last few hours." At 27,000 feet they had been feeling the shortage of oxygen very acutely: "At this great altitude it felt almost a physical impossibility to force enough oxygen into our labouring lungs, no matter how often we paused for breath . . . we were frequently forced to halt, windblown and prostrate, trying to gather enough power . . . for the next short step."[17]

So fumbling and slow had they become that, although they rose at 6:15 the next morning, they did not leave camp until 9:00 a.m., when at last, with Annullu, they began their final assault. Inching upward without oxygen equipment, "muscles aching, lungs bursting, and hearts pounding," they plugged their way slowly toward their 27,766-foot goal. A rising wind screamed across the summit, showering them with a constant spray of fine snow. They were able to progress only extremely slowly, covering just 100 feet per hour. Then, about 300 to 400 feet below the summit, Mulgrew collapsed in agony. Stabbed by a terrible pain in his right side, he lay gasping for breath, scarlet sputum spraying from his mouth and staining the snow around him.[18] He had probably suffered a blood clot in his lungs.

With Mulgrew having difficulty in moving, they struggled back to Camp Seven before nightfall, the bitter penetrating wind blowing at their backs all the while. The next morning, they started down toward Camp Six, but the descent was steep and made more difficult by the continuing bad weather. Eventually Mulgrew blacked out, and the three men became stranded at the windswept depot above Camp Six where there was no tent. Annullu, now in considerable pain himself from his cracked rib, set off down to seek help.

Soon the entire expedition would be transformed into one long rescue operation. While the assault was happening, Michael Ward, again in the role of doctor, had come up from the Makalu Col to Camp Six to attend to the Sherpa stuck there with a broken ankle. Ward had exhausted himself pioneering the route to the Makalu Col in early May, and his protracted stay on the col doing exercise tests had added to his problems.

Down on the Makalu Col, unaware of the dramatic events near the summit, Leigh Ortenburger and John Harrison began the third assault the following morning. Responding to a message from Ward over the walkie-talkie, asking for Sherpas to carry down the man with the broken ankle, they brought several extra Sherpas with them. When they got to Camp Six, they found Ward completely disoriented, perhaps succumbing to the life-threatening condition of high-altitude cerebral edema, where the brain swells and ceases to function normally. The Sherpas took Ward and the injured man down to the Makalu Col. Ward struggled into camp clinging to the arms of two Sherpas, then passed out and remained unconscious for forty-eight hours.

That same afternoon Annullu arrived down at Camp Six and gave Harrison and Ortenburger the terrible news about Peter Mulgrew. Two Sherpas were immediately sent up with a tent and some oxygen for Mulgrew and Nevison, who had been languishing 500 feet above Camp Six all afternoon, imagining they had been abandoned. On top of Mulgrew's problems, Nevison, gray-faced and dehydrated, with no stove to melt water to drink, had begun to suffer seriously from the altitude too.

The following morning, while Harrison went down from Camp Six to summon help, Ortenburger and some Sherpas went up to relieve Nevison and set about bringing down the injured Mulgrew. With the utmost difficulty Ortenburger and the Sherpa managed, with the help of oxygen, to convey Mulgrew down to Camp Six, by which time his hands, feet, and parts of his face were severely frostbitten. The next day, crawling, slithering, often unconscious, he was somehow shepherded down to Camp Five on the Makalu Col, where he arrived in a terrible state, ashen-faced and "almost lifeless."

The situation on the Makalu Col was becoming dire. Some five climbers in various stages of injury and altitude sickness were now dallying at the serious height of 24,400 feet, anoxic, bemused, and aimless, short of food, short of sleeping bags, and failing even to get a Primus stove working, so there was nothing to drink.

Down at Camp Three, physiologist John West was finding it hard to follow precisely what was happening higher up. Despite having only recently come down from the col, the physiological program complete, he now decided to go back up to see if he could help. Rounding up some Sherpas and a supply of rescue oxygen, he donned oxygen equipment himself and set off. Afterward he remembered finding the oxygen "nothing short of miraculous." "I streamed up the mountain well ahead of the Sherpas who were accompanying me, and if anybody claims that supplementary oxygen is not of great value at high altitude, don't believe them."[19]

West was one of the few expedition members who had little or no experience with climbing, but on reaching the Makalu Col he deeply impressed his ailing colleagues with the near-miraculous way in which he handled the situation. As Mike Gill later described the scene, West "swept through Camp 5 like Christ casting the money changers from the Temple."[20] Michael Ward and the other dazed climbers were brought to their senses, kitted up with oxygen sets, and dispatched down the mountain. Primus stoves were mended and lit, and snow melted for water. After helping one party of climbers down to Camp Three, West returned to the col where he treated the sick Mulgrew and directed operations to evacuate him from the mountain.

Eventually all the climbers and all the Sherpas got off Makalu without loss of life. This was an amazing achievement. The result could have been so much worse. Afterwards all the climbers paid tribute to the extraordinary part played by the non-climber in their midst.

Peter Mulgrew was gravely ill, and the doctors were convinced that his only hope of survival was to get immediate hospital treatment. So they used the radio link with Desmond Doig at the Silver Hut to summon the helicopter, and Mulgrew was flown, together with Ward and the Sherpa with a broken ankle—all watched over by West—to the hospital in Kathmandu. Had Pugh not persuaded Hillary to agree to the radio link and the helicopter, Mulgrew would have had to be carried by stretcher to Kathmandu, a trek that would have taken two weeks.

After the expedition, the climbers and the physiologists alike were left with a general view that those who had spent the winter at high altitude had not proved better able than the new arrivals to withstand the height on Makalu. Of the winter group—Ward, Gill, and Romanes—Ward was the worst affected. Gill and Romanes had had to retreat down the mountain exhausted after only one summit attempt. Three Sherpas had also become altitude-sick, one seriously.

The fresh climbers, Harrison and Ortenburger, seemed more resilient than their winter colleagues, and Ortenburger had felt strong enough to have a second try at the summit. But the other two climbers who suffered catastrophically from the altitude—Hillary and Mulgrew—had both been away for the winter, and had not returned to altitudes above 15,000 feet until mid-March. The same was true for Tom Nevison, who believed that he was suffering high-altitude pulmonary edema when he was stranded high on the mountain with Mulgrew.

Meanwhile, back at Mingbo, 30 miles away, Pugh, Lahiri, and Captain Motwani had rounded off the research program. Pugh confided in his diary, "I am well satisfied with the work we have accomplished." They left Mingbo in mid-May with fifty porters, heading for Kathmandu. They had no radio on the trek, so apart from Hillary's stroke, which had happened while they were still at the Silver Hut, they had no idea of the further dramas unfolding on Makalu, only hearing of them from Ward and West when they reached Kathmandu.[21] Nor did Pugh realize that he would soon find himself battling to prevent his expedition from being portrayed as a total failure.

24

"Gone to India. Your Dinner's in the Oven"

Griffith Pugh landed back in London on June 8, 1961, to find only one member of his family at the airport to welcome him—me, his fourteen-year-old daughter. He had been away for nearly ten months.

My mother had been expected back from India six weeks earlier, but instead of coming home she had stayed on to spend more time at the Maharishi's ashram in Rishikesh. My two elder brothers were away at school—David at a special school in Switzerland, Simon at public school in England. Five-year-old Oliver had been farmed out to cousins in Norfolk. I was the only child at day school at home. The woman my mother had employed to look after me had already moved on to her next job. Responding to a pleading telegram from my mother in India, an ancient family friend, Lady Pleasance McKenna, had stepped in to fill the unscheduled gap.

Doey's desertion of her family was the talk of our neighborhood. One of our neighbors, the wife of an architect, was so concerned about my father's plight that she took it upon herself to drive me to the airport to meet him. Although I was delighted to miss school, I was worried about how to greet my father in front of other people. Should I kiss him? How would he react if I did?

My father had been away so often that the nascent difficulties between us had not yet had a chance to blow up into full-scale hostilities. His absence on the Silver Hut expedition had come on top of the three earlier expeditions, which together with his skiing holidays and lecture tours had kept him away from home for much of my youth. I hardly knew him. When he wasn't away, he was usually deeply preoccupied with his work. Disapprove as he might that I had been expelled—after only a term—from each of the two girls' boarding schools I had been sent to at the age of thirteen (for refusing to cooperate or carry out punishments), he was too busy and too remote to take much notice, and I had ended up back where I had started, at the local day school, St. George's in Harpenden. Oliver's birth in 1955 had stimulated his sense of parenthood, and he had sent me and my brothers the occasional interesting letter from Antarctica and the Silver Hut, but I did not know him well enough to feel familiar in his company.

At the airport, it took me a few seconds even to recognize him. Watching the throngs of people walking out into the arrivals hall, my eye fell on a tall, thin man with shoulder-length light-ginger hair tied back in a straggly ponytail, who seemed familiar. Suddenly I realized it was him. Hair bleached by the Himalayan sun, face surprisingly pale and yellowish, he was dressed in the usual crumpled white shirt and beige trousers.

I do not remember our greeting. What stands out in my memory is that journalists crowded around us and we were ushered away to a room where my father was interviewed, first by the BBC and then by several journalists. Could Dr. Pugh tell them what had happened on Makalu, they asked; would Sir Edmund Hillary make a full recovery? Had the expedition been a terrible failure because of the events on Makalu?

I could see that he was getting agitated. "No," the expedition was "not a failure," he insisted. It was true that the climbers had not succeeded in their efforts to climb Makalu without oxygen, but the scientists had accomplished everything they had set out to achieve, and, yes, Hillary had made a complete recovery. The report in *The Times* the following day talked only of Hillary: "The expedition set out to discover how man would react to high altitude without the use of oxygen. During one climb Sir Edmund Hillary collapsed and had a stroke. Asked if this was due to their not taking oxygen equipment, Dr. Pugh said: 'I would not like to say that at all. We didn't go particularly high.'"[1]

Pugh was appalled at the reaction of the journalists who had ears only for stories about Hillary and Makalu, ignored Pugh's assertions that the Silver Hut science was a success, and appeared to be convinced the entire expedition had been a disastrous failure. For the first time in his life, Pugh, the man with "no concept of PR" and "absolutely no concept of pushing himself," felt a positive duty, as the leader of the scientific team, to try to ensure that his own and his team's achievements were accurately presented to the public.

Writing at once to the expedition sponsors, Field Enterprises Corporation, he urgently requested permission to hold a press conference at the MRC to publicize the success of the Silver Hut science. He was anxious, he said, to correct "an unfortunate impression in the public mind that the expedition has been a total failure on account of the events on Makalu."[2] But the sponsors wrote back, forbidding him to take any action until after the publication in the *Sunday Times* of what they described as an "excellent concluding article by Sir Edmund Hillary."

When Hillary's article appeared on July 2, it created precisely the impression of overall failure that Pugh had wanted to avoid. Furthermore, Hillary added insult to injury by leaving out Pugh's name altogether. Sir Edmund had chosen his words carefully to make it seem as if the scientific project was entirely his own. "I had always expected Makalu to be the final testing ground of my acclimatisation theories," he explained. Deploying that calculatedly disarming modesty for which he was widely admired, he freely admitted, "I was wrong, and my theories have been defeated."

Allowing the scientists no glory, he laid the blame for his and his team's failure on Makalu entirely on "the long periods we spent at 19,000 feet before the assault." The use of the first-person plural ensured that Hillary's readers would think that he—and Peter Mulgrew, who had suffered the stroke and the thrombosis on Makalu—had undermined their health by spending the winter at altitude. "This had weakened my men and made them easy targets for thrombosis and other high-altitude killers." In fact, neither Hillary nor Mulgrew had spent a single night in the Silver Hut. These supposed martyrs to the cause of science had left Mingbo in late November, and had only returned to high altitude in the middle of March.

Irritated though he was, Pugh took no action and soon became engrossed in writing up the Silver Hut research results. His young scientific team was eager to get their papers published, and he was under great pressure to work faster than usual.

At home there were just the two of us and Pleasance McKenna. My father said nothing about my mother's unexpected absence, but in the evenings he retired to the drawing room and sat for hours, listening to records over and over again. The strains of Tito Gobbi singing Scarpia in *Tosca*, Maria Callas singing *Norma* and *Traviata*, floated through the house. Sometimes when I went to call him to supper, I would find him wandering about the garden with the music booming through the window.

In the first few weeks he spent every weekend away, disappearing down the drive in his Austin-Healey convertible, which he had taken great trouble to order before he left for the Himalayas. He spent the weekends with his sisters in various parts of the country, or sailing on our boat, which was kept at Bosham Harbor on the south coast. The boat was a sleek, 98-square-foot Danish racing yacht which he had persuaded my mother to buy in the 1930s, early in their relationship.

About six weeks after his return, Griffith was on his way home from a weekend at Bosham with his friend, the millionaire furniture designer Donald Gomme, when he skidded while dicing with another car in the Sussex lanes, turning over his brand-new car. The vehicle was a write-off, and Griffith, lucky to be alive, was left lying in the road with a fractured hip.

Pleasance McKenna now found herself in a quandary. Already uneasy about my mother's absence, she did not want to be landed with the responsibility of looking after my father when he came home from the hospital. Together she and Griffith decided to send a telegram worded to guarantee that my mother would rush home at once. The message they concocted read GRIFFITH INJURED IN SERIOUS ACCIDENT STOP COME HOME IMMEDIATELY.

Deep into her meditation program, Doey was horrified by the telegram which thrust her into a frenzy of worry about whether her husband was dead or dying or forever crippled or maimed. Having no means of communicating directly with home from Rishikesh, she and Hermione sought a special audience with "Maharishi," as they called him, who perceptively reassured them that if Griffith's life was really in danger, the telegram would have said so. Doey set off for home immediately, leaving Hermione to stay on for several more weeks.

I remember feeling immensely relieved when my mother came home. The house had seemed a bleak place without her warm presence. She was a wonderful homemaker, a brilliant cook, and always full of fun and laughter. But for all her natural warmth my mother was deeply resentful about the tactics that had been used to haul her home. She blamed them on my father, and it brought out the tougher side of her nature. She cared for him dutifully while his hip mended, but they had many angry rows, their shouts reverberating throughout the house. After he was better, the rows occasionally ended in her storming out and driving off in her car. When this happened, my father would boom melodramatically: "We shall have to go onto emergency rations!" and order me to climb into our loft to retrieve the dried-meat bars he had salvaged from the Silver Hut.

But my mother always came back, usually after only a few hours. They appeared to make up and continued to coexist reasonably peaceably for some of the time. It was coexistence, though, rather than fruitful partnership. They rarely showed any affection for one another.

In the past, my mother had never seemed to mind about my father's late arrivals home from work, but they became a growing bone of contention after the Silver Hut. One day he would be shouting for his supper, demanding to know why it was late; the next, he would fail to show up until supper was ruined. A regular haunt in the early evenings was Donald Gomme's flat in Hyde Park Gate, where he would drink several whiskies before driving home somewhat unsteadily in his replacement Austin-Healey.

Donald Gomme surrounded himself with beautiful young women, as I witnessed on the few occasions I happened to be with my father when he paid Gomme a visit. The millionaire's exquisite lady friends lounged decoratively on the white-leather sofas and tiger-skin rugs adorning his ultramodern flat, nonchalantly waving their long black cigarette holders and blowing out elegant curls of smoke. They filled me with awe and, as my father quaffed his whiskey and flirted outrageously, I sat silently in teenage embarrassment, feeling exceedingly gauche and out of place. Perhaps not surprisingly my mother resented Gomme, who seldom included her in the many invitations he proffered my father.

Another of Griffith's regular haunts after work was the Hampstead home of Edward and June Posey, whom he met by chance in Kathmandu on the way to the Silver Hut. Taking a break from his last-minute preparations one day, he was using the telephoto lens of his camera to inspect a famous Buddhist temple frieze depicting different positions of sexual intercourse when a pretty young English girl with an Irish complexion and dark hair asked if she could take a look. The Poseys were in Kathmandu to bring in Nepal's first high-altitude helicopter. The three fell into conversation and subsequently became good friends. It was through Edward Posey that my father secured the helicopter link with Mingbo and the radio permit for the Silver Hut. The Poseys' London home was a charming Georgian terraced house on a steep hill in Hampstead village, close to Griffith's laboratory. Edward traveled a great deal and was frequently absent when Griffith dropped in after work to drink a few whiskies with the delightful June.

My father's newfound propensity for arriving home not just late, but drunk as well, infuriated my mother. He used to laugh it off, declaring that when he was tipsy he took the precaution of driving home in third gear. If he was suffering from double vision, he used to say, he simply drove between the two white lines he could see in the center of the road. But it was his visits to June Posey that Doey found particularly galling. One evening, when he failed to appear, she telephoned June and ordered her to "stop making Griffith drunk," but the twenty-five-year-old was most indignant at being held responsible for the behavior of a fifty-year-old man.

Less than a year after the Silver Hut, in the spring of 1962, my father came home from work one evening to find a note on the kitchen table announcing bluntly and without explanation, "Gone to India. Your dinner's in the oven." Doey had vanished.

Throughout their married life Griffith had left the management of the home and the children entirely to my mother. So busy was he with his work and his expeditions that he completely failed to notice what a raw deal he had given her. She gave him unstinting support, while he seemed oblivious to her needs. For years she had quietly sustained herself with the thought that, one day, she would break out and do something entirely for herself. The trip to India had been the consummation of that wish. Forced by my father's accident to come home before she was ready, she was determined to go back and finish her trip properly. So it was to Rishikesh that she fled, telling no one in advance, lest they try to dissuade her. Before leaving, she made all the necessary arrangements for the housekeeping and the children to be looked after, taking on a pretty French au pair girl to help care for Oliver.

She had suppressed her own needs and desires for far too long. As I discovered long afterward from the suitcase of letters that turned up unexpectedly at the Royal Geographical Society, my mother had grown up with such a low opinion of herself and was so insecure about Griffith's love for her that she had allowed herself to be browbeaten by a husband whose world revolved round satisfying his own needs. Doey married Griffith at the beginning of the war despite knowing that right up to the last minute he had been two-timing her with a girl called Carmen MacGlashan in London. Carmen was far more sophisticated and much better educated than my mother, but was most unlikely to marry a young man as socially undistinguished and poor as Griffith.

Doey suffered the first steely-cold blow of disillusionment about her marriage when she found out that Griffith, departing for his tour of duty to the Middle East in June 1940, had said good-bye to his pregnant wife in Luton and then gone secretly to London for a last fling with Carmen before joining his unit.

This shattering discovery had a disastrous impact on Doey's fragile self-esteem. However, recognizing that her husband was extremely fond of Carmen—if not in love with her—she shrank from challenging him directly about his behavior, fearing she would be treading on fire.

A year later, Doey read in a glossy social magazine, the *Tatler,* that Carmen had become engaged to another man. Unable to contain herself, she wrote to tell Griffith in a tone that illustrated her insecure state of mind all too clearly. Sparing him no details of the *Tatler* article with its "wonderful write up" about Carmen and the "lovely and glamorous" photograph of her and her handsome fiancé, Doey's letter was shot through with strained apologetic comments. "I hope it won't make you too sad," she said. And again and again she repeated, "I hope you won't mind too much. I do hope that she will be very happy & that you will not be too unhappy."

Half-triumphant and half-pleading, her letter revealed a desperate need for reassurance from her husband:

> *It makes it harder [for you] because one is always brought up to expect a lion's share of all the happiness in the world . . . Truth to tell Pug I am rather baffled by hearing of C[armen]M[acGlashan]'s wedding. I always imagined if you couldn't stick it any more with me you would marry her in the end. This complicates things, perhaps you can work it out for yourself.* [3]

No sooner had she sent it than she regretted it, apologizing abjectly in her next letter: "I hope the last letter I wrote you has gone to the bottom, as it was stupid, unkind and selfish."

Not realizing that his wife had found him out, Griffith's reply was curt and minimal rather than warm and reassuring. "You rather lectured me about Carmen, darling. Honestly I have scarcely thought of her for months. Before we were married when I saw a good deal of her in London I was very fond of her too, but since then she has gone right out of my life."[4]

Only rarely did Griffith indulge Doey in the emotional reassurance she appealed for again and again in her letters. "Are you still my amour? You are very dark about your feelings!" she asked hopefully at one point. Provoking no reaction, she tried another tack: "I have decided to give up this racket of telling you that you are not in love with me, it is very bad propaganda . . . Also I have decided to stop saying that I am stupid, ugly & inefficient. All these things you can see for yourself if you need to . . . To boast about being ugly & stupid is really the worst form of conceit."[5]

Heavily self-deprecating passages like this intruded into her otherwise witty, humorous—if occasionally slightly brittle—letters, revealing the agonizing sense of insecurity and lack of self-confidence that was always near the surface. Yet this did not prevent Griffith from writing home from Tehran in 1942, telling his wife without a trace of guilt, "I wish you were here, darling; I have quite a nice girlfriend at present, but you are incomparably nicer and will always be my true love." Her name was Ruth Lyall, and he had been wining and dining her on champagne and beef stroganoff at significant expense in all the best restaurants in Tehran. There can be few women, least of all deeply insecure women, who would be happy to hear that their absent husband has "quite a nice a girlfriend" with whom he is probably being unfaithful. Failing to respond adequately to Doey's need for reassurance from him, he expected her to be delighted that he was having such a wonderful time.

In sharp contrast, she herself did her utmost to boost his spirits whenever she sensed that he was feeling low—as when he was in trouble with the army authorities over his escape from Greece in 1941. Her reaction was to comfort him: "I do, & always shall, believe in you as a person, apart from anything between us, I believe in your courage & endurance & humour, your strength & ability to see the true value of things & your generosity & even your red hair."[6]

This was particularly generous since the accusations of desertion leveled at Griffith caused excruciating embarrassment to Doey's family. Her father, Felix, having for many years held the office of Judge Advocate General, was horrified that his own son-in-law might be facing a court-martial.

It was poor compensation for Doey to know that Griffith had no intention of ever leaving her. The problem was that he did not appear to be truly in love with her, nor did he feel bound to be faithful. In Tehran in the war he had a conversation with a friend who confided that he was falling in love with his mistress. Griffith wrote in his diary, "I told him he should stick to his wife for the sake of his two children & if necessary love outside." The concept of "loving outside" was widely accepted among men of Griffith's generation, but it was hardly calculated to meet the emotional needs of his romantic young wife.

During the war—long before Doey came into her inheritance—my father also revealed an overwhelmingly self-centered attitude toward money, spending freely on himself but showing remarkably little inclination to make any contribution to the maintenance of his wife and young son. "I'm afraid I spent over £120 in India . . . India is terribly expensive," he admitted to Doey, after splashing out on a trekking holiday in Sikkim during his leave in 1941, and went on to declare: "If you can get on all right on your money, I would send occasional cheques for any sum you need in addition, but you must let me know how much you want. I think we should save money as far as possible, for we may have to live on our savings for a time after I am demobilised."[7]

Having just spent the equivalent of seven months of his salary as a junior doctor—or approximately £4,200 in today's money—on a twelve-day holiday for himself, this showed an astonishing blindness. Doey did not criticize him, but this and similar episodes did not go unnoticed. Later, when she inherited her money, she flatly refused to give her husband access to it, which he, in turn, would find exceedingly frustrating. It would become the subject of many rows between them.

When in the late spring of 1962 Doey disappeared to India for a second time to rejoin the Maharishi, my father commented to me: "It would be better if your mother had a lover!" Her having a lover was something he might comprehend and come to terms with. The attractions of the Maharishi were much harder for him to understand. His own response to Doey's disappearance was to embark on a full-blooded affair with our au pair girl, who was thirty years his junior. As ever, he was not the man to turn his back on an opportunity when it presented itself.

Tall, with feathery blonde hair, she was about twenty years old. The early summer sunshine tanned her skin a dusky, golden color, emphasizing her light-gray eyes and clear complexion, giving her an aura of wholesome health and fitness.

I remember her one night at supper in the kitchen at home, about a month after my mother left. Throwing back her head with abandon to reveal a smoothly tanned neck and bosom, she gazed at the ceiling and declared in her thick French accent, "I want my body to be attractive to zee mens." Though I was now fifteen, I found her behavior eccentric rather than provocative, and completely failed to appreciate the effect it was having on my father.

Griffith and the au pair girl took to listening to music together after supper. One night I went into the drawing room to look for them. They weren't there. The record had reached its end and was scratching around and around on the turntable. The French windows to the garden were wide open, but there was no sign of them in the warm dusk of the summer evening.

When Doey returned in mid-July, just before the start of the school holidays, bringing with her a box of fresh mangoes, Griffith's behavior was reported to her by a neighbor who had spotted him in flagrante. The unfortunate girl was immediately bundled out of the house. On discovering later that Griffith was continuing to see her in London, Doey attempted to get her deported back to France. The affair ended but the damage was done. The betrayal was too much for her. She did not leave, but removed herself from his bedroom and went to sleep in a small room at the opposite end of our large house, never to return to my father's bed. From then on they lived parallel lives, occasionally rocking the house with their rows.

I became intensely critical of the way he treated her and did my best to persuade her to leave him. He got his own back by playing on my insecurities. Like my mother I thought of myself as stupid, ugly, and inefficient, and was very sensitive to his jibes, which often reduced me to tears. I found him nasty, cruel, and vicious. Soon I was in total rebellion. Playing truant, I was expelled from my third school. Longing to be someone else—a normal person from a normal family—I changed my name from Harriet Pugh, which I considered made me stand out, to plain Jackie Evans. Quitting my fourth school, St. Albans Girls' Grammar School, after two terms, I went to work in a local shop.

Before long I moved to London to live with my aunt. When at nineteen I asked my mother to support me while I returned to school and took my A-levels, my father was strongly opposed: "She must be thrown out on the streets where she belongs," he cried. My mother ignored him. I studied for the exams and went on to university. In all the years that followed, the grumbling hostilities between me and my father continued, and had not been put to rest when he died.

25

The Battle of the Book

If Pugh's home life, in the eighteen months after his return from the Himalayas, was not going well, the opposite was true of his work. The Silver Hut research results were received with great acclaim, and his expedition was accepted as having achieved a giant leap forward in the field of high-altitude medicine. The Silver Hut team made successful presentations in July 1961 at the prestigious J. S. Haldane Centenary Symposium at the Oxford School of Physiology, which was attended by top physiologists from all over the world. This was followed by equally well-received appearances at conferences in Europe. Silver Hut articles were given pride of place in important scientific journals.[1]

Pugh's young research team was invariably scrupulous about giving the fullest credit to their scientific leader, even when speaking about their own individual research topics, and helped to ensure that Pugh came to be regarded as one of the "fathers" of the burgeoning discipline of high-altitude medicine and physiology.

In the autumn of 1962, Professor Bruce Dill of Harvard, who had been scientific leader of the last truly landmark scientific high-altitude expedition in the 1930s, invited Pugh to lecture at many of the top universities in America. Dill had first taken an interest in the work Pugh had done in the war eighteen years previously, and Pugh was deeply gratified at having his itinerary organized by such a towering figure.

Throughout this time Pugh never lost his awareness that, for all the rows and disagreements, the Silver Hut expedition could not have taken place at all without Sir Edmund Hillary's talent for raising money. He owed a great deal to Hillary, and in every article he wrote about the Silver Hut—for either academics or lay readers—he scrupulously acknowledged Hillary's role as leader of the expedition, making it clear that it was he who had made the expedition possible.

Doey was still away in India in the summer of 1962 when Michael Ward got in touch with Pugh to tell him that Hillary's official book about the expedition, jointly written with Desmond Doig, was about to be published, without Pugh having seen a draft beforehand. Ward had written asking to see it, but Hillary had failed to reply.

Naturally Pugh wrote to Hillary at once, asking to see the manuscript before publication, but Hillary refused to show it to him.[2] Considering that the book contained a chapter on the winter phase of the expedition, when neither of the joint authors had been present at Mingbo, it was extraordinary that Hillary did not feel morally obliged to let Pugh comment on the draft.

The book was to be published by Doubleday in America and by Hodder & Stoughton in Britain. Frustrated by Hillary's silence, Ward persuaded Hodder & Stoughton to let him see the galley proofs, only to be infuriated by them. Hillary had written passages about Ward's conduct during the assault on Makalu that Ward felt were so derogatory they might seriously damage his reputation. Pugh was equally incensed to find that Hillary had set about describing the scientific element of the expedition without even mentioning Pugh's name. On the first page of the preface to *High in the Thin Cold Air,* Hillary had written: "Our primary objective, the physiological programme, was developed under the guidance of the British Medical Research Council who gave considerable aid with equipment and personnel."[3]

He was deliberately creating the impression that the Silver Hut science had been designed by Hillary, with advice from a group of unnamed professionals at the MRC. "The thread which tied the whole expedition together," he elaborated in the main text of the book—making sure his readers recognized how important the scientific side of the expedition had been—"was the physiological research into high-altitude acclimatisation, and it was in this direction that our major effort was turned."

He then went on to reinforce the impression that the Silver Hut science had all been his idea: "I planned to winter a party at a height of over 19,000 feet, something that had not been done before. By the end of the expedition we hoped to know the answer to many [physiological] questions, among them (a) what is the maximum height at which men can live at high altitudes without deterioration . . . [etc.]." Consistently failing to tell his readers that Pugh—rather than Hillary—had devised the scientific program, Hillary wrote of Pugh as if he were merely the most senior of a group of physiologists sent out by the MRC to give him a hand.

For Pugh it was an unpleasant sense of déjà vu. In August 1960, Pugh had threatened to withdraw from the expedition before it began, unless Hillary stopped referring to him in public as "my senior physiologist," which Pugh felt diminished his role as the scientific leader. Yet Hillary gave Pugh precisely that same demeaning title in the book. "My senior physiologist, Dr. Griffith Pugh, and I had discussed at some length the ideal conditions we should try to attain for setting up the physiological tests," he wrote. Had he forgotten about Pugh's ultimatum? Or was he, as Pugh suspected, deliberately underplaying Pugh's role so as to take for himself the credit for the scientific side of the expedition?

Several other self-aggrandizing passages strongly suggested the latter was the case. Hillary claimed the credit, for example, for the design of the Silver Hut. Pugh had spent six months designing the hut with architect Ezra Levin. At one point they had even consulted Pugh's friend Donald Gomme about the construction methods. As Pugh explained in his comments on the galley proofs, Hillary had been far away in New Zealand at the time, and "had virtually nothing to do with the designing and construction of the hut."[4] The New Zealander, he said, had favored quite a different "wire netting and canvas structure which Pugh would not accept." The limit of his contribution had been an exceedingly rough sketch of a possible interior that was disregarded early on. And yet, in his book, Hillary had written: "I sketched a tiny hut with eight sleeping bunks, a cooking stove, a laboratory and a snow porch entrance. Within a matter of minutes Levin had transformed this drawing into the plan of a compact hut."

The assault rations for the Makalu phase of the expedition were designed and ordered in England by Pugh, but Hillary preferred his readers to think he alone had prepared all the expedition's rations, writing, "I had devoted great care to the selection of food for both the assault phase and the period of high-altitude living."

Hillary seemed to find it impossible to concede to Pugh even a modest amount of the limelight for any aspect of his role in the expedition. Even with regard to the book, Hillary wrote that he had drawn on material written by various team members involved in each phase of the expedition—naming the contributors as Gill, Hardie, Ortenburger, Nevison, and Mulgrew. But his chapter entitled "Himalayan Winter" made use of long, verbatim quotes from the dispatches Pugh had written in the winter, without crediting him.

Pugh and Ward wrote separately to Hodder & Stoughton in England and Doubleday in the United States, demanding changes to the text. Hodder & Stoughton agreed at once, but the final decision lay with Doubleday, who refused, saying publication was too far advanced.[5] It was only under great pressure from Ward that Pugh finally sought legal advice, and, on July 31, Pugh wrote to the expedition sponsor, Field Enterprises Corporation, to get them to force Doubleday to change course:

Ward and I have seen a proof of Hillary's book and I am afraid there are some changes which simply must be made. We are both very upset that we have been in no way consulted about those phases of the expedition when we were in charge. If the book is allowed to go out unaltered I shall suffer serious damage to my professional reputation and so will Ward, and there will be a breach of the terms of the contract by which we were to be treated with fairness and dignity.[6]

Pugh closed his letter with a warning that both he and Ward had instructed lawyers, who "will be writing to the corporation."

The threatened injunction had the desired effect. After a series of transatlantic telephone calls with the sponsors and Doubleday, most—though not all—of Ward's and Pugh's proposed revisions were accepted. Pugh signed off in a letter to the sponsors, pointing out that he was still not happy: "The book is still pretty ungenerous in its treatment, but it can't be helped. I see, for instance, that Hillary still persists in claiming credit for the Silver Hut, whereas in reality he had practically nothing to do with it!"[7]

The amendments Pugh had asked for were very limited. They amounted to a paragraph in the preface, introducing himself as the leader of the scientific team, and giving the names of the scientists, which had been left out by

Hillary. He also asked for minor alterations of emphasis to make the coverage fairer, asking for Ward to be acknowledged as the leader of the successful ascent of Ama Dablam, and judiciously changing Hillary's use of the word *I* to the word *we* in many places.

Despite the contretemps over the book, Pugh continued to treat Hillary fairly. A month later, Ward, who was due to give a talk on the Makalu rescue at the Alpine Club, mischievously asked him, "Would you like me to mention that Ed had no intention of taking rescue O2 to Makalu without your insistence?"[8] But Pugh begged him not to speak of it. Ward also wanted to highlight Hillary's resistance to the rescue oxygen in an article he was submitting to the sponsors. They, of course, asked him to omit the reference.

Pugh, who had avoided telling his colleagues about his problems with Hillary during the expedition, now revealed the full story of the rescue oxygen to both Ward and to the sponsors.[9] But he agreed that Ward should not include mention of it in his article. Nor did he or Ward tell the other members of the Silver Hut team how they had had to threaten Hillary with two injunctions to force him to change the book.

When the battle of the book was over, Pugh and Hillary continued their relationship perfectly amicably, as if nothing had happened. Hillary came to England with his family in November 1962 to promote *High in the Thin Cold Air* and reported to his contact at Field Enterprises (the sponsors) that he had "descended on Griff Pugh for lunch and had a very pleasant couple of hours."[10] Pugh also wrote that he had "a very pleasant reunion with Ed and his family."[11]

Discreet though Pugh remained, neither he nor Ward was willing to abandon the issue of rescue oxygen. Invited by Laurence Kirwan to speak about the Silver Hut at the Royal Geographical Society, Pugh seized the opportunity to try to convince the climbing community to adopt more sensible, safety-conscious attitudes—even where the objective was to climb without oxygen. The meeting was chaired by Charles Evans and Sir John Hunt, and many other climbers were in the audience. In spite of his dry academic way, Pugh spoke with as much passion as he could muster about "the extreme danger of ascents above 27,000 feet without oxygen equipment, even by well-acclimatised men." "All the organs of the body are working at the limit of their capacity at these heights, and there is no margin of reserve," he told his audience: "The only safeguard against these risks is to take adequate supplies of oxygen (as was done on the present expedition) and to have them ready on the spot to meet emergencies should rescue operations become necessary."[12]

As the years passed and the fashion swung back toward small, lightly equipped "Alpine-style" Himalayan expeditions, and the number of deaths among elite climbers escalated, Pugh chose not to get involved in the lively debates about the rights and wrongs, which surfaced in the letters pages of newspapers such as *The Times*. No longer seeing it as his role to tell mountaineers what to do, he still couldn't resist the odd censorious, private dig about how many lives were being lost. Such accidents, he argued, were failures of leadership, and shouldn't be allowed to happen.

On the other hand, when interviewed by the BBC about science in mountaineering, he conceded that having been a sportsman himself, he could readily understand the climbers' motivation. "The mountaineer is not interested in the easy way," he said. "There's no challenge . . . They like to do things the hard way."[13]

26

The Four Inns Walk

After the Silver Hut, Pugh never went to extreme altitude again, but the younger members of the Silver Hut winter team continued climbing with great enthusiasm. In the spring of 1963, Barry Bishop took part in an American Everest expedition on which Tom Hornbein and Willi Unsoeld made a pioneering first ascent of Everest's difficult West Ridge, descending by the conventional southern route, completing the first full traverse of an 8,000-meter peak.

While Hornbein and Unsoeld were on their way up the last leg of the West Ridge, Bishop and his partner Lute Jerstad climbed to the summit from the south. They then descended to the South Summit where, late in the day, they waited for Hornbein and Unsoeld to join them. Two hours later, as the four men set off down the mountain in the dark, Bishop felt his strength draining away: "Our plight is precarious and we know it. With oxygen all but exhausted, and with Tom's expiring flashlight, we feel our way with cramponed feet and ice axes down the knife ridge of snow . . . In our weakened condition we can barely tell one side of the ridge from the other."[1]

At about 10:00 p.m., unable to go on, they stopped and bivouacked at 28,000 feet, a thousand feet higher than any previous Everest bivouac. The temperature was −4°F. They had no tent and they had run out of oxygen. Bishop continued: "By this time Lute and I have slipped into a stupefied fatigue. My feet have lost all feeling and the tips of my fingers are following them into numbness. We curl up in our down jackets as best we can. With his frozen fingers, Lute cannot even close his jacket. He wraps it tightly and hopes for the best."[2]

By extraordinary good luck, there was very little wind that night. If there had been, they probably wouldn't have survived. They did, but Bishop lost all his toes, and Unsoeld lost nine of his and spent a long time in the hospital, recovering.[3] Their survival intrigued Pugh, who got a firsthand account of it from Bishop. His notes of the interview included details of Bishop's clothing: "String vest, shorts and singlet; then he had a cotton and wool vest, shirt, down underclothing similar to that used in 1961 [at the Silver Hut], then short climbing trousers, down trousers and anorak. He was carrying a down jacket which he put on for the night. Boots were the same ones he used in 1961."[4]

It was all grist to the mill of Pugh's fascination with survivors of extreme conditions. A few years earlier, Pugh's old friend Jimmie Riddell from Cedars was leading a party of skiers on a high route between Saas-Fee and Zermatt in the Swiss Alps when they were pinned down by a ferocious blizzard. They were not equipped for an overnight bivouac, and the weather was so appalling that many people feared they were dead. But Riddell was the ideal person to be lost in a blizzard with. Shepherding his group into a crevasse, he kept them sheltered for twenty hours while the storm raged, and they turned up in Zermatt safe and well, once it had blown over. Hearing the story, Pugh arranged to cross-examine every member of Riddell's group.

Riddell and Bishop only confirmed for Pugh what was already perfectly obvious from polar exploration and high-altitude mountaineering: that people can survive in extreme conditions without dying of cold. Yet during the 1950s and '60s, people were regularly dying of exposure in far less severe weather in the hills and mountains of Britain.

Hill-walking and hiking had become popular pastimes in Britain. Better transportation, rising prosperity, and more leisure time allowed more and more people to visit wild, remote areas, and the number of accidents was also rising. There were no accurate figures, but estimates suggested that deaths from exposure were running at between thirty and sixty a year.[5] Why there were so many fatalities in Britain's relatively low landscape and mild climate was a mystery; despite the research carried out during and after the war, there was no consensus about how to avoid hypothermia. Worse still, effective methods of rescue, treatment, and resuscitation had not been

THE FOUR INNS WALK

established, so if exposure victims did not die on the hillside, they often succumbed while being rescued.

Pugh, with his expertise on hypothermia, was asked to join a "Working Party on Accident Prevention and Life Saving" established by the Royal College of Surgeons of England in 1961, and he soon became hooked on the subject of exposure accidents among hill-walkers and trekkers.[6]

Adventure recreation attracted more than its fair share of folk imbued with the romantic-heroic ideals that Pugh had battled with in his Everest work. Here, once again, Pugh, with his pragmatic approach and open-minded curiosity, would find himself facing opposition from old-school, antiscience stalwarts, who chose to believe that susceptibility to hypothermia was largely the result of a poor mental attitude.

It was the energetic lobbying of respected progressive educator Kurt Hahn—founder of Gordonstoun School, where the Duke of Edinburgh was educated—that had galvanized the Royal College of Surgeons into action.[7] Hahn was one of the main catalysts behind the expansion of youth adventure training in Britain after the war. An advocate of the early-morning cold bath and the tough sporting challenge, he tapped into the postwar worries of the great and the good—that young people in Britain were irredeemably "slothful," "unhealthy," "unfit," and "unruly."[8]

Hahn's answer was to bring the character-building benefits of the public-school sporting ethos to less-privileged young people through the Outward Bound movement, which he founded in 1948. Outward Bound centers in places like the Lake District and Snowdonia provided adventure-training courses usually lasting around four weeks. The veteran Alpine Club member Geoffrey Winthrop Young, onetime president of Gordonstoun, was an ardent supporter, and the legendary Everester Eric Shipton was warden of an Outward Bound center between 1953 and 1957.[9]

The Duke of Edinburgh's Award, created by Hahn in the mid-1950s and strongly supported by the duke, enabled Hahn's methods to be promoted through youth organizations such as the Boy Scouts, the Girl Guides, and the Boys Brigade, and through schools, greatly extending his reach.[10] The Everest hero Sir John Hunt helped to set it up, and was appointed its first director in 1956.[11]

But Hahn had run into the problem that the young people he was sending out on sporting adventures had been showing a distressing propensity to die of exposure. In January 1960, a party of boys with an instructor set out from the Eskdale Outward Bound center in the Lake District on a strenuous two-day hike. After a change in the weather, three boys became exhausted, and one died.[12]

The Duke of Edinburgh's Award scheme also suffered from repeated mishaps which invariably generated widespread publicity. "Youth dies on trek," the *Daily Herald* trumpeted in February 1961, after three boys on a 30-mile ramble in the Radnorshire hills were overtaken by exhaustion and one died of exposure. "They were taking part in the endurance test which forms part of the Duke of Edinburgh's scheme to encourage character, leadership and physical fitness among youngsters," the paper reported, pointedly adding that the indignant coroner had demanded: "Had there been any training leading up to this fatal exercise? . . . I want to know who sends boys out on an exercise which is apparently beyond their strength, and why."[13]

Neither John Hunt, nor the Duke of Edinburgh nor Kurt Hahn, had anticipated the high accident rates afflicting their young recruits. They were meant to be benefiting from the uplifting experience of pitting themselves against the elements, not dying.

In 1963, after three years of deliberation, the Working Party on Accident Prevention met to discuss its findings at a prestigious convention.[14] Delegates came from all the royal medical colleges, the British Medical Association, industry, the armed services, trade unions, youth movements, and five government departments. The Duke of Edinburgh attended on the first day.

Most of the speakers on youth adventure, who included Sir John Hunt, were passionately in favor of it, peppering their contributions with grand assertions. "Adventurous initiative is part of the complete man and his health," said one. "The challenge of adventure should be a necessary part of education," said another.[15]

A consensus seemed to be emerging that hypothermia accidents among the young often stemmed from the mental state of the victim. "Mountains can frighten people to death; I know of several cases where they have done this," one delegate announced firmly, adding that exposure went hand in hand with "a bad mental approach to the mountains." "[Hypothermia] is often preceded by being fed up, tired and bored . . . and being made to do something you do not want to do."[16]

Sir Arthur Porritt, the quintessentially establishment president of the Royal College of Surgeons, thought that there were five major causes of accidents—"selfishness, lack of interest in others, inefficiency, bravado and carelessness."[17]

One speaker claimed that certain types of personality, such as "extroverts" and those with a "neurotic" predisposition, were responsible for much accident-prone behavior, and argued that psychological tests to establish personality traits were "obviously going to be of great importance from the point of view of research into accidents."[18] Kurt Hahn spoke of the need for young people to undergo "physical, nervous and spiritual conditioning" before undertaking adventurous sport.

Amid all the talk of psychology, one paper stood out—namely Griffith Pugh's.[19] Setting aside all talk of character building, Pugh speculated that something as simple as wet clothes might be at the root of the hypothermia problem. There might, he said, be reasons for adopting completely new physiological—not psychological—strategies for preventing hypothermia in the field. "Experimental evidence is badly needed."

After the convention Kurt Hahn took Pugh out to lunch and invited him to be a director of one of the Outward Bound schools and a member of the Outward Bound Safety Committee.[20]

The main outcome of the convention was the establishment in early 1964 of Britain's first permanent "Commission on Accident Prevention and Life Saving." Thirty-three distinguished members of the medical profession agreed to sit on six medical subcommittees devoted to topics like road accidents, accidents in the home, heart disease, and sports and recreation. All the doctors except Pugh and one other were members or fellows of the Royal College of Physicians.[21]

The commission had not even had its first meeting before another tragedy struck: In March 1964, the annual Four Inns Walk in the northern Peak District ended in disaster with the deaths of three boys.[22] Two hundred and forty boys, between the ages of seventeen and twenty-four, took part in the tough, 45-mile competitive marathon walk organized by the Derby Rover Scouts. The race took its name from the four inns along its route—The Isle of Skye, The Snake Pass Inn, The Nag's Head, and The Cat and Fiddle.

Walking in small groups of three or four, the competitors followed a route which took them over some of the roughest moorland in Britain, at altitudes between 650 and 2,000 feet. The race was in its eighth consecutive year, and three-quarters of the walkers usually finished the course successfully. The record finishing time was seven and a half hours, though most competitors took between nine and a half and twenty-two hours.

The competition was well organized, with regular checkpoints. Most of the entrants were not competing for the first time, and rescue services were on hand. There had been a few cases of fatigue in previous years, but no serious accidents or fatalities. The only major difference from previous years was that the weather deteriorated unexpectedly during the day, bringing strong winds and rain. This year only twenty-two boys finished the course. Many became fatigued and had to drop out. And, apart from the three who died, five more became so exhausted they had to be rescued, only narrowly escaping death themselves.

The organizers were bemused. The conditions were not exceptional, and the competitors who gave evidence at the inquest said they were quite used to bad weather, though perhaps not to being out in it for such a long period.

Pugh's reaction was to drive straight to the Derbyshire Dales to look at the lie of the land. He then went on to attend the inquest at Glossop, contacting the parents of the deceased to secure more information. He followed up his enquiries with a series of experiments, and produced a report for the Accident Commission addressing the question on everyone's lips—Why had these boys died?[23]

Reviewing previous research into hypothermia and the "insulation value" of clothing, Pugh realized that, whereas the impact of wind and of wet on the warmth of clothing had been studied separately, no one had yet measured the combined effects. And no one had studied the physical impact of wearing wet clothes in windy weather.[24]

Pugh put the actual clothes worn by the three dead boys onto his experimental subjects and had them walk on treadmills in a cold chamber in differing wind speeds while being sprayed with cold water. As they walked, he measured the impact on their temperatures and the amount of energy they were using. The guinea pigs found it very unpleasant indeed.

One of Pugh's seminal discoveries was that when clothes got wet in windy conditions, their insulation value was reduced by 90 percent. The boys who died would almost have been better off naked than in the jeans they were wearing.

Once the clothes of the boys on the walk became wet, the only way to keep warm was to walk faster. The athletic, physically fit boys had no problem in doing so, and finished the race easily. But many of the competitors could not walk fast enough to keep themselves warm. When they tried they became tired and had to slow down, whereupon they got colder. Pugh had established in earlier studies that people can push themselves for long periods only at about 60 percent of their maximum capacity.

When body temperature drops too low, our bodies respond with an involuntary increase in metabolism in an attempt to warm up. Shivering is a part of this spontaneous reaction, which uses up a lot of energy in its own right, leaving even less energy for walking. Consequently the walker gets more and more exhausted. This chain of events explained why such a large number of boys in the Four Inns Walk became exhausted and dropped out.[25]

Those who struggled on despite being tired and cold became more and more tired, ever slower and ever colder. Eventually, as hypothermia progressed, their temperatures would have sunk so low that their balance and muscular control were impaired, causing them to fall over frequently, making them even slower, and further accelerating the rate at which they were cooling. It was a vicious circle.[26] The boys who died would have gradually lapsed into a stupor and have become rigid. At this point, without rescue, death would be only a short time away.

As Pugh concluded, the change in the weather, the lack of waterproof, windproof clothing, and the mistake of carrying on walking to the point of exhaustion rather than stopping and taking shelter had been a fatal combination.[27]

The first annual report of the Medical Commission on Accident Prevention opened with a brief letter from Buckingham Palace, written by the Duke of Edinburgh, saying he was "particularly interested in Dr. Pugh's report" about these "inexplicable accidents."[28] The introductory essay by the commission's scientific director, Norman Capener, also highlighted Pugh's report. "This type of research sets the pattern for many other fields in which the Medical Commission intends to work and in which physiological and psychological factors are related to the ultimate causes of accident producing circumstances."[29]

Now that Pugh had received a special mention from the duke, John Hunt asked him to help with the Duke of Edinburgh's Award Scheme. The Scout Association asked him to "look into casualties suffered by the scouts," and Kurt Hahn invited him to visit two of his Outward Bound schools to investigate which aspects of the Outward Bound regime were predisposing the recruits to hypothermia.[30] Pugh, now in his fifties, insisted on taking part in the full Outward Bound exercise himself—cold baths, long-distance hikes, and all—and came away jubilant. "I am like a boy of twenty-five. I am far fitter than most of those boys."

Shortly after the Four Inns Walk report was published in the *Lancet*, a doctor from the Anglesey General Hospital in Wales sent Pugh a collection of twenty-seven case histories of local exposure casualties. Pugh tracked down and questioned eight of them.[31] He followed up new incidents as they occurred, and embarked on new controlled experiments at his laboratory and out in the countryside with groups of Rover Scouts and schoolboys.[32] My brothers Simon and Oliver were roped in on occasion. Over the next few years he published five major academic articles and produced practical recommendations for the prevention and management of hypothermia among hill-walkers, which have been saving lives ever since.[33]

Pugh made it clear that the jeans and similar clothing typically worn by walkers at the time were quite unsuitable for walking for longer than two or three hours in wet, windy conditions. The best way to avoid hypothermia, he said, was to wear clothing that provided insulation against wind and wet—especially on the legs. Therefore walkers in remote areas should *always* carry lightweight, waterproof overgarments to be put on in the event of wind and rain, to keep the inner layers of clothing dry.[34] Calling for the development of lightweight, inexpensive emergency equipment, he also suggested walkers should carry "survival bags," and explored the idea of creating survival bags from a new, ultrathin, reflective cloth that had been developed in America for making "space blankets."[35] Today no experienced walker would set off on a long walk without lightweight, waterproof overgarments and a survival or bivouac bag.

And there was another important recommendation. "When a person shows early symptoms of exposure, the surest way of preventing disaster is to stop and camp," Pugh said. If they are unable to get off the mountain quickly, huddling together and sheltering from the wind, before the vicious circle of cold and exhaustion can set in, would give a walking group a far better chance of survival than driving themselves to exhaustion.[36] Even without waterproofs, someone caught out in the cold with wet clothes could get 50 percent more insulation from his clothes by remaining at rest than by walking on. And, if that person could get out of the wind and adopt a curled-up posture, the insulation provided by his clothes would be better still.[37]

Because the time between the onset of the first symptoms of hypothermia and outright collapse was often quite short, Pugh suggested that the rescue services should develop methods of on-the-spot resuscitation, rather than continuing with the usual practice of evacuating victims on stretchers, which was often dangerously slow.

Pugh also had an important recommendation for Kurt Hahn. Promoters of youth adventure training had always believed that sending out mixed-ability groups of young people on grueling training exercises was an ideal way of developing leadership qualities and team spirit. The stronger walkers would help and protect the weak, and this, in turn, would enhance the fellowship within the group.

Observing Outward Bound walking parties in action, Pugh found that in practice the stronger walkers tended to get fed up with the slower ones—particularly if the weather got worse and they needed to speed up to keep warm.[38] The slower walkers, who couldn't keep up, became cold and demoralized, and the group often made the fatal mistake of splitting up, leaving the slower walkers in danger of falling into the vicious cycle of exhaustion and hypothermia. This was made worse by the fact that hypothermia often affects people mentally, causing them to become aimless and apathetic, or aggressive and uncooperative, and to make bad judgments about how to behave—displaying the "bad mental attitudes" that many in the youth-training world believed to be the cause rather than a consequence of hypothermia.[39]

Pugh felt so strongly about unnecessary exposure accidents that he traveled around the country, lecturing mountain-rescue groups, adventure-training centers, Scout and youth leaders, mountain guides and police, on how to avoid and treat hypothermia. The message even got through to some vintage Everesters. A veteran of the 1933 Everest expedition—Jack Longland, Derbyshire's director of education and chairman of the National Mountaineering Centre at Plas y Brenin—wrote to applaud Pugh for publicizing "little known facts which are of great importance to all of us."[40]

Pugh was also invited to appear on radio and television programs when tragedies occurred, and became a pundit on survival. In 1973, he was positively triumphant when four sixteen-year-old boys who went missing while attempting a 50-mile walk in Snowdonia were found safe and well in their tent four days later, after the largest-ever British rescue operation. Their experiences were reenacted on a BBC Horizon program called *The Day Seemed So Good* (1974). Some commentators suggested that the boys—one of whom had become exhausted and hypothermic toward the end of the first day—ought to have made a greater effort to get off the mountain. Pugh was adamant that by sheltering in their tent and waiting to be rescued, they had behaved in an exemplary way that had kept them out of danger and had ensured their survival.

27

"Good Science and Bad Science"

In the late 1960s British trawler fishing in Icelandic waters suffered a cluster of accidents. In early 1968, three fishing trawlers from Hull sank within a week, with the loss of sixty lives. The third boat to sink—the *Ross Cleveland*—capsized suddenly in hurricane-force winds in the Icelandic fjord of Isafjordur Deep on February 4. Eight hours later a lone survivor, Harry Eddom, the "mate" of the *Ross Cleveland*, was washed ashore alongside two dead companions in a rubber lifeboat. They had drifted along the coast for 10 miles, ending up in a small fjord called Seydisfjordur.

Crawling out of the boat, Eddom pulled it ashore before setting off on foot across the boulder-strewn beach in the snow and wind. After struggling along for seven or eight hours, he spent the night sheltering in the lee of a deserted house.[1] The next day he managed to attract the attention of a shepherd boy who helped him walk to a nearby farm, where he was given food and put to bed. He was subsequently taken to the hospital, where he was found to be well except for mild frostbite in his feet. The other eighteen members of the *Ross Cleveland*'s crew all perished.

Within a few days of the extraordinary survival of Harry Eddom, Pugh flew to Iceland to find out firsthand what had happened. Pugh interviewed Eddom in the hospital, also interviewing the casualties from another British trawler, the *Notts County*, which had gone aground in the same storm. The ship had not sunk, but one of its crew had died of hypothermia. Pugh's report for the Medical Commission on Accident Prevention was published in the *British Medical Journal* in mid-March.

A seaman from the age of fifteen, Harry Eddom was a fit twenty-six-year-old with a good layer of subcutaneous fat. When he fell into the sea and was hauled onto the lifeboat by his two colleagues, he was wearing warm clothing under a two-piece, plastic-coated, waterproof overgarment known as a "duck suit." He was also wearing thigh boots. Although soaked, his clothes still provided him with a degree of insulation from the wind and the cold, which in Pugh's view was what enabled him to survive.

The rubber lifeboat had a torn canopy that was letting in wind and water. Neither of his two companions was wearing waterproofs and therefore had little hope of survival. The temperature of the air was roughly 46°F, and the water, 35°F. One of the unfortunate seamen, scantily dressed in underclothes, died of hypothermia within an hour and a half. The other, who had warm clothes but no waterproof or windproof overgarments, died after three hours. Autopsies on another five recovered bodies showed that three of the men had died of hypothermia and two had drowned.[2]

Pugh was blunt with the journalists who interviewed him about the trawler tragedy. His investigation had revealed that it was common for trawler crews to go fishing in Arctic waters, taking waterproof suits for only half the men on board (on the grounds that the other half were not expected to do deck jobs). Pugh told the science reporter of *The Times* that any trawlerman sent to north Icelandic waters without protective clothing "was more or less being condemned to death."[3]

Pugh's outspokenness did not go down well at the MRC head office, particularly as a Board of Trade inquiry into the trawler tragedies was under way, and the subject was officially *sub judice*, or officially under judicial consideration. He escaped a reprimand, however, because Sir Peter Medawar, head of the National Institute for Medical Research (NIMR), intervened. Medawar wrote to Pugh, subtly indicating that the head office was displeased, but offsetting the gentle reproof with the sympathetic remark: "I know how difficult it is to try to be reserved when newspaper men are pumping you for all they can get, so believe me when I say I have every sympathy with your predicament."[4]

MRC head-office staff members were more than mere day-to-day managers. They administered the MRC's research strategies, and were the principal channel of communication between the research scientists and the governing council. It was not a good idea to upset them. Peter Medawar, who became the director of the NIMR in 1962, was Pugh's greatest protector and his greatest champion at the MRC. Universally accepted as one of the outstanding scientists of his generation, he effectively created the science of the immunology of transplantation, for which he was jointly awarded the Nobel Prize for Medicine in 1960.[5] Heart, lung, kidney, and bone marrow transplants, which are commonplace today, owe much of their success to his pioneering work. A charismatic figure with great personal charm and a terrific sense of humor, he inspired devotion in his colleagues and was showered with many honors in his lifetime.

His respected predecessor, Sir Charles Harington, had left Pugh very much to his own devices, going out of his way to praise the quality of his research.[6] Pugh was unfailingly deferential to Harington, but Medawar was a man after his own heart. Pugh hailed from a line of physiologists who—like his great forebear, J. S. Haldane—devoted much of their efforts to solving practical problems. But the UK scientific establishment tended to look down on such mundane research; getting one's hands dirty tackling practical problems was regarded as low-level subalterns' work. It was the "pure" scientists who grappled with issues like the structure of DNA, scientists who studied fundamental issues at several levels of abstraction in the splendid isolation of their laboratories, who were regarded as the scientific elite.

Peter Medawar believed, however, that the distinction between "pure" and "applied" science was false. There were only two types of science, he said, "good science and bad science." Practical problems often provided a crucial lead to fundamental scientific principles. His own initial muse had been the question of why skin couldn't be grafted from one person to another. The search for the answer had led him into fundamental issues in human immunology which proved immensely fruitful. This was exactly how Pugh operated.

Medawar was renowned for his high intellectual standards, and shared Pugh's disapproval of research that involved "the gathering of huge amounts of information hoping something useful will come out of it."[7] Pugh's projects tended to be small, inexpensive, and focused, whereas his divisional boss, Otto Edholm, favored large, expensive projects collecting masses of data. "We had a whole aeroplane to ourselves in which we flew troops backwards and forwards to Aden," a former colleague recalled of one of those giant studies—an inquiry into heat exhaustion in soldiers. "We had fifty scientists looking after sixty soldiers. How much that cost we had no idea. But money was not a problem."[8]

Medawar took control of the NIMR at a time when Pugh's long-standing problems with Edholm were coming to a head. Pugh had been so resentful of Edholm muscling in on his Channel-swimming studies in the mid-1950s that he had given up the cold-water studies altogether. Edholm then lost interest too. Four years passed before another physiologist, William R. Keatinge, grasped the baton and took the subject forward.[9]

After the success of the Silver Hut, Pugh found it more difficult than ever to accept that Edholm deserved any authority over him. And after Sir Edmund Hillary's attempt to take the credit for the Silver Hut science, he was no longer prepared to brush off such slights and suppress his resentment as he had in the past. The resentment rose to the surface and he became extremely touchy.

While researching my father's life, I met seven physiologists who worked alongside Pugh in the 1950s and '60s.[10] Several of them told me that Pugh did not regard Edholm as a worthy boss: "I don't think Griff thought very much of Edholm," one commented. "Edholm was not the serious scientist that Griff was . . . Griff objected to being overseen . . . by Edholm, whom he thought was inferior—and he was inferior, no question about it."

Edholm was the same age as Pugh, so there was no chance of Pugh ever succeeding him. The only avenues open to him were to leave, or to break away and form his own separate unit within the MRC. The latter, however, could only be brought off with Edholm's full support, and with a great deal of politicking and schmoozing of the right people.

Pugh was at a highly productive stage in his career. His work on hypothermia and altitude had been widely acclaimed. His advice was much sought after by many influential organizations. For years he had plowed his own furrow, getting work independently of Edholm. Deeply frustrated that his professional status did not, in his view, reflect his academic achievements, he felt—rightly or wrongly—that Edholm was always there at his shoulder, waiting to move in and take credit for his work.

At the time of the Four Inns Walk, Edholm and several colleagues were also working on hypothermia on land, and Pugh became exceedingly secretive about what he was doing. When he went on field trips, he wouldn't tell

Edholm where he was going. He refused to submit his expenses to Edholm, and wouldn't allow him to see any of his research results, as was expected of all junior staff. Furthermore, he often let slip derogatory comments, which showed all too clearly that he had little academic respect for Edholm or his close collaborators. His scorn did not, of course, enhance his popularity. "Griff didn't think much of people who were less bright than he was," one colleague commented. "He was really unable to communicate with anybody except other very bright people."

Most of Edholm's team found him a considerate and supportive boss whom they remembered with affection and gratitude. As to clashes with Pugh, they felt there were faults on both sides. Edholm's greatest strength, they agreed, lay less in the originality of his own research—"one wouldn't say he was a great scientist"—than in being a networker, an "explainer of science," a mover and shaker and an excellent manager. One colleague described him as being at the center of "a huge spider's web of contacts." He sat on countless committees and public bodies, and was constantly looking for ways of promoting and expanding his division.

Like most people, however, Edholm had more than one side to him. "When he liked people—young people—then he was absolutely 100 percent," I was told. "But when he for some reason or other took exception to people, he could be absolutely vicious."

If Pugh resented Edholm, Edholm almost certainly resented Pugh for his insubordination, and for insinuating that Edholm wanted to steal his work. He, in turn, made life difficult for Pugh. He discouraged young researchers from applying to work with Pugh, telling them that he was impossible; the idea that "everyone found Pugh difficult to work with" became common currency within the division, despite clear evidence to the contrary from the Silver Hut.

The MRC's climatic chambers were in constant use by Edholm and his colleagues. When Pugh was in the midst of his studies with the Scouts, they refused to allow him access. He had to appeal to Medawar for an allocation of time. It cannot have been a healthy environment in which to work.

If Pugh wanted a change of circumstances, he should perhaps have cultivated head-office executives. Instead, he was often barely polite to them. "He could be very disparaging if he didn't agree with something," John

Brotherhood, his junior researcher, explained: "He was not an ordinary person. Just completely focused on his work. A man who was intellectually orientated. That's where he got his kicks. He was just irritated [by head office staff]—and didn't have time for anything else."

Pugh's legendary idiosyncratic habits annoyed many people, too—his late arrivals at work; his habit of blocking the exit to the parking lot with his unmistakable silver-gray sports car; his insistence on eating his lunch long after everyone else, so the ladies in the canteen felt they had to stay open late especially for him. If he wanted something, he would ignore all the proper channels and appeal directly to Medawar over Edholm's and his managers' heads.[11]

So sure was Pugh of his standing with Medawar that when his license was suspended for six months, he tried to persuade Medawar to give him a special MRC grant of £250 to cover the cost of employing a driver.[12] He felt his fieldwork with the Scouts was too important to postpone. When Medawar refused, Pugh resorted to a disguise. Dressed up in a raincoat and sunglasses, he commandeered my brother Simon's Morris Mini and drove himself around the country heedless of the fact that driving with a suspended license was a serious offense which could warrant a prison sentence.

It was perhaps not surprising that when the maverick Pugh complained bitterly about his situation to MRC officials, they were less than sympathetic. In September 1964, one MRC manager wrote to another that Pugh had contacted him to "grumble about his status and [alleged] difficulties in carrying out his work."[13]

I think I should inform you of a telephone conversation I have just had with Dr. Pugh. Dr. Pugh, who sounded most agitated, started by saying that he wanted to talk to someone about his salary; soon he switched to bitter complaints of persecution. He claimed he had absolutely no support . . . no technicians, he was being badly treated; he was sick of people riding on his work, stealing his own work and passing it off as their own; he thought he should have his own unit and refused to carry on as at present![14]

On such occasions—and there were several—the officials would inform Peter Medawar. Medawar would call Pugh over to the head office and soothe him. Pugh would be mollified and quiet down until the next time.

Medawar sympathized with his predicament and staunchly supported him. He insisted that Pugh be allowed to undertake whatever research he chose, ensured that he received regular raises in his salary, and generally looked after his interests with the establishment. He described Pugh as "one of the most distinguished members of the institute," and reminded head-office officials that his work reflected "much credit to the [MRC] since it is carried out to high scientific standards."

Perhaps it would have been better for Pugh if he had not been quite so protected by Medawar, for then he might have left the MRC and pursued his career elsewhere and avoided ending up—as one of his colleagues and great friends described him to me—"a disappointed man."

But it was not in Pugh's nature to allow petty resentments to dominate his life completely. Once again a golden opportunity was about to drop into his lap and give him a new lease on life as one of Britain's pioneering sports scientists.

28

The "Boffin" and the Altitude Olympics

In 1965 the word *altitude* was suddenly on everyone's lips. A tremendous public row had blown up about the choice of Mexico City for the 1968 Olympic Games. Encouraged by disgruntled athletes, the newspapers were outraged that the International Olympic Committee (IOC) expected top-flight sportsmen and women to perform at their peak in the rarefied atmosphere of a city located at an altitude of 7,350 feet above sea level.[1]

Mexico's altitude posed serious risks to the health of the competitors, the newspapers chorused. If Olympic athletes pushed themselves to their limits in the thin air of Mexico City—where there is 25 percent less oxygen than at sea level—the normal mechanisms protecting their bodies might fail. "There will be those who will die," Onni Niskanen, the Finnish coach of Ethiopian marathon runner Abebe Bikila, was reported to have said. Furthermore, the Games would be unfair because athletes from sea level would be at a disadvantage compared with those born and bred at higher altitudes. The "unfathomable old men of the IOC"—that "self-perpetuating and unrepresentative oligarchy"—were roundly castigated for having selected the location of the Games "in an atmosphere of party-giving and public relations flummery," without regard for the welfare of the competitors.[2] Boycotts were threatened.[3]

At first the IOC and the British Olympic Association (BOA) insisted that they had received expert advice. K. S. "Sandy" Duncan, general secretary of the BOA, wrote: "The IOC were presented with a great weight of medical opinion stressing that no danger to competitors existed and that quick acclimatization to altitude was obtainable."[4] As to the suggestions of unfairness, Avery Brundage, the chairman of the IOC, defied all the logic of international competition with the sanctimonious riposte that the point of the Olympics was "to take part rather than to win or set new records."[5]

Concrete evidence about whether there was a genuine risk to athletes' health did not in truth exist. Little research had been undertaken into the impact of altitude on athletes. A few research groups around the world—notably in Scandinavia, Italy, Denmark, and the USA—were investigating exercise physiology in relation to sports, but sports science had not yet developed into a burgeoning discipline in its own right, least of all in the UK.[6]

Eventually the BOA decided to set up a Medical Advisory Committee, asking one of the eight "unfathomable men of the IOC"—Sir Arthur Porritt—to be its chairman.[7] A former sprinter and star athlete at Oxford, Arthur Porritt had run against Harold Abrahams in the 100 meters at the 1924 Olympics, winning the bronze medal to Abrahams's gold. The race was immortalized in the film *Chariots of Fire*. Otto Edholm was invited to represent the Medical Research Council, and Griffith Pugh with his expertise on altitude was commissioned to investigate.[8]

Pugh's first point of contact with the athletes was Martin Hyman, one of the UK's leading long-distance runners. Strongly critical of what he described as the "quite appalling old boys' club" at the heart of the British sporting establishment, Hyman was chairman of the International Athletes Club, which had fomented much of the controversy over Mexico. Established in 1958 by a band of frustrated elite athletes who wanted a collective public voice, the club had become a significant pressure group. Hyman and his colleagues wanted the 1968 Games moved, but they were also acutely aware that if the Games stayed in Mexico, they would need expert advice about altitude. They suspected that the BOA intended Pugh's research to pacify them, but they agreed to cooperate. Hyman went to meet Pugh at Hampstead in the summer of 1965, and his first impression of the messy laboratory and the tousle-haired physiologist was that he had been fobbed off with a classic absentminded scientist who knew nothing about athletics.

Despite his initial doubts about Pugh, Hyman was more scientifically minded than most athletes. He and his running partner Bruce Tulloh were members of the Portsmouth Athletic Club, where they had adopted a methodical approach to training, subjecting old and new ideas to objective trials and informing themselves about the latest techniques and research.

They reaped the benefits. In five out of the six years between 1959 and 1964, Hyman was ranked one of the top five 10,000-meter runners in the world. Tulloh won the gold medal in the 5,000 meters at the European Championships of 1962. From 1961 to 1964 he was in the top six in the world. They were star members of the club—role models for the wider membership—and other runners at Portsmouth achieved outstanding success in both national and European competitions.[9] Then, as Hyman put it, "the other clubs caught up."

The Portsmouth club was not typical of the country as a whole, however. In Britain in the 1960s, Hyman told me when I met him at his home in Edinburgh, "the concept of analyzing what was needed to enable athletes to perform optimally was quite foreign to people."[10] The majority of athletes had no access to formal training, let alone training influenced by physiologists. Instead they followed training programs based on experience handed down from older athletes, and on anecdotal advice culled from sports magazines and newspapers. Most of the coaching was carried out voluntarily by ex-athletes who were not medically or scientifically trained, and many doubted whether science really had anything to offer the athlete.[11]

The better-off athletes who could afford professional coaching had typically grown up in the tradition of public-school "amateurism," which held that it was not only unsporting but also ungentlemanly to mix science with sport, or to give undue attention to training and preparation. For a long time Roger Bannister, who in 1954 ran the first mile in under 4 minutes, felt he had to hide his enthusiasm for running in order "not to appear to take games too seriously."[12] According to his running mate Christopher Chattaway, Bannister "went to great lengths to conceal the amount of training he did."[13]

Despite studying exercise physiology at the Oxford School, Bannister found it politic to use his book *First Four Minutes* to distance himself from the idea that science could be useful to sport: "Experiments in the laboratory are not of much practical value to athletes. There is in fact little scientific evidence in favor of many of the things done in training. The adaptation of the body to the stress of running is of such bewildering complexity that the athlete is forced to fall back on common sense."[14]

By the mid-1960s, however, things had moved on. Bannister had become chairman of the research committee of the newly formed Sports

Council, and the situation created by the Mexico Olympics enabled Hyman to persuade five of his fellow runners to submit themselves to Pugh's research.

The runners were still skeptical, but Pugh, an ex-Olympic sportsman who enjoyed nothing more than research in virgin territory, seized the opportunity with enthusiasm. The athletes taking part in the project—Mike Turner, John Cooke, Dominic Kelly, the brothers Gerry and Geoffrey North, and Hyman himself—were all long-distance runners of international caliber.[15] "Endurance" athletes were chosen because they were expected to suffer the most from Mexico's altitude, since they use energy derived mainly from the oxygen they breathe (aerobic exercise). By contrast, competitors in "explosive" events like sprinting or long-jumping were expected to be much less affected. They use energy stored in their muscles (anaerobic exercise) and pay back the oxygen debt later, so lack of oxygen in the atmosphere has less impact on their performances.[16] Indeed, it was predicted that sprinters would positively benefit from Mexico's altitude because the air resistance would be less than at sea level. Distance runners would gain from this too, but the benefit would be offset by the lack of oxygen.

Before starting his research, Pugh compared the results of the Pan American Games held at altitude in Mexico City in 1955 with those of the 1956 Olympics held at sea level in Melbourne.[17] Compared with Melbourne, running performances in Mexico over distances from 800 meters to 10,000 meters were progressively slower the longer the race, whereas sprint times were unaffected or slightly better. Some observers thought there had been an "abnormally high incidence of collapse in Mexico City," and there were stories of athletes blacking out and having to be revived with oxygen.[18]

Pugh's project kicked off on home turf with a four-week program to establish benchmark fitness levels and running times, followed by a further set of tests in his laboratory.[19] By this time Hyman had realized that his first impression of Pugh had been wrong. Rather than imposing preconceived ideas on the athletes, as Hyman expected, Pugh bombarded them with questions about every aspect of running and all its problems.

The first trials brought home to Pugh how lucky he was to have access to top-class athletes.[20] Elite athletes are gold-standard experimental subjects who produce remarkably consistent performances, so the research results are not distorted by the day-to-day variations that afflict lesser runners. Hyman could judge the pace at which he was running, lap by lap, to the accuracy of a second, without a watch.

Pugh was also deeply impressed by the runners' remarkable constitutions and often came home talking of their extraordinarily large hearts and blood volumes, their slow pulse rates and impressive lung capacities. So powerful were they that his usual exercise experiments on the stationary bicycle in his lab, which had never failed to bring a climber or a scientist to the point of total exhaustion, proved incapable of exhausting them.

After the four-week study, Pugh's party left for Mexico City in early November 1965. They stayed at a "comfortable" hotel near the British embassy in the center of town, in an area of wide, tree-lined boulevards, grand squares, parks, and fountains; the traffic, however, was horrendous, and the atmosphere smoggy. They spent the next four weeks carrying out more research at a running track 20 minutes' drive from their hotel and in a makeshift laboratory nearby.

The tests and experiments mirrored those the athletes had already undergone in England. They included four 3-mile running trials at weekly intervals and three sessions of 1-mile trials. At the laboratory their maximum work capacities and breathing rates were tested on the stationary bicycle with all the paraphernalia of mouthpieces, tubes, and Douglas bags. Their maximum heart rates, the levels of oxygen in their blood, their hemoglobin levels, pH levels, blood volumes, and many other variables were closely monitored before, during, and after exercise, which meant needles, more Douglas bags, wires, and electrodes. The athletes also kept records of their sleep patterns, pulse rates, food intake, and training schedules.

Most of the athletes found Pugh's tests onerous, intrusive, and unpleasant, but Pugh—a single-minded taskmaster—seemed blithely unconcerned about how his "guinea pigs" might be feeling. If an athlete collapsed from exhaustion, developed an unusual heart rhythm, or started hyperventilating in the middle of an experiment, the unfortunate man soon learned that he couldn't expect much sympathy from the physiologist. Pugh was more likely to look rather pleased and exclaim: "Oh, how very interesting, I must write that down at once."

Toughness, single-mindedness, and the ability to endure discomfort were the stock-in-trade of the distance runner, however, and Pugh generally got on well with the athletes, especially Hyman and Turner, who spent many hours discussing the mechanics of performance with him.[21]

Turner had read an article by an American exercise physiologist claiming that, contrary to conventional wisdom, the warm-up exercises practiced assiduously by most athletes were actually of little use.[22] Experiments had shown, the physiologist said, that warm-ups did not increase the temperature of the muscles nearly as much as athletes imagined. Skeptical about this, Pugh picked up a piece of wire used for measuring temperatures and pushed it clean through the bicep of his right arm, remarking as he did so that it only hurt when he pushed it in and not when it emerged on the other side. Holding a weight in his hand he then exercised his arm for 3 minutes while Turner watched the temperature monitor rise by 37°F, contradicting the recent claim. They repeated the exercise with the left arm and got the same result. It was the simplicity of Pugh's approach—the experiment that seemed completely obvious when Pugh thought of it—that impressed Turner.

On another occasion Pugh asked Hyman why, when distance runners often suffered from the heat, it was generally accepted that they ought to wear hats in hot, sunny conditions. Hats might be adding to their heat problems, he said. Obviously they wore hats to keep the sun off their heads, but Hyman had never given it much thought.

He, Pugh, and a few other runners then went to the running track, where Pugh measured how hot their heads became when running in the sun with and without hats, and found that they were 41°F hotter with hats than without them. It was enough to convince them either not to wear a hat when competing in the heat, or to wear a peaked hat with a crown made of mesh that the air could pass through.

When they first arrived in Mexico, all the athletes had felt tired and unfit. They suffered from shortness of breath, tight chests, dry mouths, and exceptionally high pulse rates when they took heavy exercise. It was several days before they felt able to resume normal training. In the first 3-mile trial, on the fourth day, they averaged around 8 percent slower than at sea level. After four weeks of acclimatization they all felt much better and their performances had greatly improved. Nevertheless, in the last 3-mile trial on the twenty-seventh day, they were still on average nearly 6 percent slower than at sea level.

If Pugh got on well with the athletes, his relationship with the BOA was quite another matter.[23] The BOA had sent out a chaperone to keep him in hand: Dr. Raymond Owen, a GP with a special interest in obstetrics and the BOA's honorary physician. Owen and his good friend, Sandy Duncan, the BOA's powerful general secretary—who had been a long jumper and captain for England in the 1938 Empire Games—were both convinced that the "alarmist press reports" had grossly exaggerated the altitude issues. They believed the research project would confirm that the athletes' main problems would be psychological rather than physical.

The British Olympic authorities, whom Owen and Duncan represented, were more adamant than most that the protests against Mexico should not succeed. Most adamant of all was the chairman of the BOA, the Marquess of Exeter, another veteran of the 1924 *Chariots of Fire* Olympics. Exeter was also president of the UK Amateur Athletics Association and a long-serving member of the International Olympic Committee. In the eyes of such establishment figures, any capitulation to the anti-Mexico lobby would open the floodgates to professional athletes who were more concerned with money and medals than with playing the game as best they could wherever they were called upon to do so.

"I cannot really feel that a physiologist is going to have much purpose," Owen had confided to Duncan before the BOA commissioned Pugh's research. Owen had been angling to carry out the research himself with a view toward obtaining the results that the BOA wanted: "If I went out myself with an athletics coach and 4–6 athletes, I could find out most of what we require to know. We would look at this thing in a practical way . . . rather than in a purely scientific way, and I am sure the results would be of more practical value to the governing bodies."[24]

But he failed to convince the Medical Advisory Committee, who feared the project would not carry sufficient weight with the public unless undertaken by an expert.

Finding himself relegated to chaperoning and "assisting" Pugh, Owen regarded him as "simply a bloody nuisance," and referred to him scornfully behind his back as "the boffin [scientist]." The dispatches he sent back to London reveal that he disliked Pugh and was deeply skeptical about his ability to find out anything useful. Determined to downplay the physical problems and highlight instead the psychological problems athletes were likely to face in Mexico, Owen assumed that psychology was completely beyond the understanding of "the boffin."[25]

The BOA had resolved to keep tight control over the publicity surrounding Pugh's project. A directive had been issued early on, stating that in London only Sandy Duncan and Arthur Gold, chairman of the Amateur Athletics Association, were permitted to speak to the press. In Mexico only Owen would be allowed to talk to journalists.

However, well before Pugh left London—indeed, as soon as the BOA announced his research project—the press descended on him in droves. Ignoring all instructions, he allowed TV crews into his laboratory to film the athletes and gave interviews to nine separate media organizations, including the BBC, the Press Association, Granada Television, and United Press International.[26] Duncan remonstrated with him but only succeeded in giving him the impression that the BOA wanted to hush up his research, then use it to cover up the altitude problems. Pugh reacted furiously, and Duncan had to pacify him.[27]

Similar disagreements arose in Mexico. Two weeks after Pugh arrived a story appeared in *The Times* quoting him as saying that "anybody who did not spend a month out here before the Olympic Games would have no chance at all of winning a gold medal in anything over 800 metres."[28] Sandy Duncan protested directly to Pugh in a letter from London.[29] But Pugh was unrepentant.[30]

Years earlier, *The Times*'s Everest contract had expressly forbidden Pugh—and the other team members—to speak publicly about their roles on the expedition. Now, toward the end of his career, he was no longer willing to keep silent, and began to reveal a surprising talent for using the media to get his voice heard.

Pugh flew back to London in early December. Having already completed his preliminary report and sent it to the BOA, he felt no qualms about telling the reporters who met him at the airport that even after four weeks the athletes in the study "were never able to run as fast as they had in England." He wasn't sure, he added, if they would regain their sea-level form even if they remained in Mexico for six months or a year.

Pugh's words did nothing to alleviate the anxiety among athletes waiting to find out what the BOA intended to do to help them. But the BOA would only comment that "a very considerable amount of data" had been collected, which would require "considerable study before final conclusions can be reached."[31]

A few weeks later, writing in the *Observer* on January 2, Christopher Brasher, Olympic gold medalist in Melbourne in 1956, and an influential member of the International Athletes Club, furiously accused the BOA of trying to hide the results of Pugh's research. Mexico was a "ghastly mistake," he roared. "The whole situation is beginning to border on farce."[32] Pugh, meanwhile, was quoted in the *Illustrated London News* as saying, "It's high time those who plan these games should stop using athletes as pawns.[33]

Finally, on January 19 the BOA's Medical Advisory Committee met to discuss the Mexico study.[34] Pugh, whose report was a pithy six pages, spoke first.[35] He had found no evidence that the athletes would die, he told the committee, but they would be slow. After four weeks of acclimatization his athletes were running 3-mile trials on average 5.7 percent slower than at sea level. Their performances had improved on average by 2.8 percent during the four weeks, and were still improving at the end—though there were individual variations. That 2.8 percent might not seem dramatic, Pugh pointed out, but in a 3-mile race it amounted to roughly 20 seconds in time, or 120 yards, "which would cover most of the field in a 5,000 metre Olympic final!" It could make the difference between coming first and coming last. In the 1-mile trials, performances had also improved, but to a lesser degree. The fact that the runners were still improving suggested they should acclimatize for a minimum of four weeks before the Games, and preferably for longer.

Dr. Owen then presented a seventeen-page report of his own.[36] Repeating many of Pugh's findings, Owen contradicted Pugh's interpretation of them. Pugh had categorically asserted that the athletes' responses to altitude were not "subjective." Owen, however, claimed that the athletes' symptoms, such as shortness of breath on exertion, "were undoubtedly psychological, although they were certainly physical as well." "To a large extent competitors will suffer those symptoms which they have been told to expect," he insisted.

Pugh had found no evidence that acclimatization reached a plateau even after twenty-eight days, yet Owen asserted that, after the first two to three weeks, acclimatization leveled off. Further improvements in performance, he said, were attributable to other factors, like improving fitness. The maximum acclimatization permitted, in his view, should be exactly twenty-four days. Staying longer would lead to "difficulties of a psychological nature," such as "boredom" and "homesickness."

The BOA was clearly determined to make as few concessions as possible to the anti-Mexico lobby, but the Medical Advisory Committee was not convinced that twenty-four days would be enough. After much debate they decided to accept Pugh's conclusions completely, and called for the athletes to be given as long as possible to acclimatize—and a minimum of a month.[37]

However, sensitive to the desires of Duncan and Owen to tread carefully on this issue, the committee agreed not to release the reports to the public, but simply to pass them on to the BOA. The BOA then instructed Owen to write a new "comprehensive official BOA report," "collating" all the results from Mexico, and, bypassing Pugh, they invited Pugh's boss Edholm to edit the report on behalf of the MRC. This ensured that the uncomfortable facts would be kept out of the public domain for a few more months.

With the facts safely under wraps, Duncan felt free to announce to *The Times* that athletes competing in "explosive" events needed *only three weeks* to acclimatize, and endurance athletes needed a *maximum* of four weeks. The BOA then formally called on the International Olympic Committee to impose a four-week limit—disregarding Pugh's and the Medical Advisory Committee's conclusion, that all types of athlete should be given as long as possible to acclimatize.[38]

The BOA's "official report," which appeared three months later (with Pugh's report discreetly tucked away at the back), proved to be a rehashed version of Dr. Owen's original account, repeating his insistence that acclimatization tailed off after the third week, and that some of the athletes' altitude symptoms were "undoubtedly psychological." His final salvo was that: "Team officials should make sure that competitors are not worried about any possible effects of altitude, as symptoms will arise if individuals are led to expect them."[39]

Pugh was intensely annoyed. "The association [BOA] have covered up the main results of the report with a mass of trivia," he told James Coote of the *Daily Telegraph*, and to the *Sunday Times* he declared that the BOA's report "was packed with pompous nonsense and insignificant statistics."[40] Finally, in a letter to Sir Arthur Porritt, he complained that the report "contravenes decisions taken by the Medical Advisory Committee," and he resigned—only to reinstate himself four days later.[41] He was reaching the breaking point.

If the BOA were trying to convince the athletes that most of their problems were psychosomatic, they were resoundingly unsuccessful. It was impossible to hide the fact that five other countries—Sweden, Japan, the USA, Germany, and Australia—had reported comparable findings to Pugh's at an international conference in Switzerland.[42]

In the run-up to the final decision of the IOC, twenty-six of Britain's most distinguished athletes and ex-athletes sent a letter to *The Times* declaring: "The International Olympic Committee must be brought to realise that its choice of Mexico City, made through giving undue weight to political and financial considerations, was a disastrous mistake and [must] be persuaded to do everything in its power to mitigate the effects."[43]

The athletes demanded that all the races longer than 800 meters be held at a separate, low-altitude venue away from Mexico City. In the *New Scientist*, Roger Bannister predicted that the Mexico Games would "damage the Olympic concept of fairness more than anything else in the history of the modern games." Demands that the venue be changed were now coming from all quarters. And yet, when the IOC met in Rome in July 1966, it insisted that Mexico would go ahead. "There's no question of any change," Avery Brundage declared. "The games belong to the world. Whether they're held north or south, east or west, in hot countries or in cold, in wet or in dry seasons, at high altitude or at low is immaterial."[44]

Above: The Queen and the Everest team at the fortieth anniversary gala party in [19]93.

Right: Members of the 1953 Everest [tea]m at Bhadgaon near Kathmandu. [lef]t to right, top row: Tom Stobart, [Gri]ffith Pugh, Wilfred Noyce, Charles [Eva]ns; middle row: George Band, [Mi]chael Ward, Ed Hillary, Tom [Bo]urdillon, Mike Westmacott; bottom [ro]w: Alf Gregory, George Lowe, John [Hu]nt, Tenzing Norgay, Charles Wylie.

[Bel]ow: Part of the Everest Icefall with [clim]bers like ants in the vast landscape.

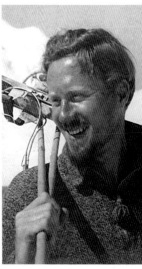

Above: Pugh in Switzerland in 1938.

Left: The Hôtel des Cèdres, Cedars, near Beirut.

Below: The ski company moves off.

mes Riddell, Chief
structor at Cedars.

Eric Shipton.

Michael Ward.

m Bourdillon.

George Band, the 1953
expedition joker.

Tom Stobart.

n Hunt, Ed Hillary, and Tenzing Norgay cope with the media at London airport after the
53 expedition.

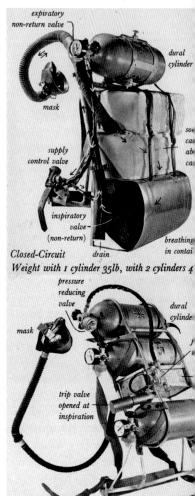

Above: Pugh at the start of the 1953 expedition, telling the locals about his exceedingly large box of scientific equipment.

Right: Illustration of closed- and open-circuit oxygen sets.

Below left: Pugh working with a Scholander Gas analyzer during the 1953 expedition.

Below right: Hillary putting on his high-altitude boots.

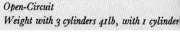

Above: The acclimatization camp at Thyangboche, March 1953.

Left: Pugh at Camp Three, testing the air in the bottom of John Hunt's lungs.

Below left: Hillary and Tenzing approaching 28,000 ft (8,534 m) on Everest.

Below right: Tenzing on the summit of Everest.

The Silver Hut.

The Nepalese pilgrim, Man Badhur, eating a glass pipette.

Skiing scientists of the Silver Hut winter party. Left to right: Jim Milledge, John West, Griffith Pugh, Michael Ward, and Mike Gill.

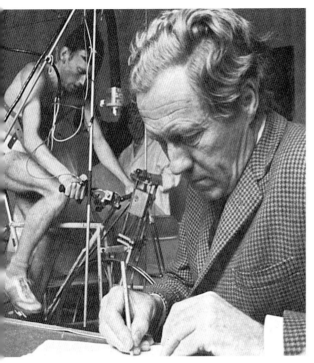

...ugh in the laboratory shed by the running track in Mexico ...ity with Mike Turner on the stationary bicycle.

...ugh and a colleague experimenting with Mike Turner.

Marathon swimmer Jason Zirganos.

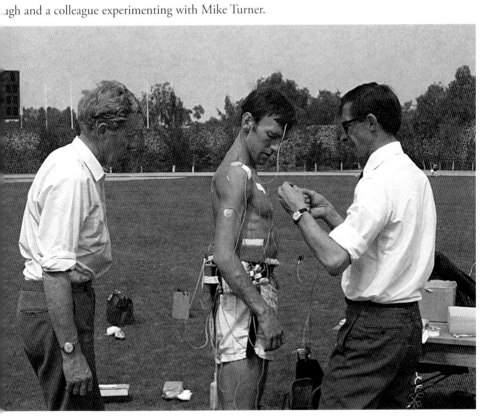

Doey in Switzerland in the mid-1930s.

One of the few photographs of Griffith and Doey together, seen here on the garden steps of Hatching Green House.

Griffith greeting his daughter, Harriet, age six, at London Airport after his return from Everest.

Putteridgebury, Doey's family home.

29

Going for Gold

The Mexico saga continued for three more years until the Games took place in 1968. During that time Pugh's relationship with the BOA became so irksome to him that he was finally driven to resign from the MRC. Yet it was also an immensely productive period for his research.[1]

After the International Olympic Committee gave the Mexico Games the go-ahead, many countries, including Russia, the United States, Poland, France, and Germany, announced that they intended to take their athletes to Mexico at least four weeks before the Games, and to offer them sessions at altitude-training centers beforehand. One of their reasons was that it was well known that people acclimatized more easily on their second and subsequent visits to altitude. The IOC was not happy. They considered altitude training to be "not in accord with the amateur traditions," and announced that any athlete who undertook more than four weeks' altitude training in a calendar year would be disqualified from the Games. In 1967 the limit was increased to six weeks—but only for 1968, the year of the Games.[2]

British athletes wanted to visit altitude-training centers too, but the BOA did its best to discourage them. Owen and Duncan issued off-putting communiqués warning that acclimatization wore off after only a few weeks. They gave lectures to athletes and officials, downplaying the impact of the altitude and the value of altitude training, and telling them that the worst problems in Mexico would be—in order of severity—boredom, sunburn, tummy upsets, and, lastly, "apprehension about the altitude."[3]

Their campaign reached its climax in May 1967 when Duncan set out the BOA's "official viewpoint" in *World Sports*, the BOA's magazine. Claiming that his conclusions were derived from the Mexico study "led" by Dr.

Pugh and Dr. Owen, Duncan asserted that there was no scientific evidence that acclimatization was more easily achieved after repeated visits to altitude. "Our research," he claimed, suggests that altitude training camps "give no great return." It was not altitude but morale that would be the main problem in Mexico City. If the "wrong climate of opinion" prevailed, athletes would come to "believe many of the remarkable scares they may read . . . If they believe . . . certain things will happen, then they are very likely to happen. Such is the power of suggestion."[4]

Pugh, meanwhile, was appearing on television promoting the opposite view. Sponsored by Independent Television, he took three runners to Font Romeu—a newly opened altitude-training center in the French Pyrenees—to give viewers a chance to see what happened to running speeds at altitude.[5]

The runners were timed running a 3-mile race at Crystal Palace, then repeating the race at Font Romeu, where their speeds dropped by similar percentages to those in Mexico.[6] Afterward Pugh wrote urging the BOA to change its stance and encourage British athletes to visit centers like Font Romeu. There would be both physiological and psychological benefits for the athletes, as well as opportunities to develop tactics to cope with altitude, he said. There was also a strong possibility that altitude training could produce improvements in performance at sea level.[7] Trying to cajole Duncan into action, he ended by pointing out that no less than fourteen other countries were sending their athletes to Font Romeu.

Even before the BOA had time to reply, Pugh gave an interview to Chris Brasher. "Shall I be blunt to the point of rudeness?" Brasher thundered in the *Observer* a few days later: "We are about to embark on the most monumental blunder that I've ever stumbled across in British sport. The greatest expert in the world on the effect of altitude on the human body sits in the laboratories of the Medical Research Council in Hampstead and says 'I feel powerless. No one has yet come to me and asked me how to train for Mexico.'"[8]

Pugh's belief that "droves of athletes should be sent to Font Romeu *NOW*" was being flatly ignored, Brasher complained, firmly pointing the finger at outdated amateur values. "It is time we stopped being supposed gentlemen and became modern realists with a professional attitude."

Duncan and Owen were furious. "A stupid article . . . since when has Pugh been an expert on athletic training!!" Duncan wrote to Owen.[9] Owen replied sarcastically: "I remember that the first time I met Pugh, he said, 'They would never have climbed Everest if it hadn't been for me, but Hillary got all the credit.' I can just imagine him saying to Chris Brasher, 'I am the greatest authority in the world on altitude, and nobody consults me on how to train!'"[10]

The athletes, however, took Pugh's advice. The International Athletes Club, sponsored by the *Daily Mirror,* the Sports Council, and the British Amateur Athletics Board took thirty "Olympic-possible" runners to Font Romeu with Pugh as an "observer," paid for by the IAC. After the trip, the athletes issued a statement calling for team doctors and coaches for Mexico to be nominated without delay, "strongly" recommending that Pugh be included.[11]

Pugh now had so much support that the BOA could no longer ignore him. An uninvited Dr. Owen had turned up at Font Romeu when Pugh was there in September, and Duncan later found himself having to join the Sports Council and the Amateur Athletics Board in funding three further trips for Pugh.

Pugh may have triumphed in one sense but, back at the MRC, head-office officials were appalled by the spat between Pugh and the sporting establishment being played out in the newspapers and on television. "Adverse publicity may prove to be a serious setback in any important field of research," they reminded Sir Peter Medawar. One official questioned whether Pugh should have leave to go to Font Romeu and was not altogether pleased when Medawar replied curtly that Dr. Pugh was "such an original that he ought more or less to be allowed to do whatever he wanted."[12]

By this time, Pugh's problems with his boss Otto Edholm had reached the breaking point. Already infuriated by Edholm's "editing" of the BOA's Mexico report, Pugh found out that in April 1967 the BOA had secretly invited Edholm—who was not an expert on altitude—to become their official altitude adviser.[13] Edholm had agreed to step in behind Pugh's back without even telling him.

After many years of simmering resentment, this was the final straw. Pugh sent Sir Peter Medawar a letter of resignation. In his letter Pugh explained how he was repeatedly being snubbed. People felt they could disregard his views. Organizations like the BOA and the Sports Council wanted to communicate with a departmental head rather than a subsidiary member of staff. "Difficult and embarrassing situations frequently arise because of my relatively subordinate position."

Though sympathetic to Pugh's problems about status, Medawar had always stopped short of pushing for him to get his own unit. When confronted with Pugh's resignation, however, he took action. Extracting Pugh from Edholm's orbit, Medawar offered him a one-man unit of his own. There would be no extra money, but Pugh leapt at the idea. Medawar pushed it through a doubtful head office by insisting that Pugh's qualities as a scientist justified the promotion:

> *Pugh . . . is a man of real distinction with an international reputation in the field of athletic physiology. His level of distinction is entirely appropriate for the head of a Lab or Division. His being awarded relatively independent status would give him extra prestige and negotiating power with the bodies who do so much to sponsor his research, like the Sports Council, British Olympic Association and International Athletics Group.*[14]

At the end of November 1967, now nearly sixty, Pugh was at last in charge of his own tiny department, which he called "the Laboratory for Field Physiology." With his newfound independence he continued working closely with the athletes and responding to the cues they gave him. In the process he made some pioneering discoveries which are still benefiting long-distance and marathon runners today.

One day Hyman chanced to tell Pugh how, when representing Britain in the 6-mile (10,000-meter) race at international "two-a-side" athletic events at the White City in the 1950s and early 1960s, he and his running partner used to take it in turns—lap on lap—to run directly in front of each other. They had a clear idea of how much energy they were saving by doing this—the equivalent of 1 second per lap. But, as Pugh realized, the energy-saving benefits of slipstreaming in running had not been measured before. Indeed, at the time, running behind a "pace setter" tended to be valued as much for its psychological benefits as for its potential for saving energy.

Pugh set up treadmills in the wind tunnels at Farnborough and at the MRC and had the athletes run one in front of the other, while he measured the energy consumptions of those in front and those behind, also exploring which position gave the most effective protection. One of his findings was that at middle-distance speeds, running approximately 1 meter behind another runner reduced the energy consumed by 6.5 percent—an advantage of about 4 seconds per lap.[15] Experience on the track showed that athletes couldn't generally run so close behind each other, but by running behind and slightly to the side, they could still gain around 1 second per lap—as Hyman had already thought.[16]

Traditionally, it was common for British runners to choose to run out in front. Some years later, before the Munich Olympics of 1972, Hyman—with his knowledge of the proven benefits of slipstreaming—tried to persuade the great British runner David Bedford that if he ran out in front for all twenty-five laps of the 10,000-meter Olympic final, he would be handing a 25-second advantage to his competitors, who would surely avail themselves of slipstreaming.[17] Just to tie with them, Bedford would have to run 25 seconds faster than them. Bedford assured Hyman that his margin of superiority was greater than that. He went on to lead the field for lap after lap, only to see five runners sweep past him in the closing stages.[18]

One of Pugh's more important projects after getting his own laboratory was specifically with marathon runners. In the mid-1960s when heat exhaustion and dehydration in athletes were still not fully understood, Olympic and British rules did not allow runners to drink during the first 10 miles of a marathon. Only three drinking stations were permitted in the entire race. Heat exhaustion—when the body's normal cooling system becomes overloaded and malfunctions—has potentially fatal results unless the victim is cooled rapidly. But when athletes collapse from heat exhaustion, they are typically shivering and have goose pimples. Instead of dousing them with cold water to cool them down, officials used to cover them in blankets to stop them shivering.

Having studied hypothermia among hill-walkers, Pugh was particularly interested in how runners coped with heat. There had been many studies of people exercising in severe heat on treadmills indoors, and in 1963 Roger Bannister had studied soldiers marching in Aden in temperatures of 90°F.[19] But no one had yet investigated what happened to marathon runners in moderate conditions outside in the open air.

Seventy runners participating in a race organized by the Road Runners' Club at Witney near Oxford in June 1967 let Pugh and a team of colleagues measure their skin and body-core temperatures. They weighed them, took urine and blood samples, and recorded their pulses, blood pressures, and temperatures before and after the race.[20] Four athletes who collapsed were subjected to especially detailed studies. In addition to the standard rectal thermometers, Pugh used a new device for measuring temperatures continuously—a radio temperature pill which the athletes swallowed. It was designed by Heinz Wolff, one of Pugh's colleagues at the MRC. The data they collected was the first such data ever published.

Athletes knew that getting too hot depressed their running performances. In 1960, athletes competing in the Rome Olympics had wanted to fly out early to acclimatize to the heat, but the BOA had insisted it was unnecessary. They were wrong. As a result most of the British runners felt they performed poorly.[21]

What Pugh showed for the first time was that, even in the relatively mild conditions of an English summer, the temperatures of long-distance runners could rise remarkably high, and being too hot and being dehydrated could slow them down. Five percent of his study group collapsed at the end of the race.

Mexico City was not expected to be significantly hotter than England, but Pugh estimated that the solar radiation would be seventeen times more intense. After two further studies at Font Romeu, Pugh predicted that heat might be almost as important as altitude in slowing marathon runners in Mexico.

A telephone call to Christopher Brasher at the *Observer* was enough to get the BOA and the Amateur Athletics Board to finance a second Mexico trip for Pugh. Two international athletes—Mike Turner and the long-distance runner Tim Johnston, who was ranked eighth in the world at 10,000 meters and tenth in the marathon—went with him and agreed to run until they collapsed from heat exhaustion.[22]

Turner ran for 18.5 miles before he collapsed, having lost 8.5 pounds—6 percent of his body weight. "You drain off all your fluid reserves and your skin dries up prickling and itching . . . I was forced to stop by sheer exhaustion," Turner said. Johnston collapsed after 14.5 miles, losing 4 percent of his body weight. His temperature had climbed to a dangerously high 106.34°F.[23] Pugh's study was the first to measure the skin and body temperatures of athletes collapsing from heat stress, and the first to describe runners experiencing one of its symptoms—"the gooseflesh syndrome."

"This heat factor is quite new," an excited Dr. Pugh was quoted telling a reporter from the *Sunday Mirror*: "We have seen long-distance runners like Jim Peters collapsing in the marathon event in Canada [in 1954], and we have proved that an important factor in this is loss of fluid and too high a temperature."[24]

After Pugh came home from Mexico, the International Athletes Club issued a leaflet to all "Olympic possibles," in which Martin Hyman set out Pugh's ideas on how to prepare for Mexico, and how to cope with the altitude, heat, and fatigue.[25]

In an era when New Zealand athletes were still wearing black running gear, Pugh suggested that British athletes should wear "white to reflect radiant heat and not dark to absorb it." Their clothes should be made of "cotton which evaporates sweat (thus cooling the body) and not artificial fibre which does not." They should "expose the maximum amount of skin"— their vests should have "very large deep arm holes and thin shoulder straps," and their shorts "should be as brief as possible, with high vertical slits at the side."

Since running shoes retained heat in the same way as hats, he suggested that the uppers should be constructed of meshed fabric to allow the air to penetrate. Also, since the rubberized Olympic track was expected to become very hot, giving the athletes blisters on the soles of their feet, the soles of their shoes should be made of rubberized spongy fabric. Before a race like the marathon, the athletes should try to find ways of "warming up" that did not increase their temperature, and they should attempt to acclimatize to heat before traveling to Mexico. "How is it possible to justify this heat scare?" Sandy Duncan retorted crossly, after seeing the leaflet: "White clothing throughout is entirely impracticable and so is cotton . . . and what pray of sunburn from these solar rays? Has Dr. Pugh ever studied a pair of athletic shorts? Anything smaller or split up higher would be indecent!"[26]

Pugh was now completely absorbed in finding ways to help marathon runners. In early 1968, Hyman recruited over fifty of the UK's top marathon runners to take part in two endurance trials. The aim was to allow Pugh to test whether the runners might "improve their performances in hot conditions by drinking a lot of water in small amounts during the race" and by "eating a diet high in carbohydrates just prior to competition [i.e., the week before]," as had recently been recommended by Swedish scientists.[27] Pugh also tested the impact of adding glucose to the drinking water.

British distance runners were used to training themselves not to drink during races—and often for several hours beforehand. It was widely believed that water made the athlete heavy, might make him want to urinate, and might give him a stitch. Machismo also played a part: Tim Johnston described himself as feeling "a bit hair shirt" about drinking while running. Athletes, like prewar British climbers, were unaware that dehydration might limit performance and cause physical damage.

The results of Pugh's research convinced him, however, that marathon runners would perform better if they drank small amounts of water whenever they wanted during a race, and that the risks of heat collapse in hot conditions would also be greatly reduced.[28] Therefore he campaigned to get marathon organizers to allow athletes to drink sufficient fluids. He even tried to get the time of the Mexico marathon changed from 3 p.m., when the sun would be at its fiercest, to a cooler part of the day. But when the British Amateur Athletics Board put this to the Olympic authorities, they were told that no one else had objected to the timing of the marathon, and in any case, Mexico City was not particularly hot.

Eventually, however, Pugh's ideas passed into common currency. Skimpy clothes, ventilated fabric, lightweight running shoes with spongy soles, and caps with meshed crowns became de rigueur. And today, marathon runners are given every opportunity to keep their bodies hydrated.

Hyman's and Turner's cooperation in the run-up to the Mexico Olympics helped make possible one of the most stimulating research periods in Pugh's life. He felt great respect for them both, and they, like the Silver Hut scientists, came to know a completely different person from the man who stormed around Hampstead in a fury, upsetting his colleagues and his managers, or who lost his temper with his daughter at home. Hyman described him as helpful, cooperative, unusually interesting, idiosyncratic, a bit helpless about day-to-day life—but never rude or inconsiderate.

After three years of athletics research, Pugh had become so enthused that he wanted to take a team of young scientists to Mexico for the Games, hoping to pounce on some collapsing marathon athletes and study them. He also wanted to investigate whether the oxygen-transport systems of successful athletes were similar to those of high-altitude natives like the Sherpas. Peter Medawar was delighted. "This is just the kind of work Pugh ought to be doing and is indeed paid to do," he told the head office, and set about obtaining Pugh an annual research budget that would prevent him from having to seek formal approval for every project.[29] Shortly before the team was due to leave for Mexico, the Mexican Olympic authorities decided to ban all research at the Games, and the project had to be canceled.

In the end, no amount of acclimatization and training could compensate fully for the impact of Mexico's altitude. Just as Pugh had predicted, some athletes achieved unprecedented success, but endurance athletes from sea level were unable to perform at their best. In many of the shorter, explosive events, records tumbled.[30] One of the memorable achievements was Bob Beaman's fantastic long jump. Assisted by the thin air—which helped the run-up and the jump itself—he jumped 29 feet, 2.5 inches, creating a record that lasted for twenty-three years.[31] *Athletics Weekly* described Mexico as "the schizophrenic games." "Altitude made such an impact that many competitors were helped to undreamt-of achievements, while lowlanders were deprived of any sporting chance of success in the long-distance races."[32]

The men's 5,000-meter race was won in the slowest time in sixteen years. The 10,000-meter race was the slowest in twenty years—almost 2 minutes slower than the world record held by Australian Ron Clarke.[33] Clarke finished sixth, collapsed after the race, and remained unconscious for 10 minutes. The five runners who finished ahead of him were all from high-altitude countries or had lived *and* trained at altitude.[34] The Mexico Games were instrumental in highlighting the potential of high-altitude runners. Today, runners from countries such as Morocco, Algeria, Kenya, Ethiopia, and parts of China dominate competitive endurance running.

30

The Restless Sharpshooter

In 1969, at the age of only fifty-four, Sir Peter Medawar suffered a catastrophic stroke while reading the Sunday lesson in Exeter Cathedral. He made a partial recovery, but in 1971 he was replaced as director of the National Institute for Medical Research by the molecular scientist, Sir Arnold Burgen.

Since establishing Pugh in his own unit, Medawar had been going out of his way to promote his work; for instance, he invited Pugh to give a colloquium on "athletic or high-performance physiology" to the 240 scientists at the NIMR's headquarters at Mill Hill.[1] The aim, he said, was to show off the "wealth of extraordinarily interesting information" Pugh's research was producing.

With the stimulus of the Mexico Olympics, sport and exercise science had become a rapidly growing international research field in which Pugh had gained a valuable foothold. He lost his great champion at the MRC just at the moment when he wanted to expand his tiny department by taking on a few bright young researchers. But, even before Medawar's departure, cold winds of change had already begun to blow on the future of applied human physiology at the NIMR.

Pugh had joined the institute at a time when the MRC was run on the "the Haldane Principle"—devised by the brilliant politician and public administrator R. B. Haldane, elder brother of the physiologist J. S. Haldane. The essence of the Haldane Principle was that research should be independent of the day-to-day concerns of politicians, and that to get the best out of scientists they must be given "the greatest degree of freedom" in the choice of the work they did.[2] Not everyone agreed with this "genius-orientated," "curiosity-led" approach, though it did produce some impressive results. MRC scientists won three Nobel Prizes in the 1950s, three in the 1960s, and two in the 1970s.[3] Crick and Watson, who discovered the molecular structure of DNA, worked at the MRC's Cavendish laboratories in Cambridge.

For the first twenty years after the war the MRC's budget had increased by roughly 10 percent a year. But with the economic decline of the late 1960s, its lavish funding was reduced.[4] At the same time, the Rothschild Report, a highly critical government review of scientific research in Britain, rejected the Haldane Principle and demanded that scientists be made more accountable for the public money spent on them.[5] The era when it had been possible for MRC researchers to behave like freewheeling gentlemen scientists was ending. Pugh was profoundly lucky to have worked in an age of scientific laissez-faire that suited his individualistic personality. Today scientists have to spend a great deal of their time justifying every penny they want to spend.

Another issue was the MRC's traditional attitude to Pugh's field of research, which it had always regarded as somewhat low-level and unscientific. It accepted that problem-solving, applied human physiology was essential to support the armed services in wartime and in the aftermath of war. In peacetime, however, it was less enthusiastic about human physiology, and since the discovery of the structure of DNA in 1953, the scientific fashion had been swinging ever more strongly toward pure research. Moving with the times, the MRC was enthusiastically "going molecular." Edholm's department, with its expensive cold chambers and large studies, seemed an ideal candidate for elimination. "This area of research appears to have acquired . . . an unfashionable image," an MRC committee reported. "It is widely but erroneously supposed to be concerned with ad hoc research on somewhat dull problems." This, they regretted, had resulted in "a shortage of able young recruits to the field."[6] While Medawar was away after his stroke, the MRC quietly decided to accept the committee's recommendation that Edholm's division be closed down when he retired in 1974. It was left up to the new director of the NIMR to decide what to do about Pugh's tiny unit.

Soon after Sir Arnold Burgen took over, a freeze on recruitment was imposed on Edholm and Pugh alike. Pugh was permitted just one short-term junior research assistant—John Brotherhood.

Undeterred, Pugh had continued his research into the energetics of walking and running, heat stress, the changes the body goes through while exercising for long periods outdoors, and many other topics.[7] Athletes, cyclists, and skiers regularly trooped to his laboratory for tests and met him at various sports grounds for outdoor trials, and he continued to publish highly original academic papers up to his retirement in 1975.[8]

However, in the late 1960s the hip he injured when he crashed his car in 1961 developed severe arthritis, causing him constant pain. Stoical and uncomplaining, he took to walking with a stick. His face, which had always looked remarkably young, became lined and weary, and he seemed to grow smaller, as if the pain was making him shrink into his body. By 1971 the hip had become so painful that he decided to have a hip replacement.

The way he made the decision typified his character. He visited the bio-engineering unit at the Institute of Orthopaedics at Stanmore Hospital to inspect the various joint systems and talk them over with the surgeon, Professor John Scales, who had developed the "Stanmore Hip System."[9] The two men emerged not only friends but also full of ideas about joint ventures.

Finding it both awkward and painful to walk with his stick, Pugh had allowed himself to become rather unfit. Yet he considered it physiologically inappropriate to go into a major operation in an unfit state, so he got himself a pair of crutches and trained himself to walk with them.

After the operation, Pugh followed his own rehabilitation program, which included exercises derived from an ancient leather-bound book of Cecchetti ballet exercises he had learned about in his youth from my mother, who had wanted to be a ballet dancer. Adapting the exercises to help him train for ski-racing in the 1930s, he had later employed them to train his commando soldiers in the Lebanon.

When he took to crutches, Pugh immediately became curious about the physiology involved. Did walking with crutches use more energy than walking normally? Did walking with a stiff leg and a stick use more energy than walking normally with an artificial hip? He found from his experiments that walking with crutches used more energy than walking normally, up to a cut-off point of 5 miles per hour, above which crutching and running used similar amounts of energy. More importantly, he demonstrated that walking with his arthritic hip consumed 50 percent more energy than walking normally after the operation. As Pugh realized, the fact that older people would need less energy to walk if they had a hip replacement could be a decisive factor in deciding whether or not to have the operation—particularly for people with afflictions like chronic lung or heart disease, which restrict oxygen intake and energy levels.

The results of the studies were published in the *Journal of Joint and Bone Surgery*.[10] Although it would be hard in today's climate to persuade an elite academic journal to publish an article about an experiment with only one subject, his findings stimulated great interest, and helped to persuade the rising generation of clinical doctors specializing in the care of older people that exercise science could be used to help orthopedic and rheumatologic patients.

In Britain today, research that does not involve large numbers of randomly selected subjects tends to be considered not worth doing. And yet much of the research carried out by physiologists of Pugh's ilk was done with only a few experimental subjects. It wasn't practical to study large numbers in the high Himalayas or Antarctica, and Pugh often deliberately chose to study small groups of exceptional people like Channel swimmers and Olympic athletes, who were not available in large numbers. His research assistant John Brotherhood remembered him saying of Edholm's huge projects: "Those people take a scatter gun approach, John, but we use a rifle. We are sharpshooters." The findings from Pugh's cold-water studies and from much of his groundbreaking work on sport and recreation were later replicated in much larger studies.

Equally characteristic of Pugh's work was the simplicity of his equipment. He preferred lightweight equipment he could carry around easily and calibrate himself to ensure that it was accurate. He aimed to be flexible, able to seize unexpected research opportunities when they came up, without sacrificing rigor. Richard Edwards, who worked with Pugh in the 1960s, told me that nowadays it would be highly unusual to embark on Pugh's type of research without having "thousands of pounds of equipment . . . and a big lot of staff." Pugh, he said, "was able to do amazing things with extremely simple equipment, through good experimental design and careful measurement." "There was something lovely about the austerity of his approach to studying things," he added a little wistfully.

Pugh returned to work after his operation, ready as ever to try out new ideas and methods. In 1972 he embarked on a highly original study of heat stress with Ray Clark, a bright young MRC researcher. Clark had used thermal photographic techniques to study aerodynamics at City University in London. Aerodynamic concepts were central to Pugh's work on the energetics of running, and the two were soon spotted deep in conversation. This provoked Clark's boss, Harold Lewis, to call the young man into his office. Pulling the door shut he told Clark, "We don't work with Griffith Pugh!" Pugh's split from Edholm's division had engendered great resentment. He and Edholm no longer spoke, and Pugh's relations with senior members of Edholm's department were frosty in the extreme.

After Lewis died in 1972, Pugh and Clark used thermal photography to make a film showing what happened to the temperature of marathon runners on a treadmill running to the point of collapse from heat exhaustion.[11] The film, which was shown on television, used nine colors for nine temperatures—from white, representing great heat, through to blue, black, and purple, representing the cooler areas. At first the runner's body was a kaleidoscope of brightly colored contours. As he exercised, the area over his abdomen could be seen cooling as the blood moved away to the working leg muscles, where the heat became concentrated. When he succumbed to heat exhaustion, his body suddenly changed color dramatically, becoming sheer dazzling white all over.

Pugh had long since given up skiing, but after his hip operation he started cycling. It gave him a joyful sense of liberation from the fetters that had curtailed his movement for the previous five years. Once again his restless mind immediately turned to the physiology of the activity. Realizing that the energy costs of cycling had not been studied since the famous physiologist Nathan Zuntz did so in 1920s, and that no one had yet measured the impact of slipstreaming on cycling—as Pugh already had on running—he was soon investigating both.[12] As was his wont, he also wanted to measure the impact of his new hobby on his own fitness and found, to his delight, that he had lost weight and gotten fitter. Previously he could only walk at 4 miles per hour; now his stride had lengthened and he could walk at 6 miles per hour. It had always been assumed that the physical atrophy suffered by the elderly was an inevitable result of aging, but Pugh saw that despite his age, his body had responded in the same way to exercise as a young person's. This suggested that the physical decline experienced by older people might be partly due to inactivity. His calls for more research and for greater attention to be given to ensuring that middle-aged and elderly people got adequate exercise was inspirational to geriatricians.[13]

In the 1960s and 1970s there were still no agreed-upon objective measures of fitness. The first study linking coronary heart disease to physical inactivity had been published as early as 1953, but the idea that exercise was necessary for health would not gain a hold on the public mind until the late 1970s and early 1980s.[14] Even in the MRC the subject was hardly taken seriously. Indeed, in 1963 Sir Peter Medawar wrote to Sir Harry Himsworth, the head of the MRC, to say that he found it "quite absurd that we should not know how important physical exercise is or even whether it is good for one."[15] Himsworth was decidedly unenthusiastic; in his view the evidence that physical exercise was necessary for health was "not really anything more than folklore."[16]

Less than a year before he was due to retire, Pugh was riding his bike up a hill near Hatching Green when he crashed into a motorcycle and broke the leg with the artificial hip. The operation to repair the damage was not a success, and Pugh ended up permanently disabled, with no proper hip joint and one leg four inches shorter than the other—not an easy situation for a man whose life had revolved around physical activity.

He disliked being confined to a bed in the hospital with his patched-up leg in traction. Having worked out that the weight of the leg itself was greater than the traction weight, he discharged himself and hobbled about on crutches with the leg dangling freely. Dedicating himself to a second program of rehabilitation, he took to elbow crutches, and eventually succeeded in going on long walks to keep fit. It was, he said, a bit like cross-country skiing. I never heard him complain about his affliction, except once, when, after being particularly nasty to my mother, he shouted at her in my hearing: "Now I'm a cripple, I suppose you're going to leave me."

The date for Pugh's retirement from the MRC came and went while he was still recovering. He returned only once to the MRC HQ on Mill Hill for a rather unceremonious farewell drinks party shared with another member of staff from a different department. Sir Arnold Burgen presided and spoke briefly about Pugh's career, and Pugh made a 5-minute speech about how the study of extremes had been the theme that had linked all his research: either extreme environmental conditions, or extreme properties in individuals. And so his career ended.

Three years later, he was sitting in the dining room at home eating lunch when he heard the news on the radio that Everest had been climbed without oxygen for the first time. He had just been telling us that they would never make it. However, when he learned that they had succeeded, he was quick to point out that Peter Habeler and Reinhold Messner had many advantages over the amateur British Everest team of 1953, as well as over Hillary and his fellow climbers on Makalu in 1961.

Habeler and Messner were professional climbers, born and bred at intermediate altitude in the Tyrolean mountains, who climbed together for fifteen years before attempting their oxygen-free ascent of Everest. During that time they had become legendary for their speed of ascent on some of the most difficult Alpine routes, frequently halving the best times achieved by their predecessors. Their superb climbing skills, speed, and strength gave them a greater margin for error by reducing the time they needed to reach a summit and get back down in relative safety.

They trained together for their Everest attempt for over a year, unlike the 1953 British team, who used the walk-in and the acclimatization period to get fit and formed most of their climbing partnerships during the expedition. Messner and Habeler also had the benefit of modern lightweight clothing, boots, crampons, and climbing equipment. Above all, they made full use of Pugh's dictum that it was vital to drink 4 liters of water a day to maintain their climbing strength. "We must drink" was their constant mantra, and much of their time when they were not climbing was spent brewing endless cups of tea sweetened with sugar.[17]

The methods they used for their superb breakthrough were remarkably similar to those Pugh had envisaged in 1959 when he suggested climbing Everest without oxygen to Hillary. He proposed that the attempt be made in two stages, with an oxygen party establishing a route to the top and putting in "all the intermediate camps." The climbers without oxygen would then make their attempt carrying no loads.[18] However, Hillary rejected the idea.

Habeler and Messner achieved the summit on the back of a successful oxygen-assisted expedition using pre-established camps. When they made their final push for the summit, a Sherpa climbed in front of them for part of the way to tread down the fresh snow on the route so they would use less effort to climb. They carried no weight; on the South Summit, Habeler flung off his light rucksack, giving up all his equipment so that he could "climb unfettered." Neither man left himself any margin for error. Both knew that they would probably die if they ran into difficulties—even minor ones. They embraced a level of risk that in 1953 would have been regarded as completely unacceptable by Sir John Hunt and his team.

Of all those who sought to ensure that Pugh's achievements were recognized, the man who tried hardest was Michael Ward, whose tireless campaign to force Sir John Hunt to acknowledge Pugh's contribution to the success on Everest made him unpopular with his fellow expedition members, who felt great loyalty for their former leader.

In 1978, after years of private criticism from Ward, Sir John Hunt published his autobiography, in which—twenty-five years after the event—he publicly admitted in print for the first, and only time, how much help he had received from Pugh: "He made a great contribution to the design of our clothing and equipment, the composition and balance of our diet and to the policy for the use of oxygen, as well as the principles of acclimatisation. All this had a powerful influence on my plans, and on our performance on the mountain."[19]

However, Michael Ward was not to be so easily satisfied. Wanting Hunt to make this admission in a wider public forum than his autobiography, Ward continued to pester and criticize him on and off for the next fifteen years.

Finally, in 1993, Hunt responded by including some words of praise for the Everest scientists in the new introduction he was writing for a paperback reprint of *The Ascent of Everest,* to mark the fortieth anniversary. Ever since then, Hunt has been credited, notably in the *Oxford Dictionary of National Biography*, for having paid "generous tribute" to Griffith Pugh.

Even so, as he had done on countless other occasions, Hunt chose words which carefully avoided giving credit to Pugh. "Today, forty years on," he wrote, "I would again like to acknowledge the contributions made by a great many people *other than those who were on the mountain* . . . I wanted *the many people who did not go to Everest*—on whose help with money, equipment and expert advice we had so greatly depended—to know how much we had valued their help." [Emphasis added.]

Pugh, of course, did go to Everest, and so was excluded from the praise that followed:

> *The part played by our scientific consultants was especially important. Their knowledge of the physiological problems of human activity and survival at high altitudes powerfully influenced the selection, manufacture and preparation of our equipment, clothing and food; their advice informed the overall planning of the expedition and decisions on the mountain.*

Asked to comment on the draft of the passage, the editor of the *Alpine Journal* pointed out to Hunt that he had made no clear reference to the research carried out specifically to help the 1953 expedition. "You might make [the scientists'] contribution sound more dynamic," she suggested. "After all, you did not really make use of scientific knowledge that already existed in a vacuum." But Hunt made no change.

Later, in May of that year, Michael Ward—unappeased—tried again. He got up at the Royal Geographical Society in front of the Queen and a large, distinguished audience and made his very public protest about the "unsung hero of Everest," stirring me to feel that one day I ought to try to write a book about my father's life.

Epilogue

Expecting the Lion's Share

While researching my father's life, I was constantly aware that I knew very little about his character as a man. Since believing, as a teenager, that my father was neither fond of nor interested in me, and that he really didn't want me around, I had shielded myself with a carapace of indifference toward him.

By refusing to think about him and refraining from having any feelings for him—not even positive dislike—I sought to exclude him from my emotional landscape, taking no interest in him or his life. He was just my remote, unsympathetic father who disapproved of me.

In 1993, at the Royal Geographical Society, when tears sprang into my eyes as I listened to Michael Ward making his speech about Griffith, it was hard to believe that I was actually feeling empathy for my father, toward whom I had supposed myself utterly indifferent.

Going back into education at nineteen, I went on to study for a degree and emerged from the University of Essex in 1970 with first-class honors in literature—a "useless subject," according to Griffith, who consistently denigrated my efforts to revive my education. I suspected him of being jealous that my mother was supporting me financially. When he was told about my first, he announced, "Of course, it's all due to me"—implying that what little diligence his daughter possessed must have been inherited from him rather than from my mother.

I was extremely fond of my mother, and after leaving home in my teens I would return to spend weekends at Hatching Green several times a year, always telling myself that I would be able to ignore my father. But Griffith found it consummately easy to penetrate my defenses, and, being a bit of a bully, he couldn't resist doing so. In truth he didn't need to say much to get me to rush off to my bedroom in tears. I was supersensitive to criticism from him. As the years went on, the frequency of my visits dwindled, only reviving after I was married and had children of my own.

In 1974 at the age of twenty-eight, I became engaged to James, whom I had met two years earlier. James followed convention by asking my father for permission to marry me. "Thank God someone's going to take that old bag off our hands," was Griffith's encouraging reply. After dinner that evening, he decided that he and James should smoke a cigar together. Reaching for the special box he kept on the sideboard, he took out one of his expensive "Hoyo de Monterrey" Havana cigars for himself, but he did not offer one to James, instead turning to my brother and saying, "Oliver, go and fetch that old box of cigars I never smoke."

Six months later, James and I were married in Chicago, where he had been posted for two years as part of his job. The ceremony was conducted by a judge at the civic center, with the judge's two secretaries as witnesses. No friends or relations were present. My parents' marriage had not presented me and my brothers with an attractive image of the married state, and I was the only one of the four of us to marry.

Over time, my father developed a certain sneaking respect for James, particularly after he became the chief executive of an "FTSE 100" company. But he could not resist commenting, "Of course, James has got where he's got by being a nice chap," implying that James owed his success not to talent or business acumen, but purely to being a likable, conventional fellow—the very opposite of Griffith himself.

Returning to England from Chicago in 1976, James and I settled in London. Our three daughters—Venetia, Lizzie, and Rosie—were born in quick succession between 1978 and 1981. My mother adored her grandchildren, and they loved her equally in return. As they grew older, James and I started going to Hatching Green more often on the weekends. Doey enjoyed taking the girls on country jaunts, and prepared all kinds of treats for them—specializing in forbidden delights like sweet chocolate drinks, which she would administer secretly with an air of great conspiracy.

Griffith spent no time with his grandchildren. He was simply a glowering presence in the background—a little envious, perhaps, of the attention my mother lavished on them. The girls themselves were completely fearless of their grandfather. They thought nothing of sneaking into his office, climbing onto his chair, and pretending to be him, infuriating him by muddling up his papers which lay around in apparent chaos, though he claimed to know exactly where everything was. They played on his stairlift and charged around the house, making a dreadful noise. When they heard him approaching—roaring his disapproval—they would skitter away to some far-off corner of the garden, giggling wildly, leaving him to reprimand the thin air. It helped that they knew he could never catch them since he was hampered by his crutches. They remember their grandfather as an "angry" but not a nasty person, grumpy but harmless, and I sometimes wondered if he wasn't secretly amused by them.

I probably gave my father good reason to be antagonistic toward me. I loathed the way he treated my mother and always took her side against him. No doubt partly projecting my own negative view of him onto her, I felt that he had curtailed her life and used her merely as his meal ticket and housekeeper. As far as I could see, all she got in return for sacrificing her life to look after him were insults and faithlessness. He continued to pursue women right up until the age of eighty, when he was overheard on the telephone telling the brothel he was about to visit, "Give me that little Malaysian one." A few minutes later he took his leave of us, saying that he was "just off to take a walk in Virginia Water," a well-known nearby beauty spot.

Though I was forced to accept that my mother admired my father and regarded him as a significant scientist, I still believed that there was no love lost between them, and that she was trapped by her good nature in a stultifying, fruitless relationship. Longing to set her free from this prison, I tried my best to persuade her to leave him. She took no notice of my efforts, but my father realized that I wanted to prise my mother away from him, and it only worsened our relationship. I never questioned why my father was like he was, though my mother often remarked that Griffith had changed a great deal as he grew older.

Not until I read the letters that turned up in the suitcase at the Royal Geographical Society did I begin to realize that I had not understood the ties that held my mother and my father together, and even less did I understand his character. But, finally, for me, the key to a deeper understanding of my father's complex, contradictory personality lay in what I discovered about his childhood. Looking back I recalled that when we were very young, Griffith had taken me and my brothers to a place that had played a defining role in forming his character as a boy—a place where he had once been truly happy.

In mid-1955, between his expeditions to Everest and Antarctica, when I was eight and my brothers David and Simon were fourteen and nine, my third brother, Oliver, was born. This event prompted a complete change in our father's character. Suddenly, he became a doting parent. He was immensely affectionate and attentive toward Oliver as a baby, and he carried his third son off to Switzerland when he was still very young and taught him to ski. This had enormous significance for me and Simon, because our father had never taken us skiing. I became prone to unreasoning rages. I remember storming through our house, slamming doors, not knowing why I felt angry. I suppose I must have been jealous.

So enthused was Griffith by his newfound sense of fatherhood that in the year after Oliver was born, he took what for him was a remarkable step. For the first and only time in his life he organized our family holiday. Usually he had nothing to do with such matters, which were left entirely to my mother. But now, in the summer of 1956, he arranged a two-week visit to Wales, where we were to stay in a vacation apartment in the servants' quarters of a large house called Rhos y Gilwen, in the midst of a country estate near the Pembrokeshire coast.

Simon and I found the house dark, dingy, and unfriendly. The apartment, way up in the eaves, was sparsely furnished and had electric lights that were hardly bright enough to read by. They flickered constantly—"because of buzzards on the lines," the landlord explained. Outside, it always seemed to be raining. A heavy mist swirled around the house.

Having gone to all the trouble to bring us to Wales, Griffith spent no time at all with us while we were there; instead, he passed his days wandering around the countryside alone, lost in a private reverie. Our tired mother was fully occupied with looking after the one-year-old baby, cooking the meals, and snatching the odd rest in between.

Left entirely to our own devices, Simon and I passed most of our time indoors, playing board games and listening to scratchy records on an old gramophone. Just occasionally we ventured out into the dripping wet garden where we were intrigued by a formidably steep, heavily wooded ravine running close by one side of the house. But all the narrow paths leading down into its misty depths were blocked by fallen branches and thick wet undergrowth, and we never got to the bottom.

When I started researching my father's life, the house and the ravine came back to haunt me.

Griffith's younger sister—my aunt Ruth—had never mentioned Rhos y Gilwen to me. Only after I started questioning her about what she could remember of her brother as a boy did she tell me a little about it. It was the house where she and Griffith spent five years of their early childhood. Ruth remembered being left in Wales at the age of three, along with Griffith, age four, when their parents, who had come over from Calcutta for their customary summer visit to the home country, rushed back to India in the late summer of 1914 at the onset of World War I. My grandmother had elected to return to India with my grandfather, rather than remain at the rented Rhos y Gilwen with her two youngest children. "No one can look after your husband," she explained in a letter to a friend, "but other people can look after your children."

The war lasted longer than anyone expected, and my grandparents did not return to Wales until 1919, after it was over. At Rhos y Gilwen, as time passed, the servants, the cook, and the farmhands were either dismissed or left of their own accord to join the war effort. Eventually the only people left in the house were the two young children and their nanny—Nanny Saunders. Five miles from the nearest village, they were isolated from the outside world and only had each other for company.

For almost five years Nanny Saunders did not have a single day off, and she invariably sent Ruth and Griffith outside in their wooden clogs to occupy themselves. All day, almost every day, they ran wild in the garden and surrounding countryside, both developing a great love of nature and the outdoors. Their only schooling was a two-hour lesson twice a week with a woman who came in from the nearest village. Ruth remembered playing in the fields, snaring rabbits, running around the tops of the slate-capped walls enclosing the vegetable garden behind the house, and, on winter evenings, sitting on a sofa, reading, by a huge fire in the hall. She and Griffith became very close and very self-sufficient, sharing a private language and doing everything together. He called her "Baby." She called him "Griffy," and regarded him as "the fount of all knowledge."

"Very thin with spindly legs, round blue eyes and fiery red hair," Griffy was in sole charge of their outdoor lives. At five he was already very bossy, liked things done his own way, and was insatiably curious—"into everything," as Ruth put it. One issue that caused arguments between them was that Griffy always wanted to go down into "the dingle"—the ravine next to the house—to do projects and experiments, and he wanted his sister on hand to help him. "We were guided by *The Scout Magazine,* and we learned to make fires and all that kind of thing," he later recalled. But Ruth found the dingle dark and sinister and seldom wanted to go there.

Ruth adored her brother and was deeply traumatized when, at the age of nine and a half, he was suddenly sent away to boarding school, and she also had to leave Rhos y Gilwen after their parents gave up the lease on the house. It felt like she was being snatched away from the Garden of Eden. Nothing was ever quite as good again. Eventually she was taken to visit her brother at school, but she found him changed and aloof, and never regained her former closeness with him.

I do not remember my father ever mentioning Rhos y Gilwen to me in his lifetime. The first time I heard him talking of it was on video in 2004, when I was loaned a tape of Griffith being interviewed at the age of eighty by one of the Silver Hut scientists, Jim Milledge. Another former colleague, Ray Clark, was doing the filming.

Viewing the tape, what struck me most was my father's transformation when he talked about his childhood. His voice softened, he chuckled with pleasure, and his face creased into smiles as he recalled his early years, running around the countryside at Rhos y Gilwen with his sister and playing in the dingle. "We were just turned loose in the morning and then we were summoned for lunch and then turned loose again," he remembered delightedly.

There was no supervision of any kind, and just this sort of jungle. It was ideal for children . . . To get us back [Nanny] blew a bugle, and when we didn't want to go back we used to tease her and say that, "Oh, we

thought it was a cow"... This was a formative time in a child's life
when he is supposed to have all this discipline and we had none... no
discipline whatever.

In 2006 I went there myself. Arriving up the tree-lined drive with dappled sunlight glinting through the leaves, I was amazed to find that the house was not the grim, unfriendly black hulk of my memory but a mellow, attractive building. At its front, wide lawns swept down to a ha-ha and meadows beyond, full of sheep and cattle. Inside, the rooms were light and well-proportioned. There was a central hall with a large fireplace and a sofa next to it where Griffith and Ruth must have sat, reading their books.

Walking around the estate I found myself picturing the two young children dashing about the fields and climbing the trees. The vegetable garden was still there behind the house, and I was shocked to see that the walls the two young children used to run along with such abandon were all of 12 feet high. It was only at this moment, when a succession of images of my father—not as my parent, but as an innocent young child racing around with his sister—crowded into my mind, that the thaw started. For the first time I began to gain a little emotional empathy for him as a person.

Lost in thought, I ventured into the dingle, setting off down a steep path to look for the mossy stream at its base. The dingle—a precipitous gash in the landscape, with ancient trees and banks of fantastical, entwined undergrowth disappearing into its invisible dark depths—proved to be a place so full of atmosphere that I was overtaken by a sense of trepidation. For years I had protected myself from being hurt by my father by keeping him out of my emotions. Now the realization that I was really beginning to penetrate the mysteries of his personality was making me fearful of how much it might hurt to allow him to exist in my mind as a sympathetic entity.

Nevertheless, I steeled myself and started to think about how his experiences in this place had helped to forge his character.

Griffith had emphasized that his life at Rhos y Gilwen had a complete absence of discipline. I think he recognized that in that lack of discipline lay the makings of the maverick adult who was never disposed to conform, and always resisted being told what to do—whether he came up against his army colonel, the long arm of the law, his boss Otto Edholm, or his

MRC managers; whether he was dealing with the Alpine Club or the British Olympic Association. The only exceptions were people like Sir Charles Harington and Sir Peter Medawar, who commanded his natural respect.

Thrown back on their own resources as young children, Ruth and my father had to become very self-reliant. For five years he spent all day, every day, deciding exactly what was to be done, with no one but his little sister to say otherwise. Therein lay the roots of a man who, later, always did things in his own way and never worried about putting his head above the parapet or standing up against the conventional view. Being cared for in his youth by a nanny who made no demands on him, and, as a young adult and the only son, having money lavished on him by his absent parents—being brought up, as Doey put it, "always to expect the lion's share"—must have encouraged that self-centered sense that the world revolved around fulfilling his needs.

I could only guess what traumas my father suffered when, already abandoned by his parents, he was plucked out of the country paradise he loved so much and thrust into the crushing world of a boys' boarding school. His comments—"The great thing about going to an English public school is that you know that nothing as bad as that can ever happen to you again," and "It took me forty years to recover from my public school"—kept echoing in my mind.

After World War I, when my father was finally reunited with his parents, he hardly recognized them. I, the unfavored daughter, felt a real sense of relief when I found this out, for it helped me to understand why he seemed such an unfeeling parent. Griffith's failure to connect with his own children ran so deep that when he took us to Wales, to the place where he had been profoundly happy as a child, he could not even bring himself to tell us about it. Far from inspiring us with his memories, he failed even to mention that he had been there before.

Although it seemed to me that my father became ever more cantankerous as time went on, Griffith did not spend the last nineteen years of his life in retirement moping about his various grievances.

In 1969, my mother's brother Sir Francis Cassel died. As the oldest son, Francis had assumed control of what remained of my grandfather's estate in Luton—a 450-acre farm with a market garden and pair of petrol stations. The farm and the businesses had become run-down, and Griffith grabbed the opportunity to step in and take over the management.[1]

Entering a completely new field once again, Griffith was soon questioning, experimenting, and measuring everything—getting back to first principles in his usual restless, ineffably curious way. He studied the composition of the soil, the properties of the wheat, the rate at which the grain metabolized in storage. He bought a mill and began grinding his own wheat and making his own bread. A land economist from Cambridge whom Griffith consulted told me that, in all his years in farming, he had never met anyone with my father's ability to get to the nub of a problem and find a simple, practical solution.

In the garages, too, he was always looking for ways to do things better, and he was always measuring—the evaporation rates of different types of fuel, the prices his competitors were charging, the temperature of the gasoline when it was delivered by tanker. The temperature was crucial. The retailer buys gasoline by volume, but it expands when it is hot, and tanker drivers can fill garage storage tanks to capacity with less gas, shortchanging the owner. Griffith would meet the tanker drivers brandishing his thermometer. If the gas was hot, he would demand compensation.

The farm, garages, and market garden prospered, but Griffith could not fully enjoy his success. He did not own the estate, nor did he have the authority of a real manager. Doey's twin brother Harold had wanted to take control of the businesses, but his sisters, Hermione and Doey, equal owners with their brother, refused to allow it—believing that he, like Francis before him, would use the estate for his own benefit while allowing it to decline. Instead, they appointed Doey the manager, with Griffith in the background, doing the work. Although they depended on my father, Hermione and Doey refused him any formal authority. He could not decide anything without their permission. This was how my mother—backed up by my aunt—repaid my father for the way he had treated her, reserving for herself complete control over everything she owned.

It was a truly poisonous situation. Sir Harold, who felt that his rightful role as head of the family had been usurped by Griffith, referred to my father behind his back as "the cuckoo," opposing every plan he came up with. Griffith would become deeply frustrated, and we always knew when he was on the warpath by the stump, stump, stump of his crutches as he followed Doey around the house, haranguing her. He had suffered the same impotence in relation to us children. My mother allowed him no say on where to educate us, whether to buy things for us, or how much or how little pocket money we should be given. His sensitivity about his lack of authority was so acute that he often surprised people by suddenly confiding, apropos of nothing, "Of course I've been unable to fulfill my function as a father because my wife has more money than me."

The other side of the coin of all this impotence was his ability to live comfortably in our large house, his lack of responsibilities, and the absence of financial worries. He had his fancy sports cars and his Hoyo cigars. And then there was his boat—largely paid for by my mother and my aunt—a 40-foot, eight-berth prototype fiberglass catamaran, which he commissioned and helped to design in the mid-1960s and spent many happy weekends and holidays sailing.

Because he had all of life's material comforts while he was still at the Medical Research Council, he had been able to behave like a gentleman scientist who cared nothing for ambition and only did his job out of personal interest. Griffith thought this was the life he wanted. He thought he didn't care about his career or his public stature. When asked by a journalist, after he retired, whether Everest had given him "more opportunities" in his profession, his immediate reaction was to protest that he had never wanted a professorship. "I didn't want a chair—I didn't want a chair," he insisted. "I had already got this beautiful house and garden. And we have never had to strain for money."

As things turned out he never got a chair—he never tried to get one—and the price he paid for failing to advance his career was that people didn't respect him in the way that he wanted. People often didn't listen to him. He was often snubbed. He was frustrated working under a boss he felt was less able than he was, and—except by the Silver Hut scientists—he was not recognized for his scientific achievements in the way that he would have liked.

I have come away from studying my father's life with a sense that, had he made different choices, a man like Griffith, with so many contradictions in his nature, might have turned out very differently.

He married Doey because she was wealthy, but she never really suited him. He was unable to make her happy or be happy with her. And in many ways her money proved to be a poisoned chalice, for it sapped his motivation to make the most of his remarkable talents. If he had married someone who demanded more of him, and if he had been forced to provide for himself and his family, to achieve a senior position at work and accept responsibility for others (as he showed he could on the Silver Hut expedition), he might have been happier, more fulfilled, and less difficult. The fact that he was never quite in charge of his own fate, either at home or at work, was a constant source of irritation to him. He wasn't suited to the subordinate roles he accepted for himself. They diminished him and, in the end, they left him—as his friend and colleague had said—"a disappointed man."

My father's funeral in 1994 at Lilley Church near Putteridge, where he married Josephine in 1939, overflowed with mourners. Even Sir John Hunt came. During the eulogy, it was not the tributes to his professional achievements that drew special warmth and recognition from the congregation but the stories of his eccentricity. It was the tales of Griffith's "never conventional and sometimes bizarre" behavior, his "assertive and at times impressionistic" driving, and the idea that he "never suffered fools gladly—indeed, never suffered fools at all" that caused murmurs of affection to ripple through the little church. Do we all enjoy a joke at a funeral? I wondered. Are people simply amused by eccentricity? Or is there a recognition at some deeper level that eccentricity is a manifestation of independence of mind, a refusal to compromise that commands both respect and affection?

I wept at my father's funeral. The people around me supposed this to be a sign of a daughter's natural grief, but my tears were not tears of grief. They were tears of anger. Anger with my father, and anger with myself for the fact that we had never achieved a proper relationship with each other. When I started writing the story of his life, I was still feeling resentful. Now, having reached the end, I am no longer angry, but grateful to Griffith for having provided me with an intensely satisfying project that has taken several years to complete—his part to be the outstanding scientist and the worthy subject, mine to be his chronicler.

The pleasure of learning about his unique talent and recording his unusual life has banished the last vestige of umbrage from his daughter's unforgiving heart and replaced it with a hope that, had he been alive, he would not have been too displeased with my efforts.

Notes

AC = Alpine Club Archives
BBC = BBC Film Archive
BL = British Library
- All references are © British Library Board

BOA = British Olympic Association Archives
- All references cite material in three uncataloged files: John le Masurier file (senior coach of the Amateur Athletics Association), plus two unnamed files containing miscellaneous Olympic material connected with the 1968 Olympic Games

BSC = University of Birmingham Special Collections
GP = Griffith Pugh (Lewis Griffith Creswell Evans Pugh)
HP = Hillary papers, Hillary, Edmund Percival, Sir. Personal papers. Auckland War Memorial Museum Library. MS 2010/1.
HTP = Private Papers belonging to Harriet Tuckey and family
IOC = International Olympic Committee
IWM = Imperial War Museum, London
MRC = Medical Research Council Head Office
MSCL = Mandeville Special Collections Library, UCSD, USA
NIMR = National Institute for Medical Research
PP = Pugh Papers (Lewis Griffith Cresswell Evans [LGCE] Pugh Papers, MSS 0491. MSCL)
RGS = Royal Geographical Society
RS = Royal Society
TNA = The National Archive, Kew, London
UCSD = University of California, San Diego
War Diary = Pugh's diaries of his experiences during World War II, in HTP
WL = Wellcome Library

PUGH'S DIARIES

War Diaries 1940–43—HTP and IWM
Cho Oyu Diary 1952—PP 33.3 and HTP
Everest Diary 1953—PP 35.13 and HTP

Antarctic Diary—1957–58—PP 3.8
Silver Hut Diary 1960–61 (Diary of the Himalayan Mountaineering and Scientific Expedition 1960–61)—PP 64.1 and HTP

ENDNOTES

Introduction: The Anniversary Lecture

1 It is "politically incorrect" to use the word conquest to describe the ascent of great mountains. Mountains, it is argued, are not conquered, they are simply climbed. However, I use the word conquest to convey something quite different—the triumph over human frailty and inadequacy in pursuit of a difficult goal. As the great climber Alfred Mummery once remarked, ". . . the essence of the sport lies, not in ascending the peak, but in struggling with and overcoming difficulties" (quoted by H. H. Tilman,1948, p. 4).

2 I have not seen a transcript of the speech, so this is not a direct quote, but as I remember it. There were seven major British expeditions to Everest in between World War I and II. There were two major Swiss expeditions in 1952. There were also maverick solo attempts on Everest in 1934, 1947, and 1951, plus a possible Russian attempt in 1952.

3 Hunt sent a copy of this letter to Pugh.

1. The Man in the Bath

1 Michael Ward kindly described for me his first and subsequent meetings with Pugh during a taped conversation at his house in 2004.

2 See Norton 1925, p. 113. The altitude record set by Lieutenant General Norton (1884–1954) in 1924, of 28,126 feet, was not exceeded until the spring of 1952, when the Swiss reached an estimated 28,210 feet. Whether they actually achieved this height has recently been disputed by Bradford Washburn (see Washburn 2003).

3 See Ruttledge 1934, p. 261. Raymond Greene (1901–1982) was a fashionable society GP doctor to the 1933 Everest expedition, and an enthusiastic climber and member of the Alpine Club. He took a close interest in the problems of altitude on Everest, and worked on improving the oxygen sets beforehand, seeking advice from J. S. Haldane and C. G. Douglas of the Oxford School of Physiology. On the 1933 expedition he took samples

of alveolar air (from the bottom of the lung) at 23,000 feet. See, for example, Greene in Ruttledge 1934 and Greene 1934 and Greene 1939.
4 Norton 1925 (I), p. 111. Also see manuscript paper by Pugh, entitled "Everest 1953 Physiological Notes" in RGS/EE/75, The Physiological Effects of Altitude.
5 Norton 1925a, p. 13.

2. Gallant Failures

1 The seven official British expeditions to Everest took place in 1921, 1922, 1924, 1933, 1935, 1936, and 1938.
2 Ruttledge 1934, p. 2.
3 Tilman 1948, p. 107, H. W. Tilman 1898–1977x9, famous climber and explorer.
4 Tilman 1948, p. 22.
5 Warren 1937, p. 139.
6 Georges Dreyer (1873–1934) was a consultant to the Royal Flying Corps during World War I (this became the RAF in 1918). He also designed the oxygen apparatus used by the Air Service, US Army. He was elected a Fellow of the Royal Society in 1921. Although some of his experiments into exercise capacity at altitude have been described as "years ahead of their time" (see West 2006), he has been largely forgotten. The use of oxygen sets for flying became widespread only in World War I, when advances in aeronautical technology produced more powerful airplanes capable of flying higher than before.
7 This comment was made after George Finch (see note 10) had spoken on oxygen at the RGS in November 1922 (see Finch 1923, p. 199). John Scott Haldane (1860–1936) of the influential Oxford School of Physiology and his colleagues made important discoveries about the relationship between carbon dioxide and the control of breathing. Haldane was famous for saving the lives of miners by proposing the use of canaries in the mines and discovering the cause of "the bends" in divers. Together with C. G. Douglas, he organized one of the earliest high-altitude scientific expeditions to Pikes Peak, Colorado, in 1911.
8 For example, Bryan Matthews was quoted in several newspapers, claiming that the combination of cold and oxygen-lack would always defeat them (see RGS/EE/65, press cuttings).

9 Some experimental oxygen was taken on the first expedition by scientist Alexander Kellas, but he died en route to the mountain and it was never used.

10 AC B 13. Farrar Letters 1919. George Ingle Finch (1888–1970) was Professor of Applied Chemistry at Imperial College, London, and was elected a Fellow of the Royal Society in 1938. Born in Australia and educated in Europe, he developed his climbing skills while studying in Zurich before moving to England in 1912.

11 Finch described his conversion to oxygen in *Mein Kampf für Everest,* published in German (in 1925), recently translated and reissued with editorial comments (see Rodway 2008). See also Unna 1921–22 and West's articles on Finch (West 2003) and on Dreyer (West 2006).

12 The Royal Aircraft Establishment at Farnborough (until 1918, the Royal Air Factory) was the RAF's main center of research and development in the country. In 1939 Farnborough's capacity for physiological research was increased with the setting up of the Royal Physiological Laboratory. Later this was transformed into the Centre for Aviation Medicine, led by Bryan Matthews.

13 Finch 1924, p. 293.

14 Finch, Geoffrey Bruce, and Corporal Tejbir demonstrated their superior speed using oxygen when they climbed from Camp Three (21,000 feet) to the North Col (23,000 feet) faster than their porters without oxygen, despite carrying greater weight than their porters (see Finch's own account in Rodway 2008, p. 141). They passed their porters again climbing from the North Col to the next camp at 25,000 feet. Delayed for a day by bad weather, they gave up their summit attempt two days later when Bruce collapsed after a fault developed in his oxygen set. Making an oxygen-free summit bid earlier on the same expedition, Mallory, Norton, and Somervell stopped at 2:15 p.m. at 26,800 feet because they were climbing too slowly to get to the top and return down to a survivable height for the night. They were exhausted, cold, and desperately thirsty. Michael Ward analyzed their experiences in Ward 2003, p. 80. (See also Unsworth 2000, pp. 85–90, and Finch 1922, p. 418, and Finch 1924, pp. 323–30.)

15 For Finch's exclusion, see West 2003; see also BL Add 63120 and Russell's introductory memoir to Finch 1924.

16 Summers 2000, p. 118.

17 Printed in Lunn 2003, p. 72. Noel Odell had been appointed oxygen officer, but delegated responsibility to Irvine.

18 The 1924 expedition was led by Edward Norton, who took on the role after the original leader, Brigadier General Bruce, went down with malaria. Norton appointed Mallory the climbing leader.

19 BL manuscript Add 61139: letter: Mallory to his wife Ruth, April 19, 1924. Norton wrote of how he tried to dissuade Mallory from choosing the inexperienced Irvine as his partner, rather than the seasoned climber Noel Odell, who was also available. Mallory said he did not want to go with Odell because Odell did not "have faith" in the oxygen, and insisted on taking Irvine. See Norton 1925(1), p. 116. Professor Noel Odell (1890–1987) was an academic geologist who worked at Harvard and Cambridge Universities during his career, and was also a renowned climber with an apparently excellent tolerance of high altitude.

20 Magdalen College Archive: Letter: Mallory to his wife Ruth, May 27, 1924.

21 Ibid.

22 Jochen Hemmleb, who searched for Mallory and Irvine's bodies in 1999, wrote afterward of the "very, very exposed" vertical walls, "intimidating" traverses that upset even experienced climbers, and the "terrifying" ridges that Mallory and Irvine would have had to cope with (see Hemmleb 1999).

23 See Norton 1925a, p. 116 and Summers 2000, p. 230.

24 See Norton 1925a, p. 14.

25 There are many descriptions of Mallory's last climb. See, for example, Gillman 2000, pp. 246–59, Summers 2000, pp. 235–50, Ward 2003, pp. 97–204, etc.

26 Finch 1939, p. 90.

27 Acclimatization enables climbers to survive and climb at heights that cause the unacclimatized (such as airline passengers exposed to sudden loss of cabin pressure) rapidly to lose consciousness and die within a few minutes.

28 Longstaff 1934, p. 103. Thomas George Longstaff (1875–1964) was the first person to climb a summit higher than 22,966 feet, the Himalayan

mountain of Trisul, in 1907. He succeeded by climbing 7,000 feet up and back in a single day.

29 Finch 1923, p. 19.

30 Dr. Raymond Greene commented on a talk given at the Alpine Club by Dr. Tom Longstaff (see Longstaff 1934, p. 108).

31 Smythe 1934, p. 443.

32 Odell 1932, pp. 91–95. Odell believed that he acquired "a very high degree of acclimatisation" by "living at an altitude of not less than 23,000 feet for eleven days" on the 1924 Everest expedition.

33 Young 1949, p. 8. Born in 1876 and educated at Marlborough, followed by Cambridge, Geoffrey Winthrop Young established a reputation as a leading climber by making a series of exceptionally difficult Alpine ascents before World War I. In his heyday a witty, dashing figure, reputedly with homosexual leanings, he regularly organized important "meets" at Penn Y Pass in Snowdonia, where top British mountaineers of his generation would join with elite, upcoming youthful climbers (such as George Mallory) for a few days of rock climbing and socializing. Young, whose climbing career was curtailed but not ended when he lost a leg in World War I, was a prolific poet and mountaineering author. He edited the *Alpine Journal* for some years, and remained an influential member of the Alpine Club until he died in 1958. His climbing manual (first published in 1920) was widely regarded as "the quintessential wisdom of mountaineering practice."

34 Ibid.

35 See Greene's comments in Ruttledge 1934(I), p. 255.

36 Greene 1974, p. 142.

37 They consulted Dr. S. S. Zilva of the Lister Institute, as indeed had the 1933 expedition under Ruttledge.

38 See Odell's comments in Tilman 1938, p. 494.

39 Finch 1923, p. 199.

40 See Smythe's comments in Tilman 1938, p. 491.

41 Longstaff 1923, p. 60.

42 See Hingston's article in Norton 1925, p. 252. Major Richard William Hingston, Royal Indian Medical Service (1887–1966).

43 See Hingston 1925, p. 11.

44 Young 1921, p. 8 (pp. 8–9 in 1949 edition).

45 From Finch's diary of the Everest Expedition of 1922, entry for April 12, 1922 (see Rodway 2008, p. 84).

46 AC B 49, Letter Smythe to Dr. C. R. Porter, August 20, 1938.

47 From Finch's diary of the Everest Expedition of 1922, entry for April 12, 1922 (see Rodway 2008, p. 84).

48 Hillary 1999, p. 69.

49 See Ruttledge 1934, p. 256.

50 Letter, Wakefield to *Alpine Journal*, Vol. 46.248/9 1934, p. 450.

51 See Warren in Ruttledge 1937, p. 218.

52 For example, Hingston wrote after the 1924 expedition, "Elaborate scientific explorations were impossible, and anything involving complicated apparatus was altogether out of the question" (see Hingston 1925, p. 4). Similarly in 1937, Dr. Charles Warren wrote, "Since the main object . . . in 1936 was to climb the mountain . . . no provision was made for scientific work to be done . . . Only very simple observations could be made" (see Warren 1937, p. 126).

53 Ibid., p. 146.

54 See Greene's comments in Tilman 1938, p. 496.

55 See also Greene 1939, p. 158.

56 Ibid.

57 Ibid.

3. Mountain of Destiny

1 See, for instance, Shipton 1969, p. 183.

2 Annapurna I is 26,493 feet. The Swiss climbed Pyramid Peak, 23,294 feet.

3 The expedition was headed by Oscar Houston and included his son Charles, H. W. Tilman, Anderson Bakewell, and Elizabeth Cowles. Departing in October 1950, they planned to follow local trails to Mount Everest to discover whether a feasible climbing route existed on the southern side (see *Berge Der Welt* 1954). Tilman's verdict was ". . . although we cannot dismiss the South Side, I think it is safe to say there is no route comparable in ease and safety at any rate up to 28,000 feet to that by the North East" (Tilman 1951).

4 In his autobiography, Shipton 1969, p. 185, Shipton wrote: "I thought it highly improbable that we would find a practicable route up the

southern side of Everest . . . Bill Tilman agreed with this opinion, and so did General Norton, who reckoned the chances against our finding a route to the South Col at forty to one."

5 Ward 1972, p. 50.

6 Ibid., p. 55. Letter Murray to Ward, May 28, 1951; W. H. Murray (1913–1996) was often described as the "Sir Galahad of the peaks."

7 RGS/EE/99: Minute Books of Mount Everest Committee and Himalayan Committee, entry for June 12, 1951.

8 TNA FO 371/92928: Letter Goodfellow to the Under Secretary of State for Foreign Affairs at the Foreign Office, June 13, 1951.

9 Ibid.: Telegram from the Community Relations Office, London, to the High Commission in Delhi, June 20, 1951.

10 Ibid.

11 Only climbers under forty years old were admitted into the group, and climbing standards were scrutinized every two years (see Ward 1972, p. 57).

12 Ibid., p. 55. The Aiguille du Dru is 12,316 feet.

13 Robert Benedict Bourdillon (1889–1971) gained a first-class degree in chemistry at Balliol College, Oxford, in 1912, and later took a medical degree, becoming a doctor in 1925. He served as an RAF test pilot from 1914–19.

14 The altitude tables produced by the International Civil Aviation Organisation are constructed using simplifying assumptions about the relationship between air pressure, humidity, and temperature and how these factors change with changing altitude, in order to provide a viable universal standard on which the altimeters of all aircraft can be calibrated. They do not show the actual physical barometric pressure on the ground, where air pressures, particularly above altitudes of 16,404 feet, vary according to the distance from the equator, being higher than predicted by the standard tables near the equator, and lower near the poles. When it was first measured in 1981, the barometric pressure on the summit of Mount Everest in good weather proved to be 17mmHG higher than the pressure predicted by the standard international altitude tables, i.e., the equivalent of Everest being 1,542 feet lower than expected. See explanation in Milledge 2006, and the articles by West 1996 and by Pugh 1957. Specialists such as meteorologists have always understood this point. Paul

Bert correctly predicted the approximate barometric pressure on the summit of Everest in 1878 (see Appendix 1, *La Pression Barométrique,* Paris), as did Alexander Kellas 1917.

15 Supplementary oxygen was first extensively used in aircraft in 1916. The apparatus was designed by R .H. Davis of the firm of Siebe Gorman and by Professor G. Dreyer at Oxford University. Siebe Gorman provided the oxygen sets for the early Everest expeditions that were adapted from Dreyer's design. These matters are very clearly explained in layman's terms in a comprehensive history of high-altitude medicine by Pugh's former colleague, Professor John West (see West 1998, p. 229).

16 As soon as Shipton took over the leadership, the committee granted the expedition £2,500, solving all of their financial problems. See RGS/EE/99: Minute Books of Mount Everest Committee and Himalayan Committee, July 19, 1951.

17 The invitation was apparently issued in response to a last-minute request, received via the New Zealand Alpine Club.

18 AC D 103: Bourdillon Diaries.

19 The India Office was the government department in London which oversaw and administered the British government in India between 1858 and 1947.

20 Ibid.: The Swiss applied again in 1926. An India Office official commented : "It is impossible not to sympathize with the [Everest] Committee's desire to achieve definitively the so-nearly-accomplished conquest of Mount Everest; and there is a distinct possibility that if a claim is not staked out without delay for a further British expedition, a Swiss or German expedition may seek facilities for an attempt on the mountain; it would be difficult to refuse the former, at any rate, any help in approaching the Tibetan Gov't unless it can truthfully be stated that a prior claim has been registered." The Hon. Sec. was warned to send in an application for the British, which was then preemptively put to Tibet before the Swiss application, on the basis that "if permission were refused to a British expedition we may assume that it would be refused to a foreign." Another file note admitted, "[T]his is not a sportsmanlike attitude, but there is a possibility of another British expedition in 1926, and we should prefer our own party to win the glory of a successful ascent."

21 Ibid.

22 *Daily Telegraph,* June 13, 1929.

23 TNA FO 371/92928: Letter Summerhayes to Murray at Foreign Office, November 26, 1951.

24 TNA FD1 9042.

25 TNA FO 371/101162.

26 TNA FO 371/101162. The note continued, "This is especially so where the Swiss were concerned, since our relations with them in the Far East were most friendly and cooperative."

27 Ibid.

28 Ibid.

4. Turf Wars

1 Letter, Pugh to his wife, October 27, 1942.

2 These experiments were carried out at the US Naval School of Aviation Medicine by Charles Houston and Richard Riley in 1944, with the ostensible aim of finding out if acclimatization could help aviators to tolerate higher altitudes (using oxygen). The experimental subjects spent a total of thirty-five days in the pressure chambers, experimenting both with and without oxygen (see West 1998, pp. 236–41). News of the research results filtered through to British climbers like Shipton and Frank Smythe, who drew a variety of conclusions. Smythe claimed Houston's experiments were ". . . of the utmost interest and explode our ideas about oxygen," and wrote excitedly to his friend Amery that Houston had shown "Oxygen when used on acclimatised men at high altitudes is useless" (AC E18: Letter, Smythe to Amery, November 5, 1946).

3 AC E18: Letter, Shipton to Donkin (Hon. Sec. of the Himalayan Committee), February 5, 1947.

4 Video interview of Pugh conducted by Jim Milledge, Professor Raymond Clarke, and Mervyn de Calcina-Goff in 1992.

5 Matthews and his team at Farnborough had greatly improved the oxygen sets used for flying by developing an "economizer," which stopped oxygen being wasted when the user was breathing out, and by creating a much-improved mask, designed by J. C. Gilson.

6 RGS/EE/99: Mount Everest Minute Books, February 24, 1948 and March 2, 1948. Greene looking at diet dropped out after a year. Russell

attended a few meetings. Lloyd produced an oxygen report in 1948 but failed to follow up.

7 See *Times* obituaries of Peter Lloyd (1907–2003), April 21 and April 30, 2003, *Daily Telegraph,* April 30, 2003, *Guardian,* May 1, 2003. Lloyd climbed in the Alps in the late twenties and early thirties and joined Bill Tilman on an Anglo-American expedition to Nanda Devi in 1936, before going to Everest in 1938.

8 Lloyd 1939, p. 87.

9 Typical of this tendency was a remark made by Lloyd at the RGS in October 1938, speaking at the end of Tilman's talk on "The Mount Everest Expedition of 1938." "I have a lot of sympathy with the sentimental objections to its use [oxygen] and would far rather see the mountain climbed without it; but on the other hand I would rather see the mountain climbed with it than not at all" (see Tilman 1938).

10 See, for example, Mangan 1981 and 2006, Girouard 1981, Porter and Wagg, 2006.

11 See for instance RGS/EE/59-60. Mount Everest Reconnaissance: Letter, Scott Russell to Kirwan, July 17, 1951.

12 Odell 1932, p. 95.

13 See Unsworth 1981, pp. 77–79, for discussion of attitudes to oxygen in the early 1920s.

14 Smythe 1942, p. 48.

15 Tilman 1948, p. 109.

16 Younghusband in Norton 1925, p. 5.

17 Younghusband in Smythe 1933, p. 1.

18 Young 1949 (7th ed.), p. 3.

19 Apart from the treasurer, R. W. Lloyd, the other committee members were all relatively passive. They attended meetings and voted, but did not do much of the work. The members of the committee are listed in note 9 of chapter 8.

20 RGS EE 62/63/64.Oxygen: "Oxygen Equipment for Everest: Notes on a meeting held on December 14, 1952," note 8. The Royal Aircraft Establishment at Farnborough was founded at the same time as the RAF itself in 1918 and carried out mechanical as well as medical research and development. In 1939 a separate Royal Physiological Laboratory was

established, which became the RAF Institute of Aviation Medicine in 1944.

21 West 2003 gives a comprehensive description of the oxygen sets. Four cylinders of compressed oxygen were carried on the climber's back. The rate at which the oxygen was delivered to the climber could be varied. A complete fully charged set weighed approximately 30 pounds. The sets included a device called an economizer that reduced waste by storing oxygen—released at a continuous rate—in a bag while the climber was breathing out.

22 The emergency oxygen in modern commercial airliners is based on the same principle as the closed-circuit.

23 Bourdillon thought that open-circuit oxygen would not significantly reduce what he called the hyperventilation of climbers, and believed that the sodium loss which resulted from "over breathing" was the underlying cause of many aspects of altitude deterioration. He explained some aspects of this theory in a brief informal paper called "Questions re: Physiological Adaption on Everest Expeditions," December 12, 1951 (in RGS EE 62/63/64.Physiology). It did not impress Professor McCance, a very eminent expert on nutrition who was asked to comment, as he made very clear in a letter to Kirwan of December 20, 1951 (in RGS/EE/ 62/63/64. Oxygen).

24 RGS/EE/62/63/64.Physiology: Letter, Lloyd to Kirwan, December 28, 1951.

25 Shipton and Ward thought they saw a route to the southwest (Shipton 1953, p. 9); Tom Bourdillon and Bill Murray were also reported to have spotted a possible route on the west side.

26 Laurence Kirwan (1907–1999) was an Oxbridge-educated archaeologist with a special interest in the Sudan and Nubia. Recruited to the RGS in 1947, he became secretary and director in 1948, remaining in the job for the next thirty years. He was the driving force behind many expeditions associated with the RGS, of which the two most famous were the Everest Expedition of 1953 and Vivian Fuchs's expedition to the Antarctic in 1957–58. He was knighted in 1972. See obituaries in *The Times*, April 22, 1999; Geographical Journal, Vol. 165.3, November 1999; *Guardian*, April 21, 1999; *Dictionary of National Biography*, Ure 2008.

27 See RGS/EE/62/63/64.Oxygen: Letter, Kirwan to Lloyd, December 20, 1951.

28 RGS/EE/62/63/64.Physiology: Letter, Lloyd to Kirwan, December 28, 1951.

29 RGS/EE/62/63/64.Physiology. This conversation is recorded in a letter from Bourdillon to Kirwan, December 23, 1951.

30 RGS/EE/62/63/64.Physiology. At Bourdillon's suggestion, Kirwan invited two experts to this meeting, Professor Robert McCance, Professor of Experimental Medicine at Cambridge, and Professor Bryan Matthews. He explained that the invitation followed discussions "in particular with Dr. R. B. Bourdillon about ways of dealing with the physiological problems of climbing Everest." See also "Note on a meeting held at the RGS on January 4, 1952," initialed "RBB," sent with a covering note to Kirwan on January 5, 1952 in same file.

31 RGS/EE/59/60.Applications for Cho Oyu Expedition: Letter, Kirwan to R. B. Bourdillon, January 17, 1952.

32 Ibid: Letter, Bourdillon to Kirwan, January 16, 1952.

33 PP 6.11 and 33.2. Bourdillon's research proposal has Pugh's handwritten additions at the bottom.

34 Professor Bryan Matthews (1906–1986) was a public-school and Cambridge-educated physiologist who developed his interest in altitude medicine while also doing important work into neurophysiology at Cambridge before World War II. He took part in the International High-Altitude Science Expedition to Chile of 1935, led by Bruce Dill, and distinguished himself by spending the longest time at high altitude, as well as making a significant scientific contribution to the expedition. After leaving Farnborough he returned to Cambridge, where he rebuilt and led an outstanding physiology department, always insisting on scientific excellence and being willing to recruit only those of exceptional academic ability. Matthews became a fellow of the Royal Society in 1940 and was knighted in 1952. See: Gray 2004 and Gray 1990.

35 RS HD/6/2/9/2/6: Letter, January 29, 1952.

5. In the Mountains of Lebanon

1 HTP War Diary, December 13, 1941.

2 i.e., Middle East Command.

3 HTP Letter, Pugh to his mother Adah, January 11, 1941. Mussolini's Italian troops occupied Albania in April 1939 and attacked Greece from Albania in October 1940. Limited British forces were deployed to Greece in November 1940, honoring the British commitment to assist Greece should it be attacked.

4 W. James Riddell (1909–2000) was a member of the British international ski team for six years. He became a professional writer after leaving Cambridge, and resumed this occupation after the war. He described his experiences at Cedars in his book *Dog in the Snow* (1957).

5 The school was established by 2nd Australian Imperial Force 1 Corps and called Middle East Ski School. Riddell was attached to the Australian army and promoted to major to set it up. When the British Ninth Army GHQ took it over a year later, it was renamed IXth Army Ski School, and finally called the Ski Wing of the Middle East Mountain Warfare Centre. The rock-climbing section, commanded and run by David Cox, was called the Mountaineering Wing.

6 HTP: Letter, Pugh to his wife, January 7, 1943.

7 HTP: War Diary, January 9, 1943.

8 HTP: War Diary, January 31, 1943.

9 See Pugh, "Physiological Commentary," 1958–59, pp. 241–44.

10 Claude Gordon Douglas (1882–1963) studied medicine at Oxford and became a fellow and lecturer in Natural Science at Oxford, remaining there for the rest of his career. He became Professor of General Metabolism in 1942, and was elected a Fellow of the Royal Society in 1922. His principal research interests were in respiratory physiology. J. S. Haldane (1860–1936) was his early mentor and remained a major influence throughout his life.

11 The 1910 expedition was led by another visionary physiologist, Nathan Zuntz.

12 See "Ski Wing Directive No. 1," February 20, 1943, in PP 49.15.

13 HTP: Letter, Pugh to his wife, March 3, 1943.

14 HTP: Letter, Pugh to his wife, April 4, 1943.

15 HTP: Pugh was paid a small sum for his invention.

16 Riddell 1995.

17 HTP: Letter, Pugh to his wife, February 14, 1943.

18 PP 24.15. See also War Office correspondence in file entitled "Equipment for Mountain Troops and Research on Mountain Warfare." TNA: FD1/6471. General Godwin-Austen became Vice Quartermaster General, War Office, in 1944. Lieutenant General Alexander Hood was Director General of Army Services 1941–48.

19 "Mountain Warfare Training Centre Ski Wing Supplement No.2: Physiology of Military Skiing," Winter 1942–44, PP 25.2.

20 A letter from Sir Alexander Hood to Sir Edward Mellanby, the head of the Medical Research Council, December 17, 1943, described Pugh as a "first class medical officer," and praised his recommendations concerning the training and equipping of mountain troops, emphasizing that they had the blessings of the War Office (see TNA: FD1/6471).

21 Pugh's unit, 140 Field Ambulance, was attached to the 44th Royal Tank Regiment, which was part of the Fourth Armoured Brigade.

22 HTP: Letter, Pugh to his wife, July 24, 1943.

23 HTP: Letter, Pugh to his wife, November 8, 1943.

24 HTP: "Mountain Warfare Training Centre Ski Wing: Final Report: Winter 1942/3," p. 6.

25 Ibid., p. 7.

26 Pugh's video interview with Milledge, December 23, 1992. British army officers as opposed to privates were much healthier and fitter, Pugh thought, not simply due to their better food and medical care but also to their basic fitness as a result of playing sports at their public schools. Before World War II there was very little scope for ordinary British people, who mostly left school at fourteen, to undertake sports of any kind. This problem was noticed and understood in the war and led to concerted efforts to provide decent facilities for sports at schools, and to bring sports to the wider population after the war.

27 Dill led the International High-Altitude Expedition to Chile of 1935—the last major scientific expedition to high altitude before World War II. See Register of Bruce Dill/Harvard Fatigue Laboratory Reprints, MSS 0517, Mandeville Special Collections Library, Geisel Library, University of California, San Diego, United States.

28 HTP: Letter, Pugh to his wife, November 8, 1943, and Letter, Lt. Col. Bruce Dill to Pugh, October 14, 1944, PP 7.5.

29 PP 9.32.

30 Letter, E. Arnold Carmichael to Sir Edward Mellanby, October 3, 1944, TNA FD1/6741. Also Mellanby's signed note recording a conversation with Crew about Pugh, October 4, 1944, TNA:FD1/6471.

31 As Mussolini's ally, Hitler came to the aid of the Italian offensive against Greece by invading Greece through Bulgaria on April 6, 1940. The German army seized Thessaloniki on April 9, entered Athens on April 27, and progressed into the Peloponnese shortly afterward. The German invasion of Greece was completed in only twenty-four days (see PP 49.13).

6. Excess Baggage

1 Alexander Kellas (1868–1921) was the son of a minor business executive. Born in Aberdeen and educated at Aberdeen Grammar School, he had spells at university in Edinburgh, London, and Heidelberg, after which he became a lecturer in chemistry at Middlesex Hospital Medical School—a job which seems to have allowed him plenty of spare time to develop a passion for the Himalayas (see West 1998, pp. 167–77).

2 Kellas's paper was discovered at the RGS and subsequently published by the physiologist and expert on high-altitude medicine, Professor John West (see West 1987 and West 1998, pp. 167–77).

3 RGS/EE/62/63/64.Physiology.

4 *The Times,* April 8, 1952.

5 Shipton 1953, p. 130. Shipton's most ardent admirers were prepared to admit that he was singularly uninterested in the planning of expeditions. Tom Bourdillon described his typically relaxed behavior on the 1951 Everest Reconnaissance: "My respect for Shipton grows. He seems astonishingly casual, never quite sure about how many porters we have or where we are going for the day, but things work out smoothly. Mike [Ward] says the same thing happened in London. He wandered about utterly vague . . . and things turned out exactly as he wanted." See Bourdillon diaries, AC D 103.

6 Hardie 2006, p. 93. Norman Hardie (b. 1924) is a New Zealand climber who spent some years living in London in the 1950s, and served briefly as secretary to the 1953 Everest expedition. Two years later, he led one of the summit pairs that succeeded in making the first ascent of Kanchenjunga.

7 RGS/EE/60.Correspondence on Planning and Equipment.

8 Cho Oyu Diary, March 27, 1952.

9 Ibid., March 31, 1952.

10 *The Times,* May 10, 1952.

11 Ibid.

12 Evans 1953, p. 10.

13 Cho Oyu Diary, April 1, 1952.

14 Ibid., April 4, 1952.

15 Greene 1974, p. 138.

16 Ibid.

17 Cho Oyu Diary, April 6, 1952.

18 Ibid., April 12, 1952.

19 Ibid., April 5, 1952.

20 Ibid., April 23, 1952.

21 Ibid., April 12, 1952.

22 Ibid., April 7, 1952.

23 Ibid.

24 Ibid., April 13, 1952.

25 For instance, in 1935 Shipton thought nothing of sending four porters on a 48-mile "double march," which they were expected to complete in a day, carrying loads (see Asthill 1935, p. 327).

26 Hunt 1953, p. 70.

27 See Pugh 1952, p. 13.

28 Cho Oyu Diary, April 17, 1952.

29 Ibid., April 19, 1952.

30 Ibid., April 18, 1952.

31 Jennifer Bourdillon kindly told me about her experiences on Cho Oyu in two taped interviews at her home in Southampton in February 2004 and July 2005.

32 Cho Oyu Diary, April 18, 1952.

7. Miserable Failure

1 He made a diagram of a typical local house with animals on the ground floor and living quarters above, and described how leaf mold was collected in baskets to use as bedding for the animals. Some of the houses had lavatories consisting of a simple opening in the floor. After being in place for some time,

the resulting compost was carried out in baskets, mostly by the women, and taken to the small fields, enclosed by stone walls, where it was distributed in neat heaps on the ground. It did not smell. The main local crop was potatoes, though maize and wheat were grown lower down. The villagers also kept yaks, goats, and chickens. Pugh decided that families probably went to bed after dark, as no lights were visible in the windows at night. There were no shops.

2 Shipton 1969, p. 207, and Shipton 1953, pp. 132–33.

3 Cho Oyu Diary, May 2, 1952.

4 Ibid., April 28, 1952.

5 Ibid.

6 Shipton behaved in the same way on the 1935 Everest expedition, which he led. The doctor, Charles Warren, wrote: "During the reconnaissance in 1935 we all suffered more or less severely with mountain sickness on reaching Tangu at 12,800 feet, and again 2 or 3 days later when crossing the Kongra La." See Warren's chapter in Ruttledge 1937. Even more striking are the anguished accounts in the diaries of individual members of the 1935 expedition (see Asthill 2005).

7 Warren 1939a, p. 108.

8 Young 1949, 7th ed., p. 6.

9 Steele 1998, pp. 234–35. Meanwhile, Tenzing Norgay, the Sherpa who got to the top of Everest in 1953, had long been conscious of the need to train for expeditions. In his autobiography he recalled: "As I had done for many years past, before big expeditions I got up early in the morning, filled a knapsack with stones, and took long walks up and down the hills round the town. I did not smoke or drink, and kept away from parties, which I usually enjoy" (Ullman 1955, p. 227).

10 Pugh 1952, p. 7. See also Evans 1953, p. 12, where Evans describes himself and Alf Gregory struggling to climb a "simple col" at 19,000 feet and envying the "easy movements" of their Sherpas up the same slope.

11 Hillary 1999, p. 88.

12 The most comprehensive account of this argument is given in Peter Steele's biography of Eric Shipton. There is still more material in the unpublished notes of the interviews with most of the members of the expedition he did for the book, which are in the Alpine Club's archives. See Steele 1998, pp. 170–72 and AC E 38.HP.

13 Hillary's Cho Oyu Diary, June 9, 1952

14 The Jasamba Camp was at 18,753 ft. (5,716 m).

15 AC E 38 1: quoted by Peter Steele.

16 Hillary 1999, p. 90.

17 Evans 1953, p. 13.

18 Cho Oyu Diary, May 12, 1952.

19 Hillary 1975, p. 140.

20 RGS/EE/62/63/64.Oxygen.

21 Bourdillon 1956, p. 167.

22 Cho Oyu Diary, May 15, 1952.

23 Ibid., May 18, 1952.

24 Ibid.

25 See AC E.38 for Steele's notes on his interviews with Lowe and others.

26 Cho Oyu Diary, May 19–20, 1952.

27 RGS/EE/75.Inclusion of a physiologist: Letter, September 24, 1952.

28 The height from bottom to top of the track, as measured by barometer, was between 280 and 285 feet.

29 This is the case when the oxygen is delivered at a standard rate, and any extra air needed is breathed in from the atmosphere. Another type of open-circuit mechanism adjusts the delivery rate of oxygen to the rate at which the climber is breathing, but makes it impossible to gauge with accuracy how long the oxygen will last.

30 Closed-circuit was also admired for preventing the loss of heat and moisture from the lungs.

31 Pugh was emphatic that the experiments with an oxygen bag could not strictly be compared with the experiments using proper open-circuit oxygen sets.

32 Short summer route used by Sherpas to reach Kathmandu from Tibet, involving glacier pass of 19,000 feet.

8. An Infusion of Strong Blood

1 RGS/EE/90.Himalayan Committee correspondence.1952. Document headed "To the Himalayan Committee," signed by E. E. Shipton, June 8. 1952.

2 Alf Gregory, who had also come home, was at the meeting too.

3 See, for example, AC P5 (3) Lloyd papers, Blakeney's "Memo on the

Everest Expedition Leadership for 1953" of November 1967.
4 AC P5 (3)Lloyd Papers. These contain full accounts of the meeting
written by several different members of the committee and various other
documents, including Secord's note to the committee. The minutes of the
meeting—RGS/EE/99—offer a heavily edited version of events.
5 He had learned this from the Swiss when he met them at Kathmandu
on the way home.
6 "Valuable opportunities for systematic research were lost," Pugh was
reported to have said, rather woodenly, "because the party had not been
briefed properly beforehand," and "had no inclination to undertake systematic work."
7 Steele 1998, p. 190. Telegram sent by Kirwan RGS/EE/68.
8 See, for example, "Everest Inviolate," *The Times,* July 25, 1952. Later
Andre Roche would tell the Alpine Club, "The success of the final assault
will depend entirely on making it possible to breathe in an atmosphere
which will permit climbers to exert normal efforts . . . The oxygen outfit we
were given may be excellent for aviators, but it was not good enough for a
climber who has to make a considerable effort" (Roche 1953, from a paper
given in January 1953).
9 Besides Basil Goodfellow, Laurence Kirwan, and Peter Lloyd, the committee at this point comprised: chairman, Claude Elliott, Provost of Eton;
Clarmont Skrine, a former consul general in Kashgar; Donald Lowndes, excolonel in the Garhwal Rifles and Himalayan plant hunter; James Wordie,
polar explorer and president of the RGS; Harry Tobin, colonel in the
Bombay Pioneers and co-founder of the Himalayan Club; Laurence Wager,
Oxford geology professor who was with Lloyd on Everest in 1938; and R.
W. Lloyd, the treasurer. The minutes of the HC meeting of 4 July (RGS/
EE/99) show that, on the basis that Shipton might not be fit enough to take
on the 1953 leadership, the committee discussed alternative leaders, including three army officers, John Hunt, Charles Wylie, and Major Roberts.
10 FD1/9042: Letter, July 11, 1952.
11 Ibid. Kirwan wrote to Sir Henry Dale, head of the Royal Society's
"Medical Research Committee." On July 14, 1952, Martin, the secretary of
the Royal Society, followed up with a letter to Sir Charles Harington (head
of the MRC's NIMR), enclosing a copy of Kirwan's letter and affirming

that "our support of this experiment seems to have been very much worthwhile . . ." NIMR. DO2 MRC Himalayan Expeditions.1952–3 (Dr. L. G. Pugh): Letter, Kirwan to Sir Henry Dale, July 11, 1952 (see also Royal Society Archive 027 RS HD/6/2/9/2/14).

12 RGS/EE/75.HAC.

13 Ibid.: The following extract from a letter Kirwan wrote to Pugh shows how he worked: "Dear Pugh . . . I sent a copy of my brief for Cherwell to Martin at the RS who passed it to Sir David Brunt who spoke to Sir James Barnes Perm. Sec. to the Air Ministry who took it up with the Director of Hygiene, Air Commodore PB Lee Potter. The Air Ministry seem anxious to help and I have arranged meeting for July 31st. Matthews will lead. PS: Will you please let me know as soon as you can when you will find it convenient to go over to Switzerland to discuss the equipment and oxygen problems with the Swiss" (written July 29, 1952, RGS/75/HAC.Oxygen subcommittee).

14 RGS/EE/75.Inclusion of Physiologist, Himsworth to Kirwan, July 15, 1952; and RGS/EE/62/63/64.Correspondence with Mr. Goodfellow: Letter, Kirwan to Goodfellow, July 16, 1952.

15 He was rejected, having failed the medical exam.

16 In his autobiography (1969, pp. 111–12), Shipton stated that it was "clear that the Committee assumed that I would lead the expedition. I had, however, given a good deal of thought to the matter and felt it right to voice certain objections." He admitted that "long involvement with a problem can easily produce rigidity of outlook," and emphasized his dislike of large expeditions, publicity, and competitiveness in mountaineering. On the other hand, he offset his "objections" by reminding the committee of his unmatched experience of the mountain itself, of high-altitude climbing, and of the Everest venture, and did not convey an overall impression that he really wanted to quit.

17 Kirwan thought Hunt should be "deputy leader," but did not push hard for this when he subsequently discovered that Shipton was strongly opposed to it (AC Archive, P5.5. Letter, Kirwan to Goodfellow, August 20, 1952). There are several detailed accounts of this period in the committee's history. For instance, the "Assistant Secretary" of the Alpine Club, T. J. Blakeney, wrote a record in 1967. Although he was not a member of the Himalayan Committee and had no vote, he attended HC meetings and kept the

minutes and wrote his record on the basis of notes taken at the time (these were later deposited in the British Library). The chairman of the committee, Charles Elliott, wrote a similarly detailed account (with the help of Basil Goodfellow) in the early 1970s, and Peter Lloyd, also a member of the committee, went through the papers again and wrote his own account in 1979 (AC Lloyd Papers P5 (9)). The various commentators agree that several of the members who attended the crucial committee meeting were still undecided. None of them knew Hunt personally except Goodfellow and Lloyd, who were not there. They were under extreme pressure to arrive at a decision about leadership, and therefore vulnerable to Kirwan's advocacy. It does not seem to have occurred to them that having pressed a somewhat diffident Shipton to take on the role of leader, they would not then be able to impose upon him their own choice of deputy leader.

18 RGS/EE/75/HAC: Letter, Matthews to Kirwan, July 30, 1952.

19 TNA FD1/9042: Letter, Matthews to Kirwan, August 1, 1952.

20 TNA FD1/9042.

21 TNA FD1/9042. Letter, Himsworth to Kirwan, August 6, 1952. Himsworth wrote: "You will of course appreciate that before a body like the Medical Research Council could agree to participate in a project of the nature proposed, they would have to satisfy themselves that the proposed expedition would provide opportunities for scientific observation of such value as to justify them in diverting some of their resources to this end, and that the expedition would be so organised that such observations could be made."

22 RGS/EE/75/HAC.Oxygen Subcommittee.

23 TNA FD1/9042.

24 This was a promise that was confirmed in writing by Kirwan, who accepted "our own obligation to take a physiologist on the preliminary acclimatisation expedition, who would subsequently move on to Everest and do what he could there within the physical limits imposed" (see TNA FD1/9042).

25 See Wylie's note to Hunt, RGS/EE/68/2.

26 RGS/EE/68.2: Letter, Goodfellow to Hunt, August 12, 1952.

27 Ibid., Letter, dated July 23, 1952. Hunt went on to say that he had reason to believe the War Office would be willing to make him available, and urged Elliott to put in a request for him soon.

28 Ibid.

29 Ibid.

30 See AC Lloyd Papers P5(3).

31 Charles Wylie told me how he accompanied Shipton to the meeting at the Alpine Club, expecting to discuss organizational and planning issues for the coming expedition. They were both surprised to see "leadership" on the agenda, as the matter was already settled. Wylie described their mutual surprise at being sent out of the room, and how after an interminable wait Shipton was called in, but came out a few minutes later white and shocked with the news that they had asked him to share the leadership with Hunt, with whom he did not feel he could work. Wylie agreed with Shipton that it was not a viable prospect, and he went back in to proffer his resignation. Later they left in a taxi, both shattered.

A common view of the sacking of Shipton was summed up by Jim Perrin, who wrote in 1985: "What emerges from close examination of relevant Himalayan Committee minutes and written submissions from its surviving members, is a bizarre tale of fudging and mudging, falsification of official minutes, unauthorised invitations, and opportunistic and desperate last-minute seizures of initiative by a particular faction. It is a perfect illustration of the cock-up rather than the conspiracy theory of history, from which little credit rebounds upon the English climbing establishment" (see Perrin 1985). More recently Ed Douglas 2003, p. 178, wrote: "Hunt . . . had been brought in as leader precisely because of his military experience, replacing Eric Shipton in a scandalously underhanded and shoddy piece of real politic which appalled Hunt as much as anyone." Isserman and Weaver 2008, p. 276, wrote that Shipton's sacking "bordered on bad faith."

9. Warts and All

1 RGS/EE/75.Reports on Apparatus: Letter, dated August 27, 1952.

2 All quotations in this section are from a taped interview of the conversation with Michael Ward at his home in Petworth in 2004.

10. "It's a Wonderful Life"

1 Cho Oyu Diary, April 24, 1952.

2 Ibid., May 16, 1952.

3 Lewis and Adah Pugh left India and came to live in London in 1940, where Lewis undertook legal work for the Privy Council.

4 Letter, Pugh to Josephine, June 3, 1942.

5 War Diary, October 5, 1941.

6 Letter, Pugh to Josephine, December 7, 1941.

7 Letter, Pugh to Josephine, 31 August 1942.

8 After the partition of Poland between Germany and Russia early in World War II, about 1.5 million people were deported from Poland, taken to Russia, and sent to labor and concentration camps all over the country. When Hitler broke his agreement with Stalin, by attacking Russia in June 1941, Russia became part of the "Grand Alliance" *against* Germany, and agreed to release all the Poles detained in Russia. Thereafter, more than 28,000 Polish evacuees from Russia passed through Tehran on their way south to the Persian Gulf. Prior to leaving, a large group of evacuees were collected together in a region east of the Caspian Sea, where typhus fever was prevalent. On the subsequent journey south, many who had so far escaped the disease now became victim to it. Arrangements were made for the reception of the sick in Tehran. The Poles, mostly soldiers, were treated at the military hospital, a combined Indian and British unit of 600 beds, 3 miles outside Tehran, called Central General Hospital, where Pugh worked.

9 Letter, Pugh to Josephine, April 27, 1942.

10 Letter, Josephine to Pugh, October 3, 1941.

11 Letter, Pugh to Josephine, October 13, 1942.

11. All Possible Steps

1 Jan Morris (formerly James Morris) described Sir John Hunt in this way when I met her at her home in Wales in November 2006.

2 RGS/EE/68.2: Letter, Hunt to Goodfellow, September 13, 1952.

3 Ibid.: Letter, Hunt to Charles Wylie, September 23, 1952.

4 RGS/EE/68.Correspondence: Letter, Wylie to Hunt, September 27, 1952. Goodfellow also wrote to Hunt on September 27, 1952: "Your ideas conform closely to ours." The commitment to take a physiologist to Everest was first mentioned by Wylie in a later letter to Hunt, dated October 3, 1952, in which he wrote: "The MRC has now asked officially for a second physiologist to accompany the party. We were previously committed to taking one as a price for MRC assistance" (see RGS/EE/68.2). Goodfellow informed Hunt of the commitment to take Pugh in briefing notes dated September 18, 1952 (see RGS/EE/66.2).

5 PP 14.8.
6 PP 35.4.
7 See RGS/EE/68.2.
8 L. G. C. E. Pugh Archive 46/15. Pugh was given access to a detailed account of the spring expedition from Dr. Chevalley, covering the period between May 19, 1952, at Camp Four, through to June 3, when they returned to the camp after their summit assault. It included descriptions of the terrain, snow conditions, progress of the climbers, how they felt, their illnesses and problems, their food and drink intakes, their use of oxygen, their sleep, etc. The paper also includes Chevalley's summary of lessons learned. Dr. Feuz of the Swiss Institute for Alpine Research gave Pugh information about the changes and improvements made as a result of the spring experience, including the full provisioning list for the autumn expedition, and so on. Pugh was able to combine the detailed knowledge derived from the Swiss experience and previous expeditions with his research results from Cho Oyu, to provide a basis for predicting the requirements of the 1953 expedition, which John Hunt was able to incorporate into his planning. A list of questions Pugh prepared to ask the Swiss is in PP 39.2. Pugh's report on his visit to the Swiss is in RGS/EE/90.Swiss Expedition Reports. In *The Ascent of Everest,* John Hunt admitted only to having made a whirlwind twenty-four-hour trip to Switzerland with Charles Evans on January 25, 1953, at which "we were shown all their [the Swiss] equipment and received a very frank and generous handover of their knowledge and experience." However, this brief later visit, after the Swiss autumn Everest attempt, was made at a time when the British preparations were almost complete, and understates the extent of the help they gave.
9 RGS/EE/68.2.
10 TNA FD1/9042.
11 RGS/EE/99. Himalayan Committee Meeting of October 9, 1952, Appendix A, clarifies this point.
12 Ward told me that he felt it was vital to make sure that Hunt understood that he needed to take the physiology seriously. He also said: "I am quite happy to tell people what to do if I think they should learn. I have always been like this."

13 See, for instance, Park in Berryman, Jack and Park 1992, p. 69, quoting from Shearman 1889, pp. 52–53; also, Wagg in Porter and Wagg 2006, quoting Woodgate 1889; and Allinson 2001, p. 20.
14 Scott Russell was married to the daughter of George Finch. He wrote a "memoir" of his father-in-law which was published as the introduction to a reissue of Finch's book, *The Making of a Mountaineer* (Bristol: Arrowsmith, 1988, p. 10). The original book came out in 1924.
15 See Lunn 1957, p. 100.
16 See Hunt's original plan in TNA FD/9042. In addition to the Cho Oyu Report, the other main sources for this chapter are the manuscript paper by Pugh, entitled "Everest 1953 Physiological Notes," submitted to the committee shortly after he returned from Cho Oyu (RGS/EE/75.The Physiological Effects of Altitude); and the manuscript of a draft book about Pugh's Everest work, which he completed in 1957, and revisited in 1978 (HTP; also different versions in PP 13.2, and AC E 36).
17 Pugh 1952, p. 35.
18 Ibid., p. 33.
19 Pugh opted for a four-week preliminary period because physiologists generally believed, and a number of studies confirmed, that acclimatization occurs rapidly during the first four weeks, then slows.
20 Their cooking stove was accidentally lost on the way up.
21 Pugh 1942, p. 11. The stoves had wickless burners protected by a cylindrical shield, inside which two water containers were heated by the hot combustion gases circulating round them. Pugh provided the general specifications, and the stoves were manufactured by C. R. Cooke of the Westcliffe Engineering Company.
22 For example, Pugh calculated that the allowance of kerosene needed for a small Primus cooker ("Primus 210") to produce 3–4 liters of water per man per day from snow was approximately three-quarters of a pint, per man, per day (see HTP unpublished book 1957, p. 75).
23 PP 35.1: Letter, Hunt to Pugh, October 18, 1952. Pugh had been working with Charles Wylie on diet since mid-September 1952. He had already designed the meal plans for different phases of the expedition, and was in the process of consulting on nutritional values and vitamin scales

with a professional dietician (Miss Grant of the London School of Hygiene and Tropical Medicine). See RGS/EE/75.Diet.

24 See accounts of these studies in Pugh 1954a and 1954b.

25 To introduce this element of choice, the assault ration packs contained more basic foods than were necessary to meet caloric needs.

26 RGS/EE/75.Diet: Letter, Band to Hillary, December 31, 1952.

27 Askew 2004.

28 See, for example, PP 35.21: Note for Hunt entitled "Oxygen for porters to enable them to make repeated ascents to South Col," and PP 31.1: Note for Hunt on Himalayan Diseases.

29 Pugh's archive papers show he had begun working on boots before the Cho Oyu expedition. He arranged, early in 1952, that a Mr. Freeborn of the British Boot, Shoe and Allied Trades Research Association, construct for him two pairs of experimental felt boots for the Cho Oyu expedition. In September 1952 they wrote asking how the boots had fared (PP 35.11).

30 "The Everest Clothing Story" in *Uniforms and Industrial Clothing Catalogue* (1954), written mainly by Pugh, gives the best account of the process of designing the boots, clothing, and other equipment for Everest.

31 Pugh learned about clo values—a technique for measuring the insulation value of clothing, perfected by Canadian research workers in the war—when he was sent on a cold-weather cruise in the Arctic by the MRC in 1949 (see note 3, chapter 17), where the design of the Canadian Navy's clothing assemblies for cold-weather duties, based on this system, struck him as "excellent" (see Belding et al. 1945).

32 PP 35.3. At Pugh's behest, the fabrics were tested for wind resistance, tear resistance, and vapor permeability by Dr. E. Kenchington at the Clothing and Equipment Physiological Research Establishment, Royal Aircraft Establishment, Farnborough. On October 24, 1952, Pugh met Kenchington at Farnborough to discuss tent fabrics, groundsheet fabrics, and cloths for windproof materials. The fabric for windproofs would be sent to Howard Flint's and Pugh would provide the design after the different types of fabric had been tested in the Alps (PP 35.3 and 4). Also PP 35.21: Letter to Pugh from the Royal Aircraft Establishment, January 9, 1952, discusses the results of the "walking in the wind experiments

wearing different types of clothing and measuring comparative oxygen consumption."

33 Pugh 1942, p. 6.

12. Opposition and Suspicion

1 RGS/EE/68.2: Letter, Goodfellow to Hunt, September 25, 1952.

2 Ibid.: Letter, Hunt to Goodfellow, September 30, 1952.

3 RGS/EE/66.8.

4 RGS/EE/68.4: December 17, 1952.

5 RGS/EE/90.Himalayan Committee correspondence 1952: Letter, dated June 8, 1952.

6 See Younghusband's speech delivered to the RGS in November 1921, printed in Geographical Journal Vol. LV111, No. 6, December 1921.

7 Quoted in Lunn 1944, p. 45. Leslie Stephen was apparently reading a paper on the first ascent of the Zinalrothorn to an Alpine Club audience.

8 Tilman 1948, p. 110.

9 AC Lloyd Papers P5 (3), "Note 4."

10 AC B 84 X11.

11 AC P 11: Letter, Norton to Hunt, January 6, 1953.

12 RGS/EE/75.Report on Apparatus: Letter, Scott Russell to Hunt, December 8, 1952. Finch had been objecting to the closed-circuit since it was first brought in, in 1936, arguing that it was bound to fail since it did not make use of the oxygen in the atmosphere, and claiming that its introduction had led to a "wasteful division of effort" between the two different oxygen systems.

13 Ibid.

14 RGS/EE/68.2: Letter, Wylie to Hunt, October 3, 1952.

15 Ibid. Hunt wrote to Lloyd: "I am very keen that [Tom] Bourdillon should be kept sweet, i.e., by continuing his present work, but answering to the Himalayan Joint Committee through you [Hunt's own underlinings]."

16 RGS/EE/75.Unmarked file: The memo, dated October 22, 1952, told Hunt that Lloyd was permitted to express his views "with reference to the practical viewpoint, but must abide by majority decisions of the [High-Altitude] Committee." Letters between Pugh's boss, Edholm, and Sir Harry Himsworth (head of the MRC) show that Lloyd's unwillingness to

subject himself to the HAC caused worries at the MRC, but was eventually resolved. On October 30, 1952, Edholm wrote to Himsworth: "Since I spoke to you last week about some of the apparent complications between the HAC and the Himalayan Committee things have improved. Lloyd, who was appointed oxygen controller by the Himalayan Committee, has clearly realised that he must not make decisions without the consent of the HAC" (see also TNA FD1/9042).

17 193,000 liters compared with 20,000 liters taken by the Swiss in the autumn of 1952, and 29,000 liters taken by the British in 1922. See account in Pugh 1954c.

18 Having seen Pugh's research, Lloyd produced his own oxygen recommendations for Hunt (see RGS/EE/68.2). Lloyd envisaged a summit assault direct from the South Col by a party who had used night oxygen. He thought they should breathe oxygen at a normal rate of 3 liters a minute, and 5 liters for the more difficult "pitches." Anticipating an overall breathing rate of 100 liters a minute when using oxygen, he predicted that climbers at 29,000 feet would be at equivalent altitudes, respectively, of 22,000 feet with supplementary oxygen at 3 liters a minute, and 18,500 feet with oxygen at 5 liters a minute. Because Lloyd's assumptions were not based on empirical tests, he thought climbers would be able to climb faster—at 750 feet per hour using oxygen—than Pugh expected, and therefore would need to take less oxygen with them than Pugh claimed. Pugh for his part had found that performances in the field on a given flow rate of oxygen fell far short of that expected from the equivalent altitude, which was merely a "convenient abstraction." He gave the example of Tom Bourdillon breathing 100 percent oxygen (a pressure higher than that present in air at sea level). Despite the amount of oxygen available, Bourdillon's intake of oxygen remained stubbornly lower than his intake of oxygen at sea level, so he did not benefit as much from the available extra oxygen as Lloyd would have assumed. See Pugh's article, "Everest 53, Physiological Notes" in RGS/EE/75.Physiological Effects of Altitude.

19 RGS/EE/99: Meeting of the Himalayan Committee of November 27, 1952.

20 RGS/EE/75.Coordination. In 1957 Pugh referred to his argument with Lloyd in an article published in the *Journal of Physiology* (Pugh 1958),

writing that to have based the oxygen requirements for 1953 on theoretical assessments of likely climbing speed and efficiency "would have led to a grossly inadequate supply of oxygen being taken. This mistake was made on previous expeditions to Mount Everest and led to arguments between physiologists and engineers [i.e., Lloyd] at the planning stage of the 1953 Everest expedition over the amount of oxygen to be sent out with the expedition and the rates of climbing to be expected from its use."

21 A letter from Pugh to Lloyd, December 13, 1952, details the faults in the Swiss apparatus (PP 35.21). An earlier letter from Pugh to "John Brown," dated August 11, 1952, says: "The Swiss were advised by Roxburgh that the set was unsuitable; however, they took it. It does not seem to have been usable at high altitude and the final attempt was made virtually without oxygen" (PP 35.21). See also West 2003. The system was chosen by Oscar Wyss, a physiologist from the University of Geneva. It was modified from an American device called the Chemox system. Besides the high resistance to breathing, the mouthpiece was rigid, preventing the head from moving so the climber couldn't look around to select the best footholds. The failure of the equipment is not usually highlighted in English or American accounts of the first Swiss Everest attempt. For example, Isserman and Weaver 2008, p. 273, state that Tenzing and Lambert continued with their summit attempt until their oxygen ran out. The authors apparently overlooked the fact that the Swiss oxygen sets could only be used when they were not climbing. The body doesn't store oxygen, so Lambert and Tenzing effectively climbed without oxygen and stopped, as they themselves testified, because they became exhausted.

22 From a taped conversation John Cotes kindly undertook with me at his home in Durham in December 2004.

23 Pugh 1952, p. 27; for example, Pugh suggested removing the cheek valves to reduce the resistance to breathing still further.

24 "Man at High Altitude," delivered by Finch on June 6, 1952, to the Royal Society (Finch 1952, p. 13). In addition, Lloyd wrote to Pugh in December 1952, raising doubts about his Cho Oyu findings and pointing to the failure of the Swiss oxygen. "I would like to be sure that we are not making a similar mistake in testing and developing the new mask." Pugh wrote a detailed letter back, explaining point by point the problems

with the Swiss oxygen equipment (see PP 35.21). Lloyd still preferred the tubes.

25 RGS/EE/75.HAC. For example, see note of December 13, 1952, in which Matthews wrote sarcastically to Hunt that he was sorry that Hunt had been unable to attend the recent High-Altitude Committee meeting because "you weren't reminded until the last moment, but I cannot agree that the notice of the meeting was short, since this date was arranged at your request at the meeting of November 24th." Matthews also noted with disapproval that the absence of the oxygen controller [Lloyd] had meant that "we couldn't discuss oxygen."

26 RGS EE 75/HAC: Letter, dated January 21, 1953.

27 Pugh quoted in Venables 1998, p. 48. Among the climbers, Hillary made the point that he did not believe Hunt was an essential ingredient to the Everest team in several publications, including in *View from the Summit,* Hillary 1999, p. 107. Shipton's biographer, Peter Steele 1998, p. 199, reported that Wylie, Ward, Gregory, Hillary, and Lowe told him in personal interviews that they believed they would have done just as well with Shipton in charge.

28 Shipton 1953, p. 137: Talk given at a meeting of the RGS on December 22, 1952.

29 PP 35.10: Letter, dated December 30, 1952.

30 RGS/EE/75.Inclusion of physiologist. After soundings taken by Kirwan, the Royal Society grant to pay for Pugh's research was confirmed on December 11, 1952, shortly after it became known that the Swiss autumn expedition had failed.

31 Hunt 1953, p. 8.

32 RGS/EE/67.5.

33 RGS/EE/66.5.

13. The Trek from Kathmandu

1 Tenzing said afterward that he refused to accept a bed out of solidarity with his fellow Sherpas.

2 In his autobiography (Ullman 1955, p. 232), Tenzing related how the Sherpas were upset because Hunt proposed to depart from the norm by not issuing their high-altitude gear until they got to Solu Khumbu, and was not intending to allow them to keep it—at least not as of right. They

were also affronted because the Sherpas were to eat different food from the Europeans.

3 Perhaps long experience of being employed as guides themselves gave the Swiss a sensitive understanding of how to make a success of the relationship with their Sherpas. "Over the years," Tenzing told Ullman in 1954, "I had liked the Swiss tremendously; I felt truly close to them and thought of them not as Sahibs or employers but as friends, and that is how it has been ever since" (Ibid., p. 111).

4 The article, based on an hourlong interview with Tenzing—one of Izzard's dispatches to the *Daily Mail*—was syndicated to the *Statesman* of Calcutta and New Delhi (see Izzard 1955, p. 95).

5 NIMR. DO2 MRC Himalayan Expeditions 1952/3: Letter, Pugh to Edholm, April 21, 1953.

6 HTP: Letter, Pugh to Josephine, March 10, 1953.

7 The late Charles Wylie, who kindly gave me a taped interview at his home in May 2004, described Pugh as "a boffin with his head way up in the clouds and very absentminded."

8 Noyce 1954, p. 20.

9 Pugh's Everest Diary, March 13, 1953. In the 1950s Sherpas would have been insulted to have been described as "coolies," but joined with the British in describing as such the low-altitude porters who were mostly Nepalese. Today, the low-altitude porters also feel insulted by the term. See Ullman 1955, in which Tenzing describes the term as having "a connotation so menial and slave-like that it is greatly resented if it is used by Westerners."

10 HTP: Letter, Pugh to Josephine, March 23, 1953.

11 Pugh in Hunt 1953, p. 275.

12 George Band explained to me that "In those days we thought it really sissy and unnecessary bulk/weight to take out tables and chairs."

13 AC P11, Letter, Hunt to his wife, March 16, 1953.

14 See Young 1949: chapter on "Management and Leadership," especially p. 30. Passages in Hunt's book, *The Ascent of Everest*, echo very closely passages in *Mountain Craft*, such as Hunt's claim on p. 6 that "The opponent was not other parties but Everest itself," as compared with Young's assertion that "The hills are our opponents, not other climbers, or even other nations" (Young 1949, p. 3).

15 From my interview with Charles Wylie in 2004.

16 The work-rate tests referred to in this context measure the amount of oxygen that is extracted from the air by the subject working at full tilt.

17 Hunt 1953, p. 71.

18 PP 35.13 Pugh Everest Diary, March 13, 1953.

19 Charles Evans's Everest Diary, June 10, 1953. Denise Evans kindly allowed me to read this diary when I visited her at her home in Capel Curig, Caernarfonshire, in December 2005.

20 Hillary 1975, p. 147.

21 Noyce 1954, p. 20.

22 Ward 1972, p. 109. Ward wrote that Tom Bourdillon "was furious both with himself for not checking the bottles regularly, and with the engineering standards that permitted such a defect." The engineering standards had been Lloyd's responsibility.

23 HTP Pugh's draft book, p. 34. Pugh notes that of the 198,000 liters of oxygen sent out with the 1953 expedition, 23,400 liters were lost due to leakage from cylinders in transit. After the successful ascent, only 15,600 liters remained unused, which "would scarcely have supplied a third assault had the second party failed to reach the summit."

24 Stobart 1958, p. 218.

25 NIMR. DO2 MRC Himalayan Expeditions 1952/3: Letter, Pugh to Edholm, April 21, 1953.

26 Pugh noted on April 7 that the climbers had used open- and closed-circuit oxygen from 17,000 to 19,000 feet, at flow rates between 2.5 and 3 liters a minute, and confirmed that the oxygen reduced fatigue and increased energy but not climbing rates. They found no difference at this stage between closed-circuit and open-circuit.

27 Lowe 1959, p. 28.

28 Hillary 1975, p. 145. Another example, from Hillary 1999, p. 100, concerns Charles Evans during the Cho Oyu expedition. Hillary wrote: "I had always regarded Charles as a very calm and non-competitive person but I suddenly realised he was rapidly overtaking me and it was turning into a race. It was too good an opportunity to miss. As we flew down, one false step would have been disastrous for us both, but when I managed to pull away from Charles, we both dropped down to a safer and more

sensible pace." Geoffrey Young's section on "walking manners" in *Mountain Craft* has some very strict things to say about climbers "afflicted" with the "racing" or "passing" manias (see Young 1949, p. 30).

29 NIMR. DO2 MRC Himalayan Expeditions 1952/3: Letter, Pugh to Edholm, April 21, 1953.

30 Stobart 1958, p. 223.

31 Pugh Everest Diary, April 13, 1953.

32 Stobart 1958, p. 228.

33 Ibid.

34 Izzard 1959, p. 170.

35 Stobart 1958, p. 229.

14. The Triumphant Ascent

1 i.e., on April 21 and 22.

2 Pugh Everest Diary, March 12, 1953.

3 Everest Diary, April 12, 1953: These were made by the firm Frankenstein and Sons in cooperation with Pugh.

4 Ibid.

5 Ibid.

6 Pugh Everest Diary, April 24, 1953.

7 Ibid., April 22, 1953.

8 Ibid., April 24, 1953.

9 NIMR MRC Himalayan Expeditions 1952/3: Letter, Pugh to Edholm, April 21, 1953.

10 Ibid.

11 Pugh Everest Diary, May 5, 1952.

12 PP 35.13.

13 NIMR. DO2 MRC Himalayan Expeditions 1952/3: Letter, Pugh to Edholm, May 4, 1953.

14 Both men returned to the Western Cwm having recovered, but neither managed to get as high as the South Col in 1953. Hunt wrote afterward, looking back at the acclimatization period, "I had the impression then, which was strengthened later, that the two newcomers to the Himalaya, George Band and Michael Westmacott, had found the altitude telling on them more than the rest of us" (Hunt 1953, p. 84).

15 Hunt consulted Pugh when he felt worried about physiological issues.

For instance, a note from Pugh at Camp Three to Hunt at advanced base camp says that data he has collected "suggests no need to worry in case of breakdown of O[pen] C[ircuit] set high up." Hunt was worried that the climbers might collapse if suddenly deprived of supplementary oxygen (PP 35.9).

16 PP 36.8.13: Minutes of the meeting of the MRC High-Altitude Committee, October 14, 1952, p. 3.

17 See RGS/EE/68/2, "Oxygen Apparatus for Everest in 1953."

18 The meeting was set up by Otto Edholm on behalf of the High-Altitude Committee. TNA FD1/9042: Letter, Edholm to Hunt, October 28, 1952. Edholm explained to Hunt: "Valuable as we expect the open-circuit sets to be, closed-circuit sets, if a proper design could be provided, would be much more useful." Afterward Hunt wrote to both Edholm and Bourdillon that "The Matthews Committee has been quite specific regarding the potential value of the closed-circuit apparatus and the consequent wisdom of having such equipment available for eventual use in the final assault." The advice of the MRC was "conclusive" as far as he was concerned, he affirmed, so if Bourdillon could produce the sets in time, he would "most readily" experiment with them on the mountain and, if they worked well, "it may well be that the closed-circuit apparatus will be used in the assault" (RGS 75. Reports on apparatus: both letters dated November 5, 1952).

19 Charles Evans's Diary.

20 Letter, Charles Wylie to Alfred Bridge, May 9, 1953, ACE27.

21 Hunt 1953, p. 147.

22 Noyce 1954, p. 149.

23 Camp Five was at 22,000 feet, and Camp Six at 23,000 feet.

24 A handwritten letter from Hunt at advanced base camp to Pugh at Camp Three, written on May 21, betrays the tension he was under. The letter begins "Dear Griff, Most Important. I am sending you the following two men who have failed us in the vital carry to the South Col." Full of underlining, the letter implores Pugh "most urgently" to send up replacements for additional lifts toward the South Col (PP 35.9).

25 None of the British climbers attempted to climb the whole of the 4,000-foot Lhotse Face without oxygen. The few who managed to climb

parts of this steep slope without oxygen were extremely proud of themselves. On one occasion Noyce climbed most of the last 1,400 feet without oxygen. Wylie managed to climb the top 500 feet without it when his oxygen ran out, and felt "strangely elated because I could now experience what the Sherpas had been going through." Bourdillon, Hillary, and Noyce climbed to Camp Seven (24,000 feet) at least once without oxygen, and Lowe worked preparing the path up the face without oxygen, mostly below 25,000 feet, but did not climb very far in one day because he was cutting steps and fixing ropes. In the previous year the Swiss climbers and their Sherpas had all climbed the entire Lhotse Face virtually without oxygen—a great feat at that time.

26 This took place on May 25.

27 Morris 1958, p. 84.

28 On the basis of new measurements using GPS, Bradford Washburn has proposed revised heights for where Hunt stopped, and for the position of Hillary and Tenzing's high camp (see Washburn 2003), but these are the historical figures.

29 RGS LJH John Hunt's Everest Diary, p. 161.

30 Pugh and Ward 1956.

31 They only had enough for part of the night.

32 Hillary's autobiography of 1999, p. 16 and p. 115, was the first of his books—written forty-six years after the event—to mention that it was Pugh who persuaded him to drink sufficient liquids on Everest. He wrote, "We had been warned by Pugh that dehydration was one of the greatest risks faced by climbers going high," and "Dr. Pugh . . . strongly emphasised the need for us to improve our liquid intake and his advice played an important part in our success."

33 Hillary, *Life* magazine, July 13, 1953, pp. 124–38.

34 Both men wore the down jackets and trousers that Pugh had helped to design. Hillary also wore Pugh's high-altitude boots, but Tenzing opted for the reindeer boots he had been given by the Swiss the previous year, which Pugh judged to be excellent. See Ward 2003, p. 31, for Hillary's clothing; Ullman 1955, p. 261, for Tenzing's.

35 Pugh 1952, p. 36.

36 Morris 1958, p. 117.

15. A Gulf of Mutual Incomprehension

1 Stobart 1958, p. 244.

2 Ward 1972, p. 147.

3 Lowe 1959, p. 30; letter home June 1, 1953.

4 AC D.103 Bourdillon's diary entry for May 30, 1953.

5 Noyce 1954, p. 167.

6 Ibid., p. 237.

7 HTP Pugh's draft book, p. 135.

8 Hunt 1993, p. 18.

9 PP 13.1.

10 *The Times,* October 22, 1953.

11 *New York Times,* December 10, 1953.

12 *The Times,* October 22, 1953.

13 Hunt's climbing journal, Kashmir 1931, quoted in Cranfield 2002, p. 7.

14 Noyce 1954, p. 13.

15 Hunt 1953, p. 231.

16 Brigadier General Bruce, who led the first Everest Expedition in 1921, gave a talk at the RGS which was preceded by a statement from the chairman, Younghusband (Bruce 1921, p. 15).

17 Hunt 1953, p. 232.

18 Ibid., p. 38.

19 Ibid., p. 50. C. R. Cooke had built the stoves to Pugh's specifications.

20 Ibid.

21 Nor did Pugh's name come up in any of the other seven appendices. In the appendix about equipment, Charles Wylie fastidiously acknowledged designers and contributors by name when describing items in which Pugh was *not* involved, such as the wireless sets. But where Pugh had played a key role, such as in the design of the high-altitude boots, the specially adapted mountain stoves, and the windproof cloth used for the clothing and tents, Wylie omitted to mention Pugh's involvement. For example, after describing the high-altitude boots in great detail, Wylie wrote that they were ". . . an illustration of the care and thought given to all our equipment by British Industry and of the value of scientific principles boldly applied with confidence based on research knowledge." This could only have been a nameless reference to Pugh's input. When I challenged

Wylie, he told me that Hunt had convinced him this was the right thing to do, though recently he had changed his mind.

22 Tilman 1953, p. 1488.

23 Pugh in Hunt 1953, p. 276.

24 Noyce 1954, p. 20.

25 Quoted in the *New Scientist* obituary of Peter Medawar, April 12, 1974.

26 Poets like William Wordsworth advocated taking cleansing breaks from harsh, materialistic, urban living to expose oneself to nature—to the "sublime" vast and magnificent landscapes of the Lake District, for instance, or the European Alps, where one could experience "transcendent" feelings and strong emotions, and be spiritually regenerated and uplifted by the sense of contact with a greater power evoked by nature. See, for example, "Lines Written a few Miles above Tintern Abbey" and "The Prelude," in both of which Wordsworth writes of the restorative powers of "mountains," "winds and sounding cataracts," which lift him above the "little enmities and low desires" of city life. Although Wordsworth died in 1850, his ideas remained extremely influential.

27 Quoted in Rose and Rose 1969, p. 58.

28 Snow 1959 (2006 reprint), p. 4. Snow first wrote on this theme in an article for the *New Statesman* in 1956. He expanded it in his 1959 Cambridge Rede Lecture, "The Two Cultures and the Scientific Revolution," and in a follow-up essay, "The Two Cultures: A Second Look," in 1963. The debate provoked by his lectures echoed an earlier debate in the 1880s between the influential poet and cultural thinker Matthew Arnold, who argued that literature, especially the classics, was the only form of education capable of producing the genuinely rounded person, and the scientist Thomas Huxley, who argued that a practical scientific education was just as good for many students as traditional learning.

16. The Golden Age

1 Just as Josephine feared, it is for this scene, rather than for his contribution to the Everest success, that Pugh is remembered. For example, at a recent Wellcome witnesses seminar on *The History of the Development of Sports Medicine in Twentieth-Century Britain* (the transcript of a Witness Seminar held by the Wellcome Trust Centre for the History of Medicine, Vol. 36, 2009, eds. Reynolds and Tansey, p. 34), one of the distinguished

participants remarked of Pugh: "When you have climbed to whatever it is, 25,000 feet, staggering back to the tents, and a physiologist wants you to do a maximum-exercise test for the next half-hour, he is probably not very popular."

2 PP 35.25.

3 RGS/EE/105.Mount Everest Committee 5.1.54.

4 RGS/EE/90.Himalayan Correspondence July–December: Note 8 of the "Notes for the Himalayan Committee Meeting of December 11, 1953," reads: "Letter from Pugh: Extract from Film Commentary. Pugh left it for long after preview; too late to alter, as 200 copies of film have gone abroad. Anyway, cost of alteration – £15."

5 PP 35.25.

6 PP 35.21.

7 Ibid.

8 PP 8.22: Pugh to *Lancet*, November 30, 1953.

9 PP 9.41. Odell to *Geographical Journal*, December 30, 1953.

10 Ibid., Pugh to Wordie, January 15, 1954.

11 Ibid.

12 Noyce 1954, p. 20.

13 Taped interview with Michael Ward.

14 In 1954 Pugh joined a working group set up under the auspices of the Ministry of Health and the MRC, to study and advise on methods of polio treatment (PP 14.7).

15 Edholm wrote of Pugh to Sir Charles Harington, director of the NIMR, "I feel he should have a real rest now. I have advised him to stay away for four weeks" (NIMR PF43 640/2).

16 PP 9.41.

17 Pugh 1954b.

18 Severinghaus 2004.

19 PP 35.2.

20 PP 46.14.

21 NIMR.CRH3 Dr. G. Pugh and Normalair Ltd.

22 NIMR Pugh Personal File. Norman Hardie described working on the oxygen with Pugh before the expedition, and also receiving advice from Pugh on high-altitude diet, to me in a series of interviews in 2008.

17. Braving the Cold

1 The historical information on hypothermia and the wartime research into this subject draws on three main sources, most importantly Paton 2001, along with Keatinge 1969 and Edholm and Bacharach 1965.

2 Glaser 1950.

3 Pugh, "Medical Research Council: Physiologist's Report, RN Cold-Weather Cruise 1949," unpublished booklet HTP.

4 Hardy and Soderstrom 1938, p. 494. This caused a stir at the time, but it later emerged that another scientist, H. Bordier 1898, had made the same measurements much earlier using different techniques, and had found beef muscle to have thermal conductivity 1.8 times that of beef fat, which agreed with Pugh's findings about human fat.

5 Hatfield and Pugh 1951.

6 For instance, a report on shipwreck survival by G. W. Molnar (1946) stated that at average temperatures of 60°F, people immersed in the sea did not usually survive longer than five hours even when their heads were supported above water by life jackets.

7 Rockett 1956, p. 181.

8 Zirganos finished the swim in 6 hours, 50 minutes.

9 See modern assessment of Pugh's Channel-swimming studies in Glickman et al. 2003.

10 Pugh and Edholm 1955. As Pugh pointed out, these findings did not apply to marathon swimmers like Jason Zirganos, who were fat and well-insulated.

11 See, for example, Keatinge 1969.

12 Pugh's observations included measuring their fat, their rectal and muscle temperatures, their oxygen consumption while swimming, their food consumption, etc.

13 Interview between Jim Milledge and Pugh, 1993.

14 Orr Reynolds was also a prominent figure in the US Physiological Society.

15 *Symposium on the Problems of Mountain Altitudes, 1955,* jointly sponsored by the White Mountain Research Station and the University of California. Pugh kept a diary of this trip (HTP).

16 The other funders were the Rockefeller Foundation and the US National Science Foundation. Records held by MSCL.

17 The European hut, the Capanna Regina Margherita (15,000 feet), erected in the 1880s on a peak of the Monte Rosa, and also used for physiological research, was still higher.

18 Nello Pace (1916–1995) was an outstanding environmental physiologist at the University of California at Berkeley. William Siri (1919–2004) was a leading researcher in biophysics at Lawrence Berkeley National Laboratory—the Donner Laboratory. He led the American attempt on Makalu in 1954, and went on to study the effects of altitude and oxygen deprivation on the human body as deputy leader of the first American expedition to Mount Everest in 1963.

19 Pugh 1955 and Pugh 1960.

20 Ibid.

18. "Your Natures Are So Completely Different"

1 Medawar 1986 (paperback edition, 1988), p. 149.

2 MRC P28/311 Pugh, Dr., L. G. C. E., Dr. F. H. K. Green, assistant secretary at the MRC, later secretary of the Wellcome Trust, repeatedly tried to persuade Pugh to take the MRCP. In a minute to a colleague in July 1954, he wrote: "I suggested to Pugh that he should explore the possibility of presenting an account of his Everest work as a thesis for the MRCP."

3 Sir Ernest Cassel (1852–1921) was involved in many large financial projects, including the financing of the Aswan Dam, the Mexican Central Railway, many American railway projects, gold and diamond mining in South Africa, and the Swedish iron ore industry. He gave away at least £2 million to charitable causes, including the founding of two hospitals—£2 million in 1910 would be roughly equivalent to £145 million in 2007 (see *Economic History Service*, www.measuringworth.com)—and died in 1921, leaving an estate of £7 million. In 1878 Cassel married Annette Maxwell, who died in 1881, leaving one daughter, Maud. Maud's marriage to Wilfred Ashley produced two daughters of whom the elder, Edwina, married Lord Louis Mountbatten shortly after inheriting the lion's share of her grandfather's fortune. Felix Cassel's mother, Wilhelmina (1847–1925), was married to a mysterious figure called Schoenbrunn. The history of the marriage has remained shrouded in secrecy, and no one in my family knows whether we have any ancestors in Germany (see Allfrey 1991 and Rubin 2004).

4 The association between rubella and the variety of problems now known as "congenital rubella syndrome" was recognized by the Australian doctor, Norman McAllister Gregg (1892–1966). See *Australian Dictionary of National Biography,* Melbourne University Press 1996, pp. 325–27.

5 HTP: Letter, Doey to Pugh, January 26, 1942.

6 HTP: Letter, Pugh to Doey, June 27, 1944.

7 "Report of the Mental Deficiency Committee, being a Joint Committee of the Board of Education and the Board of Control," London HMSO, 1929, known as "The Wood Report" and "Report of the Departmental Committee on Sterilisation," Cmmd 4485, 1934. See also introductory article by Macnicol 1983.

8 Napsbury Psychiatric Hospital, as it later became known, near St. Albans, Hertfordshire, was finally closed down in 1999.

19. A Man in a Hurry

1 PP 35.10.

2 Hardie 2009, p. 109, quoting Hillary and Lowe.

3 Hillary 1955, p. 62.

4 Johnston 2005, p. 82.

5 Hillary 1975, p. 22.

6 Ibid., p. 25.

7 Hillary 1955, p. 5.

8 RGS/EE/86&87.Press Cuttings: *South Wales Argos,* October 23, 1953.

9 This story was told to me by Norman Hardie, who was a good friend of Jim McFarlane. See also Johnston 2005, p. 84.

10 Hillary 1975, p. 182.

11 Ibid., p. 183.

12 Hardie 2006, p. 108.

13 Hillary 1999, p. 121.

14 Ibid.

15 Fuchs's Trans-Antarctic Expedition was an independent enterprise, financed mainly by charitable funds. It was loosely associated with the "International Geophysical Year," under which a large number of nations agreed to put aside their differences for a period of eighteen months (July 1957–December 1958) and release their scientists to cooperate in a joint effort to advance the world's geophysical knowledge. Scientists from

sixty-four countries took part, and some 4,000 research stations were set up throughout the world. Antarctica was one of the key focus points. In a frenzy of scientific activity, twelve different countries set up more than fifty overwintering bases there, to which they sent out numerous scientists. Fuchs himself (1908–1999) was a geological scientist who conceived of the idea of repeating Shackleton's attempt at traversing Antarctica while working as field commander of the British Falkland Islands Dependency Survey (see *The Times* obituary, November 13, 1999, and Clarkson's article on Fuchs in the *Dictionary of National Biography* 2004).

16 See note 15 above.

17 Before leaving for Antarctica, Fuchs, Hillary, Lowe, and several other members of the Trans-Antarctic Expedition went to Pugh's laboratory in London to have benchmark measurements taken.

18 Hut Point was the name given to the tip of the peninsula where Captain Scott established his shore base during the *Discovery* expedition of 1901–03. The sea inlet is known as McMurdo Sound. Jim Adam had been seconded to Edholm's division at the MRC by the navy.

19 Hillary 1955, p. 63.

20 Hillary 1999, p.8 8.

21 A high concentration of red blood corpuscles is less advantageous to the high-altitude climber than common sense might suggest, partly because it tends to make the blood more syrupy and viscous, increasing the risk of blood clots and high-altitude strokes. On Cho Oyu and Everest, Pugh had begun to make some of the earliest comparisons between the British climbers and the native Sherpas and porters. He had noticed that the Sherpas performed better at altitude than most of the British, yet consistently showed significantly lower hemoglobin levels than the British. In an academic paper (Pugh 1954e) published a year before Hillary's book came out, Pugh wrote that he had found "no obvious relationship between haemoglobin levels and physical performance." Pugh's measurements were the first observation of a phenomenon which is now thought to indicate that Sherpas are better adapted to altitude than lowlanders.

22 Squadron Leader John Claydon (later Wing Commander) kindly gave me a recorded interview when I visited him at his home in Christchurch, New Zealand, in 2007. Claydon, who had been left in charge of Scott

Base, told me that Hillary's plans to go to the Pole were actually well under way long before he reached Depot 700. He said, "We got to Depot 480 and before I left Ed took me aside and said, 'John, I want to tell you something in absolute confidence. Have you got sufficient fuel to bring the fuel to me at 700?' He told me he was heading for the Pole and asked if I had enough fuel. I said 'no.'" The fuel was eventually obtained from the Americans and flown to Depot 700 by Claydon.

23 Pugh was clear that Hillary was "forbidden" to go to the Pole directly by a telegram from Fuchs, which explicitly told him to abandon his idea of reaching the Pole (quoted in Hillary 1999, p. 225, Corgi paperback version), and indirectly by a preceding telegram from the Ross Sea Committee, which instructed him to ascertain and act in accord with Fuchs's wishes, whatever they might be (quoted in Hillary 1999, pp. 219–20). Almost a year earlier, in March 1957, Hillary had already proposed to Fuchs a range of extracurricular activities he wanted to undertake at Depot 700, but Fuchs forbade him to do anything beyond establishing the depot. "From then on," Hillary wrote, "I decided I would largely ignore the instructions of the Ross Sea Committee, and, as leader in the field, make whatever decisions I regarded as appropriate" (Hillary 1999, p. 186.) After hearing the news of Hillary's arrival at the Pole while in the NZ radio room at Scott Base, Pugh reported in his diary: "H has disregarded both Ross Sea Committee and Fuchs' signals" (Pugh's Antarctic Diary, January 4, 1958). John Claydon, who made Hillary's project possible by flying out the fuel he needed, commented to me, "Quite simply it was a dirty trick, Ed going to the Pole. It wasn't his place to go there . . . a lot of people think it was a good thing for Ed to do—to oppose authority and take the mickey out of the British and all the rest of it . . . The Brits were offended . . . and quite frankly, it beggared the expedition because the whole objective was the crossing of Antarctica with Hillary providing the support—an exact replica of what Shackleton had planned . . . Anyway, I think that as soon as [Ed] was selected, with the kind of bloke he is, before he left NZ, he thought, 'I'm going to be the bloke.' I think that Ed was just conserving his resources. He was sitting back there and just waiting until he got his turn and then, phew."

24 See, for example, articles in *The Times* on January 7 and 8, 1958.

25 *Paris Match,* January 18, 1958.

26 Hillary 1961, p. 210.

27 During my visit to New Zealand in 2007, I was told by several of those involved at the time that Hillary's dash for the Pole was still a matter of controversy in New Zealand. Three of the scientific members of Hillary's team complained that they were unable to carry out their pre-agreed research program because Hillary requisitioned the NZ tractors they had been promised for his race to the Pole. Furthermore, when Murray Ellis, who traveled to Depot 700 with Hillary's group, asked Hillary to release him so he could join his scientific colleagues to carry out a prearranged mapping and surveying project, Hillary persuaded Ellis to forgo his project and join the race to the Pole instead, by threatening to go anyway with Peter Mulgrew as his only companion (see Hillary 1999, p. 20). Hillary lacked the skills to keep the vehicles going, and would have put himself in significant danger if Ellis, who was a skilled mechanic, had refused to accompany him. Afterward, it is said that Ellis never fully forgave Hillary for preventing him from using the unique opportunity to do his research. The residual resentment felt by Fuchs and others about Hillary's behavior is discussed at length in Dodds 2005.

20. Everest without Oxygen

1 See Hillary 1975, pp. 233–35.

2 PP 42.10.756: Cover letter dated April 6, 1959.

3 PP 42.10.748: Letter, Hillary to Pugh, February 16, 1959.

4 From a taped interview kindly given to me by Hillary's friend, climber Mike Gill.

5 Pugh in Edholm and Bacharach 1965, p. 121.

6 This expedition was described by its leader in Dill 1980. See also West 1998, pp. 219–27. Pugh also often wrote about it (see, for example, Pugh 1969c).

7 WL Pugh ref.8525. Before leaving for Antarctica Pugh had been planning an Anglo-American scientific expedition to Kamet in 1959 or 1960. Will Siri and Nello Pace had expressed interest in taking part. He had applied to the Mount Everest Foundation for a grant, but he omitted to fill in the section of the application form requiring him to list his qualifications to lead a scientific expedition to high altitude. No doubt he felt that

the MEF ought to know who he was. The result was that the foundation refused even to consider his application.

8 PP 42.10.750: Letter, Pugh to Hillary, April 6, 1959.

9 Ibid.: Letter, Hillary to Pugh, April 19, 1959.

10 Ibid.: Letter, Hillary to Pugh, September 19, 1959.

11 Ibid., p. 763.

12 Hillary describes this episode in his books of 1975, p. 235, and 1999, p. 241.

13 Copy in PP 42.10.766.

14 Izzard 1955.

15 See Ward 1972, p. 157. Notwithstanding Ward's memory of being invited onto the expedition at a very early stage by Pugh and Hillary together, Hillary later objected to being asked to pay Ward's salary, writing to Pugh, "I am afraid we will not be able to afford the luxury of Mike Ward. Mike could be very useful, but I do not regard his inclusion as sufficiently essential to pay £1,000 for it." However, Pugh wanted Ward on the expedition, and he was included nonetheless (PP 42.10.a792).

16 HP MS 2010/1 NLZ folder 2.NLI folder 1.Sheet 9: Letter, Pugh to Hillary, 1959.

17 PP 42.10.771 "Notes after a consultation with Sir Edmund Hillary," October 19, 1959.

18 Ward and Milledge 2002, p. 84.

19 Milledge 1993, p. 173.

20 Hillary and Doig 1962, p. 167.

21 PP 42.6 and 10.785. Pugh first approached Mr. Comrie, head of the Government's Department of Scientific and Industrial Research. A minute of their first meeting (which Ward also attended) shows they discussed the location of the hut, the likely weather conditions, and the dimensions, including factors like sleeping area and bunks. Comrie then sent Pugh on to architect Ezra Levin. The hut was described in the *Marley News,* No. 28, October 1969, in an article entitled "Highest Building in the World."

22 Hillary and Doig 1962, p. 171.

21. "Only If I Have Complete Control"

1 HP MS 2010/1: Letter, Hillary to Pugh, August 18, 1960.

2 Silver Hut Diary, October 1, 1960.

3 Silver Hut Diary, October 17, 1960.

4 Doig and Perkins made a Yeti scalp of their own from Thar goat skin. A Thar goat is a Himalayan mountain goat with a thick, woolly, reddish to dark-brown coat.

5 Pugh to Doey, October 31, 1960.

6 HTP: Hillary and Doig 1962, p. 167.

7 Hardie described his experiences of the Silver Hut to me during several meetings in 2005 and 2006. He also wrote about them in a chapter on the Silver Hut expedition in his book published in 2006, pp. 192–217. Pugh often commented in admiration that Hardie did a remarkable job delivering the complete set of Silver Hut parts to Mingbo undamaged.

8 Hillary and Doig 1962, p. 170.

9 PP 42.7.639 Being in some respects shy, he would have found it hard to muscle in on Hillary's group without being invited.

10 HTP: Letter, Pugh to Doey, November 10, 1960.

11 Silver Hut Diary entries for November 7–15, 1960.

12 HTP: Letter, Pugh to Doey, November 10, 1960.

13 Ibid. The full passage says, "E is a hopeless leader but good at forging on. He turns out to be much too small a man for an expedition like this, which includes a number of older & more experienced men as well as the young climbers. I have been unable to fathom his true intentions and he won't give direct answers to my questions. For example, I cannot get him to give a direct yes or no about the radio communication & the use of helicopter. I expect he feels ashamed secretly about going back to NZ and wants to keep things as dark as possible while he is away. He seems unable to delegate authority & yet does not communicate his plans, so none of us know where we are. No doubt I shall have to have another straight talk with him soon and, if the result is not satisfactory, return home. So anything may happen."

14 Silver Hut Diary entries for November 7–15, 1960. See also Pugh's notes, PP 42.7.639–40.

15 Pugh had grouped the physiological equipment by procedure: All the items needed for respiratory gas analysis had been packed together, and so on. Three further lists provided a record of the contents case by case, a full general alphabetical inventory, and, lastly, a classified catalog according to procedure. His complaint was that Hillary put the wrong people in charge

of the repacking; instead of Mike Gill, who understood the system, he gave the job to Milledge and Nevison.

16 Since they lacked radio contact with Kathmandu, a desperate message was sent by runner to Namche Bazar. From there they put in a request to the officer in charge of the military radio post to send a message by Morse to Kathmandu, and from there a cable was sent to the MRC in London. See unpublished draft article "Himalayan Scientific and Mountaineering Expedition 1960/61 from Dr. L. G. C. E. Pugh" HTP.

17 PP 42.7.639–40.

18 Hillary 1975, p. 243.

19 Silver Hut Diary, November 7–15, 1960.

20 Hillary 1975, p. 243.

21 Silver Hut Diary, November 15, 1960. Pugh wrote: "Yesterday I was present at a long meeting between Desmond Doig & Z [presumably meaning some] of the Khumjung village elders sitting on furs round the charcoal brazier. The meeting lasted all of 2 hours & they agreed to hand over their Yeti scalp on already agreed conditions (6,000RN & a new school) providing that the remaining opposition can be bought off which would require 500RN." Later the deposit was raised to 8,000 rupees.

22 PP 27.18.

23 HTP: Letter, Pugh to Doey, November 25, 1960.

24 Pugh observed in his Antarctic studies into carbon monoxide poisoning that the gas is about twice as poisonous at 15,000 feet as it is at sea level (see Pugh 1959b).

25 Gill 1969, pp. 134–35.

26 HTP: Letter, Pugh to Doey, December 28, 1960.

22. Winter in the Silver Hut

1 Pugh 1963. Man Badhur was also able to generate heat, increasing his body temperature without shivering.

2 West, "A Memoir: Highs and Lows in Three Countries, 2003," John B. West papers, MSCL.

3 West 1985, p. 82.

4 HTP: Draft paper, Pugh, L. G. C. E., "Himalayan Scientific and Mountaineering Expedition: A Report from the Leader of the Scientific Team, October 6, 1960."

5 Ibid.

6 Pugh summarized the work and the main results of the expedition in Pugh 1961, Pugh 1962a, b, c, Pugh 1964b, Pugh 1965b, and Pugh 1969. For a general account of the expedition and the scientific findings, see West 1998, chapter 10, and Milledge 1982 and 2002.

7 Milledge 1993, p. 173.

8 West 1985, p. 79.

9 Gill's psychometric tests were devised in collaboration with the MRC Unit for Applied Physiology at the Department of Applied Psychology at Cambridge. See draft article: "Himalayan Scientific and Mountaineering Expedition 1960/61 from Dr. L. G. C. E. Pugh, Leader of the Wintering Party: Mingbo December 22, 1960" (HTP).

10 They had slide rules and miniature mechanical calculators called Curtas, first introduced in 1948, to help them.

11 HTP: Draft "Scientific Leader's dispatch" written by Pugh, January 10, 1961. The serow goat is an ancient species of goat native to Asia.

12 HTP: Letter, Pugh to Doey, January 22, 1961.

13 See undated copy of this letter in PP 42.7.318.

14 Ibid.

15 PP 42.7.536.

16 HTP: Letter, Edholm to Pugh, February 9, 1961.

17 On March 1, 1961, Pugh's diary notes, "Ed bringing in the O2 after all." He later sent Hillary the detailed research program for Makalu with a note, saying, "I enclose for your information the programme of work envisaged for Makalu. It was fully discussed and agreed before winding up the Silver Hut. Details will naturally have to be fitted in with your plans" (PP 42.7).

18 Ward and Gill earlier made the first ascent of a fluted ice peak behind the Silver Hut which they named Rakpa Peak. It had 60-degree slopes near the top. Also Milledge made the first ascent of Puma Dablam (20,879 feet).

19 The sixth wife was Gita Bannerjee, wife of Doig's assistant, Bhannu. Lila Bishop and Betty Milledge had been living in Kathmandu throughout the expedition. Irene Ortenburger and June Mulgrew came in with Hillary.

20 HTP: Letter, Pugh to Doey (undated).

23. Disaster on Makalu

1 PP 42.8: Draft article by Hillary, dated July 1961.

2 Silver Hut Diary, April 10, 1961.

3 Hillary and Doig 1962, p. 212.

4 Ibid.

5 Ibid., p. 215.

6 Mulgrew 1964, p. 86.

7 Hillary and Doig 1962, p. 216.

8 Ibid., p. 221.

9 Silver Hut Diary, April 9, 1961.

10 Ibid., April 16, 1961: "I had by this time more or less decided I should have to give up the idea of going to Makalu. It would need 10 days travelling at heights up to 20,000 feet & really very little to show for it. My plan is to stay here, take down all the equipment, pack it & take it out to Kathmandu before the monsoon. I should also like 14 days to coordinate & copy out all the results."

11 Ibid., April 30, 1961.

12 PP 42.7.551: Letter, Doig to Pugh, May 1, 1961.

13 Sukhamay Lahiri and the Indian army doctor Captain Motwani were not invited to Makalu, and Barry Bishop decided not to go because his glaciology project was unfinished.

14 HTP: Quote from Ward's draft article, "The Uses of Adversity."

15 Gill 1969, p. 152. The descriptions of the Makalu assault that follow are mainly drawn from the following sources: Gill 1969, chapter 13; Mulgrew 1964, chapters 6, 7, and 8; Harrison 1961; and Ward, draft article "The Uses of Adversity" (1962 HTP).

16 See description in Mulgrew 1964, p. 105.

17 Mulgrew 1964, p. 108.

18 West describes Mulgrew's affliction as "probably a pulmonary embolus" (see West 1998, p. 297).

19 West, "A Memoir: Highs and Lows in Three Countries, 2003," John B. West papers, MSCL.

20 Gill 1969, p. 156.

21 In the spring, the Silver Hut had begun to look as if it was precariously perched on stilts because the snow surface on which it stood had melted,

leaving intact only a pillar of snow beneath each of the supporting jacks. Hillary donated it to the Himalayan Mountaineering Training Institute of Darjeeling. A team of Sherpas led by the institute's director, Tenzing Norgay of Everest fame, came to collect it, and it was eventually reassembled at the institute's training camp in Sikkim, where it remains to this day.

24. "Gone to India. Your Dinner's in the Oven"

1 *The Times,* June 9, 1961.
2 PP 42.8.646, June 15, 1961.
3 HTP: Letter, 26 September 1941.
4 HTP: Letter, 26 December 1941.
5 Undated letter.
6 HTP: Letter, 1 November 1941.
7 HTP: Letter, October 5, 1941.

25. The Battle of the Book

1 A complete list of all the publications which came out of the expedition is in West 1993, pp. 200–01.
2 PP 27.18: Pugh's letter to Hillary, dated June 27, 1962, 764; Hillary's reply, July 12, 1962, 763. By way of explanation, Hillary told Pugh, "Having completed the manuscript as best I can, I don't have a great deal to do with any further arrangements."
3 Ibid.: This file contains copies of galley proofs and Pugh's suggested alterations.
4 Ibid.
5 Ibid.
6 Ibid.: Letter, Pugh to Dienhart (PR Director of Field Enterprises), July 31, 1962. In England Hodder & Stoughton agreed immediately to make any changes that would render the book more accurate.
7 Ibid.: Letter, September 27, 1962.
8 Ibid.
9 PP 42.9: Letters, Pugh to Ward, September 25, 1962, 400, and Pugh to Dienhart, September 27, 1952, 399.
10 Ibid.: Letter, Hillary to Dienhart, December 6, 1962, 130.
11 Ibid.: Letter, Pugh to Dienhart, January 4, 1963, 139.
12 *Geographical Journal,* 128.4. December 1962, pp. 447–56.

13 *The Other Side of the Mountain*, BBC Wales 1978.

26. The Four Inns Walk

1 Bishop 1963. This expedition is also described in Hornbein's famous book, written in 1965.

2 Ibid.

3 Forty-one years earlier, in 1922, George Finch, Captain Bruce, and the Gurkha Tejbir Bura survived for two nights in a flimsy tent in appalling weather on the north side of Everest at 25,500 feet. Finch believed that one of the reasons he and his companions survived was that they were able to breathe supplementary oxygen at a low rate from their oxygen sets.

4 PP 23.10: Pugh's record of his conversation with Bishop, dated December 4, 1963, tells of how the two parties had had no contact for several days, but Bishop decided he and his partner must wait for Hornbein and Unsoeld, who joined them two hours later. Pugh wrote, "I had the impression that Hornbein and his companion owe their lives to Bishop because they would not have been able to find their way down in the dark, and the smallest error would have been irretrievable, as they could not have ascended again without oxygen equipment."

5 This estimate should only be regarded as giving a general impression of the size of the problem, which all commentators agreed was rapidly getting worse. Pugh quoted the number of thirty to sixty a year in a letter to the chairman of the Derbyshire Adventure Club Mountain Rescue Team (see PP 7.16.147).

6 As well as a complete lack of national statistics, there also had been no formal medical appraisal of accident prevention in Britain, where killer diseases like tuberculosis had tended to steal the limelight. However, since World War II, "the scourge of disease" had been lifted by antibiotics, and people were becoming more aware that significant numbers of deaths and injuries were being caused by accidents. The working party's own first estimates suggested that 20,000 people were dying in accidents every year, with 300,000 suffering serious injury. See WL SA/MWF/FSO/1. See also Foreword by Capener to Hunt 1965, pp. ix–xii.

7 Kurt Hahn (1886–1974) learned about the English public school system when studying at Oxford between 1904–06 and 1910–14, before returning to Germany where he had been born and brought up. He founded a public

school called Salem in Germany in conjunction with Prince Max of Baden, because, he claimed, of his disappointment in the qualities of leadership he perceived in contemporary German society. The school occupied part of the prince's castle home at Lake Constance, and the prince's son, Berthold, Margrave of Baden, was the first pupil. Berthold later married the second sister of Prince Philip of Greece, who in turn married Princess Elizabeth, heir to the British throne. The Jewish Hahn was forced to leave Germany in 1933, and subsequently started Gordonstoun in Scotland, with help and support from distinguished well-wishers such as William Temple (Archbishop of Canterbury), Lord Tweedsmuir (John Buchan), and G. M. Trevelyan. The progressive principles on which Salem and Gordonstoun were founded are described in Stewart 1972 and Brereton 1968. It would be wrong to characterize the school as solely preoccupied with physical or athletic aspects of education. There was a concerted attempt to develop the whole person, with emphasis given particularly to self-discipline, enterprise, physical fitness, service to the community, craftsmanship, and compassion. See also Wedell 2004. Prince Philip began his education at Salem, moving to Gordonstoun when Hahn left Germany. The Royal Family has been sending its children there ever since.

8 This was seen as a result of the ending of the war, the impending end to National Service, the advent of television, and a general shortage of sporting and recreational facilities. See, for example, Justin Evans 1974, p. 22.

9 The movement spread to forty countries throughout the world.

10 The Award Scheme provided a program of activities leading to a hierarchy of awards and was intended to be used as a resource by existing youth organizations to supplement their own activities. Hahn's objectives, if not his precise methods, echoed those of Baden Powell's earlier Boy Scout movement, which also deliberately set out to promulgate traditional public-school values among young people of all social classes. Baden Powell first published *Scouting for Boys* in 1908, and the first official Scout Camp was held in the same year. Springhall 1977, p. 64, argues that the Scout movement had its roots in the ethos of "muscular Christianity," which dominated British public schools in the last quarter of the nineteenth century and in the intellectual climate of the UK in the 1900s. One admiring commentator remarked of the Scouts, "In the next generation there should

be no overgrown lad standing on street corners idly and foolishly, gaping after they know not what. There will be a new race of boys in England when the Scouts of today have little Scouts of their own."

11 Hunt 1978, pp. 127–30.

12 See Pugh 1966, p. 126, "Incident 19."

13 *Daily Herald,* February 21, 1961. PP 61.5 has a collection of newspaper articles on deaths from hypothermia.

14 "Convention on Accident Prevention and Life Saving," organized by the Royal College of Surgeons, May 14, 1963.

15 See Hunt 1965, p. 228, for papers given at the convention. One delegate alone showed signs of doubt when he announced, "There is an attitude amongst many people that by shoving poor characters into the mountains you will transform them into first class characters. This is not so . . ."

16 Ibid., p. 229.

17 See Sir Arthur Porritt's speech of welcome at the opening of the convention (Ibid., p. 5). Sir Arthur Porritt (1900–1994) was a distinguished surgeon, former Oxford athlete, and Olympic sprinter. As the only man ever to be president of the Royal College of Surgeons and the British Medical Association simultaneously, he was a prominent establishment figure.

18 Furneaux, W. D., "Psychology of Adolescent Misadventure," Ibid., p. 240.

19 Ibid., pp. 224–27.

20 PP 6.43.56.

21 WL SA/MWF/F20/1.

22 See "Scouts Die, Two Lost on Moor," *The Times,* March 16, 1964. The competition took place on March 14–15, 1964.

23 Pugh 1964a.

24 Pugh frequently referred to the work of: Adolph and Molnar 1946, who studied nude subjects performing on ergometers in various weather conditions; Belding et al. 1945, who studied clothing test methods in the United States during the war and the effects of exercise on the insulation value of clothing; Breckenridge and Woodcock 1950, who measured the effect of wind on the insulation value of military cold-weather uniforms; Hall and Polte 1956, who measured the effects of wetting on the insulation value of clothing; and (occasionally) German hypothermia experiments

carried out on Dachau prisoners and later investigated and published after the war by Major L. Alexander 1946 etc.

25 In a later article (Pugh 1967c) Pugh wrote, "The metabolic response to cold during exercise was approximately equal to that brought about by a 300kg increase in work load, and amounted to 15–20% of the subjects' estimated maximum O2 intake." When a subject "was exercising at a given work rate in the wet cold situation his oxygen intake was 50% higher than it was at the same work rate in dry conditions."

26 Pugh 1964a, p. 1212.

27 The association between the quantity of subcutaneous fat and resistance to cooling in water was well understood by this time. Pugh's research into hill-walkers showed that there was no similar relationship between fat and cold resistance when walkers' clothes were dry, but when their clothes became wet in windy conditions, they got into a similar situation to people in water, and fat appeared to become a helpful factor in keeping them warm. Many of the hypothermia victims studied by Pugh turned out to be very thin (see Pugh 1966a).

28 WL SA/MWF/F20/1: Medical Committee on Accident Prevention: Annual Report 1964–1965.

29 Ibid., p. 12.

30 MRC P28/311: Pugh, Dr. L. G. C. E.: Letter, Peter Medawar to J. C. R. Hudson, June 3, 1964; letter Peter Medawar to D. J. Cawthron, July 13, 1964.

31 Pugh 1966a, p. 123. Pugh's informant was Dr. I. Jones, resident casualty officer at the Caernarvon and Anglesey General Hospital in 1966.

32 PP 6.43.

33 Pugh collaborated on hypothermia with Kenneth Cooper of the MRC's Body Temperature Research Unit at the Radcliffe Infirmary, Oxford, with whom he discussed methods of resuscitation (PP 6.43), and Cooper also helped with some of Pugh's field studies. The results were published in Pugh 1964, 1966a, 1966b, 1968, and 1969.

34 Pugh 1966a, p. 29.

35 PP 61.6.

36 Ibid.

37 Pugh 1967, p. 336.

38 Pugh 1966, p. 129.

39 Pugh 1967c, p. 333. Pugh also criticized the youth-adventure community for subjecting young people to exhausting trials of strength beyond their physical abilities. See letter to *The Times,* PP 10.16.

40 PP 59.8.367: Letter from Jack Longland to Pugh, October 2, 1964. See also correspondence in PP 7.16. Most often cited were: Pugh's insistence that walkers and hikers should always carry suitable protective clothing; his advice to set up an emergency camp and wait to be rescued when problems arose; and his suggestions for the treatment and resuscitation of exposure cases on the spot, by mountain rescue teams.

27. "Good Science and Bad Science"

1 Pugh 1968, pp. 826–27.

2 Ibid., p. 829.

3 *Times Saturday Review,* February 24, 1968.

4 PP 8.39.255: February 26, 1968.

5 Medawar, Sir Peter (1915–1987). Born in Rio de Janeiro, Brazil, Medawar was educated in England at Marlborough College (in common with Geoffrey Winthrop Young, John Hunt, Michael Ward, and Charles Wylie). He said of his former school, "I was uniformly unhappy from beginning to end surrounded by pedants and pederasts" (Temple 1984, p. 14). He went on to gain a first-class degree in zoology at Oxford in 1935, and it was at Oxford that he later carried out the research that won him the Nobel Prize he shared with Australian immunologist Sir MacFarlane Burnet. Medawar was a Fellow of the Royal Society, receiving its Copley Medal in 1969, and was knighted in 1965.

6 MRC P28/311 Pugh, Dr. L. G. C. E. Harington described Pugh as "a highly individualist worker who pursues his own line. Pugh's work is in my opinion of high value and his reputation as an authority on respiratory physiology in connection with high-altitude work speaks for itself."

7 Mitchison 1990, p. 284.

8 Taped interview which Professor Rainer Goldsmith kindly gave me at his home in Derby in July 2004.

9 The baton was taken up by W. R. Keatinge at the MRC's Body Temperature Unit in Oxford. Keatinge later moved to the London Hospital, where he had large water tanks installed in his laboratory and continued

the immersion research under the sponsorship of the MRC's Royal Navy Personnel Research Committee. The experiments which Keatinge, who became a world expert on hypothermia, did at the end of the 1960s confirmed many of Pugh's earlier findings, such as the importance of subcutaneous fat in insulating the body against cold in water, and the finding that heat was better conserved if people kept still rather than attempting to swim. See Keatinge 1969. (Information from a taped personal interview the late W. R. Keatinge kindly gave me at his home in November 2007.)
10 They included Professor Heinz Wolff, Professor Rainer Goldsmith, Jim Adam, Professor Ray Clark, John Brotherhood, Professor Mervyn Davies, and Dr. David Jones.
11 See examples in NIMR.PF43 640/2 Pugh Personal File.
12 PP 8.39.249: Letter, Pugh to Medawar, April 26, 1967.
13 MRC P28/311 Pugh, Dr. L. G. C. E.
14 Ibid.

28. The "Boffin" and the Altitude Olympics

1 The IOC is the self-appointed, self-recruited voluntary body which governs the worldwide Olympic movement. The Olympic movement embraces individual national Olympic associations, such as the British Olympic Association, in each of the participating countries, though these associations are not "represented" on the central governing committee. The movement also embraces a plethora of voluntary bodies representing individual sports in each country, such as the Amateur Athletics Association and the Amateur Rowing Association in the UK, as well as a series of umbrella federations representing the individual sports at an international level (see Krotee 1988).
2 B. Glanville, "The Old Men of the IOC," *Sunday Times,* June 11, 1961.
3 Peter Wilson, "Our Boxers May Pull Out of the Olympics," *Sunday Mirror,* January 1966.
4 Duncan 1967. Wrynn 2006, pp. 1156–57, describes the bidding process. The Mexicans accompanied their bid with a plethora of research results, which purported to refute any possibility that the athletes could be harmed by the intermediate altitude of Mexico, and explicitly claimed, "The altitude of Mexico City permits a rapid adaptation of normal persons and does not impair in any way the capacity to carry out physical work or

sporting events" (*The Organisation,* Organising Committee of the Games of the XIX Olympiad). This was not in line with conventional medical opinion about the effects of altitude on physical performance, so the committee cannot have consulted very widely.

5 Quoted from BBC interview with Patrick Smith; see Smith 1966.

6 Examples of researchers are Margaria and Cerretelli in Italy; Per-Olaf Astrand, Christensen, and Avrill Karlsson in Scandinavia; Karpovich, Jokl and others in the United States. In the UK, MRC HQ files at the National Archives (FD23/88 and 89) show sports science was patchy, uncoordinated, and limited in scope.

7 BOA LM "Minutes of the Meeting of the Medical Advisory Committee held at St. Mary's Hospital on Monday, March 8, 1965." The committee was set up at the request of the British Empire and Commonwealth Games Council for England and the BOA, and its initial remit was to give advice on the Commonwealth Games due to be held in Jamaica in 1966, and the Mexico Olympics of 1968. Porritt was elected onto the IOC in 1934 and retired in 1967. He was also involved with the British Association of Sport and Medicine under the auspices of which the BOA's medical committee was formed.

8 In the wider medical community it had long been taken for granted that acclimatization improved physical performance at altitude, as the normal processes such as increase in breathing rates, increased blood volume, and numbers of red blood cells, etc., brought about a corresponding increase in maximum oxygen intake. But this view had been challenged by Italian physiologists Cerretelli and Margaria 1961, and Cerretelli 1964, who had compared published data on the maximum oxygen uptakes of groups of people exposed to simulated altitudes in pressure chambers with the maximum oxygen uptakes of acclimatized visitors to altitude, such as mountaineers. According to their findings, as altitude increased, there were greater reductions in the maximum oxygen uptakes in the acclimatized subjects than in the unacclimatized subjects. This implied that the limitation of performance imposed by altitude was not influenced by acclimatization. Pugh in Pugh 1967 objected that different groups of subjects were compared at sea level and at altitude. The BOA's Medical Advisory Committee decided to commission Pugh's Mexico study in preference to joining in with the

so-called experimental "little Olympics," which were staged in Mexico City by the Mexican organizing committee in 1965, 1966, and 1967, to try to offset some of the criticism of the 1968 Olympic venue.

9 Out of Portsmouth's total membership of thirty-four distance runners—which included Hyman, Tulloh, the Cooke brothers, Tim Johnston, and other top-grade athletes—seventeen represented either Great Britain or England or both. In the International European Cross-Country Championships of January 1963, Portsmouth's A team took 1st, 2nd, 4th, and 5th places, and Portsmouth's B team won the "open" race at the end, for which all the teams were eligible. See James Coote, "Portsmouth Snatch all the Honours," *Daily Telegraph,* January 25, 1963. A profile of the club, "Take Eight Good Runners," was published in *World Sports* (1965).

10 Martin Hyman kindly gave me two taped interviews in Edinburgh, as well as several written communications. The quotations attributed to him come from the interviews.

11 See, for example, Berryman 1992, p. 83 and p. 88.

12 Bannister 1954, p. 62.

13 Booth 1999, p. 96.

14 Bannister 1955, p. 121.

15 Mike Turner described them respectively as: a professional student, a bricklayer, an area sales manager, a salesman, a local government officer, and a schoolteacher. Turner himself was an English cross-country international and vice president of Cambridge University Hare and Hounds Cross-Country Club; he used to be described as "just below" Olympic standard. The North brothers were members of the Belgrave Harriers. In April 1975 *Athletics Weekly* dubbed Gerry North Britain's most consistently successful cross-country runner since the war. Dominic Kelly, youngest of three famous running brothers, was also a cross-country international for Derby. Hyman and Cooke, who came third in the International Cross-Country Championship in 1964, ran for Portsmouth Athletics Club.

16 Pugh described these contrasting processes in an article (Pugh 1967, p. 629), on the effect of altitude on athletic performance, written explicitly for laypeople, as follows: "The energy released in muscular work is supplied by the chemical breakdown of adenosine-triphosphate (ATP) in the muscles. The breakdown process does not require oxygen, but oxygen is

used in the complex series of chemical reactions associated with recovery. In continuous 'steady state' exercise the processes of breakdown and recovery balance [each other], and oxygen is absorbed by the body at a steady rate, which is directly proportional to the work rate. This is known as aerobic metabolism. In short-term high-intensity exercise the release of energy by breakdown of ATP far outstrips the body's capacity to absorb oxygen, and the oxygen needed for recovery is absorbed mainly after the exercise. This type of metabolism is known as anaerobic metabolism. The extra oxygen absorbed during recovery, which is in excess of normal resting oxygen consumption, is known as the recovery oxygen, and is equal to the 'oxygen debt' incurred during the exercise. In most athletic events energy is provided by a combination of anaerobic and aerobic metabolism; the shorter the event, the greater the anaerobic component; the longer the event, the greater the dependence on aerobic metabolism and oxygen intake." The "oxygen debt" can be measured by comparing the athlete's oxygen intake in a given time of 40 to 50 minutes, while he is at rest before and after the race. Pugh's measurements of this aspect of post-race recovery suggested that the process of building up oxygen debt was not significantly altered in Mexico City, as compared with sea level, which tended to confirm that sprint athletes would be relatively unaffected by the lower atmospheric pressure of Mexico City.

17 Pugh, *Nature*, 1965, pp. 1397–98. Pugh emphasized that these figures should be treated as a rough estimation.

18 Cervantes and Karpovich 1964.

19 One of Pugh's most comprehensive accounts of the Mexico study is an article entitled "Athletes at Altitude," published in the *Journal of Physiology* (Pugh 1967, pp. 619–45). Pugh took advice from the Amateur Athletics Association coach John Le Masurier and from the athletes themselves about the best way to estimate their average running performances at sea level for comparison with those at altitude in Mexico, taking into account factors like the weather, the state of the track, and the athlete's physical condition. The results were then tested in two timed 3-mile trials over the next four weeks so Pugh could satisfy himself that his athletes really could produce repeatable performances.

20 Carried out with the help of the Amateur Athletics Association's senior coach John Le Masurier.

21 As Martin Hyman put it, "To race to the limits of his ability, a distance runner needs to endure progressively increasing discomfort and to concentrate increasingly hard to avoid slowing down." Turner described athletes like himself as people who could endure a greater degree of pain than the man in the street.

22 Karpovich 1956.

23 For an academic account of the difficulties between Pugh and the BOA, see Heggie 2008.

24 BOA LM 157: Letter, Owen to Duncan, May 5, 1965.

25 These letters, mostly handwritten, are in the BOA archives.

26 BOA 1.6.

27 BOA 3.26: "I had a real upper and downer with Pugh on the phone and we both agreed we were quite intolerable to each other. Then he quietened down," Duncan reported to Owen.

28 *The Times,* November 20, 1965.

29 BOA 1.47: Letter, Duncan to Pugh, November 22, 1965.

30 BOA 1.81: Letter, Pugh to Duncan, November 24, 1965 and BSC SC1/2 1834.

31 BOA 1.58.

32 Brasher, "The Tragi-Comedy of Mexico," *Observer,* January 2, 1966.

33 Dudley Doust, "Olympic Hazard: High-Altitude Tests in Mexico," *Illustrated London News,* January 1, 1966.

34 BOA LM: Minutes of a meeting of the Medical Advisory Committee to the British Olympic Association, January 19, 1966.

35 HTP: (Manuscript) copy of Pugh's report, "British Olympic Association Investigation into Mexico City: Preliminary Report to the Medical Committee," 1965.

36 BOA 2.

37 BOA LM 1372 Minutes of the Medical Advisory Committee, January 19, 1966.

38 "Britain Calls for Limit on High-Altitude Training," *The Times,* February 3, 1966.

39 BOA 2.108. BOA Report Conclusion No. 4.

40 *Daily Telegraph,* April 11, 1966; *Sunday Times,* April 16, 1966.

41 MRC P28/311 Pugh, Dr. L. G. C. E.

42 Symposium on Sports in Medium Altitude, Magglingen, Switzerland, December 15–19, 1965.

43 "Olympic Games in Mexico—Effects of High Altitude," *The Times,* April 16, 1966.

44 Quoted from Patrick Smith's "Dispatch from Rome," April 21, 1966 (Transcribed by Bush House Transcribing Unit) YFN 24697.

29. Going for Gold

1 NIMR.AR 17-AR33: Laboratory for Field Physiology. Manuscript, "Review of Research" for MRC Annual Report.

2 "Training Camps," *Olympic Review,* October 1, 1967, p. 22.

3 A copy of lecture delivered to the Fencing Association is in BOA 1.109.

4 Ibid., p. 15.

5 Font Romeu is at 6,000 feet.

6 The 7.5 percent decrease in performance was similar to that in Mexico City in 1965 (8.5 percent). The small difference is probably accounted for by the fact that Font Romeu is 1,500 feet lower than Mexico City.

7 BOA LM 1212: Letter, Pugh to Duncan, May 25, 1967. Pugh wrote, "The extra strain on the respiratory and circulatory systems at altitude may well increase the development of these systems, which would result in lasting improvement at sea level. No satisfactory data are available on this question at present."

8 *Observer,* May 28, 1967, "Let's stop being gentlemen!"

9 BOA LM 1213: Letter, Duncan to Owen, May 30, 1967.

10 Ibid.: Letter, Owen to Duncan, May 31, 1967.

11 PP 62.10: 453, See IAC statement dated September 12, 1967.

12 MRC P28/311: Pugh, Dr. L. G. C. E., Lush to Medawar, July 12, 1967.

13 BOA LM 1252: Letter, Edholm to Duncan, April 5, 1967. Also BOA LM1247 shows they gave Edholm the Olympic Medical Archives and various foreign reports on altitude research to consider. He happily agreed to take on the role of their altitude adviser.

14 MRC P28/311 Pugh, Dr. L. G. C. E.

15 Pugh 1970 and Pugh 1971.

16 That is to say, they could save the amount of energy used by running for 1 second.

17 Born in 1949, David Bedford was a top distance runner in the 1970s who set a new world record for the 10,000 meters in 1973, which he held until 1977. In the 1972 Olympics he was twelfth in the 5,000 meters and sixth in the 10,000 meters. He is currently one of the directors of the London Marathon.

18 Wallechinsky 2000.

19 See Menier and Pugh 1968. Pugh's MRC colleague R. H. Fox had discussed the thermal aspects of marathon running at the time of the Rome Olympics (see Fox 1960 and Bannister 1959). But no research had been done on marathon runners in the field, and very little was known about the physiological factors limiting athletic performance in endurance running.

20 Pugh, Corbett, and Johnston 1967b.

21 TNA FD23/88 and 89. Duncan ignored warnings about the need for acclimatization to heat from Roger Bannister, John Cotes, and others before the Rome Olympics.

22 Tim Johnston of Portsmouth Athletic Club represented England in the International Cross-Country Championships seven times, coming second in 1967. He broke the world track record for 30 kilometers in 1965 and came eighth in the 1968 Olympic marathon. He was ranked tenth-best marathon runner in the world, and eighth in the world for the 10,000 meters in 1968.

23 Pugh 1972 and manuscript report in HTP: "International Athletes Club Altitude Research Projects, 1967, Font Romeu, Mexico City," p. 32. Once having stopped running due to incipient heat exhaustion, the runners could still walk unaided, but if they tried to stand still they collapsed.

24 See "Beat this for courage!," *Sunday Mirror,* November 5, 1967.

25 PP 58.6.271, BOA 1.

26 BOA 1 32: Duncan's handwritten comments on the IAC leaflet.

27 "The Bracknell Tests" in *Road Runner's News Letter* No. 65, April 1968, and No. 68, April 1969.

28 Pugh 1972a.

29 NIMR.AR17-AR33 Laboratory for Field Physiology.

30 World records were achieved in the men's 100 meters, 200 meters, 400 meters, and both relay races (see Wallechinsky 2000).

31 Wilber 2004, p. xvi, writes of Beaman's jump, which beat the world record by 22 inches: "Years later, biomechanical engineers calculated that

about 5.9 inches of the margin by which Beaman broke the long jump world record was due solely to altitude and its favourable effect on approach speed and reduction of aerodynamic drag during the aerial phase of the jump."
32 *Athletics Weekly,* November 9, 1968.
33 Wallechinsky 2000, p. xxviii.
34 Frisancho 1993, p. 269, writes of the 10,000-meter race, "First was Naftali Temu from Kenya (1500m–2000m), second Mamo Wolde from Ethiopia (2000m–2500m), third Mohamed Gammoudi from Tunisia (1500m–2000m), fourth Juan Martinez from Mexico (2380m), and fifth Nikolay Sviridov from Leninakan [USSR] (1500m)."

30. The Restless Sharpshooter
1 NIMR.AR17-AR33 Laboratory for Field Physiology.
2 This idea was reaffirmed in "Memorandum on the Provisions of the Ministry of Health Bill 1919 Cmd. 69, 1919," in which Lord Addison wrote, "Any body of men engaged upon scientific research in medicine or in any other field should be given the widest possible freedom to make their new discoveries."
3 The Nobel Prize winners included: Martin 1952, Krebs 1953, and Sanger 1958; Medawar 1960 (shared with Australian immunologist, Sir MacFarlane Burnet); Crick and Watson 1962; and Perutz and Kendrew 1962.
4 "National Institute of Medical Research Annual Report," 1973–74, p. 9.
5 The review of the way the government funded and organized pure and applied research was carried out by Lord Victor Rothschild, chairman of Edward Heath's Central Policy Review Staff. Rothschild introduced the idea that government departments should enter into a "customer con-tractor" relationship with the science councils, commissioning their own applied research to meet their needs. In the first instance this led to 25 percent of the MRC's budget being taken away and given to the Department of Health and Social Services.
6 NIMR. Future of Human Physiology: Council Sub-Committee on Human Physiology Report, June 17, 1970, paragraph 13.
7 Pugh, Turner, and Johnston 1968b, Pugh 1969a.
8 See examples in NIMR. AR17-AR33 Laboratory for Field Physiology: Manuscript "Review of Research" for MRC Annual Report.

9 Professor John Scales (1920–2004) developed this system at the Royal National Orthopaedic Hospital, Stanmore, and the Institute of Orthopaedics, University of London. The first hip replacement using this method was carried out in 1963.

10 Pugh 1973.

11 In the project Pugh calculated mean, overall skin temperatures from the thermocouple readings of the exercising subjects in the normal way, while Clark estimated average skin temperatures from the thermo-vision images, and they were able to show the two methods yielded comparable results, confirming the validity of the technique (see Clark, Mullan, and Pugh 1974 and 1977).

12 Helped by his research assistant John Brotherhood and a group of competition cyclists, Pugh (1974a) published the first-ever assessments of the energy saved by slipstreaming in cycling.

13 Archie Young, Professor of Geriatric Medicine at University of Edinburgh Medical School, Edinburgh Royal Infirmary, kindly told me about his memories of Pugh in 2007, and made this point to me.

14 TNA 23/88 809 Morris 1957. This study of London busmen revealed a substantial difference in risk between drivers (sedentary) and conductors (who ran up and down the stairs of London's double-decker buses).

15 TNA FD 23/89 777. The letter, dated February 14, 1963, continued, ". . . and whether indulgence in exercise of various kinds has any notable effect on morbidity rates, life expectancies, etc."

16 TNA FD 23/89 781: Meeting between Himsworth, Edholm, and Whitney to discuss future work on human physiology, May 16, 1963.

17 See Messner 1979, p. 172, and Habeler 1979, p. 164.

18 PP 42.10.756.

19 Hunt 1978, p. 115.

Epilogue: Expecting the Lion's Share

1 Besides the main farm at Putteridge, which was about 350 acres, Pugh persuaded Doey and Hermione to buy a second, similar-size farm in 1973 at Eltisley, near Cambridge, in order to introduce economies of scale. The two garages were "twins" on either side of the A404 main road between Luton and Hitchin. They had four petrol pumps each.

Bibliography

Alexander, L. "Medical Science Under Dictatorship," *New England Medical Journal*, 241, (1949), pp. 39–47.

Allfrey, Anthony. *Edward VII and his Jewish Court*. London: Weidenfeld & Nicolson, 1991.

Allinson, Lincoln. *Amateurism in Sport*. London: Frank Cass, 2001.

Ashley Cooper, Anthony, 3rd Earl of Shaftesbury. *Characteristics of Men, Manners, Opinions and Times* (1711), ed. Robertson. New York: Bobbs-Merrill, 1964.

Askew, W. E. "Food for High-Altitude Expeditions: Pugh Got It Right in 1954—A Commentary on the Report by L. G. C. E. Pugh: 'Himalayan Rations with Special Reference to the 1953 Expedition to Mount Everest,' *Wilderness and Environmental Medicine* 15 (2004), pp. 125–34.

Asthill, T. *Mount Everest: The Reconnaissance, 1935*. Published by the author, 2005.

Baker, Norman. "Whose Hegemony? The Origins of the Amateur Ethos in Nineteenth-Century English Society," *Sport in History*, Vol. 24, No. 1 (2004), pp. 1–16.

Band, George. *Everest*. London: HarperCollins, 2003.

———. "Hunt, (Henry Cecil) John, Baron Hunt (1910–1998)." *Oxford Dictionary of National Biography*. Oxford University Press, 2004 (online edition, May 2006).

———. *Summit: 150 Years of the Alpine Club*. London: HarperCollins, 2006.

Bannister, Dr. Roger. *First Four Minutes*. London: Putnam, 1955.

———. "Acute Anhidrotic Heat Exhaustion," *Lancet*, Vol. 274, 7098 (September 12, 1959), pp. 313–16.

———. "Athletics at Altitude," *New Scientist* (April 28, 1966).

Belding, H. S., R. C. Darling, D. R. Griffin, S. Robinson, E. S. Turrell. "Evaluation of Thermal Insulation Provided by Clothing," in *Clothing Test Methods*, L. H. Newburgh and A. M. Harris (eds.). Washington, DC: US National Research Council, 1945.

Berryman, Jack, and R. J. Park (eds.). *Sport and Exercise Science*. Chicago: University of Illinois Press, 1992.

Bishop, Barry C. "Wintering in the High Himalayas," *National Geographic*, Vol. 122, No. 4 (October 1963).

———. "How We Climbed Everest," *National Geographic*, Vol. 124 (November 5, 1963).

Black, D., and Sir J. Gray. "Sir Harold Percival Himsworth KCB (1905–1933)," *Biographical Memoirs of Fellows of the Royal Society*, Vol. 41 (November 1995), pp. 201–18.

Booth, C. "Sir Harold Himsworth," *Proceedings of the American Philosophical Society*, Vol. 141, No. 1 (March 1997), pp. 85–87.

———. "McMichael, Sir John (1904–1993)." *Oxford Dictionary of National Biography*. Oxford: Oxford University Press, 2004.

Booth, Dick. *The Impossible Hero: A Biography of Gordon "Puff Puff" Pirie*. London: Corsica Press, 1999.

Bordier, H. "Sur la mesure comparative de la conductibilité calarifique des tissus de l'organisme," *Arch Physiol* (Paris) 1898 (5) 10: 17–27.

Bourdillon, Jennifer. *Visit to the Sherpas*. London: Collins, 1956.

Bowman, W. E. *The Ascent of Rum Doodle*. London: Max Parrish and Co., Ltd., 1956.

Brailsford, Dennis. *British Sport: A Social History*. Cambridge: Lutterworth, 1992.

Breckenridge, J. R., and A. H. Woodcock. "Effects of Wind on Insulation of Arctic Clothing, Environmental Protection Section," Quartermaster Climatic Research Laboratory, Report 164 (1950).

Brereton, Henry L. *Gordonstoun: Ancient Estate and Modern School*. London: Chambers, 1968.

British Olympic Association. "Report of the Medical Research Project into Effects of Altitude in Mexico City in 1965," London (April 1966).

Bruce, Brigadier General, The Hon C. G. "Mount Everest," *Geographical Journal*, Vol. LVII.1 (January 1921).

———. "The Mount Everest Expedition of 1922," *Geographical Journal*, Vol. LX, No. 6 (December 1922), pp. 385–422.

———. *The Assault on Mount Everest 1922*. London: Edward Arnold, 1923.

Burton, Alan, and Otto G. Edholm. *Man in a Cold Environment*. London: Edward Arnold, 1955.

Cannon, P., and W. R. Keatinge. "The Metabolic Rate and Heat Loss of Fat and Thin Men in Heat Balance in Cold and Warm Water," *Journal of Physiology*, 154 (1960), pp. 329–44.

Capes, Geoff. *Big Shot*. London: Stanley Paul, 1981.

Cerretelli, P., and R. Margaria. "Maximum Oxygen Consumption at Altitude," *European Journal of Applied Physiology and Occupational Physiology*, 18 (1961), pp. 460–64.

———. "Work Capacity and Its Limiting Factors at High Altitude: Discussion," in *The Physiological Effects of High Altitude*, Weihe, W. H. (ed.). London: Pergamon Press, 1964, pp. 242–47.

Cervantes, J., and P. Karpovich. "Effect of Altitude on Athletic Performance," *Research Quarterly*, 35 (October 1964), Supplement, pp. 446–48.

Chrenko, F. A., and L. G. C. E. Pugh. "The Contribution of Solar Radiation to the Thermal Environment of Man in Antarctica," Proceedings of the Royal Society of London, Series B, Biological Sciences, Vol. 155, No. 959 (November 21, 1961), pp. 234–65.

Clark, R. P., B. J. Mullen, L. G. C. E. Pugh. "Skin Temperature during Running: A Study Using Infra-Red Colour Thermography," *Journal of Physiology*, 267 (1977), pp. 53–62.

Clark, R. P., B. J. Mullen, L. G. C. E. Pugh, and N. Toy. "Heat Losses from the Moving Limbs in Running: The Pendulum Effect," *Proceedings of the Physiological Society* (March 1974), pp. 22–23.

Clarkson, P. "Fuchs, Sir Vivian Ernest (1908–1999)." *Oxford Dictionary of National Biography*. Oxford: Oxford University Press, 2004.

Cranfield, Ingrid (ed.). *Inspiring Achievement: The Life and Work of John Hunt*. Cumbria, England: Institute for Outdoor Learning, 2002.

Dill, D. B. "Ten Men on a Mountain," in *Environmental Physiology: Aging, Heat and Altitude*, edited by Horvath, S. M., and H. K. Yousef. New York: Elsevier/North Holland, 1980.

Dodds, Klaus. "The Great Trek: New Zealand and the British/Commonwealth 1955–58 Trans-Antarctic Expedition," in *Journal of Imperial and Commonwealth History*, Vol. 33, No. 1 (January 2005), pp. 93–114.

Douglas, E. *Tenzing, Hero of Everest.* Washington, DC: National Geographic Society, 2003.

Duncan, K. S. "Our Aim—The Will to Win," *World Sports: The Official Magazine of the British Olympic Association,* London (May 1997), pp. 14–15.

Dutton, D. J. "Marples, (Alfred) Ernest, Baron Marples (1907–1978)." *Oxford Dictionary of National Biography.* Oxford University Press, 2004 (online edition, May 2006).

Edholm, Dr. O. G., and A. L. Bacharach (eds.). *The Physiology of Human Survival.* London and New York: Academic Press, 1965.

Engel, Claire. *History of Mountaineering in the Alps.* London: Allen & Unwin, 1948.

Evans, R. C. "The Cho Oyu Expedition, 1952," *Alpine Journal,* Vol. L1X, 286 (May 1953), pp. 9–18.

———. "The New Zealand Himalayan Expedition," *Geographical Journal,* Vol. CXXI, Part 2 (June 1955).

———. *Kangchenjunga, The Untrodden Peak.* London: Hodder & Stoughton, 1955.

Finch, G. I. "The Mount Everest Expedition of 1922: The Second High Climb," *Geographical Journal,* LX, No. 6 (December 1922), pp. 413–22.

———. "The Second Attempt," in Bruce (1923), pp. 227–61.

———. "Equipment for High Altitude Mountaineering with Special Reference to Climbing Mount Everest," *Geographical Journal,* LX1.3 (March 1923), pp. 194–207.

———. *The Making of a Mountaineer.* London: Arrowsmith, 1924 (reprinted with introductory memoir by Scott Russell, Bristol: Arrowsmith, 1988).

———. "Oxygen and Mount Everest," *Alpine Journal,* No. 51 (1939), pp. 89–90.

———. "Man at High Altitude," RS Friday evening discourse, June 6, 1952.

Fleming, Fergus. *Killing Dragons: The Conquest of the Alps.* London: Granta, 2000.

Fogg, G. E. *A History of Antarctic Science.* Cambridge: Cambridge University Press, 1992.

Fox, W. R. "Heat Stress and Athletics," *Ergonomics,* 3 (1960), pp. 307–13.

Frisancho, R. A. *Human Adaptation and Accommodation.* Ann Arbor: University of Michigan Press, 1993.

Gill, Michael. *Mountain Midsummer: Climbing in Four Continents.* London and Auckland: Hodder & Stoughton, 1969.

Gillman, P. "The English Said the Swiss Couldn't Do It; It Was War," *Sunday Times Magazine,* May 4, 2003.

Gillman, P., and L. Gillman. *The Wildest Dream.* Seattle: The Mountaineers, 2000.

Girouard, Mark. *The Return to Camelot.* New Haven and London: Yale University Press, 1981.

Glaser, E. M. "Immersion and Survival in Cold Water," *Nature,* Vol. 166 (December 23, 1950), p. 1068.

Glickman, E. L., E. Potkanowicz, and R. Otterstetter. "Pugh and Edholm's 'The Physiology of Channel Swimmers'—A Commentary," *Wilderness and Environmental Medicine,* 15 (2003), pp. 38–39.

Gray, J. "Bryan Harold Cabot Matthews, June 14, 1906–July 23, 1986," *Biographical Memoirs of Fellows of the Royal Society,* Vol. 35 (March 1990), pp. 265–79.

———. "Matthews, Sir Bryan Harold Cabot (1906–1986)." *Oxford Dictionary of National Biography.* Oxford: Oxford University Press, 2004.

Greene, Raymond, "Some Medical Aspects," in Ruttledge (1934 (1)), pp. 247–69.

———. "Observations on the Composition of Alveolar Air on Everest, 1933," *Journal of Physiology,* 82(4) (November 12, 1934), pp. 481–85.

———. "Scientific Research in the Region of Mount Everest," *Nature,* 144 (July 22, 1939), pp. 158–59.

———. *Moments of Being.* London: Heinemann, 1974.

Habeler, Peter. *Everest, Impossible Victory,* translated by David Heald. London: Arlington Books, 1979 (first published 1978).

Hall, J. F., Jr., and J. W. Polte. "Effect of Water Content and Compression on Clothing Insulation," *Journal of Applied Physiology,* 8.539 (1956).

Hanessian, J. "National Interests in Antarctica," in Hatherton (1965), pp. 3–51.

Hansen, Peter. "Albert Smith, the Alpine Club, and the Invention of Mountaineering in Mid-Victorian Britain," *Journal of British Studies*, 34 (July 1995), pp. 300–24.

———. "Partners: Guides and Sherpas in the Alps and Himalayas, 1850s–1950s," in Elsner, Jas, and Joan Pau Rubies (eds.), *Voyages and Visions: Towards a Cultural History of Travel*. London: Reaktion Books, 1999.

———. "Coronation Everest: The Empire and Commonwealth in the 'Second Elizabethan Age,'" in Ward, Stuart (ed.), *British Culture and the End of Empire*. Manchester: Manchester University Press, 2001.

Hardie, N. *On My Own Two Feet: The Life of a Mountaineer*. Christchurch, New Zealand: Canterbury University Press, 2006.

Hardy, J. D., and G. F. Soderstrom. "Heat loss from the human body and peripheral blood flow at temperatures of 22°C–35°C," *Journal of Nutrition* 16 (5) (1938), p. 494.

Harrison, J. "Makalu," *New Zealand Alpine Journal* (1961), pp. 41–49.

Hatfield, H. S., and L. G. C. E. Pugh. "Thermal Conductivity of Human Fat and Muscle," *Nature* 168 (November 24, 1951), pp. 918–19.

Hatherton, Trevor (ed.) *Antarctica*. Reed A.H. and A.W., Auckland, New Zealand 1965

Heggie, Vanessa. "'Only the British Appear to be Making a Fuss': The Science of Success and the Myth of Amateurism at the Mexico Olympics," *Sport in History*, Vol. 28.2 (2008), pp. 213–35.

Hemmleb, J., L. Johnson, and E. Simonson. *Ghosts of Everest: The Authorised Story of the Search for Mallory and Irving*. London: Macmillan, 1999.

Hillary, Sir Edmund. In *Life* (July 13, 1953), pp. 124–38.

———. *High Adventure*. London: Hodder & Stoughton, 1955 (references to page numbers in Bloomsbury Paperback reissue of 2003).

———. *No Latitude for Error*. London: Hodder & Stoughton, 1961.

———. *Nothing Venture, Nothing Win*. London: Hodder & Stoughton, 1975.

———. *View from the Summit*. London: Doubleday, 1999.

Hillary, Sir E., and D. Doig. *High in the Thin Cold Air*. London: Hodder & Stoughton, 1963 (first published in 1962 by Field Enterprises Educational Corporation).

Himsworth, Harold. "Society and the Advancement of Natural Knowledge," *British Medical Journal*, Vol. II (December 15, 1962), pp. 1557–63.

——. *The Development and Organisation of Scientific Knowledge*. London: Heinemann, 1970.

——. "Harington, Sir Charles Robert (1897–1972)," rev. *Oxford Dictionary of National Biography*. Oxford: Oxford University Press, 2004.

Hingston, Major R. W. G. "Physiological Difficulties in the Ascent of Mount Everest," *Geographical Journal*, Vol. LXV.1 (January 1925), pp. 4–23.

Hinks, A. R. "The Mount Everest Expedition," *Geographical Journal*, Vol. LIX, No. 5 (May 1922), pp. 379–83.

Hornbein, Thomas F. *Everest: The West Ridge*. San Francisco: The Sierra Club, 1965.

Hunt, Sir John H. *Ascent of Everest*. London: Hodder & Stoughton, 1953.

Hunt, John H. (ed.). *Accident Prevention and Life Saving: Papers Given at a Convention Held at the College of Surgeons of England, May 1963*. London: Livingstone, 1965.

Hunt, Sir J. *Life is Meeting*. London: Hodder & Stoughton, 1978.

——. "Letters from Everest," in *Alpine Journal*, Vol. 98, No. 342 (1993), pp. 10–21.

Huntford, Roland. *The Race to the South Pole*. London: Hodder & Stoughton, 1979.

Hyman, Dorothy. *Sprint to Fame*. London: Stanley Paul, 1964.

International Symposium on Exercise and Sports Physiology, Netaji Subhas National Institute of Sports, Patiala, India (October 28–30, 1974).

Isserman, M., and S. Weaver. *Fallen Giants*. New Haven and London: Yale University Press, 2008.

Izzard, Ralph. *The Abominable Snowman Adventure*. London: Hodder & Stoughton, 1955.

——. *The Innocent on Everest*. London: Hodder & Stoughton, 1955.

Johnston, Alexa. *Sir Edmund Hillary: An Extraordinary Life*. Auckland, New Zealand: Penguin/Viking, 2005.

Jones, Max. *The Last Great Quest: Captain Scott's Antarctic Sacrifice*. Oxford: Oxford University Press, 2003.

Justin Evans, H. *Service to Sport: The Story of the CCPR, 1935–1972*. London: Pelham Books, 1974.

Karpovich, P. V., and C. Hale. "Effect of Warming Up upon Physical Performance," *Journal of the American Medical Association (JAMA)*, vol. 162 (1956), pp. 1117–19.

Keatinge, W. R. "Death after Shipwreck," *Lancet*, 2 (1965), pp. 1537–41.

———. *Survival in Cold Water: The Physiology and Treatment of Immersion Hypothermia and of Drowning*. London: Blackwell Scientific Publications, 1969 (reprinted version, 1978).

Kellas, A. M. "A Consideration of the Possibility of Ascending the Loftier Himalaya," *Geographical Journal*, 49 (1917), pp. 26–47.

———. "A Consideration of the Possibility of Ascending Mount Everest," with an introduction by John West, *High Altitude Medicine and Biology*, 2(3) (September 1, 2001), pp. 427–29.

Kinloch, A. J. "Norman Adrian De Bruyne, November 8, 1904–March 7, 1997," *Biographical Memoirs of Fellows of the Royal Society*, Vol. 46 (November 2000), pp. 126–43.

Kirkam, N. F. "Mountain Accidents and Mountain Rescue in Great Britain," *BMJ*, 1 (1966), pp. 162–64.

Krotee, M. L. "An Organisational Analysis of the International Olympic Committee," chapter 8 in Segrave and Chu (1988), pp. 113–48.

Kurz, Marcel. "Mount Everest: A Century of History," in Kurz (ed.), *The Mountain World*, London: Allen & Unwin, 1953, pp. 17–34.

Landsborough Thomson, A. *Half a Century of Medical Research*. London: Medical Research Council, 1987.

Lloyd, Peter. "Oxygen on Mount Everest, 1938," *Alpine Journal*, No. 51 (1939), pp. 85–89.

Longland, Jack. "Between the Wars: 1919–1939," *Alpine Journal*, Vol. 62, 295 (1957), pp. 83–97.

Longstaff, T. G. "Some Aspects of the Everest Problem," *Alpine Journal*, Vol. 35, 226/227 (1923), pp. 57–68.

———. "Lessons from the Mount Everest Expedition of 1933," *Alpine Journal*, Vol. 46.248/249 (1934), pp. 102–10.

Lovesey, Peter. *The Official Centenary History of the Amateur Athletics Association*. Enfield and Middlesex: Guinness Superlatives Ltd., 1979 (reprinted 1980).

Lowe, George. *Because It Is There*. London: Cassell, 1959.

Lunn, Arnold. *Switzerland and the English*. London: Eyre and Spottiswoode, 1944.

———. *A Century of British Mountaineering*. London: Allen & Unwin, 1957.

Lunn, Peter. "Andrew Irvine's Missing Letters from Everest," *Kandahar Review*, London (2003), pp. 71–74.

Mackenzie, M. *In the Footsteps of Mallory and Irvine*. London: John Murray, 2009.

Macnicol, J. "Eugenics, Medicine and Mental Deficiency: An Introduction," *Oxford Review of Education*, Vol. 9, No. 3 (1983).

Mallory, G. "The First High Climb," in Bruce, "The Assault on Mount Everest 1922," *Geographical Journal*, Vol. LX, No. 6 (December 1922), pp. 400–12.

———. "The Third Attempt," in Bruce, *The Assault on Mount Everest 1922*. London: Edward Arnold, 1923, pp. 273–95.

Mangan, J. A. *Athleticism in the Victorian and Edwardian Public School*. Cambridge: Press Syndicate of the University of Cambridge, 1981.

———. (ed.). *A Sport-Loving Society: Victorian and Edwardian Middle-Class England at Play*. London: Routledge, 2006.

Margaria, R. "Capacity and Power of the Energy Processes in Muscle Activity: Their Practical Relevance in Athletics," *European Journal of Applied Physiology*, 25(4) (December 1968), pp. 352–60.

Mason, Kenneth. *Abode of Snow*. London: Diadem Books, 1987.

Mason, Tony (ed.). *Sport in Britain: A Social History*. Cambridge: Cambridge University Press, 1989.

Medawar, Sir Peter. *The Art of the Soluble*. Oxford: Oxford University Press, 1986 (paperback edition, 1988).

———. *Memoir of a Thinking Radish*. Oxford: Oxford University Press, 1986 (paperback edition, 1988).

Menier, D. R., and L. G. C. E. Pugh. "Oxygen Intake during Walking and Running," *Journal of Physiology*, 197 (1968), pp. 717–21.

Messner, Reinhold. *Everest: Expedition to the Ultimate*. Munich: MBLV Verlagsgessellschaft MbH, 1978 (English translation by Salkeld, Audrey (1979); London: Kaye and Ward, 1979).

Milledge, J. S. "The Silver Hut Expedition," in Sutton, John R., Norman L. Jones, and Charles Houston (eds.), *Hypoxia: Man at Altitude*, New York: Thieme Stratton Inc, 1982.

————. "Dr. Griffith CE Pugh, Field Physiologist," in *Hypoxia and Molecular Medicine*, edited by Sutton, Houston and Coates, 1993, pp. 171–75.

————. "Lessons from History: The Silver Hut Expedition—A Commentary 40 Years On," *Wilderness and Environmental Medicine*, 13 (2002), pp. 55–56.

————. "Altitude Medicine and Physiology Including Heat and Cold: A Review," *Travel Medicine and Infectious Disease*, 4, Elsevier (2006), pp. 223–37.

Mitchison, N. A. "Peter Brian Medawar, February 28, 1915–October 2, 1987," *Biographical Memoirs of the Fellows of the Royal Society*, Vol. 35 (March 1990), pp. 282–301.

Molnar, G. W. "Survival of Hypothermia by Men Immersed in the Ocean," *Journal of the American Physiological Association*, Vol. 131 (1942), pp. 1046–50.

Morris, James. *Coronation Everest*. London: Faber & Faber, 1958.

Morris, J. N. *Uses of Epidemiology*. Edinburgh: Livingstone, 1957.

Morris, Peter J. "Porritt, Arthur Espie, Baron Porritt (1900–1994)," *Oxford Dictionary of National Biography*, Oxford: Oxford University Press, 2004.

Mumm, A. L. *Alpine Club Register, 1857–1890*, 3 Vols. London: 1923–28.

Murray, W. H. *The Story of Everest*. London: J. M. Dent, 1953.

————. *The Evidence of Things Not Seen*. London: Baton Wicks, 2002.

Newburgh, L. H., and M. Harris (eds.). *Clothing Test Methods*. Washington, DC: National Research Council, Pub. No. 390, 1945.

Norton, E. F. *The Fight for Everest 1924*. London: Edward Arnold, 1925 (page numbers from reprint, Pilgrim's Publishing, 2002).

———. "The Problem of Mount Everest," *Alpine Journal*, Vol. XXXVII, No. 230 (May 1925a), pp. 1–38 (read before the Alpine Club, December 15, 1924).

Noyce, Wilfred. *South Col: One Man's Personal Adventure on Everest*. London: Heinemann, 1954.

Odell, N. E. "High Altitude and Oxygen," *Himalayan Journal*, Vol. 4 (1932), pp. 91–95.

Park, Roberta J. "Athletes and Their Training in Britain and America, 1800–1914," in *Sport and Exercise Science*, Berryman, Jack, and R. J. Park (eds.). Chicago: University of Illinois Press, 1992.

Parsons, M., and M. Rose. *Invisible on Everest*. Philadelphia: Old City Publishing, 2003.

Paton, Bruce C. "Cold Casualties and Conquests: The Effects of Cold on Warfare," chapter 10 in Pandolf and Kent, *Medical Aspects of Harsh Environments*, Textbooks of Military Medicine, Vol. 1, Washington, DC: Borden Institute, 2001, pp. 313–39.

Perrin, Jim. Introduction to Shipton, Eric, *The Six Mountain Travel Books*, London: Diadem Books, 1985.

Pirie, Gordon. *Running Wild*. London: W. H. Allen, 1961.

Porter, D., and S. Wagg. "Introduction," *Sport in History*, 26–3 (2006), pp. 345–51 (special issue on amateurism in sports).

Priestley, R. *South: The Race to the Pole*. Cambridge: Cambridge University Press, 2000.

Pugh, Lewis Griffith Cresswell Evans. *British Himalayan Expedition to Cho Oyu, 1952*, A Report to the Medical Research Council (unpublished manuscript).

———. "Technique Employed for Measuring Respiratory Exchanges on Mount Everest," *Journal of Physiology*, 123 (1953), pp. 25–26.

———. "Himalayan Rations with Special Reference to the 1953 Everest Expedition," *Proceedings of the Nutrition Society*, 13 (1954a), pp. 60–69.

———. "Food Consumption and Energy Balance at Various Altitudes," Swiss Foundation for Alpine Research, 1 (1954b), pp. 75–80.

———. "Scientific Aspects of the Expedition to Mount Everest, 1953," *Geographical Journal*, Vol. CXX, Part 2 (June 1954c).

———. "The Effects of Oxygen on Acclimatised Men at High Altitude," *Proceedings of the Royal Society*, B 143 (1954d), pp. 14–17.

———. "Haemoglobin Levels on the British Himalayan Expedition to Cho Oyu in 1952 and Everest in 1953," *Journal of Physiology*, 126 (1954e), pp. 38–39.

———. "Oxygen on Everest," *Middlesex Hospital Journal*, 54 (1954f), pp. 4–6.

———. "Notes on Temperatures and Snow Conditions in the Everest Region in Spring 1952 and 1953," *British Journal of Glaciology*, Vol. 2, No. 15 (1954g), pp. 363–65.

———. "Resting Ventilation and Alveolar Air on Mount Everest: With Remarks on the Relation of Barometric Pressure to Mountains," *Journal of Physiology*, 135 (1957), pp. 590–610.

———. "Physiological Commentary" in *The British Ski Year Book* (ed., Sir Arnold Lunn), Vol. XVIII (1958–59), pp. 241–44.

———. "Muscular Exercise on Mount Everest," *Journal of Physiology*, 141 (1958), pp. 233–61.

———. "Carbon Monoxide Content of the Blood and Other Observations on Weddell Seals," *Nature*, Vol. 183, No. 4654 (January 10, 1959a) pp. 74–76.

———. "Carbon Monoxide Hazard in Antarctica," *BMJ* (January 24, 1959b), pp. 192–96.

———. "Science in the Himalaya," *Nature*, Vol. 191, No. 4787 (July 29, 1961), pp. 429–31.

———. "Physiological and Medical Aspects of the Himalayan Scientific and Mountaineering Expedition, 1960–61," *BMJ* (September 8, 1962a), pp. 621–27.

———. "Himalayan Scientific and Mountaineering Expedition, 1960/61: The Scientific Programme," *The Geographical Journal*, Vol. 128, No. 4 (December 1962c), pp. 447–56.

———. "Tolerance to Extreme Cold in a Nepalese Pilgrim," *Journal of Applied Physiology*, Vol. 18 (1963), pp. 1234–38.

———. "Deaths from Exposure on Four Inns Walking Competition, March 14–15, 1964: Report to Medical Commission on Accident Prevention," *Lancet*, 13 (May 30, 1964a), pp. 1210–12.

————. "Man at High Altitude," chapter 3 in *The Scientific Basis of Medicine Annual Reviews* (1964b), pp. 32–54.

————. "Altitude and Athletic Performance," *Nature*, 207.5004 (September 25, 1965a), pp. 1397–98.

————. "Effect of Altitude on Athletic Performance," *Kandahar Review*, Vol. V, No. 1 (October 1965b), pp. 63–65.

————. "High Altitudes," chapter 5 in Edholm, Dr. O. G., and A. L. Bacharach (eds.), *The Physiology of Human Survival*, London and New York: Academic Press, 1965c.

————. "Accidental Hypothermia in Walkers, Climbers and Campers: Report to the Commission on Accident Prevention," *BMJ*, 1 (January 15, 1966a), pp. 123–29.

————. "Clothing Insulation and Accidental Hypothermia in Youth," *Nature*, Vol. 5030 (March 26, 1966b), pp. 1281–85.

————. "Athletes at Altitude," *Journal of Physiology*, 192 (1967a), pp. 619–46.

————. "Cold, Stress and Muscular Exercise, with Special Reference to Accidental Hypothermia," *BMJ*, 2 (1967c), pp. 333–37.

————. "Isafjordur Trawler Disaster: Medical Aspects," *BMJ*, 1 (March 30, 1968), pp. 826–29.

————. "Thermal, Metabolic, Blood, and Circulatory Adjustments in Prolonged Outdoor Exercise," *BMJ*, 2 (June 14, 1969a), pp. 657–62.

————. "Athletes at Altitude: Lessons of the 1968 Olympic Games," *Transactions of the Medical Society of London*, 85 (1969b), pp. 76–83.

————. "Man at High Altitude," *Journal of the Royal College of Physicians*, 3 (1969c), pp. 385–97.

————. "Oxygen Intake in Track and Treadmill Running with Observations on the Effect of Air Resistance," *Journal of Physiology*, 207 (1970), pp. 823–25.

————. "The Influence of Wind Resistance in Running and Walking and the Mechanical Efficiency of Work against Horizontal or Vertical Forces," *Journal of Physiology*, 213 (1971), pp. 255–76.

————. "The Logistics of the Polar Journeys of Scott, Shackleton and Amundsen," *Proceedings of the Royal Society of Medicine*, Vol. 65 (January 1972), pp. 42–47.

———. "The Gooseflesh Syndrome (Acute Anhidrotic Heat Exhaustion) in Long Distance Runners," *British Journal of Physical Education* (March 1972a).

———. "Fitness Tests on Skiers Training for the British Women's Alpine Ski Team," *Kandahar Review* (1972b), pp. 39–47.

———. "The Oxygen Intake and Energy Cost of Walking Before and After Unilateral Hip Replacement, with Some Observations on the Use of Crutches," *Journal of Joint and Bone Surgery*, British Volume 55(4) (November 1973), pp. 742–45.

———. "The Relation of Oxygen Intake and Speed in Competition Cycling and Comparative Observations on the Bicycle Ergometer," *Journal of Physiology*, 241 (1974a), pp. 795–808.

———. "Air Resistance in Sport, with a Note on the Effect of Altitude," *International Symposium on Exercise and Sports Physiology*, Netaji Subhas National Institute of Sports, Patiala, India (October 28–30, 1974b).

———. "Mount Cho Oyu, 1952, and Mount Everest, 1953," in Sutton, J. R., N. L. Jones, and C. S. Houston (eds.), *Hypoxia: Man at High Altitude*, New York: Thieme-Stratton, 1982.

———. "Everest 1953 Reminiscences," *Alpine Journal*, Vol. 98, No. 342 (1993).

Pugh, L. G. C. E., et al. *Mountain Warfare Training Centre Ski Wing: Final Report*, 6913/PME/.1996.D/200.6.43 (Winter 1942–43).

Pugh, L. G. C. E., and F. A. Chrenko. "Observations on the Effects of Solar Radiation Inside Tents in Antarctica," *Annals of Occupational Hygiene*, Vol. 5 (1962b), pp. 1–5.

Pugh, L. G. C. E., J. L. Corbett, and R. H. Johnson. "Rectal Temperatures, Weight Losses and Sweat Rates in Marathon Running," *Journal of Applied Physiology*, Vol. 23, No. 3 (September 1967b), pp. 347–532.

Pugh, L. G. C. E., and O. G. Edholm. "The Physiology of Channel Swimmers," *Lancet* (October 8, 1955), pp. 761–69.

Pugh, L. G. C. E., and M. P. Ward. "Some Effects of High Altitude on Man," *Lancet* (December 1, 1956), pp. 1115–21.

Rennie, Drummond. "The Incidence, Importance and Prophylaxis of Acute Mountain Sickness," *Lancet* (November 1976), pp. 1149–55.

Riddell, James. *Dog in the Snow*. London: Michael Joseph, 1957.

Riddell, W. J., "In Memoriam," Obituary for Griffith Pugh, *Alpine Journal*, Vol. 100.344 (1995).

Ring, Jim. *How the English Made the Alps*. London: John Murray, 2000.

Riordan, James. "Amateurism, Sport and the Left: Amateurism for All Versus Amateur Elitism," *Sport in History*, 26:3 (2006), pp. 468–83.

Robertson, D. *Mallory*. London: Faber & Faber, 1969.

Robertson, John M. (ed.). *Characteristics of Men, Manners and Opinions* (1711). Indianapolis and New York: Bobbs-Merrill, 1964.

Roche, André. "The Swiss Everest Expedition: Spring 1952," *Alpine Journal*, Vol. LIX.286 (May 1953), pp. 1–8.

Rockett, Sam. *It's Cold in the Channel*. London: Hutchinson, 1956.

Rodway, George. *George Ingle Finch's The Struggle for Everest*. Herefordshire: Carreg, 2008.

Rose, Hilary, and Steven Rose. *Science and Society*. London: Allen Lane, The Penguin Press, 1969.

Rothschild Report: "The Organisation and Management of Government Research and Development," in *Cabinet Office: A Framework for Government Research and Development*. London: HMSO, November 1971.

Roxburgh, H. L. "Oxygen Equipment for Climbing Mount Everest," *Geographical Journal*, 109 (1947), pp. 207–16.

Royal College of Surgeons of England. *Working Party on Accident Prevention and Life Saving*, 1961–63.

Rubin, G. R. "Cassel, Sir Felix Maximilian Schoenbrunn, First Baronet (1869–1953)." *Oxford Dictionary of National Biography*, Oxford: Oxford University Press (September 2004).

Ruskin, John. *The Works of John Ruskin* (Library Edition, edited by Cook and Wedderburn). London: George Allen, 1903.

Ruttledge, Hugh. "The Mount Everest Expedition, 1933," *Alpine Journal*, Vol. 45 (1933).

———. "The Mount Everest Expedition, 1933," *Geographical Journal*, Vol. LXXXIII (January 1934a).

———. *Everest 1933*. London: Hodder & Stoughton, 1934.

———. *Everest: The Unfinished Adventure*. London: Hodder & Stoughton, 1937.

Segrave, Jeffrey O., and Donald Chu (eds.). *The Olympic Games in Transition*. Champaign, IL: Human Kinetics Books, 1988.

Severinghaus, John W. "Sightings," *High Altitude Medicine & Biology*, 5(4) (Winter 2004), pp. 389–94.

Shearman, Sir M. *Athletics and Football*. London: Longmans, Green and Co., 1887.

Shipton, Eric. "Expedition to Cho Oyu: Mr. Shipton's Himalayan Objective," *The Times* (April 8, 1952).

———. "Approach to the Himalayas, British Party's Progress, April 17th," *The Times* (May 10, 1952).

———. "The Expedition to Cho Oyu," *Geographical Journal*, Vol. CXIX.2 (June 2, 1953), pp. 129–39.

———. *That Untravelled World*. London: Hodder & Stoughton, 1969.

Smith, Patrick, "International Olympic Committee Meets," BBC Dispatch from Rome, N.277 (April 21, 1966).

Smythe, F. S. *Kamet Conquered*. London: Gollancz, 1933.

———. "Everest: The Final Problem," published as a letter to the editor, *Alpine Journal*, Vol. 46, 248/249 (1934), pp. 442–46.

———. *British Mountaineers*. London: Collins, 1942.

Snow, C. P. "The Two Cultures," *New Statesman and Nation* (October 6, 1956), pp. 413–14.

———. *The Two Cultures and the Scientific Revolution* (reprint with an introduction by Stefan Collini, Cambridge University Press, 1998).

Springhall, J. *Youth, Empire and Society: British Youth Movements 1883–1940*. Beckenham: Croom Helm, 1977.

Steele, P. *Eric Shipton: Everest and Beyond*. London: Constable, 1998.

Stephen, L. *Some Early Impressions*. London: Hogarth Press, 1924.

Stewart, W. A. C. *Progressives and Radicals in English Education, 1750–1970*. London: Macmillan, 1972.

Stobart, Tom. *Adventurer's Eye: Autobiography of the Everest Film Man*. London: Odhams Press, 1958.

Strachey, Lytton. *Eminent Victorians*. London: Chatto and Windus, 1918.

Summers, Julie. *Fearless on Everest*. London: Weidenfeld & Nicolson, 2000 (paperback edition, Phoenix, 2001).

Sutherland, Andrew. "Why are So Many People Dying On Everest?" *BMJ*, 333:452 (August 26, 2006).

Taylor, D. J. *On the Corinthian Spirit: The Decline in Amateurism in Sport.* London: Yellow Jersey Press, 2006.

Temple, Robert. "Sir Peter Medawar," *New Scientist*, No. 1405 (April 12, 1984), pp. 14–20.

Thane, P. "Cassel, Sir Ernest Joseph (1852–1921)." *Oxford Dictionary of National Biography*, Oxford: Oxford University Press (September 2004).

Tilman, H. W. "The Mount Everest Expedition of 1938," *Geographical Journal*, Vol. XCII.6 (December 1938), pp. 480–98.

———. *Mount Everest 1938.* Cambridge: Cambridge University Press, 1948.

———. "The Annapurna Himal and the South Side of Everest," *Alpine Journal*, Vol. 28 (May 1951).

———. "Seventh Time Lucky," *Time and Tide* (November 14, 1953).

Ullman, J. R. *Man of Everest: The Autobiography of Tenzing* (told to James Ramsay Ullman). London: Harrap, 1955.

Unna, P. J. "The Oxygen Equipment of the 1922 Everest Expedition," *Alpine Journal*, 34 (1921–22), pp. 235–50.

Unsworth, Walt. *Everest.* London: Baton Wicks, 1981 (revised edition, 2000).

Ure, John. "Kirwan, Sir (Archibald) Laurence Patrick (1907–1999)." *Oxford Dictionary of National Biography*, Oxford: Oxford University Press, 2004.

Venables, Stephen. "Everest Forty-Five Years On," *Saga* (August 1998), pp. 46–48.

Wagg, Stephen. "'Base Mechanic Arms'?, British Rowing, Some Ducks and the Shifting Politics of Amateurism," *Sport in History*, Vol. 26, No. 3 (December 2006), pp. 520–39.

Wakefield, A. E. "The Health of the Everest Expeditions," *Alpine Journal*, Vol. 46, 248–9 (1934), pp. 449–51.

Wallechinsky, David. *The Complete Book of the Olympics.* London: Aurum Press, 2000.

Ward, Michael. *In This Short Span.* London: Gollancz, 1972.

———. "Thermal Balance and Its Regulation," chapter 23 in Ward, Milledge, and West, *High Altitude Medicine and Physiology*, Philadelphia: University of Pennsylvania Press, 1987.

———. "Everest 1951: The Footprints Attributed to the Yeti—Myth and Reality," *Wilderness and Environmental Medicine*, 8 (1997), pp. 29–32.

———. *Everest: A Thousand Years of Exploration.* Glasgow: Ernest Press, 2003.

Ward, Michael, J. S. Milledge, and J. B. West. *High Altitude Medicine and Biology.* Philadelphia: University of Pennsylvania Press, 1989.

Warren, Dr. C. B. "The Medical and Physiological Aspects of the Mount Everest Expeditions," *Geographical Journal*, Vol. XC, No. 2 (August 1937).

———. "Physiology," in Ruttledge (1937), pp. 218–45.

———. "Mount Everest in 1938," *St. Bartholomew's Hospital Journal* (February 1939a).

———. "Mountain Sickness and the Physiological Problems of High Altitude Mountaineering," *Alpine Journal*, Vol. 51, No. 259 (November 1939b), pp. 271–83.

Washburn, Bradford. "The Location of Camp IX," *Alpine Journal*, 108 (2003), pp. 20–21.

Wedell, G. "Hahn, Kurt Matthias Robert Martin (1886–1974)," *Oxford Dictionary of National Biography*, Oxford: Oxford University Press (September 2004).

West, John B. *Everest: The Testing Place.* New York: McGraw-Hill, 1985.

———. "Alexander M. Kellas and the Physiological Challenge of Mt. Everest," *Journal of Applied Physiology*, Vol. 6387, Issue 1 (1987), pp. 3–11.

———. "The Silver Hut Expedition, High-Altitude Field Expeditions, and Low Pressure Chamber Simulations," chapter 19 in Sutton, John, Charles Houston, and Geoffrey Coates (eds.), "Hypoxia and Molecular Medicine: Proceedings of the 8th International Hypoxia Symposium held at Lake Louise, Canada, February 9–13, 1993."

———. "Prediction of Barometric Pressures at High Altitudes with the Use of Model Atmospheres," *Journal of Applied Physiology*, 81:1850–1854 (1996).

———. *High Life: A History of High Altitude Physiology and Medicine.* New York: American Physiological Society, OUP, 1998.

———. "Failure on Everest: The Oxygen Equipment of the 1952 Swiss Everest Expedition," *High Altitude Medicine and Biology*, Vol. 4, No. 1 (Spring 2003), pp. 39–43.

———. "George I. Finch and His Pioneering Use of Oxygen for Climbing at Extreme Altitudes," *Journal of Applied Physiology*, 94(5) (May 1, 2003), pp. 1702–13.

———. "Georges Dreyer (1873–1934) and a Forgotten Episode of Respiratory Physiology at Oxford," *Journal of Medical Biography*, 14 (3) (2006), pp. 140–49.

Wilber, Randall L. *Altitude Training and Athletic Performance.* Champaign, IL: Human Kinetics, 2004.

Wilson, Claude. "Valedictory Address," *Alpine Journal*, Vol. 44, No. 244/245 (1932), p. 12.

Windsor, J., and G. Rodway. "English Air: The Story of the 1922 Mt. Everest Oxygen Apparatus," *Wilderness and Environmental Medicine*, 20 (2009), pp. 83–88.

Woodgate, W. *Boating.* London: Longman, Green and Co., 1889.

Wrynn, Alison M. "'A Debt Was Paid Off in Tears': Science, IOC Politics and the Debate about High Altitude in the 1968 Mexico Olympics," *International Journal of the History of Sport*, Vol. 23, No. 7 (November 2006), pp. 1152–72.

Wyss-Dunant, Eduard. "The First Swiss Expedition to Mount Everest, 1952," *Geographical Journal*, Vol. CXIX (September 3, 1953).

Young, David. *The Olympic Myth of Greek Amateur Athletics.* Chicago: Ares, 1984.

Young, Geoffrey Winthrop. *Mountain Craft*, 2nd edition. London: Methuen, 1921 (7th edition, 1949, first published 1920).

———. "Club and Climbers 1880–1900," in *Alpine Centenary, 1857–1957, Alpine Journal*, Vol. 66, No. 295 (November 1957), pp. 52–61.

ACKNOWLEDGMENTS

John Hunt hoped that the conquest of Everest would inspire people all over the world to find Everest quests of their own. Writing this book has seemed like my own personal Everest quest. When I started, I felt completely overwhelmed and bewildered by the size of the task. Without the help, encouragement, and sheer human kindness shown to me by a huge array of friendly people, I would not have been able to do it. I want to convey my grateful thanks to all those people.

Throughout the researching and writing of this book I have been lucky enough to be able to seek the help and advice of a group of my father's former colleagues, some of whom have sadly since died. For their huge contribution, and for much more, I owe heartfelt thanks to Professor John West and his wife, Penny; Dr. Jim Milledge and his wife, Pat; the late Dr. Michael Ward and his wife, Jane; the late Professor Richard Edwards and his wife, Eleri; Norman and Enid Hardie; Martin Hyman; Mike Gill; Dr. Mike Turner; Tim Johnston; Dr. David Jones; Professor Craig Sharp; Professor Raymond Clark; Mervyn de Calcina-Goff; John Brotherhood; the late Professor Sukhamay Lahiri and his wife, Krishna; Professor Bruce Paton; and Professor Rainer Goldsmith. They shared their memories of Griffith with me, helped to steer me toward a basic understanding of some of his main scientific achievements, patiently answered my layman's questions about physiology, climbing, and athletics, opened doors, and generally provided unfailing encouragement and support. They were also kind enough to give up their time to read and comment on draft chapters at various stages of their evolution. However, I hasten to add that the opinions and conclusions expressed in the book, as well as any mistakes that, despite my best efforts, will inevitably have made their way into the text, are all entirely my own.

I also owe a big debt of gratitude to Colonel James Adam and his wife, Lucy; Hans Amstutz; Tony Asthill; the late Daphne Baker; the late George Band and his wife, Susan; Sir Roger Bannister; Clara Barell; Joyce Beacon; Felix Beardmore-Gray of Horris Hill School; Irene Beardsley; Lila Bishop; Jennifer Bourdillon; the late Juliet Browne; Hillary Buzzard; the late Ione Cassel; Tim Cassel; Lord and Lady Chorley; Wing Commander John Claydon; Liz and Sarah Clifton; Mick Conefrey; the late Michael Corfield; Dr.

John Cotes; Tony and Lynne Crisp; Leslie Dandy; Geoff and Jackie David-son; Professor Mervyn Davies and his wife, Jackie; Colonel Henry Day; the late Ann Veronica Dodkins; Diana Eden; Patrick Fagan; Dr. Ruedi Fassbind and his wife, Jacqueline; Ivor and Ann Faulconer; Duncan Geddes; Maria Goldberger; Oliver Greene; Alf Gregory; Teddy Harding; Luli Harvey; Dicon Hesketh-Prichard; Mary Hess; the late Dr. Heylings and his grandson, Johnny; the late Sir Edmund Hillary and Lady Hillary; Bodil Hinterer; Tom Hornbein; Dulcibel Jenkins; David Jones; the late Professor W. R. Keatinge; Alexandre Koutaissoff; Eve Lee; Diana Lees Jones; Professor Ian Little; Dr. Brian Lloyd; George Lowe; Peter Lunn; Chloe MacCarthy; Maureen McK-enna; Jürg Marmet; Johanna Merz; Jan Morris; Sandy Munro; Joy Neale; Gerry North; Katharina Odermatt; Victoria and John Phillips; Edward Posey; June Posey; George Pownall; George Rodway; the late Joan Royle; Bill Ruthven of the Mount Everest Foundation; the late Belinda Ryan; Gina Sopwith; Bella Spurrier; the late Lady Sara Stephens; Anna Swan; Alan Tuff-nell; Bruce Tulloh; Robert Underwood; Dayle Vargus of Harrow School; the late Michael Westmacott; Professor Edward Williams; Professor Heinz Wolff; Sheila Wright; the late Charles Wylie; and Professor Archie Young.

Special thanks to Dame Denise Evans, widow of Charles Evans, for let-ting me read Charles's private diaries of the Cho Oyu and Everest expedi-tions; Jane Ward, for giving me access to her husband's unpublished Everest Diary and his correspondence with my father and for much helpful advice; Peter Gillman, for sharing information and generously lending me his taped interview with my father; and to Ray Clarke, Jim Milledge, and Mervyn Goff, for giving me an invaluable copy of their video interview of my father. Thanks also to Vanessa Heggie for showing me her article on the Olympic movement before it was published, and directing me to the British Olympic Association archive; to Geraldine Thomas and Tessa Morgan, for advice on matters psychological; to Rich Brown, for help with the photos; to Johanna Merz, for showing me correspondence between herself and John Hunt; to Peter Steele, for allowing me access to his papers at the Alpine Club; and to Annabel Nichol and Mike Grocott, for allowing me access to symposia on high-altitude medicine and physiology.

I would also like to thank the staff of the archives and libraries I have used for my research, especially Margaret Ecclestone; Glyn Hughes; Yvonne

Sibbold; Peter Rowland and Tadeusz Hudowski at the Alpine Club; Sarah Strong, Joy Wheeler, Eugene Rae, Janet Turner, Julie Carrington, and Jamie Owen at the Royal Geographical Society; the staff of the British Library; Amy Terriere and her colleagues at the British Olympic Association archives; Bruce Ralston of Auckland Museum, New Zealand; the staff of the University of Birmingham Special Collections; Rosa Parker and Thelma Kingsley at the Medical Research Council; the BBC Film Archive; Frank Norman and colleagues at the library and archive of the National Institute for Medical Research; the staff of the Imperial War Museum; Lynda Claassen and Steve Coy and their colleagues at the Mandeville Special Collections Library in San Diego; staff at the Royal Society Archive and the National Archives at Kew; the Wellcome library and archive; and Elizabeth Hussey, keeper of the British Ski Club archives.

If it hadn't been for my family and the selfless support of my friends, especially Airdre Taylor, Nell Smith, and Mary Green, who have patiently counseled, inspired, listened, and advised; read, reread, and edited drafts; and encouraged and indulged my obsession for the last eight years, I would not have been able to write the book.

James, my husband, has been my beloved mainstay throughout the whole long saga. Venetia, Lizzie, and Rosie, my children, have held faith and encouraged me through all the highs and lows. My brothers Simon and Oliver have transcribed my father's diaries and the family letters, helped with the archive research, attended some of the interviews, and scrutinized and discussed every draft with me.

Venetia Lascelles, David Lascelles, Auriol Stephens, Sir John Ashworth, Professor Hugh Stephenson, Penny West, Nina and Mike Beasley, and Mike Morrison have all given up their precious time to read and make invaluable comments on the full manuscript, and Professor Bruce Paton has been good-hearted enough to read the full text with an editor's eye and suggest many editorial changes. Winning the Biographers Club Tony Lothian Prize in 2009 gave me the courage and self-confidence to continue with the book when I might have given up. I also owe colossal thanks to my agent, Anthony Sheil, and my publishers, Judith Kendra and Susan Lascelles.

Most importantly I want to thank my brilliant, incisive editor, David Smith, whose help and guidance were to my mind akin to the role my father played in helping the British to climb Everest—without him this book would not have seen the light of day. It was a joy to work with him; he understood what I wanted to say almost better than I did myself.

The author and publisher would like to thank the following for permission to use copyright material, referenced in full in the Notes and Bibliography: The Alpine Club Archives; the British Library; the British Olympic Association Archives (BOA), for extracts from the John le Masurier file (senior coach of the Amateur Athletics Association) and files containing miscellaneous Olympic material connected with the 1968 Olympic Games; Peter Hillary and Sarah Hillary, for extracts from the late Sir Edmund Hillary's private diaries and his books; Sue Leyden and family, for extracts from *Ascent of Everest* and *Life is Meeting* by the late Sir John Hunt; the Medical Research Council for permission to reproduce extracts and images from Pugh's pension file (the MRC does not endorse any views or opinions expressed or inferred by the author); Jan Morris, for extracts from Coronation Everest (Faber & Faber, 2003); the National Archives at Kew; National Geographic, for extracts from "How We Climbed Everest" (1963) by Barry Bishop; the Royal Commission on Accident Prevention, Royal College of Surgeons, London; the Royal Geographical Society; Peter Steele, for use of material in the Alpine Club's Shipton archive; Julie Summers, for extracts from *Fearless on Everest: The Quest for Sandy Irvine* (Weidenfeld & Nicolson, 2000); the Wellcome Library and Archive. While every effort has been made to trace all copyright holders, if any have been inadvertently overlooked, the author and publisher will be pleased to make the necessary arrangement at the first opportunity.

INDEX